AGINCOURT

AGINCOURT

HENRY V AND THE BATTLE
THAT MADE ENGLAND

JULIET BARKER

LITTLE, BROWN AND COMPANY
NEW YORK   BOSTON

Little, Brown and Company
Hachette Book Group USA
1271 Avenue of the Americas, New York, NY 10020
Visit our Web site at www.HachetteBookGroupUSA.com

First U.S. Edition: June 2006
First published in Great Britain in October 2005 by Little, Brown

Library of Congress Cataloging-in-Publication Data

Barker, Juliet.
    Agincourt : Henry V and the battle that made England /
Juliet Barker — 1st ed.
        p. cm.
    Originally published: London, 2005.
    Includes bibliographical references and index.
    ISBN-10: 0-316-01503-2 (hardcover)
    ISBN-13: 978-0-316-01503-5 (hardcover)
    1. Henry V, King of England, 1387–1422. 2. Agincourt, Battle of,
Agincourt, France, 1415. 3. Great Britain — History, Military —
1066–1485. 4. France — History, Military — 1328–1589. I. Title.

DA256.B37 2006
944'.02542 — dc22

                                                            2006002034

            10   9   8   7   6   5   4   3

                        Q-MART

            Printed in the United States of America

CONTENTS

PART III
THE AFTERMATH OF BATTLE

PREFACE

As first light dawned on the morning of 25 October 1415, two armies faced each other across a plateau in an obscure corner of north-eastern France. The contrast between them could not have been greater. On one side stood the bedraggled remnants of an English army that had invaded Normandy ten weeks earlier and, in a major blow to French pride, captured the strategically important town and port of Harfleur. The siege had taken its toll, however, and of the twelve thousand fighting men who had embarked on the expedition, only half that number were now assembled on the field of Agincourt. Of these, only nine hundred were men-at-arms, the human tanks of their day, clad from head to toe in plate armour and universally regarded as the elite of the military world. The rest were English and Welsh archers, who wore only the minimum of defensive armour and carried the longbow, a weapon virtually unique to their island. Many of them were suffering from the dysentery that had also incapacitated their comrades: all were exhausted and half-starved after a gruelling eighteen-day march through almost two hundred and fifty miles of hostile terrain, during which they had been constantly harassed, attacked and deflected from their course by the enemy. Even the weather had been against them, biting winds and constant heavy rain adding to their misery as they trudged from Harfleur towards the safety of English-held Calais.

Facing them — and blocking their route to Calais — was a French army that outnumbered them by at least four to one and possibly as much as six to one. Galvanised by the desire to revenge the loss of Harfleur, the chivalry of France had turned up in their thousands from every part of northern France and some from even further afield. So many men-at-arms had answered the call that it was decided to dispense with the services of some of the less well-equipped city militiamen and crossbowmen, and reinforcements continued to arrive even after the battle had begun. With a few notable exceptions, every princeling with a trace of royal blood in his veins was present, together with all the greatest military officers of France. Well rested, well fed, well armed, fighting on their own territory on a site that they had chosen themselves, this army could be forgiven for thinking that the result of the battle was a foregone conclusion.

Yet some four hours later, in defiance of all logic and the received military wisdom of the time, the English were victorious and the fields of Agincourt were covered with what one observer graphically described as "the masses, the mounds, and the heaps of the slain."[1] Perhaps most astonishing of all was the fact that virtually all the dead were French: "almost the whole nobility among the soldiery of France" had been killed,[2] including the dukes of Alençon, Bar and Brabant, eight counts, a viscount and an archbishop, together with the constable, admiral, master of the crossbowmen and *prévôt* of marshals of the French army. Several hundred more, among them the dukes of Orléans and Bourbon, the counts of Richemont, Eu and Vendôme, and the celebrated chivalric hero Marshal Boucicaut, were prisoners in English hands. The English, by contrast, had lost only two noblemen, Edward, duke of York, and Michael, earl of Suffolk, a handful of men-at-arms and perhaps a hundred archers. The English victory was so unexpected and so overwhelming in its scale that contemporaries could only ascribe it to God.

For Henry V, however, the battle of Agincourt was not just a divine affirmation of the justice of his cause. It was also the culmination of a carefully planned campaign, preceded by years of meticulous preparation. To see the battle in this context is to understand not only the determination and single-mindedness of the principal human architect of the victory but also the reason why, against all the odds, he was victorious. For these reasons, therefore, this book is not merely a study of the military campaign to which this battle was the dramatic denouement. *Agincourt* also aims to set the scene in which such a conflict was possible and to explain why, given the character of Henry V, it was almost inevitable. The book falls into three parts. The first deals with the inexorable countdown to war as Henry stamped his authority on his own kingdom, exploited the internal divisions caused by the French civil wars to his own advantage and engaged in diplomacy to ensure that France's traditional allies did not come to her aid when he attacked. The second part of the book follows the campaign itself, from the moment Henry gave the signal that launched the invasion, through the siege and fall of Harfleur, the increasingly desperate march to Calais, the battle and, finally, the formal concession of defeat by the French heralds. The third part examines the impact of the battle on the victors, on the families of those who lost their lives and on the prisoners, some of whom were to endure years in foreign captivity. It also looks briefly at the wider historical consequences of Agincourt and at the literature that this spectacular victory inspired.

It is no coincidence that many authors have been prompted to write about Agincourt in times of war. When national morale is low and victory seems uncertain or far off, it is useful to be reminded that resourcefulness and determination can sometimes be more important than sheer weight of numbers. On the other hand, writing in such circumstances makes it easy to fall into the propaganda trap, and much of the historical and literary response to Agincourt has been one-sided, politically motivated or simply jingoistic, portraying the battle as a victory of stout-hearted, no-nonsense English commoners over lily-livered, unmanly, foppish French aristocrats. Writing in the aftermath of 9/11 and the invasions of Afghanistan and Iraq by the Americans, the British and their allies, it is impossible not to be struck by the echoes from six centuries ago. But while human nature does not change, the circumstances in which we live and fight our wars do, and it would be wrong to draw too close analogies between the past and the present.

In writing this book, I hope to have done something towards creating a more balanced view of the battle and the events leading up to it. Inevitably, the fact that English administrative, financial and family records have been preserved in far greater numbers than similar ones in France (where most were destroyed during the French Revolution) means that greater emphasis is placed on the English experience, though this is not necessarily inappropriate, given that Henry V was the aggressor. The fascination of the English material is its detail: we learn of the young earl marshal's purchase of new armour and equipment (including a pavilion to stable his horses and a new seat for his latrine) for his first military campaign; of the vast household, including everyone from heralds and minstrels to scullery servants and torchbearers, which accompanied the king himself; of the unprecedented expenditure in hiring armourers, fletchers and, most significantly, foreign gunners to operate Henry's huge train of cannon and artillery.

What we can piece together from the French sources makes it clear that, contrary to popular belief, there was a brave and concerted effort on the part of many of those living in northern France to resist the English invasion. The extraordinary story of the unsung hero Raoul, sire de Gaucourt, is a case in point.* If he is remembered at all, even in his own country, it is only as the friend and companion-in-arms of Joan of Arc. Yet a host of scattered references reveal that this former crusader not only succeeded in getting a relief force into Harfleur under the nose of Henry V but also conducted a long and gallant defense of the town which foiled the king's plans for the next stage of his invasion. His subsequent treatment by Henry V and his own sense of knightly duty, which obliged him to surrender himself into English custody because he had given his word to do so, make him a figure of compelling interest. The cult of chivalry has

---

*Although I have anglicized all the titles held by Frenchmen throughout this book, there is no satisfactory English equivalent for "sire de," which I have therefore retained.

often been misunderstood, misinterpreted and derided as hope-lessly romantic by historians, but Raoul de Gaucourt was a liv-ing example of the way that it informed and determined the conduct of medieval men-at-arms. And he was not alone. The great tragedy of Agincourt for the French was not just that so many of them were killed, but that so many of them had altruis-tically put aside bitter personal and political differences to unite in defence of their country and lost their lives as a result.

Military historians, rightly, have an exhaustive interest in battle formations, positions and tactics but sometimes seem to forget that the chess pieces on the board are human beings, each with their own distinctive character and history, even if the future is not always theirs. All too often medieval men-at-arms are depicted as little more than brutal thugs, unthinking killing machines, motivated solely by lust for blood and plunder. Yet on the field of Agincourt we find many highly intelligent, literate and sensitive men: Edward, duke of York, and Thomas Morstede wrote the standard fifteenth-century treatises in English on hunting and surgery respectively; Charles, duke of Orléans, was a gifted writer of courtly love lyrics; Jean le Févre de St Remy and Jehan Waurin became the chivalric historians and chroni-clers of their age; Ghillebert de Lannoy a celebrated traveller, diplomat and moralist.

At an altogether different level, we can occasionally catch a poignant insight into the impact of war on less notable people: an esquire desperately trying to raise money on the eve of the expedition by pawning his possessions; two Welshmen perform-ing a pilgrimage "in fulfilment of vows made on the battlefield"; the unfortunate Frenchman left without heirs because his four sons were all killed at Agincourt; the mother of seven children who, six months after the battle, had no income and did not know whether she was a wife or a widow because her husband's body could not be found; the anonymous English chaplain, author of the most vivid, detailed and personal account of the campaign, who sat trembling with fear in the baggage train as the battle raged around him.

It is the personal stories of individuals such as these which make Agincourt live again for me.

A NOTE TO THE TEXT

In order to make the quotations from contemporary sources more easily understood, I have translated those in medieval French and Latin into English and modernized archaic English passages. For authenticity's sake, however, I have kept the pre-decimal references to pounds, shillings and pence. In the fifteenth century, one pound sterling (£1) was divided not just into twenty shillings (20s), or two hundred and forty pence (240d), but also into six parts: one sixth (3s 4d) was known as a crown, a third (6s 8d) as a noble and two thirds (13s 4d) as a mark. To give the reader a rough idea of the current values of these sums, I have used figures supplied by the Office for National Statistics, which equate £1 in 1415 with £414 ($666.54) in 1999.

PART I

THE ROAD TO AGINCOURT

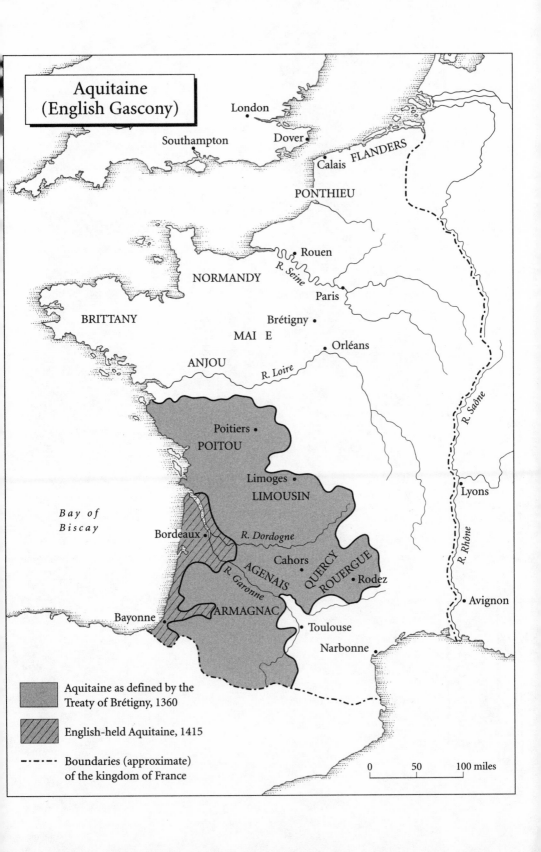

Aquitaine
(English Gascony)

London

Southampton

Dover

Calais   FLANDERS

PONTHIEU

Rouen

R. Seine

NORMANDY

Paris

BRITTANY

Brétigny

MAI E

Orléans

ANJOU

R. Loire

R. Saône

Poitiers

POITOU

Limoges

LIMOUSIN

Lyons

Bay of
Biscay

Bordeaux

R. Dordogne

Cahors

AGENAIS   QUERCY

ROUERGUE   Rodez

R. Garonne

R. Rhône

Avignon

Bayonne

ARMAGNAC

Toulouse

Narbonne

Aquitaine as defined by the
Treaty of Brétigny, 1360

English-held Aquitaine, 1415

Boundaries (approximate)
of the kingdom of France

0   50   100 miles

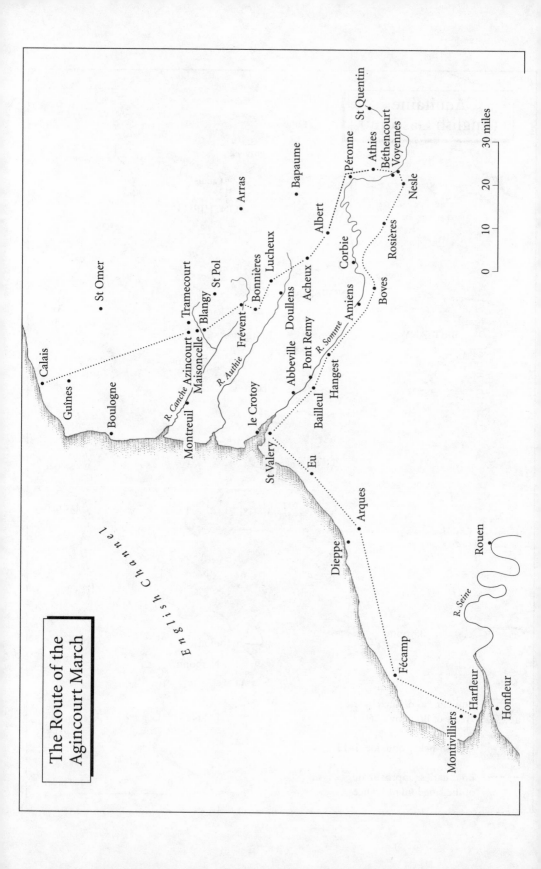

The Route of the
Agincourt March

English Channel

Calais
Guînes
Boulogne
St Omer

Montreuil
R. Canche
Azincourt
Tramecourt
Maisoncelle
Blangy
St Pol
Arras

R. Authie
Frévent
Bonnières
Lucheux
Bapaume

le Crotoy

Abbeville
Doullens
Pont Remy
Acheux
Albert
St Valery
Bailleul
Hangest
R. Somme
Amiens
Corbie
Péronne
St Quentin
Athies
Béthencourt
Voyennes
Eu
Boves
Rosières
Nesle

Arques

Dieppe

Fécamp

Montivilliers
Harfleur
Honfleur
R. Seine
Rouen

0   10   20   30 miles

Figure 1: The French royal succession and Edward III's claim to the throne of France

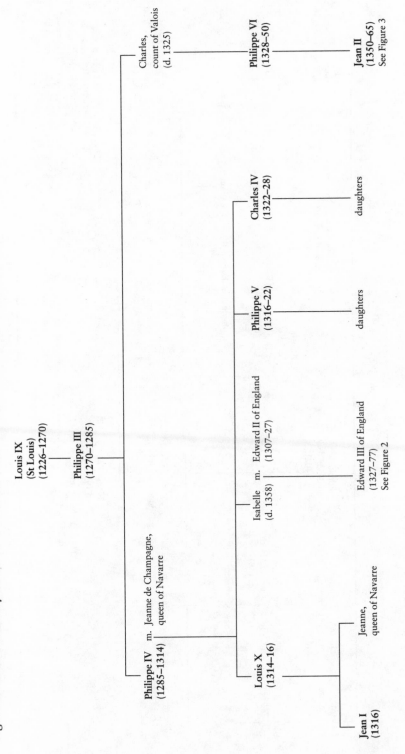

Figure 2: The English royal line from Edward III

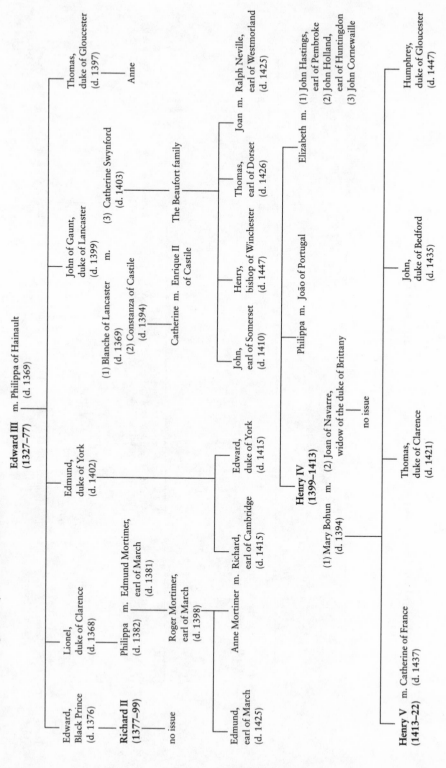

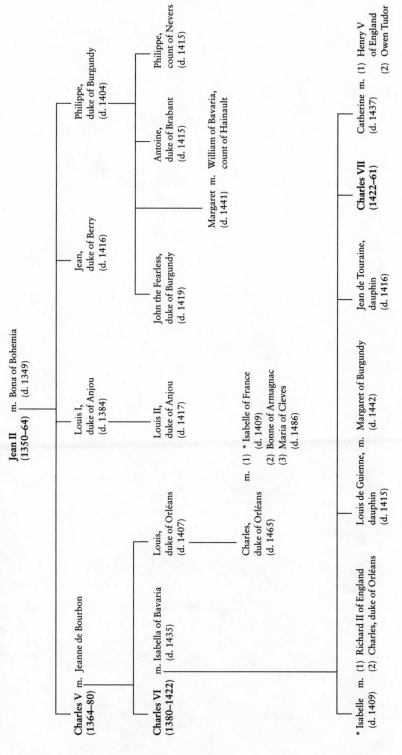

Figure 3: The French royal line: the House of Valois

CHAPTER ONE

JUST RIGHTS AND INHERITANCES

The last letter that Henry V sent to Charles VI of France before he launched the Agincourt campaign was an ultimatum, its opening lines, which in most medieval correspondence were an opportunity for flowery compliments, characteristically abrupt and to the point. "To the most serene prince Charles, our cousin and adversary of France, Henry by the grace of God king of England and France. To give to each that which is his own is a work of inspiration and of wise counsel." Henry had done everything in his power to procure peace between the two realms, he declared, but he did not lack the courage to fight to the death for justice. His just rights and inheritances had been seized from him by violence and withheld for too long: it was his duty to recover them. Since he could not obtain justice by peaceable means, he would have to resort to force of arms. "By the bowels of Jesus Christ," he pleaded, "Friend, render what you owe."[1]

Henry V was undoubtedly an opportunist, in the sense that he was remarkably clever at identifying the chance to turn something to his own advantage. Was he also an opportunist in the more negative sense of the word, a man prepared to put expediency before principle? Had he really been deprived of his "just rights and inheritances"? If so, what were they and was it necessary for him to go to war to win them back? To answer those questions, we have to go back almost exactly 350 years before the Agincourt campaign, to another, even more momentous invasion.

In 1066, at the battle of Hastings in southeast England, the Normans conquered the Anglo-Saxons and crowned their own duke, William the Conqueror, as king of England. Though the kingdom continued to be governed separately and independently from Normandy, socially, culturally and, to a much lesser extent, politically, England effectively became part of the continent for the next one and a half centuries. William and his Anglo-Norman aristocracy held lands and office on both sides of the Channel and were equally at home in either place. French became the dominant language in England, though Latin remained the choice of official documents and the Church, and Anglo-Saxon lingered on in vernacular speech, particularly among the illiterate. Cathedrals and castles were built as the visible symbols of a newly powerful and dynamic system of lordship in Church and state.

The new technique of fighting which had won the battle of Hastings for the Normans was also adopted in England; instead of standing or riding and hurling the lance overarm, these new warriors, the knights, charged on horseback with the lance tucked beneath the arm, so that the weight of both horse and rider was behind the blow and the weapon was reusable. Though it required discipline and training, giving rise to the birth of tournaments and the cult of chivalry, a charge by massed ranks of knights with their lances couched in this way was irresistible. Anna Comnena, the Byzantine princess who witnessed its devastating effect during the First Crusade, claimed that it could "make a hole in the wall of Babylon."[2]

Intimately connected with these military developments was the arrival — via William the Conqueror — of the feudal system of land tenure, which provided the knights to do the fighting by creating a chain of dependent lordships with the king at its head. Immediately beneath him in the hierarchy were his tenants-in-chief, each of whom had to perform a personal act of homage, acknowledging that he was the king's vassal, or liege man, and that he owed him certain services. The most important of these was the obligation to provide a certain number of knights for the royal army whenever called upon to do so. In order to fulfil this duty, the tenants-in-chief granted parcels of their own land to dependent knights upon the same conditions, so that a further relationship of lord and vassal was created. Though it quickly became the accepted practice that the eldest son of a tenant succeeded his father, this was not an automatic right and it had to be paid for by a fine. If the heir was under twenty-one, the lands returned to the lord for the period of his minority, but a vassal of any age could be deprived of his lands permanently if he committed an act contrary to his lord's interests. The feudal system underpinned the entire structure of Anglo-Norman society, just as it did in France, and if abused it could cause serious tension.

The cracks took some time to show. Pressure began to build in the twelfth century. The marriage in 1152 of Henry II of England and Eleanor of Aquitaine created a huge Angevin empire, which covered almost half of modern France as well as England and Wales. It encompassed Normandy, Aquitaine, Anjou, Maine, Touraine and Poitou — virtually all of western France apart from Brittany. Such an extensive, wealthy and powerful lordship was a threat, politically and militarily, to the authority and prestige of an increasingly ambitious French monarchy, which launched a series of invasions and conquests. Over time, virtually all of the Angevin inheritance was lost, including Normandy itself in 1204. All that then remained in English hands was the duchy of Aquitaine, a narrow strip of sparsely populated, wine-producing land on the western seaboard of France. Otherwise known as Gascony, or Guienne, it had no exceptional value, except for the strategic importance of its principal ports of Bordeaux and Bayonne, but it was a constant source of friction between the French and English monarchies.[3]

The status of the duchy increasingly became the subject of dispute. The French claimed that the duke of Aquitaine was a peer of France, that he held his duchy as a vassal of the French crown and that he therefore had to pay personal homage for it to the king of France — in other words, that a classic feudal relationship existed, binding the English king-duke by ties of loyalty to serve the French king in times of war and, more importantly, establishing a superior lordship to which his Gascon subjects could appeal over his head. This was unacceptable to the dignity of the kings of England, who counter-claimed that they held the duchy in full sovereignty and recognized no superior authority but that of God. The Gascons, not unnaturally, exploited the situation to their own advantage, relying on their duke to defend them against repeated French invasions and yet appealing against him to the ultimate court of France, the Paris Parlement, whenever they felt threatened by his authority.[4]

A situation that had long been smouldering burst into flame in 1337 when Philippe VI of France exercised his feudal authority to declare that Edward III was a disobedient vassal and that Aquitaine was duly confiscated. This had happened twice before, in 1294 and 1324, resulting each time in a brief and inconclusive war. The difference this time was that Edward III's response was to challenge the legitimacy not of the king's decision, but of the king himself. He assumed the arms and title of king of France as his own and adopted the motto "Dieu et mon droit," for God and my right, the right being his claim to the French crown. It was a move that transformed a relatively small-scale feudal conflict into a major dynastic dispute.[5]

Edward III was able to claim the throne by right of inheritance from his grandfather, Philippe IV of France, but he owed it to a Templar curse. Philippe IV was ambitious, quarrelsome and always chronically short of money. Expedients such as expelling the Jews from France and confiscating their debts made temporary contributions towards replenishing his coffers and whetted his appetite for bigger game. His choice of his next victim was as bold as his action was ruthless. The Knights Templar was the oldest military order in Christendom, founded in 1119 to defend the fledgling Crusader states in the Holy Land. It was also one of the richest of all religious orders; the generosity of the pious had enabled it to amass enormous wealth in lands, property and goods throughout Europe, but especially in

France. The *raison d'être* for these powerful monk-knights had disappeared, however, when the city of Acre, the last Christian outpost in the Holy Land, fell to the Saracens in 1291. Philippe acted swiftly and without warning: on a single night he seized the Temple treasury in Paris and ordered the arrest of every Templar in the country. With the aid of a reluctant but compliant pope (a French puppet whom he had installed under his thumb at Avignon), he set about the total destruction of the order. Its members were accused individually and collectively of sorcery, heresy, blasphemy and sexual perversion. As there was no evidence to support the charges, proof was obtained by confessions extorted from hapless Templars. Many died as they were tortured; some committed suicide; more than half of the 122 who admitted their supposed crimes later courageously withdrew their confessions and were burnt alive as relapsed heretics. Among this last group was Jacques de Molay, Grand Master of the order, who was burnt at the stake before the Cathedral of Notre Dame in Paris in March 1314. As the flames consumed him, de Molay's last act was to defy his persecutors. He proclaimed the innocence of the Templars, cursed the king and his descendants to the thirteenth generation and prophesied that king and pope would join him before the throne of judgement within a year. The prophecy was spectacularly fulfilled. Eight months later, both Philippe IV (aged forty-six) and his tool Clement V (aged fifty) were indeed dead, and within fourteen years so were the three sons and grandson who succeeded Philippe. The ancient line of Capetian monarchs died with them.[6]

In 1328, therefore, the throne of France stood empty and there was no obvious candidate to succeed. Those with the strongest claim, because they were Philippe IV's direct descendants, were his grandchildren Jeanne, the daughter of his eldest son, and Edward III, the son of his daughter Isabelle. In practice, however, neither was acceptable to the French: Jeanne because she was a woman and Edward because he was king of England. The unfortunate Jeanne had been deprived of her inheritance once before. When her brother had died, she had been only four years old and her uncle had seized the throne;

ironically, a few years later, exactly the same fate would befall his own young daughters. Since no one wanted a minor sovereign, let alone a female one, the precedent set by these usurpations of 1316 and 1321 was later justified and legitimised by the invention of the Salic Law, which declared that women could not succeed to the crown of France. Nicely dressed up with an entirely spurious ancestry dating back to the eighth century and Carolingian times, the new law was applied retrospectively. It therefore excluded Jeanne permanently, but it made no mention of whether the right to succeed could be passed down through the female line. Edward III could therefore still legitimately claim to be the rightful heir. In 1328, however, his rights were purely academic. At the age of sixteen, he was still a minor and a powerless pawn in the hands of his mother, Queen Isabelle, and her lover, Roger Mortimer, a notorious pair who had compelled his father, Edward II, to abdicate and then procured his murder.

In any case, Edward III was pre-empted by yet another coup. Philippe IV's nephew, the preferred candidate of the French, seized the moment and was crowned Philippe VI. It was thus the Valois dynasty, not the Plantagenets, who replaced the Capetians as kings of France. There was nothing unusual in this sequence of events. It was a drama that had been played out all over Europe many times before and one on which the curtain would rise many times again. But on this particular occasion, the consequences were to extend far beyond anything that any of those immediately involved could have imagined. Edward III's decision to enforce his claim by force of arms launched the Hundred Years War, a conflict that would last for five generations, cause untold deaths and destruction, and embroil France, England and most of their neighbours as well. Even if Edward III's claim to the French throne was only revived as a cynical counter-ploy for the confiscation of his duchy of Aquitaine, it was sufficiently valid to convince many Frenchmen, as well as Englishmen, of the justice of his cause. Undoubtedly some of them were "persuaded" purely out of self-interest.[7]

Until Henry V came on the scene, the closest the English came to achieving their objectives was the Treaty of Brétigny. This was drawn up in 1360 when, as a result of Edward III's spectacular victories at the battles of Crécy (1346) and Poitiers (1356), France was in turmoil and its king, Jean II, a prisoner in English hands. In return for Edward III renouncing his claims to the French throne, Normandy, Anjou and Maine, the French agreed that he should hold Aquitaine, Poitou, Ponthieu, Guînes and Calais (captured by the English in 1347) in full sovereignty; Edward was also to receive an enormous ransom of three million gold crowns for the release of Jean II. The treaty was a diplomatic triumph for the English, but it had an Achilles heel. A clause regarding the reciprocal renunciation of claims to the crown of France and to sovereignty over Aquitaine was taken out of the final text and put into a separate document, which was to be ratified only after certain territories had been placed in English hands. Despite the clear intention of both kings that the terms of the treaty should be fulfilled, formal written ratification of this second document never took place. As a consequence, Bolognese lawyers acting for Jean II's successor were able to argue that the treaty was null and void. It was a lesson Edward's great-grandson, Henry V, would take to heart: his embassies would always include experts in the civil law to ensure that any future agreements were legally watertight.[8]

Whether Edward III and his successors, particularly Henry V, were sincere in their belief that they were the rightful kings of France, or were simply using the claim as a lever with which to extract more practical concessions, has been the subject of much unresolved debate. Edward III muddied the waters by performing homage (kneeling before the French king and acknowledging his allegiance to him in a formal public ceremony) for Aquitaine to Philippe VI in 1329,[9] and even at Brétigny he was prepared to accept considerably less than he had originally demanded. Pragmatism was preferable to the unattainable. Indeed, until 1419, when Henry V began to achieve the impossible, the utmost extent of English ambition was the restoration of the old Angevin empire.[10] Edward III's grandson Richard II, who succeeded him in 1377, had no use for the title of king of France, except as an empty verbal flourish on official documents, seals and coins. He was determined to obtain peace and to that end he was even prepared to make concessions on Aquitaine, proposing to separate the duchy from the crown by giving it to his uncle John of Gaunt. This would have ended the problem of an English king having to perform homage to a French one (no one in England would object to a duke, even a royal one, doing so) and would have ensured that the duchy remained under English influence. The Gascons, however, would have none of it. They wanted to remain a crown possession, believing that it would need the full resources of the English king to prevent Aquitaine from being annexed by the French. The most Richard was able to achieve was a truce which was to last for twenty-eight years, until 1426, cemented by his own marriage to Isabelle, the six-year-old daughter of Charles VI of France. (Richard was then a twenty-nine-year-old widower.)[11]

Had Richard survived and had children by Isabelle, peace with France might have been a genuine option, but in 1399 he was deposed in a military coup by his cousin Henry Bolingbroke, and died in prison suspiciously soon afterwards. As the son of John of Gaunt and grandson of Edward III, Henry IV inherited the claim to the French throne, but he had neither the means nor the leisure to pursue it. His first priority was to establish his rule in England in the face of repeated conspiracies and rebellions. Nevertheless, it was clear from the start that there would be no long-lasting peace. The French refused to recognize Henry as king of England, and the king of France's brother Louis, duke of Orléans, twice challenged him to a personal duel over his usurpation. French forces invaded Aquitaine and threatened Calais and there were tit-for-tat raids on either side of the Channel in which undefended towns were burnt and plundered and enemy shipping was seized.[12]

Henry IV's usurpation also sealed the fate of Richard II's poor child-widow. Like so many medieval women bought and sold into marriage as hostages for political alliances, she had served her purpose and, at ten years of age, was now redundant. Henry toyed with the idea of marrying her to one of his own sons (raising the interesting possibility that the wife of the future Henry V could have been the older sister of the woman who eventually did become his queen), but there was more to be gained from keeping the English princes available on the international marriage market. Isabelle was therefore sent back to France, where she was promptly betrothed to her cousin Charles, son and heir of Louis d'Orléans; married for the second time at sixteen, she died, aged nineteen, shortly after giving birth to his daughter.[13]

Louis d'Orléans took advantage of Henry's preoccupation with his domestic problems to invade Aquitaine in alliance with Jean, count of Alençon, and two disaffected Gascons, Bernard, count of Armagnac, and Charles d'Albret, who, as constable of France, held the highest military office in that kingdom. Though they failed to take the principal towns, they succeeded in annexing large areas of the duchy and there was every possibility that English rule in Aquitaine would come to a premature end.[14] It was at this juncture that an event took place which was to transform the fortunes of both England and France. In November 1407 Louis d'Orléans was assassinated. His murderer was his cousin John the Fearless, duke of Burgundy, one of the richest, most powerful and, in an age not noted for the delicacy of its morals, most unscrupulous of all the princes of France.

The murder was the culmination of a bitter personal feud between the two dukes, both of whom had been ambitious to fill the vacuum at the heart of power in France caused by the intermittent madness of Charles VI.[15] Louis, as we have seen, had married his eldest son to Charles's daughter Isabelle; John the Fearless secured a double alliance, marrying his only son to another of Charles's daughters, and his own daughter Margaret of Burgundy to the dauphin. Nevertheless, for some years before his murder, Louis d'Orléans had possessed the upper hand, controlling the king's person, diverting royal revenues into his own pocket and, it was said, enjoying the queen too. ("Monsieur le duc d'Orléans is young and likes playing dice and whoring," a contemporary remarked.)[16] John the Fearless was determined to acquire these benefits, including, so it was said, the queen's favors, for himself. When his political machinations failed to achieve the desired objects, he resorted to murder, hiring a band of assassins who ambushed the duke one evening as he made his way home through the streets of Paris after visiting the queen. They struck him from his horse, cut off the hand with which he tried to stave off their blows and split his head in two, spilling his brains on the pavement.

The action was so blatant and the murderer himself so shockingly unrepentant that the remaining French princes were reduced to paralysis. The duchess of Orléans demanded justice, but the only person in a position to enforce punishment against so powerful a magnate was the king and he was incapable. The dauphin, who might have acted in his father's place, was son-in-law of the murderer and, in any case, a child of ten. As there was no one willing or able to take a stand against him, John the Fearless was literally able to get away with murder. He swept unopposed into Paris and by the end of 1409 he was king of France in all but name.[17]

This monopoly of power would not go unchallenged for long; Burgundy had removed one opponent only for another, more fearsome, to rise in his place. Charles d'Orléans had been a day short of his thirteenth birthday when his father was assassinated. Though he had then been compelled to swear publicly on the Gospels in the cathedral of Chartres that he would forgive the murder, revenge was never far from his thoughts and actions. Within two years he had signed a military pact with Bernard, count of Armagnac, and within three he had not only engineered an anti-Burgundian alliance with the dukes of Berry, Bourbon and Brittany and the counts of Armagnac, Alençon and Clermont but also led their combined armies to the gates of Paris to remove the king and the dauphin from John the Fearless's control.[18] This was merely a preliminary skirmish in what was to become a major civil war, pitting the Burgundians and their allies against the Orléanists or Armagnacs, as they were called by their contemporaries after Charles d'Orléans married the count's daughter in 1410. The two sides were irreconcilable. This was not just a struggle for power but a bitter personal quarrel in which nothing less than the trial and punishment (preferably by death) of John the Fearless would satisfy the Armagnacs for the murder of Louis d'Orléans; such an outcome was, of course, unthinkable to the Burgundians. Their hatred of each other was so great that in their search for allies, both sides were prepared to overlook their shared dislike of the English. Indeed, they were even prepared to buy the support of the king of England at the price of recognising his "just rights and inheritances," including, eventually, his title to the throne of France.

Such an opportunity was irresistible to the English, though deciding which party to aid was more difficult. In 1411, when the duke of Burgundy formally sought English assistance for the first time, Henry IV and his council were by no means unanimous in their opinion. Alliance with the Armagnacs offered the possibility of regaining through negotiation those areas of Aquitaine which had been lost to Louis d'Orléans, Charles d'Albret and the counts of Armagnac and Alençon in 1403–7. On the other hand, alliance with John the Fearless, whose Burgundian dominions included the Low Countries, might achieve the same object (though by military means) and would certainly give additional protection and advantages to vital English trading interests in Flanders, Brabant and Hainault.

The decision was complicated by the fact that Henry IV, like Charles VI of France, was not in a position to exercise personal rule. Though he was not insane, like Charles, he had suffered many bouts of debilitating illness since 1405. What was actually wrong with him is a subject of speculation and it says much for the medieval frame of mind that whatever the diagnoses, contemporaries all agreed that his sickness was a divine punishment for having usurped the throne. The king himself seems to have thought so too, beginning his will with the self-abasing words, "I, Henry, sinful wretch" and referring to "the life I have mispended."[19] As a result of his incapacity, his eldest son, the future Henry V, had gradually come to assume a dominant role on the royal council. In the light of his later campaigns in France, it is significant that in 1411 it was his decision to intervene on behalf of the duke of Burgundy.

Exactly what John the Fearless offered as an inducement is not clear, though Armagnac propaganda was quick to suggest that he had promised to hand over four of the main Flemish ports to the English, which would have been an attractive proposal if it were true. All that is known for certain is that negotiations were begun for a marriage between Prince Henry and one of the duke's daughters, and in October 1411 one of the prince's most trusted lieutenants, Thomas, earl of Arundel, was dispatched with a substantial army to France. These English forces played an important part in the successful campaign to lift the Armagnac blockade of Paris, participated in the Burgundian victory at the battle of St Cloud, and before the end of the year had entered Paris with a triumphant John the Fearless.[20]

Having achieved so much militarily, it might have been thought that the English would reap the diplomatic and political benefits of their alliance with the duke. Yet before Arundel's expedition had even returned home, Henry IV's council had performed a quite astonishing volte-face and thrown in their lot with the Armagnacs. There were two reasons for this. The first was that the increasingly desperate Armagnac princes now made a better offer than the duke of Burgundy: they agreed to reconquer, with their own troops and at their own expense, the whole duchy of Aquitaine as defined by the Treaty of Brétigny, to hand it over to Henry IV in full sovereignty and to do homage to him for the lands they themselves held there. In return, the English were to send an army, four thousand strong, at French expense, to help them defeat the duke of Burgundy and bring him to justice.[21]

The magnitude of what was on offer might well have been sufficient temptation to persuade the English to change their alliance, but there was a second reason that influenced the decision. Prince Henry's domination of the royal council had come to an abrupt end in the winter of 1411 because, it would seem, the ailing Henry IV now suspected the loyalty and ambition of his eldest son. Colourful tales were certainly in circulation. According to one contemporary chronicler, the dying king told his confessor that he repented his usurpation but could not undo it because "my children will not suffer that the kingship goes out of our lineage."[22] Another story, which was later taken up by Shakespeare, was first reported by the Burgundian chronicler Enguerrand de Monstrelet in the 1440s. The prince, he said, had removed the crown from beside his father's bed, thinking that Henry IV was already dead, only to be caught red-handed when his father awoke from sleep and challenged him for being presumptuous.[23] Whether or not such incidents actually took place (and it is difficult to see how either chronicler could have obtained his information), they were anecdotal versions of an undoubted truth, which was that in 1412 the prince felt compelled to issue an open letter protesting his innocence and loyalty in the face of rumours that he was plotting to seize the throne.[24]

Was there any substance to these rumours? Henry IV's prolonged ill-health had already prompted the suggestion that he should abdicate in favor of his eldest son and he clearly resented Prince Henry's popularity and influence at court, in Parliament and in the country. The prince, for his part, may have feared that, one way or another, he might be disinherited in favor of his next brother Thomas, for whom their father appears to have had a decided preference. Thomas, supported by Henry IV's oldest friend and ally Thomas Arundel, archbishop of Canterbury, now replaced Prince Henry as the key figure on the royal council, effectively excluding the heir to the throne from government and completely overturning his policies. Henry's natural place as leader of the military expedition to France on behalf of the Armagnacs was first allotted to him, then taken away and given to his brother; shortly afterwards, Thomas was created duke of Clarence and appointed the king's lieutenant in Aquitaine, even though Henry had been duke of Aquitaine since his father's coronation. To add insult to these not insignificant injuries, Henry was also falsely accused of having misappropriated the wages of the Calais garrison.

In the circumstances, it is not surprising that the prince suspected that there was an orchestrated campaign at court to undermine him and perhaps settle the succession on Clarence. Rumours that he had been plotting to seize the throne may have been deliberately circulated as part of that campaign, and the fact that the prince felt the need to deny them at all, let alone publicly and in writing, suggests that he was fully alive to the seriousness of his situation. In his open letter, he demanded that his father should seek out the troublemakers, dismiss them from office and punish them, all of which Henry IV agreed to do, but did not. Yet despite all the provocation, Prince Henry did not resort to violence. Always a patient man, he had no need to grasp by force what would eventually come to him in the course of nature. In the meantime, he could do nothing but await with trepidation the outcome of his brother's expedition to France. A brilliant success would enhance Clarence's reputation and might threaten his own position further; an abject failure might vindicate his own decision to side with the Burgundians but would have serious repercussions at home and abroad.[25]

Clarence sailed from Southampton on 10 August 1412 with one thousand men-at-arms and three thousand archers and landed at St-Vaast-la-Hougue in Normandy. Among his commanders were three members of the extended royal family who were to play a leading role in the Agincourt campaign three years later: his father's cousin Edward, duke of York; his father's half-brother Sir Thomas Beaufort, newly created earl of Dorset; and his uncle by marriage Sir John Cornewaille,[26] who was one of the greatest knights of his generation. Such a prestigious army should have carried all before it, but Clarence was never the luckiest of leaders. Even before he set foot on French soil, the Armagnacs and Burgundians had secretly come to terms with each other and there was no need for his services. By the time he learnt that the Armagnac princes had unilaterally renounced their alliance it was too late; he was already at Blois, their appointed rendezvous, and he angrily demanded that they honour their obligation. To buy him off the Armagnacs had to agree to pay a total of 210,000 gold crowns, offering as immediate security plate, jewels and seven hostages, including Charles d'Orléans' unfortunate twelve-year-old brother, Jean, count of Angoulême, who was to remain a prisoner in English hands, forgotten and unredeemed, until 1445. Clarence then marched his army, unopposed and living off the land, to Aquitaine, where he spent the winter negotiating alliances with the local Armagnac leaders and preparing for the possibility of another campaign the following spring.[27]

Clarence's expedition was not the military and political triumph he and his father had hoped for, but neither was it a complete disaster. He had failed to realize English ambitions for the restoration of a larger Aquitaine and it would prove well-nigh impossible to extract the sums promised by the Armagnac leaders. On the other hand, he had demonstrated the weakness of a divided France and that it was possible for an English army to march unscathed and without resistance from Normandy to Aquitaine. If nothing else, he had provided his more able brother with a model for the Agincourt campaign.

CHAPTER TWO

A KING'S APPRENTICESHIP

On 20 March 1413 Henry IV died at Westminster Abbey in the Jerusalem Chamber, thereby fulfilling (in the tenuous way of most medieval prophecies) the prediction that he would die "in the Holy Land." The dazzling young hero, renowned for his personal prowess as a crusader and jouster and for his lavish patronage of the arts, died a broken man, unlamented and unrespected, at the age of only forty-six. He had kept his stolen crown by a combination of luck, ruthlessness and success in battle. He had even succeeded in passing it on to his son. In almost every other respect he had failed. He left the government heavily in debt, the royal council and the wider nobility riven with faction and intrigue, the country plagued by violent disorder and the Church under threat at home from heresy and abroad from schism. In the circumstances, it was probably fortunate that Clarence was still in Aquitaine and powerless to take advantage of the situation to hinder his brother's accession.[1]

Henry V was determined that his reign would mark a sea-change in the fortunes of the English monarchy. Although he had not been born to be king, he had, quite literally, received a textbook training for his future role. Books of advice on this subject, known as mirrors for princes, had a long tradition dating back to classical times, and an English version, written by Thomas Hoccleve, a clerk of the privy seal (one of the departments of state) and part-time poet, had been dedicated to Henry himself when he was prince of Wales.[2] Christine de Pizan, an Italian-born French poet and author of books on chivalry, had written a similar work for the dauphin Louis, in which she recommended that moral virtues as well as practical skills should be taught, stressing above all the importance of acquiring discipline, humanistic learning and early experience in the workings of government.[3] In all these things the new king excelled.

Henry V had been brought up to be literate and numerate to an unusual degree, probably because he was the son and grandson of two great patrons of literature, chivalry and learning. John of Gaunt was famously an early patron of the court poet Geoffrey Chaucer (who became his brother-in-law), a patronage that was continued by Henry IV. After Chaucer's death, Henry IV offered his position to Christine de Pizan, no doubt hoping that as she was a widow and her only child, her sixteen-year-old son, was effectively a hostage in his household, she could be persuaded to agree. If so, he completely misjudged this redoubtable woman, who had once replied to criticism "that it was inappropriate for a woman to be learned, as it was so rare . . . that it was even less fitting for a man to be ignorant, as it was so common." De Pizan had no intention of becoming the English court poet but "feigned acquiescence in order to obtain my son's return . . . after laborious manoeuvres on my part and the expedition of some of my works, my son received permission to come home so he could accompany me on a journey I have yet to make."[4] Not surprisingly, she later became one of the bitterest and most vocal critics of Henry V and the English invasions of France.

The new king was the eldest of Henry IV's six surviving children by his first wife, Mary de Bohun, daughter and co-heiress of Humphrey, earl of Hereford. He was born at his father's castle at Monmouth, in Wales, but because no one expected the boy to become king of England, his date of birth was not formally recorded. The likeliest date, given in a horoscope cast for him later in life, was 16 September 1386.[5] From an early age, Henry was able to read and write fluently in English, French and Latin, and like his two youngest brothers, John, duke of Bedford, and Humphrey, duke of Gloucester, both noted bibliophiles, he built up a considerable, if conventional, personal library of classical, historical and theological texts. His taste sometimes ran in a lighter vein, for he is known to have commissioned copies of books on hunting and his personal copy of Chaucer's poem *Troylus and Cryseyde* still survives.[6] He also "delighted in songe and musicall Instruments." Perhaps because of his Welsh upbringing, he had a particular affinity for the harp, which he learnt to play in childhood; years later, his harp would accompany him on campaign, as did his band of minstrels and the musicians of his chapel. He even composed music: a complex setting of part of the liturgy, the *Gloria*, for three voices by "Roy Henry" is attributed to him.[7]

In addition to his artistic and literary pursuits, Henry had received a solid grounding in the art of war. Every chivalric treatise had always placed great emphasis on the importance of learning to bear arms from the earliest age; Henry possessed a sword at the age of twelve, and his own son, Henry VI, would be given eight before he reached the age of ten, "some greater and some smaller, for to learn the king to play in his tender age."[8] Hunting in all its forms was strongly recommended by chivalric writers as the perfect preparation for military life. The typical argument was put forward in the first half of the fourteenth century by Alfonso XI, who found time between ruling his kingdom of Castile and fighting the Moors to write a book about the sport.

> For a knight should always engage in anything to do with arms and chivalry, and if he cannot do so in war, he should do so in activities which resemble war. And the chase is most similar to war, for these reasons: war demands expense, met without complaint; one must be well horsed and well armed; one must be vigorous, and do without sleep, suffer lack of good food and drink, rise early, sometimes have a poor bed, undergo cold and heat, and conceal one's fear.[9]

Different types of hunting required different skills, all relevant to warfare, including knowledge of the quarry's habits, handling a pack of hounds, complete control of an often-frightened horse and the use of various weapons, including spears and swords to perform the kill. In England, uniquely, deer were also hunted on foot with bow and arrow. This was particularly significant because deer hunting was exclusively an aristocratic sport. On the continent, archery was looked down upon as the preserve of townsmen and the lower ranks of society, but every English nobleman, including the king himself, had to be capable of handling a longbow and crossbow, and skill in the art was highly prized. "I know little of hunting with the bow," remarked Gaston Phoebus, count of Foix, in southernmost France, who wrote the standard hunting treatise of the late fourteenth century: "if you want to know more, you had best go to England, where it is a way of life."[10] The consequences of this English obsession were to be felt at Agincourt.

If hunting introduced young men to some of the physical and mental skills required for a military career, mock combat honed and perfected them. Three hundred years and more since the introduction of the massed charge with couched lance, this form of fighting was still relevant to the battlefield and therefore had to be practised in jousts and tournaments. An international tourneying circuit had existed since at least the twelfth century and young Englishmen eager to make a name for themselves regularly travelled to France, Spain, Portugal and, to a lesser extent, Germany and Italy, to take part in these games. The English borders with France and Scotland were fertile ground for those seeking adventures of this kind because they provided a natural meeting place for knights from enemy nations.[11]

Although there is no record of Henry V participating in a public joust or tournament, he must have learnt to fight in such combats, which were organised and supervised by professional heralds and judged by older, more experienced knights; together they enforced a strict set of rules designed to prevent death or serious injury. The joust would have taught him to handle his lance in individual encounters on horseback; the less highly regulated tournament went a stage further, involving groups of combatants on horseback, often beginning with a massed charge with the couched lance, which then gave way to the real business of sword fighting, thereby more closely emulating the experience of genuine battle. He would also have been familiar with a relatively new development, the feat of arms, in which two opponents fought several types of course: a set on horseback with the lance, followed by a set each with the sword, the axe and the dagger, all fought on foot. This training was crucial since it had become accepted practice that the knights and esquires should dismount for battle and stand with the archers, "and always a great number of gentlemen did so in order that the common soldiers might be reassured and fight better." Philippe de Commynes, who made this comment at the turn of the sixteenth century, also observed that it was Henry V and the English who had introduced this particular tactic to France.[12] He was wrong, but it is significant that this was his perception.

The reason why Henry V, unlike his father, does not appear to have taken part in any public forms of mock combat is that he was too busy with the real thing. According to contemporary chivalric treatises, this was actually more praiseworthy. Geoffroi de Charny, for example, who carried the battle standard of France, the oriflamme, at Crécy and died in its defence, wrote in his *Book of Chivalry* that it was honourable to joust, even more honourable to tourney, but most honourable of all to fight in war.[13] It was not pursuit of honour that led Henry to begin his professional military career before he reached the age of fourteen: it was necessity. His father's usurpation of the crown was repeatedly challenged by armed revolt and for at least the first six years of his reign the kingdom was in a state of constant unrest and even open war. Henry's role in these events was mapped out for him at his father's coronation in October 1399. Even though he had only celebrated his thirteenth birthday a month previously, he was one of the young men chosen for the customary honour of being knighted on the eve of the coronation. Knighthoods conferred on such occasions were highly prized because they occurred so rarely and because they were accompanied by unusual pageantry and religious ritual. The ceremony took place in the Tower of London, where each candidate took a symbolic bath to wash away his sins, was dressed in white robes to signify purity and a red cloak to represent his willingness to shed his blood, and then spent the night in a vigil of prayer watching over his arms in the chapel. The next day, having heard mass, the candidate's sword (double-edged to represent justice and loyalty) was girded about his waist, and his gold spurs, symbolising that he would be as swift to obey God's commandments as his pricked charger, were fastened to his heels. Finally, he received from the new king the *collée*, a light tap with the hand or sword, which was the last blow he was ever to receive without returning it.[14]

Having been admitted to the order of knighthood, as befitted his new princely status, Henry had also borne one of the four swords of state at his father's coronation: significantly, he chose, or was chosen, to carry the sword representing justice. A few weeks later Parliament officially decreed that he should be known as "Prince of Wales, duke of Aquitaine, Lancaster and Cornwall, earl of Chester, and heir apparent to the kingdom of England."[15] These were not simply empty titles: even at this early age, Henry was expected to share the burden of his father's crown and take personal responsibility for the security and administration of his own domains. When he sought aid to recover Conwy Castle in north Wales from rebel hands, for instance, his father informed him in no uncertain terms that the castle had fallen through the negligence of one of the prince's officers and it was the prince's responsibility to recover it.

Henry's right to two of his most important titles was soon to be challenged. In September 1400 Owain Glyn Dŵr, lord of Glyndyfrdwy in north Wales, declared himself prince of Wales and began a rebellion that would not be quelled until 1409. In 1402, the dauphin was proclaimed duke of Guienne (the French name for Aquitaine) and his uncle, Louis d'Orléans, launched an aggressive campaign of conquest in the duchy.[16] Though the threat to Aquitaine was as great as that to Wales, the problems of the rebellious principality had to take precedence since they were literally closer to home.

Medieval Wales was a country united by language but physically divided in two. The Normans, demonstrating yet again their remarkable capacity for private enterprise, aggression and colonisation, had extended their conquest of England into south Wales by the early years of the twelfth century, but their cavalry tactics were inappropriate for the mountainous north. This part of the country therefore retained its independence and its distinctive Celtic customs until the end of the thirteenth century. Edward I's conquest of north Wales was as ruthless and efficient as that of the Normans in the south: the native Welsh were expelled to make way for the building of castles and new towns, which were colonised by English settlers, and all public offices were put into English hands. As late as 1402, in response to petitions from the House of Commons, Henry IV's Parliament was still enacting racially discriminatory legislation that prohibited Welshmen from holding office in Wales or from acting as deputies and even from purchasing lands or properties within English boroughs in Wales.[17]

Owain Glyn Dŵr's revolt began as a private property dispute between himself and his Anglo-Welsh neighbour Reginald Gray, lord of Ruthin, but it swiftly escalated into a national rebellion because it tapped into both anti-English sentiment in Wales and hostility to the new Lancastrian monarchy in England. Perhaps the most dangerous point came in 1403 when the greatest and most powerful family in the north of England, the Percys, joined forces with Glyn Dŵr. The Percys had been among Henry IV's closest allies and had played a major role in helping him to the throne. Henry Percy, earl of Northumberland, had been rewarded with the posts of constable of England and warden of the west march of Scotland; his son, the Harry "Hotspur" later made famous by Shakespeare, had been made warden of the east march and justiciar (chief minister) of north Wales; and Henry's brother Thomas Percy, earl of Worcester, became admiral of England, steward of the royal household, king's lieutenant in south Wales and governor to the prince of Wales. This formidable alliance now determined to depose Henry IV and replace him with the twelve-year-old Edmund Mortimer, earl of March. (Mortimer's claim to the English throne was better than Henry IV's, since he was descended from an elder son of Edward III; the Mortimers had twice been recognised formally by the childless Richard II as his heirs, but when Richard was deposed in 1399, the earl was a child of eight whose rights were as easily swept aside as those of the young French princesses in 1316 and 1321.)[18]

The alliance between the Percys and Glyn Dŵr gave Prince Henry his first experience of what was a relatively rare event, even in medieval times: a full-scale pitched battle. It was to be a salutary experience. A force of some four thousand rebels, led by Hotspur, took up a defensive position on a ridge three miles outside the town of Shrewsbury; the king and his son marched out of the town with an army some five thousand strong. Last-minute negotiations having failed to avert conflict, the battle began about midday on 21 July 1403 with a hail of arrows from the veteran bowmen of the prince's own county of Cheshire. Unfortunately for him, they had taken the rebel side and he was on the receiving end. As the royal army struggled up the slope, the Welsh and Cheshire archers drew "so fast that . . . the sun which at that time was bright and clear then lost its brightness so thick were the arrows" and Henry's men fell "as fast as leaves fall in autumn after the hoar-frost." An arrow struck the sixteen-year-old prince full in the face but he refused to withdraw, fearing the effect it would have on his men. Instead he led the fierce hand-to-hand fighting that continued till nightfall, by which time Hotspur was dead, his uncle Thomas, earl of Worcester, was a prisoner and the Percy rebellion was over.[19]

Henry had survived his first major battle but his powers of endurance were to be tested further. A way had to be found of extracting the arrow that had entered his face on the left side of his nose. The shaft was successfully removed but the arrowhead remained embedded six inches deep in the bone at the back of his skull. Various "wise leeches" or doctors were consulted and advised "drinks and other cures," all of which failed. In the end it was the king's surgeon, a convicted (but pardoned) coiner of false money, John Bradmore, who saved the prince and the day. He devised a small pair of hollow tongs the width of the arrowhead with a screw-like thread at the end of each arm and a separate screw mechanism running through the centre. The wound had to be enlarged and deepened before the tongs could be inserted and this was done by means of a series of increasingly large and long probes made from "the pith of old elder, well dried and well stitched in purified linen cloth . . . [and] infused with rose honey." When Bradmore judged that he had reached the bottom of the wound, he introduced the tongs at the same angle as the arrow had entered, placed the screw in the centre and manoeuvred the instrument into the socket of the arrowhead. "Then, by moving it to and fro, little by little (with the help of God) I extracted the arrowhead." He cleansed the wound by washing it out with white wine and placed into it new probes made of wads of flax soaked in a cleansing ointment, which he had prepared from an unlikely combination of bread sops, barley, honey and turpentine oil. These he replaced every two days with shorter wads until, on the twentieth day, he was able to announce with justified pride that "the wound was perfectly well cleansed." A final application of "dark ointment" to regenerate the flesh completed the process.[20]

The pain the prince must have suffered in the course of this lengthy operation is unimaginable: basic anaesthesia, based on plasters of opium, henbane, laudanum or hemlock, was understood and practised in medieval times but it was unpredictable and inefficient. It says something for Henry's constitution that he survived the operation and avoided septicaemia afterwards. A wound of such magnitude in such a prominent place would surely have scarred the prince for life, but no mention of any blemish of this kind is made by contemporaries, though it is possibly the reason why Henry's only surviving portrait shows him in profile, rather than in the three-quarter-face position favoured by all other medieval English kings.[21]

If nothing else, the battle of Shrewsbury must have taught Henry the value of archers and surgeons; both would be deployed in numbers at Agincourt. Nevertheless, Shrewsbury was an exceptional event, and for most of the best part of a decade that Henry spent campaigning in Wales, he was preoccupied with the far more mundane and tedious business of besieging castles, routing out rebels and, worst of all, ensuring that his men were paid and supplied. Letters written to his father at this time reveal that the prince had become a competent, if battle-hardened, veteran, who thought nothing of burning and laying waste rebel-held territory, pausing only to comment, without irony, that it was "a fine and populous country." When a rebel chieftain was captured and offered to raise five hundred pounds within a fortnight for his ransom, Henry casually informed his father that "we couldn't accept it, so we killed him." The authentic voice of the pious victor of Agincourt also rings out in his announcement of a defeat inflicted by his household on a superior force of rebels: "it is proof that Victory does not depend on a multitude of people but, as was well demonstrated in that place, on the power of God."[22]

In the longer term, victory required not only military success but also the establishment of peace. Here, too, the prince showed his mettle, building up around him a tightly knit group of tried and trusted councillors, retainers and servants, most of whom were to serve him for the rest of his life. Foremost among these were two young soldier-aristocrats who had much in common with the young prince and became his loyal retainers. Thomas Fitzalan, earl of Arundel, was five years older, Richard Beauchamp, earl of Warwick, four: both, like Henry himself, were sons of the so-called Appellant earls, who had challenged Richard II's autocratic style of government and reaped a bitter harvest in consequence. Arundel's father had been executed, Warwick's sentenced to life imprisonment, Henry's exiled: all had had their estates forfeited by Richard II and, after his deposition, restored by Henry IV. Arundel and Warwick had distinguished military lineages, their ancestors having fought with Henry's at Crécy and Poitiers, and both were knighted with Prince Henry on the eve of Henry IV's coronation. As they each owned extensive estates in Wales, they were involved in the military campaigns against Owain Glyn Dŵr from the start, and Warwick, who distinguished himself at the battle of Shrewsbury, was rewarded by being made a Knight of the Garter at the age of twenty-one. Arundel, as we have seen, was entrusted with the leadership of the expedition to France in aid of the duke of Burgundy in 1411; Warwick accompanied him and both men were present at the battle of St Cloud. The two earls would play important roles in the Agincourt campaign but, by an ironic twist of fate, would both be deprived of the opportunity to take part in the greatest military victory of Henry's reign.[23]

Aristocrats like Arundel, Warwick and Edward, duke of York, who all had landowning interests in Wales and on its borders, were Henry's natural allies, but he did not neglect the lesser men, the knights and esquires from Herefordshire and Shropshire, who also had an interest in pacifying their troublesome neighbour. His appointments to key offices in Wales were usually made from this highly experienced group of soldiers-cum-administrators, whose local knowledge was invaluable, but he was also prepared to promote Welshmen who had proved their worth and loyalty, despite parliamentary enactments to the contrary. Royal finances in Wales were restored by two equally judicious appointments which reflect the prince's willingness to draw on expertise wherever he found it. John Merbury, who would recruit twenty men-at-arms and five hundred archers from south Wales for the Agincourt campaign, was a self-made Herefordshire esquire who had a history of long and loyal service to both John of Gaunt and Henry IV. Thomas Walton, on the other hand, was a clergyman, a young Cambridge graduate and honorary canon of St John's at Chester, whom Henry plucked from obscurity.[24] Talent, rather than status or connections, was the key to advancement in Henry's administration.

Victory also depended on money, but this was in short supply. Henry IV seems to have had little grasp of financial affairs and, despite having promised to avoid the profligacy that had made Richard II so unpopular, he could not afford to "live of his own," especially when he had to reward his supporters and suppress rebellion out of his personal income. This meant that he had to go cap in hand to an increasingly irritated Parliament to seek taxes and subsidies, which did nothing to improve either his popularity or his credibility as a reformist monarch. His reluctance, or inability, to commit enough money to the Welsh wars was one of the principal reasons why they dragged on for so long.

Prince Henry's campaigns in Wales were constantly hampered by shortage of funds. Repeated requests for more men, supplies and money were never met in full, and the prince and his officers complained incessantly that their forces were on the brink of mutiny or desertion because their wages had not been paid. In 1403 Henry pawned his own stock of "little jewels" to aid the besieged castles of Harlech and Aberystwyth and in 1405 Lord Grey of Codnor was so short of money to pay his soldiers' wages that he had to pawn his own armour. Edward, duke of York, the prince's justiciar of south Wales, tried to raise funds to pay his men at Carmarthen by obtaining loans, but was refused by everyone he approached because they had not yet been repaid earlier loans made to the crown; to keep his men in place he had to promise them on his word "as a true gentle-man" that, if no other means could be found to pay them, he would put the revenues from his Yorkshire estates at their disposal. At times the prince was even reduced to threatening that he would have to abandon the country to the rebels: "without man-power we cannot do more than any other man of lesser estate," he warned his father.[25]

The lessons of this hand-to-mouth existence were obvious and Henry was swift to learn them. In complete contrast to his father, financial prudence, economy and strategic planning were to be his watchwords. As early as 1403 he embarked on a series of measures to increase his revenues from his duchy of Cornwall and earldom of Chester, increasing rents, taking back under his own management lands that had been rented out and substantially reducing the number of annuities he paid from local revenues. The gradual reconquest of his lands in Wales also made a steady and increasing contribution to his purse, so that after 1409 he could look to an annual income of some eighteen hundred pounds from south Wales and thirteen hundred from north Wales, compared to a paltry five hundred pounds from each when he first received the principality.[26]

Such financial wisdom could not help but endear the prince to the same parliaments that groaned over his father's mismanagement of money. Parliament was under no obligation to grant the monarch any taxation, except in exceptional cases for the defence of the realm. In practice, it was the decision of the House of Commons whether to grant taxation or not; it also decided at what level taxation should be set. As Henry V's reign would show, its members were not always reluctant to do so and they could be generous. What they expected in return was value for money or, as they termed it, "good governance." In this respect, Henry IV repeatedly drew down their ire by assigning money they had voted for the defence of Calais or Aquitaine or the war in Wales to other ends, such as the payment of annuities for his supporters. To an unprecedented degree, the Commons was outspoken in its criticism, insisting that taxes should be spent on the purpose for which they had been granted, demanding that the king should reduce the size and reform the character of his household and requiring oversight of his appointments to his council. Henry IV's response to this hectoring was counterproductive: he promised compliance and did nothing, thereby adding untrustworthiness to the list of grievances against him. The Commons reacted by attaching increasingly stringent conditions to its grants, not only bypassing the royal exchequer by appointing special treasurers for war, but also insisting that their accounts should be audited and presented for parliamentary approval.[27]

The genuine fear that the monarchy would go bankrupt was not without basis, as we have seen from the extraordinary measures to which Prince Henry and his officers in Wales had been obliged to resort to finance the war there. Nor was royal insolvency without precedent. In 1340 the strains of financing the war against France had bankrupted Edward III and ruined the two Florentine banking houses on whose loans he defaulted.[28] In granting Henry IV a subsidy in 1406, Parliament inflicted its severest humiliation yet on the king, the appointment of a council with powers to oversee royal government and control its expenditure. It is a telling indication of the high opinion in which Prince Henry was already held that he was appointed to its head. A year later the council had done its job so effectively that the Commons passed a vote of thanks to the prince for his service in Wales, where the end of the rebellion was in sight, and, more pragmatically, granted a further half-subsidy.[29]

As Henry's presence in Wales became less necessary, he was able to devote more time to the council and acquire that early experience in the workings of government which Christine de Pizan had recommended. Despite the fact that the appointment of the council had been forced upon the king by Parliament, it was composed almost entirely of his friends. It included at least two men who had shared his exile: Thomas Arundel, the archbishop of Canterbury, who had crowned him king and was now chancellor of England; and Sir John Tiptoft, one of his household knights, who had served as a Member of Parliament for Huntingdonshire since 1402 and speaker of the House of Commons in 1405–6, who became treasurer of England. The new council also included the king's closest family, upon whom he had relied heavily when his own sons were too young to take an active role in politics. These were his three half-brothers — John Beaufort, earl of Somerset; Thomas Beaufort, earl of Dorset; and Henry Beaufort, bishop of Winchester — and their cousin and retainer Thomas Chaucer, the son of the poet, who was speaker of the House of Commons in the parliaments of 1407, 1410 and 1411. (The Beauforts, together with their sister Joan, who was married to Ralph Neville, earl of Westmorland, were the illegitimate children of John of Gaunt and his mistress Catherine Swynford, whom Gaunt belatedly married in 1396. Their offspring were then legitimised by the papacy and by a royal patent approved in Parliament, though they were formally excluded from succession to the throne.[30])

Apart from Archbishop Arundel, with whom Prince Henry seems to have quarrelled irrevocably, probably over their differing attitudes towards France, and John Beaufort, earl of Somerset, who died in 1410, all these men were to remain trusted advisors of the future king. The Beauforts' influence, in particular, was extremely important in helping to shape Henry's priorities and his role as both prince and king. John and Thomas Beaufort were active soldiers and veterans of the Welsh campaigns; perhaps more importantly, both men served as admiral of England and captain of Calais, roles which made them passionate advocates for the defence of the seas and for the protection of English trading interests with Flanders. This alone was sufficient to recommend them to the House of Commons, where there was a powerful merchant lobby, but their success in performing their duties also earned them parliamentary approval. Their brother Henry Beaufort was an extraordinary man whose wealth, power and influence were matched only by his ambition, energy and ability, enabling him to straddle the secular and ecclesiastical worlds with equal success. At the age of twenty-two he had been elected chancellor of Oxford University, a year later he obtained his first bishopric (which did not stop him fathering a bastard on Archbishop Arundel's widowed sister) and in 1409, when he was still only thirty-two, he was appointed a cardinal a latere by the schismatic pope in Rome, Gregory XII. An assiduous attender of royal council meetings, he served his first stint as chancellor of England in 1402–5 and paved the way to his future role as moneylender-in-chief to the crown with a loan of two thousand marks for the defence of the seas and Calais. The identification of the Beauforts with the concerns of the House of Commons gave them both an ear and a voice in the lower house, but because they never lost the confidence of the king they were able to act as intermediaries between the two. The more receptive prince gained proportionately, being fully informed on opinions within the Commons and also acquiring friends and advocates there.[31]

Through his close association on the council with the Beauforts and the two speakers of the House of Commons, Tiptoft and Chaucer, Prince Henry managed to achieve the amicable working relationship with Parliament which had eluded his father (and, indeed, Richard II). He had effectively demonstrated his capacity to rule wisely, particularly during the two years when he had enjoyed complete control of the council. In that period he had re-established the royal finances by a mixture of retrenchment, prioritised and targeted expenditure and careful audit work. The security of the kingdom had been enhanced by the suppression of the Welsh revolt and by strengthening the key garrisons in that principality, at Calais and in the northern marches with men, ordnance and supplies. The alliance with the duke of Burgundy, which had resulted in Thomas, earl of Arundel's expedition into France, had demonstrated that he appreciated the value of English trading interests in Flanders. On a different level, but almost as important as these practical proofs of Prince Henry's abilities, was his determination to dissociate himself publicly from the "fair words and broken promises"[32] that had characterised his father's dealings with Parliament and to establish a reputation for himself as a man who did not give his word lightly but, when he did, took pride in keeping it.

When Henry IV died after years of chronic illness, in March 1413, his eldest son and heir was twenty-six years old. He had served a long and hard apprenticeship for kingship, but along the way he had gained invaluable experience as soldier, diplomat and politician. He was now at the peak of his powers. In the circumstances, it was not surprising that his accession was widely anticipated as the dawning of a new hope and a brighter future.

CHAPTER THREE

A MOST CHRISTIAN KING

The day of Henry V's coronation, Passion Sunday, 9 April 1413, would long be remembered for the savagery of the storms that ravaged the kingdom, "with driving snow which covered the country's mountains, burying men and animals and houses, and, astonishingly, even inundating the valleys and fenlands, creating great danger and much loss of life."[1] For an age that saw the hand of God in everything, this was not a good omen, but Henry V was not a man to let superstition of this kind stand in his way. Precisely because he was the son of a usurper, he was determined to establish the legitimacy of his kingship beyond all doubt. To do this, he deliberately set out to be the perfect medieval monarch and the coronation was a key element in his strategy.

The ceremony itself was traditionally regarded as one of the holy sacraments of the Church. The most important elements were the anointing with unction, which conferred divine and temporal authority upon the new king, and the coronation oath. The act of anointing had taken on a deeper meaning since the "discovery" of a sacred oil which, according to legend, had been given to St Thomas Becket by the Virgin Mary, who promised him that a king anointed with it would recover Normandy and the lands of Aquitaine which had been lost by his ancestors, drive the infidel from the Holy Land and become the greatest of all kings. The oil had then remained hidden away until it was "rediscovered" in the Tower of London by Archbishop Thomas Arundel, just in time for Henry IV's coronation. The whole story was clearly a piece of Lancastrian propaganda, but neither this, nor the fact that Henry IV failed to fulfil the prophecy, deterred his son (and grandson) from using the oil at his own coronation. The small print of the legend rather forlornly specified that Normandy and Aquitaine would be recovered "peacefully" and "without force."[2]

The second strand to the coronation ceremony placed equal emphasis on the duties of kingship. This was the coronation oath, sworn at the altar, in which the king promised to uphold the laws, protect the Church and do right and equal justice to all. Significantly, Henry IV had chosen to rely on this aspect of the coronation to justify his usurpation, accusing Richard II of breaking his oath to provide the country with "good governance" and therefore committing perjury that rendered him unfit to be a king. The idea that kingship was a contract between king and people, rather than an inalienable right, was not new, but Henry IV had taken it a step further, and even so ardent a pro-Lancastrian as the chronicler John Capgrave had to admit that he had succeeded Richard II "not so much by right of descent as by the election of the people." The danger of Henry relying so heavily on the duties instead of the rights of kingship was immediately apparent. He had made himself a hostage to fortune, and throughout his reign his own failure to live up to his promises would be used repeatedly as an excuse for every sort of opposition.[3]

It was typical of Henry V that he was able to take two essentially flawed concepts and turn them into a position of strength. In his own mind there was no question but that he was divinely appointed to rule and, like Richard II, he insisted on the dignity due not to himself, but to his office. Richard had required his courtiers to fall to their knees whenever he looked at them; Henry, according to at least one source, would not allow anyone to look him in the eye and deprived his French marshal of his office for having the temerity to do so. Although Henry's personal preference seems to have been for a simple, almost austere way of life, he took great care to appear in the full panoply of state whenever he considered it necessary. As we shall see, he would receive the formal surrender of the "rebel" town of Harfleur, for instance, in a pavilion on top of a hill (so that he could look down on the defeated Frenchmen as they approached him), sitting on his throne under a canopy, or cloth of estate, made of gold and fine linen, with his triumphal helm bearing his crown held aloft on a lance by his side. Yet when he actually entered the town for the first time, he dismounted and walked barefoot to the parish church of St Martin, in the manner of a humble pilgrim or penitent, to give thanks to God "for his good fortune."[4]

Henry's ability to distinguish between himself as a man and as the incumbent and upholder of his office also impressed his contemporaries: unlike most modern commentators, they were able to see that his invasions of France were not made out of egotism or the desire for personal aggrandisement, but rather because he wanted, and considered it his duty, to recover the "just rights and inheritances" of the crown. On the other hand, both contemporaries and modern commentators alike have sometimes been confused by the expression of this dual personality: the affable, straight-talking and companionable soldier "Harry" could swiftly become the cold, ruthless and haughty autocrat if he felt that the line had been crossed and unacceptable liberties were being taken.[5]

Henry's character and bearing deeply impressed even his enemies. The French ambassadors sent to negotiate with him some years later came away singing his praises. They described him as being tall and distinguished in person, with the proud bearing of a prince, but nevertheless treating everyone, regardless of rank, with the same kindly affability and courtesy. Unlike most men, he did not indulge in lengthy speeches or casual profanity. His answers were always short and to the point: "that is impossible" or "do that," he would say, and if an oath were required, he would invoke the names of Christ and his saints. What they most admired was his ability to maintain the same calm, equable spirit in good times and bad. He took military setbacks in his stride, encouraging his soldiers by telling them that "as you know, the fortunes of war vary: but if you desire a good outcome, you must keep your courage intact."[6] It was a philosophy that would serve him, and his men, well on the Agincourt campaign.

The chroniclers' stories of Henry's wild, misspent youth and his dramatic conversion at his coronation into a sober, just and righteous king were mostly written long after his reign was over and, although they have acquired a veneer of historicity because they were taken up by Shakespeare, the only contemporary hint of even the slightest misconduct is a comment by his friend Richard Courtenay, bishop of Norwich, that he believed that Henry had been chaste since he had become king.[7] What is important about these stories is not so much their truth, but that they represent in anecdotal form the spiritual experience of the coronation: the anointing transformed an ordinary man into a unique being, part man, part clergyman, who was chosen by God to be his representative on earth.

Despite his belief in his divinely constituted authority, Henry also placed unprecedented emphasis on his coronation oath as the central theme of his kingship. Unlike his father, he treated it "almost as a manifesto, a programme for government,"[8] and he was committed to its implementation. He would uphold the laws, protect the Church and do right and equal justice to all. From the moment he succeeded to the throne, he made it clear that he was prepared to draw a line under the events of the previous two decades. Among the young nobles whom he selected for knighting on the eve of his coronation were at least five of the sons and heirs of men who had died in, or been executed for, rebellion against Henry IV. The most important of these was the twenty-one-year-old Edmund Mortimer, earl of March, who had been recognised by Richard II as his heir and, as a child, had twice been the focus of rebel attempts to depose Henry IV in his favour. He had spent most of his childhood in captivity but from 1409 he had lived in the less formal prison of the future Henry V's own household, where, although he was unable to come and go as he pleased, he was in every other respect treated like any aristocratic member of the royal court. Henry now trusted him sufficiently not only to free and knight him but also to restore all his lands and allow Mortimer to take his place in the first parliament of the new reign. Although two years later he would be involved on the fringes of the only aristocratic plot against Henry V, his sense of personal obligation was such that he revealed it to the king and remained both loyal and active in royal service for the rest of his life.[9]

Henry's generosity towards another potential rival, the twenty-three-year-old John Mowbray, also paid dividends. The son of the man whose bitter personal quarrel with Henry's own father had led to their joint banishment by Richard II, and younger brother of Thomas Mowbray, whom Henry IV had executed for treason in 1405, he had not been allowed to inherit his lands until a fortnight before Henry IV's death. On his accession, Henry V immediately restored to him the family's hereditary title of earl marshal. This was not an empty honour and the timing of its reinstatement was sensitively done because it enabled Mowbray to play his important traditional role at the coronation, demonstrating publicly that the feud which had plagued both their houses was at an end. Negotiations for similar restorations of titles and lands were also begun for Henry Percy, nineteen-year-old son of "Hotspur" and grandson of the earl of Northumberland, both of whom had died in rebellion against Henry IV, and for the eighteen-year-old John Holland, son of the earl of Huntingdon executed by Henry IV in 1400.[10]

In his choice of councillors and officers of state the new king also displayed both wisdom and tact, building round him a team upon whom the success of the Agincourt expedition would depend. He was always prepared to promote talent wherever he found it, keeping on those who had served his father well, whether they were career civil servants, such as John Wakering, the keeper of the chancery rolls, whom he would promote to the bishopric of Norwich in 1416, or aristocrats, like Ralph Neville, earl of Westmorland, who was confirmed in his office as warden of the west marches of Scotland.

On the other hand, key posts were also given to those who had been part of his inner circle as prince of Wales. His half-uncle and long-term ally Henry Beaufort, bishop of Winchester, was appointed chancellor of England and keeper of the Great

Seal on the first day of the new reign, ousting the sixty-year-old Archbishop Arundel. This combined office made Beaufort the most powerful government minister in the kingdom. As chancellor he controlled the office which issued all the writs in the king's name by which government business was carried out. The Great Seal, which was attached to these orders, was instantly recognisable (even to the illiterate) as the official seal of England whose authority outranked that of any other individual or department of state. Thomas, earl of Arundel (the archbishop's nephew), replaced Sir John Pelham as treasurer of England and was also appointed to maintain the country's first line of defence from invasion as warden of the Cinque Ports and constable of Dover. Richard Beauchamp, the young earl of Warwick, who had already demonstrated outstanding negotiating skills as well as military ones, was immediately employed on several sensitive diplomatic missions and, at the beginning of 1414, would be entrusted with the strategically important post of captain of Calais.[11]

Almost as important as this choice of advisors was Henry's refusal to promote those who might have expected office, honour and profit from the new king. Henry Beaufort's financial skills, powers of oratory and influence in the House of Commons made him an exemplary chancellor, but the post was not enough to satisfy his limitless ambition. When Archbishop Arundel died on 19 February 1414, Beaufort expected to be rewarded with the see of Canterbury. Instead, Henry appointed a man who was both a relative newcomer and, compared to the aristocratic Arundel and Beaufort, an outsider. Henry Chichele was the sort of clergyman whom the new king liked to have around him. A Londoner, whose brothers were eminent aldermen in the City, he was an Oxford graduate and an expert in civil law who had served on an embassy to France, as king's proctor in Rome and as a delegate to the general council of the Church at Pisa. Since 1408 he had been bishop of St David's in Wales and in 1410–11 he had served on the royal council when it was headed by Henry as prince of Wales. Significantly, he had not attended after Henry's removal, indicating that he was already identified as one of the prince's men.

Fifty-two years of age when he was appointed to Canterbury, Chichele had a wealth of experience as an administrator and a diplomat, but in two important aspects he was the antithesis of the king's half-uncle. First, he was solid, dependable and tactful, a servant of the Church and king, rather than of his own personal ambition. Second, unlike the flamboyant and worldly Beaufort, he was genuinely pious, with a touch of that severe self-discipline and restraint which Henry shared and admired in others. Henry's own piety would not allow him to appoint as leader of the Church in England a man who did not have the spiritual interests of that Church at heart. Chichele amply repaid Henry's trust by the quiet efficiency with which he led both diplomatic embassies and Church affairs. His appointment also served as a warning shot across the bows that the new king would not allow anyone, however high his rank or long his service, to presume upon his favour. It was a lesson Beaufort should have learnt in 1414 but would have to be taught more harshly a few years later.[12]

The most significant person to be excluded from Henry V's inner circles and favour was his brother Thomas, duke of Clarence. Despite the fact that for the first eight years of Henry's reign Clarence was next in line to the throne, he was never appointed regent, never received a major independent military command and was never given a significant position of trust. Although he set off for home as soon as news of Henry IV's death reached Aquitaine, he did not arrive in time for his brother's coronation. He was thus accidentally deprived of the opportunity to carry out his duties as steward and constable of England at the ceremony. And, shortly after his return, he was deliberately deprived of his office as king's lieutenant in Aquitaine, which was given to his half-uncle Thomas Beaufort, earl of Dorset, who had remained in the duchy with Edward, duke of York. Not long afterwards, he lost the captaincy of Calais to the earl of Warwick, though he remained captain of the less important adjacent territory of Guînes.[13]

Although Henry carefully avoided humiliating Clarence by compensating him for the loss of his offices with a handsome pension of two thousand marks, the new king's determination to foster a spirit of reconciliation does not seem to have genuinely embraced his brother. Was Henry being vindictive? Was Clarence being punished, even persecuted, for having been his father's favourite? His treatment is in marked contrast to that meted out to his younger brothers. John, who was twenty-four at Henry V's accession, was allowed to remain in office as warden of the east marches of Scotland and twenty-two-year-old Humphrey was appointed chamberlain of England. They each received advancement at Henry's hands too: John was created duke of Bedford and Humphrey duke of Gloucester on 16 May 1414. More significantly, both men would serve as regents in England while Henry was away fighting in France.[14]

Hot-headed, quarrelsome and lacking in judgement, Clarence had never made any secret of his support for the Armagnacs. Indeed, it was typical of the man that in 1412, not content with just leading a military expedition to their assistance, he had also taken the step of forming an intimate personal bond with their leader. Reserving only his allegiance to the king of England (who was then his father, not his brother), Clarence had sworn a formal oath to become the brother-in-arms of Charles d'Orléans, promising to "serve him, aid him, counsel him, and protect his honour and well-being in all ways and to the best of his powers."[15] The kindest interpretation of this action is that it was indiscreet, but Clarence had compromised himself further during the winter of 1412–13 by forming military alliances in Aquitaine with Bernard, count of Armagnac, and Charles d'Albret.

Clarence's commitment to the Armagnacs raised suspicions that he was trying to carve out a principality of his own. Indeed, this may have been his father's intention when he appointed Clarence his lieutenant in Aquitaine in the first place, for there was, as we have seen, a precedent in Richard II's plans to hive the duchy off from the crown and bestow it on John of Gaunt. And if Henry gave up his own title of duke of Aquitaine to his brother when he became king, it would resolve the problem of homage once and for all, since there could be no objection to Clarence and his heirs doing homage to the king of France. A proposal of this nature might also be traded for a recognition of increased rights and expanded boundaries in Aquitaine, which had always been the principal aim of Henry IV's foreign policy. But Henry V had no intention of relinquishing his duchy to anyone, since to do so would undermine his own claim to the rest of his "just rights and inheritances" in France.[16]

One of Henry V's first acts as king was to offer the olive branch in the form of a general pardon for all treasons, rebellions and felonies committed in his father's reign to anyone who cared to seek it. "Whereas we are mindful of the many great misfortunes which have arisen out of faction . . . ," he proclaimed, "we have firmly resolved, since it would be pleasing to God and most conducive to the preservation of good order, that as God's pardon has been freely bestowed on us, we should allow all the subjects of our kingdom . . . who so desire, to drink from the cup of our mercy." Suing for a pardon did not necessarily imply guilt. It is difficult to believe that the elderly bishop of Hereford, a former royal confessor, really needed his pardon "for all treasons, murders, rapes, rebellions, insurrections, felonies, conspiracies, trespasses, offences, negligencies, extortions, misprisions, ignorances, contempts, concealments and deceptions committed by him, except murders after 19 November." Nevertheless, a pardon was a useful insurance policy in uncertain times and the response — some 750 individual pardons were issued before the end of the year — suggests that this conciliatory gesture was welcomed in many quarters.[17]

Within a few days of his accession, Henry dispatched Thomas, earl of Arundel, to Wales with special powers to receive former rebels into the king's grace and to grant them pardons at his discretion. The results were spectacular. Six hundred inhabitants of Merionethshire appeared before Arundel admitting that they deserved death as traitors but asking for mercy; when he granted them a communal pardon on Henry's behalf, they fell on their knees and thanked God for the magnanimity of their king. More than fifty condemned rebels from Kidwelly were also spared death, fined and had their lands restored. This granting of pardons and restoration of lands to former rebels was not simply an act of royal mercy and charity. It was also highly profitable. In just two years Henry raised more than five thousand pounds — well over four million dollars in today's currency — from fines collected from his Welsh lands.[18]

While it might be tempting to see fund-raising as the real reason for the whole exercise, it was nevertheless true that the pardons and restorations allowed those Welshmen who had been tempted to rebel to put the past behind them and make a clean start. The success of this policy was demonstrated by the fact that, although Owain Glyn Dŵr was still at large in the mountains (and never would be captured), at no time was he ever able to attract enough malcontents to raise the standard of revolt again. Significantly, too, there was a genuine attempt to pursue and punish corrupt royal officials who had abused their powers in the principality. Thomas Barneby, the chamberlain of north Wales, at first successfully evaded indictment by bribery, but Henry's commissioners did not give up and a few months later he had to face thirty charges of extortion and embezzlement and was removed from office. Another royal official, Sir John Scudamore, the steward of Kidwelly, was similarly deprived of his post, even though it had been granted to him for life.[19] Such actions did much to redress the balance: the king might penalise those who had rebelled against his authority, but he was also prepared to punish those who had abused it. Henry was demonstrably carrying out his oath to do right and equal justice for all in Wales. It was a policy that clearly won him friends in the principality, judging by the huge numbers of Welshmen who signed up for the Agincourt campaign.

The same was true of the rest of his kingdom. Violence against persons and property, riots and disorder, were endemic in medieval England.[20] The principal reason for this was not simply that society was naturally more criminal, but rather an inability to obtain justice, which encouraged those who perceived themselves to be victims to seek redress or revenge themselves. Since there was neither a police force nor a public prosecution service to investigate crimes or indict criminals, the judicial process relied almost entirely on local men (and they were nearly always men) who served as jurors, sheriffs or justices of the peace. Inevitably, these were also the people most vulnerable to bribery, corruption and intimidation because they were dependent for their offices on the goodwill, power and patronage of the magnates and aristocrats, the super-rich whose landholdings and influence crossed county boundaries and ultimately led to the fount of all good things, the royal court and the king himself.

In Shropshire, where the most powerful magnate was Thomas, earl of Arundel, one of Henry V's closest friends, a small group of his retainers had acquired a stranglehold on local administration. Their crimes ranged from the obvious — peculation, extortion, terrorising and destroying the countryside at the head of armed bands of men — to the ingeniously devious, such as securing the appointment of their opponents to the unpopular post of tax-collectors. Henry IV had not dared to intervene for fear of offending Arundel, whose support was essential in crushing the Welsh revolt, but Henry V had no such qualms. He appointed a special commission of central court justices from the king's bench at Westminster with extraordinary powers to suppress the disorder in Shropshire. This was a bold move (commissions of this type had roused such violent popular opposition under Richard II that Henry IV had been afraid to use them and had never allowed the king's bench to leave Westminster), but it proved its worth immediately. Over the course of the summer of 1414, almost eighteen hundred indictments were received and proceedings were begun against sixteen hundred individuals.[21] The seven leading culprits were prosecuted, found guilty and forced to give bonds for the enormous sum of £200 each (the equivalent of $133,300 today) to keep the peace in future. Arundel himself was obliged to give a further bond of £3000 ($2,012,500 today) as a pledge for their good behaviour. This alone was a powerful demonstration that Arundel's friendship with the king did not allow him, or his retainers, to be above the law.

In less sure hands, such exemplary punishment meted out to a powerful aristocrat and his supporters would probably have provoked a hostile reaction, possibly even armed revolt. The success of Henry's policy is therefore all the more remarkable, particularly as the experience in Shropshire was repeated throughout the rest of the country. The knights and esquires of the shires, who should have been the natural upholders of local justice, were specifically targeted by Henry's special courts and made to pay the price for deviating from that role. Critically, however, it was not such a high price that it drove them into opposition. Even Arundel's notorious band of seven was given a second chance. They all received pardons and, more importantly, redeemed themselves by active military service: six of them served in Arundel's retinue on the Agincourt campaign; the seventh remained at home as a captain entrusted with the guardianship of the Welsh marches.[22] Many of their own servants, who had also been indicted for the same offences, played a vital role as archers at Agincourt.

Henry was also prepared to intervene personally to resolve disputes before they spiralled out of control. A revealing anecdote in an English chronicle proves that it was a far more terrifying experience to have to answer to the king in person than to his courts. Two feuding knights from Yorkshire and Lancashire were ordered before the king when he was just sitting down to dinner. Whose men are you? he asked them. Yours, they replied. And whose men had they raised to fight in their quarrel? Yours, they replied again. "& what authority or comaundement had ye, to raise up my men or my peeple, to fyght & slay eache othyr for your quarel?" Henry demanded, adding that "in this ye are worthy to die." Unable to answer, the two knights humbly begged his pardon. Henry then swore "by the feith that he owed to God and to Seint George" that if they could not resolve their quarrel before he had finished his dish of oysters, "they should be hanged both two." Faced with such a choice, the knights were immediately persuaded to settle their differences, but they were not yet off the hook. The king swore his favourite oath again and told them that if they, or any other lord within or without his realm "whatsomeever they were," ever caused any insurrection or death of his subjects again, "they should die, accordyng to the lawe."[23] By sheer force of personality, Henry succeeded in establishing and keeping the king's peace to a degree that was unprecedented, especially for a monarch who spent much of his reign absent from his kingdom. In doing so, he earned himself a reputation that extended far beyond the shores of England and even eclipsed his military successes in contemporary eyes. "He was a prince of justice, not only in himself, for the sake of example, but also towards others, according to equity and right," wrote the Burgundian chronicler, Georges Chastellain; "he upheld no one through favour, nor did he allow wrong to go unpunished out of kinship."[24]

Given Henry's determination to promote reconciliation and restore peace and order to the country, it is ironic that the first serious challenge to his authority came not from one of his father's enemies but from a trusted member of his own household. Sir John Oldcastle was a veteran of the Welsh wars who had served as a Member of Parliament for, and sheriff of, his home county of Herefordshire. It is a measure of Henry's confidence in him that in 1411 Oldcastle had been chosen as one of the leaders of Arundel's expedition to France to aid the Burgundians.[25] Like many of the wealthy, literate and intelligent knights attached to the royal court under Richard II and Henry IV, Oldcastle had strong Lollard sympathies, and it was these that brought him into trouble. Lollardy was a precursor of the Protestant faith. Its roots lay in anticlericalism — anger and frustration at the wealth and privileges enjoyed by the Church and the inadequacy and corruption of its ministers — which had been strengthened by the growth in literacy among the gentry and urban middle classes. Knights, esquires, merchants, tradesmen and their wives who were capable of reading their own Bibles and, increasingly, owned or had access to a copy in English, were inclined to be more critical of the Church's failure to measure up to the apostolic standards of the New Testament. More importantly, instead of simply looking to reform the Church, they were also starting to develop an alternative theology that made the Bible the sole authority for the Christian faith, rather than the Church and its hierarchy. They began to question, and even to deny, the central teachings of the Church. The most extreme among them believed that the Church had no valid role to play as an intermediary between the individual and God. They therefore rejected the seven sacraments performed by priests (baptism, confession, eucharist, confirmation, marriage, ordination and extreme unction) and anything which relied on the intercession of saints, such as praying to them, venerating their images or even going on pilgrimage. In the forthright words of Hawisia Mone, a convicted Lollard in the diocese of Norwich, going on pilgrimage served no purpose except to enrich priests "that be too riche and to make gay tapsters and proude ostelers." On the evidence of his *Canterbury Tales*, one feels that Chaucer might not have entirely disagreed with this statement.[26]

The problem with identifying Lollardy as heresy was that it included many shades of opinion, not all of which fell outside the pale of orthodoxy. Even the new king's loyalty to the Church could not be taken for granted. His grandfather, John of Gaunt, had been an early patron of John Wycliffe, the Oxford theologian who is regarded as the father of English Lollardy, and employed him to write tracts attacking papal supremacy and clerical immunity from taxation. The Lollards themselves believed that they had enjoyed the support of Henry IV, and Thomas, duke of Clarence, owned a copy of the Wycliffite Bible.[27]

Oldcastle's heretical views were not in doubt. He was the "principal receiver, patron, protector, and defender" of Lollardy in England and was in touch with similar movements abroad: he had even offered the military support of his own followers to King Wenceslaus, who was carrying out a programme of seizure of Church lands in Bohemia.[28] Tried and convicted of heresy, Oldcastle refused to renounce his faith and was sentenced to be burnt at the stake. At the king's express request, a stay of execution was granted so that Henry could try to persuade his friend to submit, but before the forty days' grace had elapsed, Oldcastle escaped from the Tower of London.[29]

It was at this point that what should have been a purely religious affair became a political one. Instead of going into hiding or fleeing abroad, Oldcastle decided to stage a *coup d'état*.[30] The plot was to capture the king and his brothers by disguising himself and a group of his fellow conspirators as mummers for the annual Twelfth Night celebrations at Eltham Palace in January 1414. At the same time, Lollards from all over the country were to gather in St Giles's Field, just outside the city gates, ready to take London by force. These plans were foiled by

Henry's spies, who discovered the plot and forewarned the king. (They, and two informers, were swiftly and generously rewarded by the king.)[31] The court removed from Eltham and as the little bands of Lollards, armed with swords and bows, drifted into St Giles's Field from as far away as Leicestershire and Derby, they were ambushed and overpowered. Oldcastle's predictions that one hundred thousand men would rally to his cause were hopelessly exaggerated. Some seventy or eighty were captured, of whom forty-five were promptly executed as traitors; significantly, only seven were burnt as heretics.

It rapidly became apparent that Oldcastle's revolt had little popular support, and having reacted swiftly and harshly to the initial threat Henry was now prepared to be merciful to the individuals involved. On 28 March 1414 he issued a general pardon to all rebels who submitted before Midsummer and in the following December he extended this to include those still in prison and even to Oldcastle himself, who had escaped capture and gone into hiding.[32]

Oldcastle's revolt had precisely the opposite effect to the one that he had intended. Lollardy did not become a national state-endorsed religion, nor could it be any longer regarded as purely a Church affair that was irrelevant to the secular authorities. Instead, it had now become synonymous with treason and rebellion. One of the first acts passed by the next parliament which met at Leicester in 1414, just after the revolt, required all royal officials, from the chancellor right down to the king's bailiffs, to investigate heresy and assist the ecclesiastical courts in bringing Lollards to justice. This resulted in a significant increase in heresy trials, convictions and burnings at the stake. Lollardy did not die out altogether, but it was disgraced, discredited and driven deeper underground.[33]

The crushing of Oldcastle's revolt marked the victory of orthodoxy over heterodoxy. It was also a personal triumph for Henry V. He had survived an attempted coup by acting decisively, and in the process he had placed the Church under an obligation to himself which he did not hesitate to call in. The Agincourt campaign would be financed from the coffers of the English clergy and supported by the Church's prayers, blessings and propaganda. The new king had demonstrably fulfilled his coronation oath to defend the Church and would continue to do so. Even Thomas Arundel, the archbishop of Canterbury, was forced to admit (perhaps through gritted teeth) that Henry V was "the most Christian king in Christ, our most noble king, the zealous supporter of the laws of Christ."[34] It was an accolade that would be repeatedly bestowed by many contemporaries and it was a significant one: it was yet another title that Henry V had taken from the king of France.[35]

❖ CHAPTER FOUR ❖

THE DIPLOMATIC EFFORT

Henry V had been king of England for only a few weeks when there was a dramatic turn of events in France. The uneasy peace that had existed between Armagnacs and Burgundians since the previous autumn exploded in the sort of mob violence which would be a hallmark of the French Revolution in the 1790s. On 28 April 1413 a Parisian rabble burst into the dauphin's palace, the Hôtel de Guienne, overcame his guards and seized the dauphin himself. Not long afterwards the same fate befell his parents, and the king, again in a scene that strikingly anticipated the 1790s, was forced to put on the revolutionary emblem, the white hood.[1]

The revolt was led by one Simon Caboche, who, aptly enough, was a butcher by trade. It rapidly emerged that like most Parisians he was also a Burgundian by sympathy. All the Armagnacs who held senior positions in the royal households, including Edouard, duke of Bar, Louis, duke of Bavaria (who was the queen's brother), and thirteen or fourteen of the queen's ladies-in-waiting, were thrown into prison; some were murdered, others were executed, all were replaced by Burgundians. It was, as one Burgundian sympathiser coolly remarked, the best thing that had happened in Paris for the past twenty years.[2]

John the Fearless may have instigated these events because he felt he was losing control of his sixteen-year-old son-in-law, the dauphin, who was showing increasing signs of independence and had just dismissed his Burgundian chancellor. If he did, he was soon to reap the whirlwind. The dauphin bitterly resented the public humiliation that he had been forced to endure and determined to ally himself more firmly with the Armagnacs. And in May, his father, Charles VI, unexpectedly recovered his sanity. It was only a temporary reprieve, but it was enough to allow him to take advantage of a reaction against the bloodiness of the Cabochien coup to impose an equally temporary peace.[3] By August, it was clear that the Armagnacs, with the help of the dauphin, were regaining control of Paris. Their device, or badge, emblazoned with the words "the right way," began to reappear throughout the city and was again worn openly on their supporters' clothing. The dauphin ordered the arrest of some of the most prominent Cabochiens and began replacing Burgundian officials with Armagnacs once more. In the face of growing rumours that John the Fearless himself would be seized and made to stand trial for the murder of Louis d'Orléans, the duke decided that discretion was the better part of valour and took flight for Flanders. He did so without seeking the king's permission to leave, as he was obliged to do, and, as his chancellor wrote with barely disguised pique to the duchess, "without telling me or his other officials, whom he has left in this town you can imagine in what peril."[4]

For the moment, the Armagnacs enjoyed the sweet taste of victory again. Charles, duke of Orléans, made a triumphal entry into Paris, riding side by side with the dukes of Anjou and Bourbon and the count of Alençon. They were joined a little later by the two Gascons who had proved such a thorn in the side of the English in Aquitaine, Charles d'Orléans' father-in-law, Bernard, count of Armagnac, and Charles d'Albret, who was now restored to his post as constable of France. Although peace was officially proclaimed, all Paris was full of armed men, and every single official appointed by the duke of Burgundy was ousted and replaced by an Armagnac.[5]

On 8 February 1414 John the Fearless appeared before the gates of Paris at the head of a large army. He claimed that he had come at the dauphin's request and flourished, as proof, letters from his son-in-law begging to be rescued from the Armagnacs. The letters were forgeries but they fooled most contemporary chroniclers (and some later historians). They did not, however, spark the uprising in Paris that the duke needed to gain entry to the city. Even though the terrified citizens, unable to go out to work in the fields as they usually did, were struck down with a fever and cough so severe that men were made impotent and pregnant women aborted, the gates of Paris remained firmly shut against him. After two weeks of frustration, the duke abandoned the siege and decamped back to Arras.[6]

Flushed with this success, the Armagnacs decided to take the war out to the enemy. The king had once more relapsed into a madness that was probably more comfortable than the insanity going on around him. Royal letters were therefore issued in his name, laying open the way for the prosecution of Louis d'Orléans' murderer, and on 2 March 1414 war was declared on the duke of Burgundy. The Armagnacs marched out of Paris, taking with them the king and the dauphin.

With the king, who was once more wearing the badge of the Armagnacs, went the oriflamme,[7] the sacred standard of France, which was only ever carried when the king himself was present in battle. With the dauphin, who was "in a jovial mood," went "a handsome standard covered in beaten gold and adorned with a K, a swan [cigne] and an L," a punning reference to La Cassinelle, a very beautiful girl in the queen's household, who was "as good-natured as she was good-looking," and with whom the dauphin was passionately in love. Since being "good-natured" was a medieval euphemism for being of easy virtue, the dauphin's jovial mood is easily explained. What is more, by riding out under a device referring to his mistress he was able to combine paying lip-service to the chivalric ideal of fighting for the love of a woman with the altogether more satisfying notion that, in doing so, he was also insulting both his wife and his father-in-law. (The duke of Burgundy did not have much luck with his sons-in-law. Another daughter, Catherine, who had been offered as a potential bride to both Philippe d'Orléans [Charles's younger brother] and Henry V of England, was married at the age of ten to the son of Louis, duke of Anjou, and sent to live at the Angevin court. Three years later, in the wake of John the Fearless's flight from Paris and having spent all the dowry she brought with her, the duke of Anjou decided to join the Armagnacs. Catherine was therefore surplus to requirements and was unceremoniously and humiliatingly returned to her father "like a pauper." As her husband was even younger than she was, it was likely that the marriage was unconsummated and therefore not legally binding, but it made her position difficult with regard to future marriages. Though she bore the family burden of being extremely ugly — a Burgundian would be punished for describing her and her sister as looking like a couple of baby owls without feathers — her repudiation was an extreme and unusual act of cruelty aimed at her father, rather than herself. The innocent victim of these politically motivated posturings was said to have died of grief and shame soon afterwards; it was certainly true that she never remarried.)[8]

The dauphin's enthusiasm for making war on his father-in-law was not, apparently, shared by the royal military officers: the constable of France, Charles d'Albret, managed to break his leg and the admiral, Jacques de Châtillon, was similarly immobilised by a fortunately timed attack of gout. The first objective of the Armagnac army was to recover the towns of Compiègne and Soissons, which John the Fearless had seized on his way to Paris earlier in the year. Compiègne was taken relatively easily, but Soissons, where the Armagnac sympathies of the town were held in check by a Burgundian garrison in the castle, proved to be an altogether more bloody affair.

The garrison was commanded by Enguerrand de Bournonville, "an outstandingly good man-at-arms and a great captain," who had carried out many "fine deeds of arms against the enemies of my lord of Burgundy." He was a veteran of the battle of Othée in 1408, in which Burgundian forces had defeated the men of Liège, and of St Cloud in 1411, in which he had commanded a division against the Armagnacs. Bournonville had only a small force of men-at-arms from Picardy and Artois, reinforced with a group of English mercenaries, with which to defend both castle and town, but he refused to surrender. Faced with a besieging army and a hostile town, Bournonville carried out a heroic defence that ultimately proved futile. Soissons was taken by storm; Bournonville himself was captured and immediately executed. Though Burgundian partisans depicted this as a breach of chivalric conventions and an act of private vengeance by Jean, duke of Bourbon, whose bastard brother was killed by a crossbowman during the siege, Bournonville had been captured in arms against his king and was technically a rebel. According to the laws of war, therefore, his execution was entirely justified. His courage and loyalty on the scaffold nevertheless ensured him a deserved place in the history books. Bournonville asked for a drink and then declared, "Lord God, I ask your forgiveness for all my sins, and I thank you with all my heart that I die here for my true Lord. I ask you, gentlemen, to punish the traitors who have basely betrayed me, and I drink to my lord of Burgundy and to all his well-wishers, to the spite of all his enemies."[9]

Bournonville's execution was just the beginning. Despite the fact that some of the citizens of Soissons had colluded with the Armagnacs and actively assisted in its capture, the city was sacked with a savagery that became almost legendary. The men were slaughtered, the women, including nuns, were raped, and churches were ransacked for their treasure. The Armagnacs, it was said, behaved worse than Saracens, and more than one chronicler would conclude that the defeat at Agincourt, which was inflicted on the feast day of the cobbler-saints of Soissons the following year, was divine retribution for their crimes against the city. It would become a common refrain that nothing the English inflicted on the long-suffering inhabitants of northern France would exceed the miseries enacted upon them by their own fellow-countrymen.[10]

After the brutal sacking of Soissons, the Armagnacs swept into the heartlands of the duke of Burgundy's territories and laid siege to Arras, "the shield, the wall and the defence of Western Flanders."[11] This time, however, they found a rock-solid defence and no traitors within the city's walls. The siege petered out amidst a failure of money, supplies and will, exacerbated by an outbreak of dysentery, the scourge of besieging armies. But

John the Fearless was sufficiently alarmed to be persuaded of the need to come to terms again. On 4 September 1414, acting through his brother Antoine, duke of Brabant, and his sister Margaret, wife of William, count of Hainault, Holland and Zeeland, he agreed the Peace of Arras, which was to end all military activity, offer an amnesty to those involved on both sides and prohibit all partisan behaviour. Neither side had any intention of keeping the treaty, but it allowed another temporary cessation of hostilities without loss of face for either party. Indeed, John the Fearless managed to avoid swearing to keep the peace in person for almost ten months and when he eventually did so, on 30 July 1415, it was so hedged about with conditions that it was almost meaningless.[12]

As John the Fearless was well aware, by the time he actually put pen to paper the Peace of Arras was an irrelevance. Just across the Channel, Henry V had gathered one of the biggest invasion fleets ever seen and was poised to set sail for France.

English military intervention in France had been likely ever since Henry V's accession; after all, he had been intimately involved in the earl of Arundel's expedition of 1411 and also, as the French mistakenly believed, in Clarence's expedition the following year. What no one, except perhaps Henry himself, expected was that this time the English would not be invited in to assist one or other of the warring parties, but would invade independently, unannounced and entirely for their own ends. So intent were the French princes on pursuing their own private quarrels that this simply did not occur to them. They would pay dearly for their lack of imagination.

Henry had been waiting and preparing for just such an opportunity from the moment he ascended the throne. Although the establishment of law and order in his own kingdom was a priority, it was not the only one and would constantly vie for his attention with foreign policy. Unlike his father, Henry did not simply react to events on the continent but actively sought to influence them. The new king had two objectives: to neutralise those maritime nations that had traditionally allied with France against England and to protect English merchant shipping and coastal towns from attack.

The Spanish kingdom of Castile had consistently aided the French against the English, despite the fact that its co-regent, the widowed Queen Catherine, was Henry IV's half-sister.[13] Castilian galleys had frequently preyed on English shipping as it made its way to and from Aquitaine, and a small Castilian fleet under the command of "the unconquered knight" Don Pero Niño had made a series of raids on Bordeaux, Jersey and the south-west coast of England in the early 1400s, stealing ships, looting and burning the towns and killing their inhabitants. The new king now signed truces with Castile, appointing arbitrators to settle disputes and claims arising from both sides and holding out the prospect of a final peace in continuing negotiations. It was typical of Henry V that he did not allow breaches of the truces to go unchallenged, even if they were committed by his own side. As early as 17 May 1413 he ordered the release of two Spanish ships, the *Seynt Pere de Seynt Mayo en Biskay* and the *Saint Pere*, together with their cargoes, which had been captured and taken to Southampton by his own ship, the *Gabriel de la Tour*.[14] This conciliatory policy achieved its short-term objective of preventing any Castilian intervention in English affairs.

"The greatest rovers and the greatest thieves," according to a contemporary political song, were not the Spanish but the Bretons. Although geographically part of France, Brittany was virtually an independent state, with its own administrative and judicial systems, a small standing army and its own currency. For centuries the duchy had enjoyed close political ties with England. Henry II's son Geoffrey had been count of Brittany in the twelfth century, young Breton princes had been brought up in the English royal household in the thirteenth century, English soldiers and mercenaries had played a decisive role in the Breton civil wars of the fourteenth century and as recently as 1403 Henry IV had married Joan of Navarre, the widow of Jean V, duke of Brittany. Despite these close links and English dependence on the importation of salt from Bourgneuf Bay,[15] relations between the merchants and seamen of the two nations had been distinctly adversarial. The rich pickings to be had from the commercial shipping ploughing regularly up and down the Channel were a great temptation to Breton and Devonshire pirates and the retaliatory seizure of ships and cargoes by both sides in pursuance of unpaid debts threatened to spiral out of control.

Henry V was determined to clamp down on piracy. Negotiations with the duke of Brittany resulted in January 1414 in a renewal and extension of the ten-year truce that had been agreed two years earlier. Keepers and enforcers of the truce were appointed on either side, with the result that English prisoners from London, Fowey and Calais were released and English ships from Bridgewater, Exeter, Saltash, Bristol and Lowestoft were returned, as were Breton ships held at Hamble, Fowey, Winchelsea and Rye.[16] This was all standard practice, but Henry V was prepared to go a stage further in demonstrating his determination to enforce the treaty. In Devon alone, some 150 indictments for piracy were brought and around twenty ship-owners were charged. Among them were some of the most important and influential people in the county, including three former mayors of Dartmouth, all of whom had sat as Members of Parliament, and one of whom was deputy admiral for Devon. Like those convicted of criminal offences in the shires, they would also be given a second chance. They were allowed to sue for pardon and, with a nice irony, at least one would later lend his king an ex-pirate vessel, the *Craccher*, to patrol and help safeguard the seas during his campaigns in France.[17]

The unusual vigour with which Henry prosecuted those individuals guilty of breaking his truces was a clear indication of the depth of his commitment to keeping the peace with his maritime neighbours,[18] but his reasoning was not entirely altruistic. The keeping of the seas was not just a matter of preserving order: it could have serious diplomatic consequences. Breaches of truces and safe-conducts threatened good relations with the Bretons, the Castilians and the Flemish which he needed to cultivate in the hope of detaching them from their traditional alliances with France. The newly negotiated truces with Brittany provided an excuse for the inclusion of clauses in which the duke unilaterally agreed not to receive or help any English traitors, exiles or pirates, and, more significantly, not to receive or help any armed enemies of Henry V, nor to allow any of his own subjects to join the king's enemies. These undertakings would have

serious implications for the role of Brittany during the Agincourt campaign.[19]

The same thinking guided Henry's negotiations with the duke
of Burgundy, which were intimately connected with his separate
discussions with the king of France and the Armagnacs. The
greater significance of the relationship with Burgundy was
reflected in Henry's choice of ambassadors. Instead of the relatively humble knights and clerks who had negotiated the truces
with Castile and Brittany, he employed a glittering array of
some of the most eminent in the land. Richard, earl of Warwick,
and Henry, Lord Scrope of Masham, were both veterans of
important diplomatic embassies abroad, Henry Chichele, the
future archbishop of Canterbury, was an expert in civil law and
drafting treaties, and William, Lord Zouche of Harringworth,
was lieutenant of Calais. All were tried and trusted members of
the king's inner circle, and each of them brought experience and
special skills to the negotiating table.

That such high-powered envoys should be sent to Calais
merely to arbitrate and settle any disputes arising from the existing truces between England and Flanders, as they were nominally empowered to do, aroused suspicion. The fact that the
English envoys chose to spend a considerable amount of time in
the duke of Burgundy's company — and that he actually paid
out more than seven hundred pounds for them to travel between Calais and Bruges — added to the rumours. The Armagnacs now in control of Paris believed that an alliance had
already been concluded between the duke and the English. If
any secret deal was reached, however, there is no official record
of it, though at least one contemporary chronicler got wind of
discussions about a proposed marriage between Henry and one
of the duke's daughters.[20]

In fact, while English commercial interests in Flanders were a
powerful argument for siding with John the Fearless, Henry was
not yet ready to commit himself to a formal alliance with either
party. The short-term aim of his policy towards France was
simple, even though his methods were not: he wanted to exploit
the divisions between Burgundians and Armagnacs to obtain
the best possible outcome for himself. In this he was not very

different from his predecessors, except that the focus of their attention since the 1370s had always been Aquitaine. Henry was more ambitious. When his ambassadors met those of the king of France at Leulinghen, near Boulogne, in September 1413, they began a lengthy lecture on Edward III's claim to the throne of France and the unfulfilled terms of the Treaty of Brétigny. They even produced a selection of "most beautiful and notable books" to back up their demands with documentary evidence. (One can see the lawyer Chichele's guiding hand in this reliance on historical text.) The French responded by quoting Salic Law and denying that the kings of England were even legitimate dukes of Aquitaine, let alone kings of France. In the stalemate that followed, all that could be agreed was a temporary truce to last for eight months.[21] An interesting side-light on these abortive negotiations was the English insistence that all the conversations and subsequent documentation should be conducted in Latin, even though French was the customary language of diplomacy. Already, it would seem, the English were asserting their Anglo-Saxon superiority and pretending that they did not understand French.

Before the year was out, a batch of Armagnac ambassadors, headed by Guillaume Boisratier, archbishop of Bourges, and Charles d'Albret, constable of France, had arrived in London. This time, the English appeared more conciliatory and a new truce was agreed to last for one year from 2 February 1414 to 2 February 1415. Although the English had previously insisted on their right to help their own allies despite the truces — which the alarmed Armagnacs must have interpreted as evidence of a secret arrangement with the Burgundians — they now agreed that all the allies and subjects of England and France should also be bound by these agreements. (The list included the duke of Brittany and also the duke of Burgundy's subjects, the count of Hainault, Holland and Zeeland, and the duke of Brabant, but not the duke of Burgundy himself.) The spat over whether the proceedings should be recorded in Latin or French was repeated but resolved with the decision that, in future, all treaties between the two nations should be in both languages.[22]

Henry was prepared to make these minor concessions because

the truces were useful and because he had his eye on the bigger picture. The French ambassadors had also been empowered to discuss a lasting peace and, "for the avoidance of bloodshed," Henry declared himself ready to hear what they had to offer. He even agreed that the best prospect for securing peace was that he should marry Charles VI's eleven-year-old daughter, Catherine, and undertook not to marry anyone else for the next three months while negotiations continued. Four days after the truces were signed, Henry appointed a low-key embassy to France, headed by Henry, Lord Scrope, which had powers to negotiate a peace, arrange the marriage and, if necessary, extend the period during which Henry had promised to remain single.[23]

As Henry had undoubtedly intended, his willingness to discuss peace lulled the Armagnacs into a false sense of security. Throughout the entire period of the negotiations, they also derived additional hope from the presence in Paris of Edward, duke of York, who was believed to favour an Armagnac alliance and the marriage with Catherine of France. The duke was actually on his way home from Aquitaine, but he lingered for five months in Paris, where he was assiduously courted and fêted by his Armagnac hosts. No expense was spared and the duke even received substantial sums of money due to him from the Armagnac princes after Clarence's abortive expedition of 1412.[24] Unfortunately for them, they had overestimated the duke's influence at the English court; more seriously, they had also misjudged Henry V's intentions.

The apparently favourable progress of negotiations between the English and the Armagnacs caused alarm and consternation in the Burgundian camp. John the Fearless's situation had become increasingly desperate after his failed siege of Paris and his subsequent flight to Flanders. As the Armagnac army swept into the heartland of his territory in the summer of 1414, he knew that if he was to obtain English support, he would have to raise the stakes. He therefore sent ambassadors to England, empowering them to repeat the offer to Henry V of one of his daughters in marriage, but also to arrange an offensive and defensive alliance between the two countries. The terms he proposed were that, on request, each of them should supply the other with five hundred men-at-arms or a thousand archers for three months without payment; that the duke would help Henry to conquer the territories of the count of Armagnac, Charles d'Albret and the count of Angoulême; and that the duke and the king would mount a joint campaign to conquer the lands of the dukes of Orléans, Anjou and Bourbon and the counts of Alençon, Vertus and Eu. It was also suggested that neither party would make an alliance with any of these dukes or counts without the consent of the other and that the Anglo-Burgundian alliance would be aimed against all except the king of France, the dauphin, their successors, the duke's close family, including his brothers, Antoine, duke of Brabant, and Philippe de Nevers, the king of Spain and the duke of Brittany.[25]

These were tempting terms for Henry and he had no hesitation in appointing envoys to discuss them. Henry, Lord Scrope, and Sir Hugh Mortimer, who had just returned from arranging the king's marriage with Catherine of France, now found themselves simultaneously arranging his marriage with Catherine of Burgundy.[26] They were joined on this embassy by three of Henry's most trusted servants, Thomas Chaucer, Philip Morgan, a lawyer and future bishop of Worcester, and John Hovyngham, an archdeacon of Durham, who was the workhorse of most of Henry's diplomatic missions.[27] These ambassadors clearly suspected that the Burgundian terms were unworkable and that the feudal loyalty that the duke owed to the king of France would, in the field, take precedence over his convenient alliance with the king of England. Where, then, would that leave an English army in the midst of a campaign against the Armagnacs? Scrope and his fellow envoys were not reassured by the equivocal replies they received to their questions. The most startling aspect of the proposed alliance, however, was not mentioned in the official account of the negotiations. Henry had actually given his ambassadors full powers "to seek, obtain and receive the faith and liege homage of the duke of Burgundy, for himself and his heirs, to us and our heirs, and to receive him as our vassal." Such homage could only have been given if Henry had persuaded the duke to renounce his allegiance to Charles VI and recognise his own title as the true king of France. Duplicitous and treacherous though John the Fearless undoubtedly was, his quarrel was not with Charles VI himself, but with the men surrounding him, and he was not yet prepared to betray his sovereign for an English alliance.[28]

Even without homage, the duke of Burgundy's offers considerably strengthened Henry's bargaining position with the Armagnacs. He was now able to take a discernibly sterner tone, referring to Charles VI as "our adversary of France" and demanding the restoration of his just rights and inheritances. It is even possible that he considered that the moment had now come when he could launch his invasion of France. At some point in the spring of 1414, Henry had called a meeting at Westminster of the great council of the realm, consisting of all the senior members of the aristocracy and the Church, to discuss and approve a resolution to go to war. Far from slavishly backing the idea, the lords of the great council delivered something of a reproof to their king, urging him that he should "in so high a matter begin nothing" except what was pleasing to God and would avoid the spilling of Christian blood. They urged him to negotiate further, to moderate his claims and to ensure that if he had to go to war it should only be because all other reasonable avenues had been exhausted and he had been denied "right and reason."[29]

Henry responded by appointing yet another embassy, this time a high-profile one, led by Richard Courtenay, bishop of Norwich, Thomas Langley, bishop of Durham, and Thomas Montagu, earl of Salisbury. On their arrival in Paris, Courtenay made the now customary claim for the throne of France, but then, almost in the same breath, acknowledged that this was unacceptable to the French and offered to compromise: Henry would accept Normandy, Touraine, Anjou, Maine, Brittany, Flanders and a fully restored duchy of Aquitaine in full sovereignty, together with the lordship of Provence, the one million six hundred thousand crowns outstanding from the ransom of Jean II of France and two million crowns as dowry for the Princess Catherine. The Armagnacs, who had heard most of this before and regarded it simply as an opening gambit in the diplomatic game for Catherine's marriage, responded by repeating the offer they had made in 1412 of an enlarged Aquitaine (though the thorny question of homage was left unaddressed), plus a dowry of six hundred thousand crowns.[30]

These were generous terms so far as the Armagnacs were concerned, but they were derisory compared to what Henry had claimed. It was this disparity — combined with some highly effective English propaganda — which led to the famous incident of the tennis balls. As told by Shakespeare, the dauphin responded to Henry's demands by mocking his supposedly wild youth and sending him some tennis balls to play with, prompting Henry's defiant reply:

> *When we have match'd our rackets to these balls,*
> *We will, in France, by God's grace, play a set*
> *Shall strike his father's crown into the hazard.*[31]

In fact, the dauphin, who was almost ten years younger than Henry, had nothing to do with these negotiations and was actually away from Paris campaigning against the duke of Burgundy when the embassy took place. Had he really sent tennis balls, especially to Henry V, who was notoriously prickly on the subject of his dignity, the insult would have been a major diplomatic incident and brought the negotiations to an abrupt end. This simply did not happen. Nevertheless, the tennis balls story found its way into some contemporary chronicles, and all English sources are unanimous in describing the French as mocking Henry's claims and ridiculing the king himself; the ambassadors, according to one chronicler, "were treated with derision."[32] This was all patently untrue, but it was a convenient fiction that would whip up anti-French sentiment and help justify the English invasion of the following year.

The Peace of Arras in September 1414 put a temporary stop to hostilities between the Armagnacs and Burgundians and for the time being ended the duke of Burgundy's need for military assistance. The terms of the military alliance that he had proposed to Henry were quietly dropped, though negotiations continued and the duke's behaviour during the build-up to the battle of Agincourt suggests that he had given at least a tacit assurance that he would do nothing to hinder the English invasion. He would not be the first or last to hope that foreign troops would destroy his enemies for him.

The same high-powered English embassy, led by the bishops of Norwich and Durham but with the substitution of the king's half-uncle, Thomas Beaufort, earl of Dorset, for the earl of Salisbury, returned to Paris in February 1415. Once again, they were received with great honour, and took their place in the public celebrations to mark the Peace of Arras. They attended feasts, watched Charles VI (despite his madness) joust against the count of Alençon, who had just been created a duke, and, more significantly, saw a friendly joust between Charles, duke of Orléans, and the duke of Burgundy's brother Antoine. A few days later, they were also present to observe the performance of a challenge by three Portuguese knights against three French; as the Portuguese were long-term allies of the English, they were led into the field by the earl of Dorset, who then had the mortification of watching them being defeated.[33]

Despite the festivities, the serious business of the embassy was not neglected. The French were convinced that Henry V's territorial demands were simply posturing and that the marriage would go ahead and resolve everything, not least because the English ambassadors now agreed to discuss the two questions separately. The English made some show of compromise, reducing their demand to a million crowns for Princess Catherine's dowry, but the French refused to rise above eight hundred thousand and were not prepared to make any more concessions. The English declared themselves unable to agree to such terms without further authorisation (the standard diplomatic excuse for bringing negotiations to an end) and returned home empty-handed.[34]

Henry V had not expected any other outcome. Four days before the French made their final offer, he had summoned the mayor and aldermen of London into his presence at the Tower and informed them that he intended to cross the sea to recover his rights by conquest.[35]

It had always been unlikely that Henry would achieve all that he wanted in France through diplomacy alone. It is impossible to guess what concessions would have been enough to buy him off, but the marriage with Princess Catherine was certainly an indispensable condition: it was the only way that Henry could ensure that any lands he acquired in France would pass to his heirs by right of inheritance, as well as by legal treaty or conquest. As the son of a usurper himself, he understood all too well the necessity of securing the legitimacy of his future line. Though he also entertained (simultaneously) proposals of marriage with the daughters of the duke of Burgundy, the king of Aragon and the king of Portugal,[36] these were never anything more than a polite detour along the road to diplomatic alliance.

What territorial concessions would have satisfied him? An enlarged Aquitaine, restored to the boundaries set by the Treaty of Brétigny, which had been the goal of his predecessors, was clearly not enough. The Armagnacs offered him this in the summer of 1414 — as did John the Fearless, implicitly, with his proposal to assist Henry in conquering the lands of the count of Armagnac, Charles d'Albret and the count of Angoulême.[37] Henry seems to have taken this restoration for granted. His ambitions were, instead, focused on creating a cross-Channel empire centred on Calais, and expanding westwards and southwards into Normandy and eastwards into Picardy and western Flanders. An English dominion of this size on French soil and flanked on either side by two friendly powers, Brittany and the Burgundian-controlled Low Countries, would have enormous strategic value. It would allow the English complete control over both the Straits of Dover and the Channel, safeguarding the merchant shipping of England and her allies and opening up potential new markets in the north of France. It would also give Henry command over the two most important waterways of France, the rivers Seine and Somme, enabling him to restrict the flow of goods and travellers into the interior at will. Finally, it would also place a further barrier, beyond the Channel, between France and Scotland, two ancient allies that were united in their enmity to England.

CHAPTER FIVE

SCOTS AND PLOTS

Scotland had always been regarded as the French back door into England. The "auld alliance" between the two countries had been mutually beneficial. The French could rely on the Scots invading England from the north whenever the English themselves attacked France; the Scots, on the other hand, were able to maintain their own independence because the English were so preoccupied with their French ambitions. Unlike the Welsh, the Scots were very much part of the European chivalric tradition and could match the English tactic for tactic; their mercenaries were as active and as feared as English ones. The porous nature of the border between England and Scotland made it virtually impossible to police effectively, so if Henry was to make any sort of intervention in France, he needed to ensure that the border was secure and that the Scots stayed at home.

Although English kings had from time to time demanded homage from Scottish kings, Scotland at this time was an independent kingdom with its own monarchy and parliament. Like England and France, it had suffered from the incapacity of its kings and the mutually destructive power struggles between its magnates. Relations with England had deteriorated since the accession of Henry IV, who had begun his reign by demanding that Robert III do homage to him as king of England and by invading Scotland as far as Edinburgh. On 14 September 1402 Harry "Hotspur" Percy had inflicted a crushing defeat on the Scots at the battle of Homildon Hill. Seven Scottish magnates were killed and twenty-eight captured, including Murdoch, earl of Fife, the son and heir of the duke of Albany, the de facto regent of Scotland.[1]

Murdoch was handed over to Henry IV, but Percy had refused to surrender his other most valuable captive, the earl of Douglas. When Percy himself had raised the standard of revolt against Henry IV in 1403, he made an alliance with the Scots and Douglas fought on his side at the battle of Shrewsbury, where he was again captured and joined Murdoch as the king's prisoner. Though negotiations for Douglas's ransom continued fitfully for a number of years, he did not obtain his freedom until 1409, and then it was only by the shameful expedient of breaking his parole, "contrary to knightly honour," and refusing to return to his English prison. (Having sworn to serve Henry IV and his sons for the rest of his life, he promptly broke this oath also.) The more honourable, if perhaps more foolish, Murdoch remained a prisoner in England for the rest of Henry IV's reign.[2]

When the second Percy rebellion failed in 1405, Hotspur's father, the earl of Northumberland, fled to Scotland with his eleven-year-old grandson Henry Percy. The boy was sent to St Andrews to be brought up with James Stewart, the son and heir of the king of Scotland, who was the same age. At the beginning of 1406, the dying king, fearing that his son's life was all that stood between the duke of Albany and the Scottish throne, decided to send James to France. The boy was hidden on board the *Maryenknyght*, a merchant ship from Danzig carrying wool and hides, and sailed from North Berwick. Unfortunately for him and for Scotland, the *Maryenknyght* was captured off the Yorkshire coast by Norfolk pirates, and the heir to the throne of Scotland joined the heir of the duke of Albany and the earl of Douglas in an English prison. He was to remain there for the next eighteen years.[3] Henry IV now held all the cards.

Robert III died within a few days of his son's capture and although the captive James was recognised as king by the council-general of Scotland, his uncle, the duke of Albany, was appointed governor of the kingdom and set about converting it into his personal fiefdom. In his negotiations with England, Albany's aim was to obtain the release of his own son, Murdoch, earl of Fife, and leave James in captivity, though he could not do this too overtly for fear of alienating those loyal to the new king. A five-year truce was finally agreed in May 1412 and preparations were put in train for the release of James and Murdoch the following spring. All these arrangements were stalled by the death of Henry IV in March 1413.[4]

During the last few weeks of Henry IV's life, bills had been circulating in London alleging that Richard II, the king whom Henry had deposed and murdered, was still alive and would return from Scotland to reclaim his throne. Immediately after his coronation, Henry V ordered the arrest of the chief conspirators, including the man who had put his name to the bills, John Whitelock, a former yeoman of Richard II's household, and Sir Andrew Hake, a Scottish knight, who had been involved in a plot against Henry IV in 1399.[5]

The conspirators had taken sanctuary in Westminster Abbey — an additional insult to Henry V, whose coronation took place in the Abbey church while they were there. Sanctuary was supposed to be inviolable,[6] affording the protection of the Church for forty days to anyone seeking refuge, and the sanctuary at Westminster was the holiest of holies. (It was a moot point whether the Whitelock conspirators could be forcibly removed or not, but there were more subtle ways of obtaining the desired result: in an earlier, similar case one malefactor was arrested when he left the sanctuary of St Mary Somerset in London to use a privy a hundred yards away.[7])

In June 1413, and within days of a second set of Whitelock's bills appearing on church doors in London, the conspirators were arrested and found themselves in the Tower. Much to Henry V's fury, Whitelock escaped before he could be sent for trial and was never recaptured. Hake and another of the conspirators were set free on terms which suggest that they turned king's evidence and were perhaps to be employed as double agents. The only real casualty of the whole affair was the unfortunate prison warden who had helped Whitelock escape: he was drawn, hanged and quartered as a traitor, and his head was posted on one of the Tower gates as a warning to the rest of the prison staff that dereliction of duty would not be tolerated.[8]

The Whitelock affair, like Oldcastle's revolt, had been nipped in the bud by Henry V's prompt and decisive actions, but it confirmed the dangers of allowing people to believe that Richard II might still be alive. Before the end of the year, therefore, Henry had arranged that Richard's body, which had been interred in the Priory church of the Black Friars at King's Langley, should be reburied in Westminster Abbey. It had been Richard's own wish that he should be buried in the tomb he had erected in the choir of the Abbey for himself and Anne of Bohemia, his beloved queen who had pre-deceased him. Now Henry arranged that the body, placed in a new coffin on a bier draped with black velvet, should be carried the twenty miles from Langley to Westminster. With characteristic parsimony, he borrowed the banners he had had made for his own father's funeral at Canterbury Cathedral for the procession, but otherwise the obsequies were performed as lavishly as Richard himself had laid down in his will. The corpse was escorted by a crowd of bishops, abbots, knights and esquires, and received at the Abbey by Henry himself, who ordered that four tapers should burn continually at the tomb and that there should be a weekly dirge, requiem mass and distribution of money to the poor in Richard's name. This ceremonial reburial, carried out with all due honour and splendour, was widely applauded as an act of personal piety on the part of the new king, in which he had tried to make amends for his father's usurpation and murder of Richard II.[9] This was undoubtedly true. It was also just as true that the very public display of the king's corpse, over the course of the several days that it took for the funeral procession to wend its way to Westminster, was calculated to prove, once and for all, that Richard II was dead. His ghost would not be laid so easily, but it was already beginning to sleep more quietly.

The Whitelock affair underlined the importance of coming to

some sort of terms with the Scots as swiftly as possible. On the very first day of his reign, Henry had sent King James and Murdoch, earl of Fife, to the Tower of London, where they were to remain in secure custody for the best part of the next two years. On the same day, Henry's brother John, duke of Bedford, and Ralph Neville, earl of Westmorland, were confirmed in their offices as wardens of the Scottish marches and a programme of reinforcing and repairing the northern border castles was put in place. These aggressive tactics persuaded the governor of Scotland, the duke of Albany, that it was in his best interests to renew the truces between the two countries in the summer of 1413, and in February 1414 the Scots were also included in the general truce between England, France and their allies, which was to last for a year.[10]

Making a truce and keeping it were two different things. It was virtually impossible to rein in the unruly marcher lords who existed in a constant state of warfare with their neighbours on the other side of the border. The twice-perjured earl of Douglas was the main culprit on the Scottish side, raiding and burning English towns almost at will.[11] Henry V realised that the most effective way of preventing this was to restore the defence of the northern marches to their traditional keeper, a Percy earl of Northumberland, so long as the loyalty of that earl was beyond doubt. Given the recent history of the Percy clan, this was a bold initiative and an extremely risky one. There were simply no guarantees that Hotspur's heir would be any more loyal than his father or grandfather. What is more, the restoration of the Percys was likely to alienate their ancient rivals in the north, the Nevilles, whose loyalty to the Lancastrian kings had been unswerving.

Henry's solution to these problems was complicated and ingenious. In November 1414 he sanctioned a petition in Parliament that would allow Percy to sue for his restoration to the title and estates of the earldom of Northumberland, which had been forfeited by his grandfather on his conviction for treason. Negotiations were then put in place for Percy to be exchanged for Murdoch, earl of Fife. (Neither Albany nor Henry V had any wish to exchange him for King James, whose return to Scotland would certainly end Albany's rule as governor and might end the factional struggles that had divided and weakened the realm.) As Murdoch had been captured in war, his release was also dependent on the payment of a ransom, for which Henry demanded ten thousand pounds. This amount was not to be paid by the Scots directly but by Percy, giving the king a financial hold over him which might be perceived as a bond for his good behaviour. Henry also arranged (with Percy's consent) that Percy should marry Eleanor Despenser, the widowed daughter of Ralph Neville, earl of Westmorland, and Joan Beaufort, Henry's own half-aunt.[12] The marriage was prestigious enough to satisfy Percy's honour and had the added advantage of compensating the Nevilles. Most important of all, it laid the foundations for a lasting peace between the two rival families, which could only benefit the short- and long-term stability and security of the northern marches.

But for once, Henry's carefully laid plans miscarried. Murdoch was released from the Tower in May 1415 into the custody of two esquires, who were entrusted with escorting him to the northern borders. As they travelled through Yorkshire, they were attacked by an armed band led by an outlawed Lollard knight from Easington in Craven, Sir Thomas Talbot, and Murdoch was "feloniously abducted." Almost as unlikely as the abduction itself was its resolution. After spending a week in captivity, Murdoch was miraculously rescued by another Craven esquire, Ralph Pudsey, whom a grateful Henry rewarded with an annuity of twenty-five pounds for life. He was then handed over to the earl of Westmorland for safekeeping but the moment had passed and the delayed exchange did not take place until some nine months later.[13]

The timing of this whole episode could not have been worse. The failure to hand over Murdoch provoked outrage in Scotland and played straight into the hands of the French, who already had ambassadors in Perth trying to persuade the duke of Albany to attack England. At the moment Henry most needed peace in the northern marches, the Scots were literally on the war path. On 22 July 1415 a large Scottish force crossed the border into Northumberland and after a fiercely fought

battle at Yeavering was heavily defeated by Sir Robert Umfraville, the constable of Warkworth Castle. Another force, led by
the earl of Douglas, succeeded in penetrating as far as Westmorland and burnt the market town of Penrith before turning back.
A retaliatory raid by the English from the western marches targeted and burnt the Scottish town of Dumfries. Only a few days
before he set sail for France, Henry dispatched three experienced negotiators to secure a renewal of the truces and ordered
all the local militias to be alert and ready to march against the
Scots at his brother's command, "as the king has particular
information that those enemies and their adherents are purpos-
ing shortly with no small power to invade the realm by divers
coasts . . . to do therein what mischief they may." Nevertheless,
he was sufficiently confident about the Scottish situation not to
delay his voyage. His judgement was justified, for there was no
serious incident during his absence from the realm, and what
trouble did occur was confined to the Scottish marches, where
local troops contained and dealt with it. But Murdoch and
Percy would have to wait for their release until he had finished
his business in France.[14]

Henry V had spent so long planning his expedition in such
meticulous detail and had tried to anticipate every eventuality
so carefully that the crisis which befell him just before he set
sail must have shaken him to the core. On 31 July 1415, the
day before a general embarkation was due to take place at
Southampton, Edmund Mortimer, the young earl of March,
came to the king and confessed that there was a plot afoot to
depose Henry and put March himself on the throne. The main
conspirator was Richard, earl of Cambridge, the younger
brother of Edward, duke of York, and a cousin of the king's
own father. Accused with him was a knight from Northumberland, Sir Thomas Grey of Heton, and a clutch of other northern
knights, including Sir Robert Umfraville, Sir John Widdrington,
John, Lord Clifford and, most shockingly of all, one of Henry's
trusted advisors, Henry, Lord Scrope. The aim, as Cambridge
later confessed, was to take the earl of March to Wales and
there proclaim him king. While an uprising was being fostered

in Wales with the aid of the fugitive rebel leader Owain Glyn Dŵr, the Scots were to invade northern England, bringing with them both Henry Percy and the "Mommet," a Richard II impersonator, who were to be exchanged for Murdoch, earl of Fife. The Scots were to be assisted in their invasion by Umfraville and Widdrington, who had charge of several strategically important border castles and their garrisons, and the return of Percy would persuade the north to rise in rebellion. The rest of England would fall to the combined forces of the conspirators and the Lollards, who would rally once again to their outlawed leader, Sir John Oldcastle. Attacked on all sides, "Harry of Lancaster," the "usurper of Yngland," would thus be swept away and replaced by the legitimate heir to the throne.[15]

It would be easy to dismiss the entire plot as the work of fantasists. Could anyone seriously believe that it might be possible to bring all these disparate elements together to form a cohesive and invincible army? Did anyone really think that the twenty-three-year-old earl of March, whom one of his fellow conspirators contemptuously referred to as nothing "but a hogge," would make a better king than Henry V? What had the Scots (or, for that matter, Percy and Murdoch) to gain from treating with the rebels rather than the king? The common view among historians appears to be that there was never any chance that Cambridge's "hare-brained scheme" would come to fruition.[16] Nevertheless, unlikely though it may seem, there are several indications to suggest that the web of conspiracy had indeed spread along the lines Cambridge had envisaged.[17]

The conspiracy — aptly described as "an epilogue to the story of the reign of Henry IV,"[18] rather than a reaction to that of Henry V — was in many respects a replay of the Percy rebellions of 1403 and 1405 and a typical medieval aristocratic revolt. Edmund Mortimer had long been a focus for disaffection, simply because of his birth and his standing as the acknowledged heir of Richard II. Grey, Clifford and Scrope were all related to both Cambridge and Percy by marriage, and Scrope was also the nephew of the archbishop of York, whom Henry IV had executed for treason in 1405. Family networks and loyalties clearly played their part in drawing men into the conspiracy, but they cannot explain why they were prepared to risk their lives and fortunes to overthrow the Lancastrian regime that had been in power for sixteen years. Some contemporaries, baffled especially by Scrope's involvement, believed that they had been corrupted by French gold. This was not impossible, for both Cambridge and Grey were in severe financial difficulties that their expenditure on preparations for the Agincourt expedition could only have compounded. What is more, the French ambassadors were still in England in July and knew of rumours that there might be a rebellion in favour of either the earl of March or the duke of Clarence once Henry V had left the country.[19] Supporting such a rebellion — and such rumours — was in France's interest, even if it only temporarily delayed or diverted Henry from his purpose.

Henry's reaction on learning of the plot was characteristically swift and ruthless. He at once ordered the arrest of Cambridge, Scrope and Grey, and before night fell all three were imprisoned in the new tower at Southampton Castle and a ten-strong commission, led by John Mowbray, the earl marshal, who was responsible for military discipline, had been appointed to investigate the allegations. Two days later, on 2 August 1415, the three men were indicted for high treason. The principal charge against them, however, went far beyond the treasonable acts of which Cambridge and Grey were undoubtedly guilty. They were accused specifically of having plotted to assassinate the king, his brothers and other subjects of the king in Southampton. Though the death of the king, and perhaps his brothers, might have been inferred from a successful usurpation, their assassination does not appear to have featured in any of the conspirators' plans, and was probably an invention designed to secure a swift conviction. Cambridge and Grey pleaded guilty, but Scrope demonstrated greater courage and probity. He denied absolutely any involvement in an assassination plot, or indeed any other plot, and claimed that his only crime had been that he knew about the conspiracy but had failed to tell the king.

On the strength of his confession, Grey was condemned to

death and beheaded the same day. Both Cambridge and Scrope claimed their legal right to be tried by their peers. This was quickly and easily arranged, for most of the aristocracy were in Southampton, waiting to embark for France. On 5 August twenty peers, including the king's brothers Clarence, who presided over the court, and Gloucester, gathered in Southampton Castle to pass judgement on the accused men. (Cambridge's elder brother, the duke of York, should have had a place on the tribunal, but was excused.)

The verdict was a foregone conclusion and unanimous. Cambridge and Scrope were condemned to be drawn, hanged and beheaded. Henry graciously remitted the sentence of hanging and spared Cambridge, as he had Grey, the humiliation of being drawn, or dragged through the public streets to his place of execution.[20] Cambridge wrote a grovelling letter after his condemnation, addressed to "Mine most dreadful and sovereign liege Lord," beseeching the king to spare him. He even had the temerity to borrow his brother-in-law's excuse, claiming that all the offences he had committed were caused "by the stirring of other folk egging me thereto." It availed him nothing, and on 5 August Cambridge paid for his treason with his life. Two days later Edmund Mortimer received a royal pardon, on the grounds that the conspirators had taken advantage of his innocence.[21]

Scrope, however, had to suffer the full rigour of the law. The reason for this is not entirely clear. Henry may not have believed his professions of innocence: if French gold had underwritten the plot, then Scrope, who had played a crucial role in delicate diplomatic missions abroad, was the obvious person to have negotiated a treasonous deal. His disloyalty certainly caused the king the greatest personal pain, and as a Knight of the Garter (the most illustrious order of knights) he also deserved greater punishment for betraying the high standards of his order. Alternatively, the reason may have been that he alone refused to confess to having committed high treason. Concealing treason fell outside the provisions of the Statute of Treasons and was therefore effectively a new category of crime.[22]

The Cambridge plot could easily have jeopardised the entire

Agincourt campaign. Nevertheless, all those involved on the fringes of the plot escaped investigation, punishment or even recrimination. Henry had made his point in his usual way, making an example of the leading figures and giving the benefit of the doubt to the rest, who were thus enabled to redeem themselves on the campaign to come.[23]

✤ CHAPTER SIX ✤

"HE WHO DESIRES PEACE, LET HIM PREPARE FOR WAR"[1]

Throughout the entire period of diplomatic negotiations between England, France and her allies, Henry V had been steadily preparing for war. The castles on the northern borders had all been repaired, reinforced and regarrisoned at Henry's accession. Calais, too, underwent a major programme of rebuilding in anticipation of the role it would inevitably play during an English invasion of France. In 1413 commissioners were appointed to investigate the state of the defences of the town and the other fortresses in the Pas-de-Calais. New orders were issued to ensure that all houses were roofed with slate or tiles, rather than the cheaper thatch of straw or reeds which was so vulnerable to fire, especially during a siege. The king's carpenter in Calais was ordered to hire men, and by August he had a master-carpenter and thirty-two ordinary carpenters on his books, the latter being paid eight pence a day for their work. At Guînes, the moat and a ditch were cleared of the debris that always accumulated in such places in times of peace, the defences were reinforced and a new watch tower was built.[2]

The appointment of one of Henry's most trusted lieutenants, the earl of Warwick, as captain of Calais in 1414 marked a second stage of increased activity. A commission of inquiry was appointed to investigate alleged frauds committed by the four men responsible for supplying Calais with arms, building materials and victuals during the reign of Henry IV. The new supplier immediately applied himself to building up stockpiles of all these necessary items, including massive quantities of Gascon and Portuguese wine, salted beef, pork and herrings, which could all be kept for long periods of time if the town found itself under siege or its supply lines cut.[3] On his appointment, the earl had undertaken to ensure that the Calais garrison was manned, in time of war, by 240 men-at-arms and between 274 and 334 archers, at least half of whom, in both categories, were to be mounted. Additionally, he was to have four mounted scouts, forty crossbowmen, thirty-three carpenters, twenty masons, a plumber, a tiler, an artillery specialist and a "purveyor of stuff," or quartermaster. More troops were also stationed within the town of Calais, though these were not the responsibility of the captain of the castle.[4]

Similar activity had also been taking place in England, where the coastal defences of towns such as Portsmouth and Southampton were strengthened with new towers. A major programme of rebuilding at Southampton had started in the 1380s, when there was a threat of a repeat of the French raid of 1338, which had destroyed almost half the town. Southampton had then been vulnerable to attack from the sea, because its city walls had been built only on the landward side. As a consequence of such disasters and the growing commercial prosperity of ports and market towns, a change in defence strategy had been required. It was no longer acceptable for the civilian population of a town to have to flee with their families and animals into the safety of a castle when threatened. The new generation of wealthy citizens, merchants and burghers, who had invested heavily in valuable goods and substantial properties, demanded that they too should be protected and that the town itself should be fortified. Thus, by the end of the fourteenth century, Southampton was completely encircled, not just with moats, ditches and embankments, but with stone curtain walls, behind the battlements of which archers could shelter and take fire. Towers defended the key sites and, in response to the increasing importance of artillery, arrow-slits were converted to take small cannon; one new tower even had a vaulted ceiling so that it had the potential to take the weight of heavier cannon on its roof. (Similar conversions for guns were also undertaken nearby at Portchester Castle, Winchester and Carisbrooke Castle.) That artillery was starting to make a substantial contribution to defence is indicated by the somewhat startling appointment of a chaplain, Thomas Tredington, "to serve the king in his new tower of Southampton, both to celebrate the divine services and to keep the armour, artillery, victuals and guns for its garrison and defence. He is retained for this service expressly because he is an expert in guns and the management of artillery."[5]

Recognising the importance of Southampton's new fortifications because the town was "so near the enemy," Henry V contributed to them both indirectly and directly. In the December parliament of 1414, he heard a petition from the mayor and burgesses complaining that they could not afford the cost of their new defences and seeking a reduction in the rents they had to pay to the king's stepmother Joan of Navarre. Acknowledging the justice of their case, Henry offered either to persuade Joan to remit most of the rents or take them into his own hands and reduce them himself if she would not. He also built another new tower, the God's House Tower, which became the residence of the town gunner and his arsenal; projecting out of the town wall, it was built primarily to protect the sluices beneath it, whose function was to control the water levels in the moats that were the first line of defense.[6]

Although most major towns and ports had their own gun and weapon stores, the national arsenal was housed in the Tower of London. Preparations for restocking this had begun almost from the very moment Henry V had succeeded to the throne. On 10 May 1413 he had forbidden the sale of bows, arrows, arms and artillery to the Scots and other foreign enemies, and a month later he appointed a fletcher, Nicholas Mynot, to be keeper of the king's arrows in the Tower. Mynot himself set to work making arrows, and orders were placed with other London fletchers, such as Stephen Seler, who was paid £37 10s (just under $25,000 at current values) in August 1413 for supplying twelve thousand arrows.[7] This was but one of many commissions over the next two years.

Arrows were produced in sheaves of twenty-four. Each archer was normally armed with between sixty and seventy-two arrows, carrying two sheaves in his canvas quiver and the rest stuck in his belt, ready for immediate action. Additional supplies were carried on wagons and boys were employed to act as runners to bring more arrows to the archers on demand. Though a spent arrow might be recovered and reused,[8] this was both dangerous and impractical during combat, especially given that the archer's greatest strength was his speed of fire: an archer who could not fire ten aimed arrows per minute was not considered fit for military service. In a battle situation therefore the arrows he carried were only enough to keep him supplied for a seven-minute bombardment at most. Since the normal rate of fire by professional archers could rise as high as twenty per minute, his supply might last him for only half that time. The scale of the demand and the sheer logistics involved in providing sufficient arrows for an entire military campaign were thus enormous, hence the need to begin stockpiling early.[9]

There were two types of arrow in common use for military purposes at the time of Agincourt. The first was for long-range use, had a wooden shaft over thirty inches long made from a light wood, such as poplar, and an iron arrowhead shaped almost like an aeroplane, its "wings" bent back to form barbs, which lodged in the victim's flesh. It was highly effective against unarmoured men and horses up to a distance of around three hundred yards, especially in a co-ordinated volley. The second kind of arrow had been developed in response to the introduction of plate armour. It had a slightly shorter and heavier shaft, often made from ash, and a fearsome arrowhead called a bodkin, which, as its name suggests, was like a long, thick needle with a hardened and sharpened point. Fired at a closer range of less than 150 yards, these arrows could even penetrate the thickened steel of a helmet.[10]

Arrowheads intended for use in war were forged with a surprising degree of sophistication, the hardened steel of the tips and the edges enclosing a softer iron core which absorbed the shock of impact and made the shaft less likely to split or break off. Military arrows used flights made out of goose feathers, which were fixed to the shaft with glue and bound in place with thread. At times of crisis, the king would send an order out to the shires to provide goose feathers and, though no such order is extant for the Agincourt campaign, in December 1418 Henry V commanded his sheriffs to find him 1,190,000 by Michaelmas. A similar exercise in February 1417 was limited to the twenty southern shires and to six feathers from every goose, but these had to be at the Tower within six weeks of the command going out.[11]

In England and Wales, the preferred bow for military purposes was the longbow, as distinct from the crossbow. The latter never gained any great popularity in England, except for hunting animals, though it was extensively used in Europe from at least the mid-eleventh century. The Genoese, in particular, were renowned crossbowmen and regularly served as mercenaries in French armies. The advantages of the crossbow were threefold. It required comparatively little training and physical strength to be operated, it could be put into the shooting position and held there till needed, and its highly effective use of the power of torque — a winding mechanism was used to bend the bow — produced greater impact over a longer range, especially after the introduction of steel crossbows in the fifteenth century. Its great disadvantage was that it was slow and cumbersome in action: the ability to draw a weight of a thousand pounds did not compensate for being able to shoot only two quarrels or bolts a minute, especially in the heat of battle.[12]

Longbows were not only lighter and faster to operate, but also considerably cheaper to make than crossbows. Prices in 1413–15 ranged from less than 1s to just over 2s, at a time when an ordinary archer earned 6d, or half 1s, a day on campaign. The quality of a bow depended on the wood from which it was made. Every English schoolchild knows the story that the ancient yew trees, which grow in so many local churchyards, were planted to provide the archers of England with bows. In fact, English yew was an unsuitable material for bow-making because the changeable climate encouraged its tendency to twist as it grows. (Church property was, in any case, exempt from requisitioning; when Nicholas Frost, the king's bowyer, was empowered to acquire anything belonging to the bowyers' trade, including "the timber called bowestaves," just before the Agincourt campaign, he was not allowed to encroach on Church land.)[13]

The best bow-staves were cut from a single piece of straight-grained yew, imported from Spain, Italy or Scandinavia, and shaved into shape. Unstrung, the bow would be some six feet long and tapered, with the softer, more flexible sap-wood on the outside and a thicker layer of heart-wood on the inside, a combination that gave the bow its natural elasticity. Nocks made of horn were glued at either end to hold the string, and the whole bow was given several layers of protective wax or oil sealant. A regular maintenance regime of waxing and polishing ensured that the bow did not dry out or crack under the pressure of being strung or fired. Bow-strings, made of hemp or gut, were also waxed or oiled to keep them weather-proof, though this was not always successful. At the battle of Crécy in 1346, the Genoese crossbowmen found out to their cost that the pouring rain had soaked their bow-strings, so that they "could not stretch the cords to the bows so shrunken were they . . . they could not shoot a single bolt." The English, perhaps because they were more accustomed to rain, had learnt how to deal with such possibilities. According to the French chronicler Jean de Vennette, they "protected their bows by putting the strings on their heads under their helmets," a habit that is said to have given rise to the expression "keep it under your hat."[14]

Archaeological evidence from the wreck of the Tudor warship the *Mary Rose* suggests that the commonest draw-weight of a medieval English military longbow was between 150 and 160 pounds and that it was capable of firing an arrow weighing 4 ounces over a distance of 240 yards. To achieve this, regular use was essential. In 1410 Henry IV had reissued Edward III's act of 1363 which made archery practice compulsory for all able-bodied men between the ages of sixteen and sixty; every Sunday and feast day they were to go to the butts, the local shooting ranges, where targets were set up over measured dis-

tances, to "learn and practise the art of shooting . . . whence by
God's help came forth honour to the kingdom and advantage to
the king in his actions of war." Novices would begin with light-
weight bows and arrows, progressing to heavier ones as their
skill and strength increased. "I had my bows made me according to my age and strength," wrote Hugh Latimer, the English
bishop who was martyred for his Protestant beliefs in 1555; "as
I increased in them, so my bows were made bigger and bigger,
for men never shoot well, unless they be brought up to it." He
had learnt, he said, "how to draw, how to lay my body in my
bow, and not to draw with strength of arms as other nations do,
but with strength of the body." The twisted spines and increased
bone density of the over-developed shoulders, upper arms and
elbows of the *Mary Rose* archers are testimony to the physical
effort required to use the military longbow.[15] They also explain
why English archers were feared throughout Europe.

Henry V was not prepared to rely entirely on his archers for
the Agincourt campaign. His experience of warfare in Wales
had taught him the value of siege-craft and the importance of
artillery. Although cannons had been around since at least the
1320s (and Roger Bacon, an English Franciscan monk, had discovered how to make gunpowder more than half a century before that), gun technology was still in its infancy. In yet another
example of an unholy alliance between Church and state, the
skills involved in casting cannons originated, and were honed,
in the foundries that made church bells. The reason for this
becomes clearer when one realises that the earliest cannons were
bell-shaped and made of bronze or brass; the bolts they fired
were also made of bronze. By the beginning of the fifteenth century, the longer, more familiar tubular design had developed. By
the time of the Agincourt campaign, cannons were usually made
from long iron strips, heated and hammered together round a
removable wooden core and bound round with iron hoops to
form the barrel. The guns were breech loading and, depending
on the size of the cannon, fired anything from lead pellets, like
grapeshot, to round stone balls, which weighed between 5 and
850 pounds. A second separate metal chamber, also tubular in
shape, was packed with gunpowder, plugged with a wooden

bung and placed behind the barrel on a hollowed-out wooden frame. The cannon was now ready for firing through a touch-hole in the second chamber, but the whole process was so slow and inaccurate that a single shot a day was not uncommon. One gunner who managed to hit three different targets on the same day was assumed to be in league with the devil and sent off on pilgrimage to redeem himself.[16]

Large ordnance was hugely expensive to make. A single cannon made in Bristol by John Stevens, and laboriously hauled overland to London for the Agincourt campaign, cost Henry V £107 10s 8d. The scale of the investment required in artillery is indicated by Christine de Pizan, in her authoritative treatise, *The Book of Deeds of Arms and of Chivalry*, written in 1410. She suggested that anyone planning to besiege a stronghold on a river or by the sea (as Henry was) needed to have 248 cannons, capable of firing stones weighing between one hundred and five hundred pounds, together with thirty thousand pounds of gun-powder, five thousand sacks of charcoal, twenty three-legged braziers with handles for lighting the fuses and twenty bellows. A reinforced cart would be required to transport each cannon, plus a further twenty-five, each pulled by three horses, to carry their supplies. Again, the logistical problems involved in acquir-ing and, above all, transporting artillery were tremendous. In the fifteenth century, large artillery pieces could be moved an average of only seven and a half miles a day, and in 1409 the great cannon of Auxonne, which weighed some 7700 pounds, managed only three miles a day. Travelling by sea or river was faster and easier, but guns still had to be brought to the port of embarkation and moved into position at the end of their voyage.[17]

On 22 September 1414, as Henry's preparations for war stepped up a gear, he commanded Nicholas Merbury, master of the king's "works, military engines and guns, and of all our ord-nance for war," to find as many stone masons, carpenters, sawyers, joiners and workmen as were "necessary for the con-struction of the said guns," together with timber, iron and any-thing else he required for them, including transport. A similar order addressed to William Wodeward, "ffounder," and Gerard

Sprunk, authorised them to collect copper, brass, bronze, iron and all other kinds of metal to make "certain guns" for the king, but also to restock his kitchen with pots, bowls and kettles for the campaign. Four days later, the king addressed a writ to all the collectors of customs and subsidies and transport wardens in ports throughout the kingdom, prohibiting the exportation of "gunpoudre" without a special licence. This was done "for certain causes," the mysterious phrase that Henry frequently employed as a somewhat transparent cover for his military preparations.[18]

William Merssh, the king's smith at the Tower, was also busy, and as early as February 1414 was looking to employ more workmen to make guns and other ironwork. This was despite the fact that his wife, Margaret, was a professional blacksmith in her own right, who worked alongside her husband in the Tower forge. Payments made to her include one of 35s (almost $1,200 at today's values) for eighteen pairs of fetters and eight pairs of manacles. Though it flies in the face of modern misconceptions about the medieval period, women were expected to work at their husband's trade. The Ordinance of Founders of 1390, for instance, stipulated that each master smith could employ only one apprentice, but a special exemption was granted for one man to have two, "because he has no wife." Her female status did not protect the wife of a "smytheman" from having to do hard labour: she was expected to break up rock, work the bellows and smelt ore. Although she was paid for these tasks, she normally earned only a twelfth of his wage, receiving 1d for his every 1s.[19]

Smelting iron was a filthy business, as well as a back-breaking one. Iron ore was readily available in almost every English county, and was used to produce nails, horseshoes and tools; better-quality imported iron from Normandy, Spain and Sweden was used for siege engines and weapons. To make iron, crushed iron ore would be layered with charcoal in furnaces that needed to be kept at very high temperatures to extract the molten metal. Steel, which was increasingly used for armour and weapons, was made by a more complex and highly skilled procedure. The iron was sprinkled with a mixture of burnt ox-horn and salt, or, alternatively, smeared with pig fat and covered with strips of goat leather or clay; this was heated red hot, then plunged into water or urine (animal or human) to cool down and harden. It was perhaps not surprising that the records of the city of London were full of complaints about "the great nuisance, noise and alarm experienced in divers ways" by those living close to forges. A particular fear was fire because sparks "so vigorously issued forth from the chimneys," but the noise levels could be intolerable. The neighbours of one armourer, Stephen atte Fryth', complained that

> the blows of the sledge-hammers when the great pieces of iron called "Osmond" are being wrought into "brestplates," "quy-sers," "jambers" and other pieces of armour, shake the stone and earthen party-walls of the plaintiffs' house so that they are in danger of collapsing, and disturb the rest of the plaintiffs and their servants, day and night, and spoil the wine and ale in their cellar, and the stench of the smoke from the sea-coal used in the forge penetrates their hall and chambers.[20]

There had always been forges in the Tower of London and female blacksmiths working there too. During Edward III's Crécy campaign, Katherine of Bury, the mother of the king's smith, was paid 8d a day to "keep up the King's forge in the Tower and carry on the work of the forge" while her son was with the king in France; she was probably highly experienced, for she was also the widow of Walter of Bury, who had been the king's smith for nine years. This precedent suggests that it is possible that Margaret Merssh also ran her husband's forge in the Tower while he was away on the Agincourt campaign. The female blacksmith was clearly not a woman to be trifled with: in medieval literary tradition, she had a particularly evil reputation and, like Eve before her, the sins of the world were laid at her feet. The story was that the blacksmith who was asked to make the nails for Christ's crucifixion could not bring himself to do it and feigned an injury to his hand. His wife had no such qualms, took over his forge and made the nails herself.[21]

The greatest problem facing Henry V was not so much

acquiring the materials of war, but transporting them. An invasion of France, of necessity, demanded the use of ships, and when Henry came to the throne in 1413 the royal fleet consisted of precisely six vessels. His great-grandfather, Edward III, upon whom Henry so often seems to have modelled himself, had been able to call on between forty and fifty royal ships throughout his long reign. Within four years of Richard II's accession, only five remained, and by 1380 four of these had been sold off to pay Edward III's debts. Henry IV's fleet never exceeded six ships and was sometimes reduced to two. Both kings had been forced to rely on seizing privately owned merchant vessels to supplement their fleet when required. This had caused considerable anger and hostility, not least because, until 1380, there was no compensation paid to the ship-owners. Under pressure from the House of Commons, Richard II had then agreed that 3s 4d would be paid for every quarter-ton of carrying capacity, but the usual payment rarely exceeded a paltry 2s and was regularly the subject of bitter complaints in Parliament. Another cause of tension was that the wages of seamen were not always paid from the date of their being pressed into service but from the day they actually sailed.[22]

Henry V's reign marked a revolution in the fortunes of the royal fleet. The six ships he had inherited in 1413 had become twelve by 1415 and thirty-four by the time he began his second invasion of France in 1417. The architects of this transformation were a clergyman and a draper. William Catton became clerk of the king's ships in July 1413, and, like all his predecessors in the post, was a civil servant in minor orders.[23] William Soper, who replaced him in 1420, was a wealthy merchant and Member of Parliament from Southampton with extensive shipping interests. Within weeks of his appointment, Catton was given authority to obtain all the materials, sailors and workmen he needed to perform the task of repairing and building up the king's navy. Soper became officially involved in February 1414, when he obtained a similar commission for the specific purpose of "the making and amending of a great ship of Spain at Southampton."[24]

No doubt at least in part because William Soper was based

there, Southampton became in effect Henry's royal dockyard. The port enjoyed great natural advantages: protected from the Channel by the Isle of Wight, the sheltered waters of the Hamble estuary, Southampton Water and the Solent provided a mass of natural harbours and easy access to the French coast that lay opposite. On its doorstep was a seemingly limitless supply of timber from the New Forest for the building and maintenance of the king's ships. Soper added a new dock and storehouse at Southampton and built more storehouses and wooden defences for the ships under construction at Hamble. For the first time, the English had a naval dockyard that was beginning to rival the great fourteenth-century French shipyards at Rouen.[25]

Rebuilding a ship on the frame of an old one was a common maritime practice in the medieval period and indeed for many centuries afterwards. It was a cost-effective exercise, allowing for the sale of all the old scrap and outdated fittings, while reducing the investment needed for timber and other materials that could be reused. Much of Henry's new fleet was built in this way, and as a high proportion of the vessels were captured as a result of either war or letters of marque (documents issued by countries authorizing private citizens to seize goods and property of another nation), this substantially increased the savings to be gained. The cost of rebuilding Soper's Spanish ship, the *Seynt Cler de Ispan*, as the *Holy Ghost*, and refitting a Breton ship, which had been seized as a prize, as the *Gabriel*, amounted to only £2027 4s 11½d. This compared favourably to the sums in excess of £4500 (excluding gifts of almost four thousand oak trees and equipment from captured shipping) spent building Henry's biggest new ship, the 1400-ton *Gracedieu*, from scratch.[26]

Unfortunately, neither the *Holy Ghost* nor the *Gracedieu* would be ready in time for the Agincourt campaign. Despite Catton's and Soper's best efforts, it was not easy finding and keeping skilled and reliable shipbuilders. On at least two occasions the king ordered the arrest and imprisonment of carpenters and sailors "because they did not obey the command of our Lord the King for the making of his great ship at Southampton" and "had departed without leave after receiving their wages."

Henry's purpose in all this was not to build up an invasion fleet as such: the magnitude of the transport required for a relatively short time and limited purpose made that impractical. His priority was rather to have on call a number of royal ships that would be responsible for safeguarding the seas. When they were not engaged on royal business, the vessels were put to commercial use: they regularly did the Bordeaux run to bring back wine and even hauled coal from Newcastle to sell in London. So successful was Catton in hiring them out between 1413 and 1415 that he earned as much from these efforts as he received from the exchequer for his royal duties. Nevertheless, their primary purpose was to patrol the Channel and the eastern seaboard, protecting merchant shipping from the depredations of French, Breton and Scottish pirates, and acting as a deterrent to Castilian and Genoese fighting ships employed or sponsored by the French.[27]

On 9 February 1415 Henry V ordered that crews, including not just sailors but also carpenters, were to be impressed for seven of his ships, the *Thomas, Trinité, Marie, Philip, Katherine, Gabriel* and *Le Poul,* which were all called *"de la Tour,"* perhaps indicating that, like the king's armoury, they were based at the Tower of London. A month later, the privy council decreed that during the king's forthcoming absence from the realm a squadron of twenty-four ships should patrol the sea from Orford Ness in Suffolk to Berwick in Northumberland, and the much shorter distance from Plymouth to the Isle of Wight. It was calculated that a total of two thousand men would be needed to man this fleet, just over half of them sailors, the rest of them divided equally between men-at-arms and archers.[28]

The reason so many soldiers were required was that even at sea fighting was mainly on foot and at close quarters. The king's biggest ship in 1416 carried only seven guns, and given their slow rate of fire and inaccuracy they served a very limited purpose. Fire-arrows and Greek fire (a lost medieval recipe for a chemical fire that was inextinguishable in water) were more effective weapons but were used sparingly because the objective of most medieval sea battles, as on land, was not to destroy but to capture. Most engagements were therefore fought by coming alongside an enemy ship with grappling irons and boarding her. Imitating land warfare still further, fighting ships, unlike purely commercial vessels, had small wooden castles at both prow and stern, which created offensive and defensive vantage points for the men-at-arms and archers in case of attack.[29]

Even with a newly revitalised and rapidly expanding royal fleet, Henry had nothing like enough ships to transport his armies and his equipment. On 18 March 1415 he therefore commissioned Richard Clyderowe and Simon Flete to go to Holland and Zeeland with all possible speed. There they were to treat "in the best and most discreet way they can" with the owners and masters of ships, hire them for the king's service and send them to the ports of London, Sandwich and Winchelsea. Clyderowe and Flete were presumably chosen for this task because both had shipping connections: Clyderowe had been a former victualler of Calais and Flete would be sent later in the summer to the duke of Brittany to settle disputes about piracy and breaches of the truce. Flete was perhaps unable to fulfil this earlier commission, for when it was reissued on 4 April his name was replaced by that of Reginald Curteys, another former supplier of Calais.[30]

What is interesting about this mission is that it could not have happened without the consent of the duke of Burgundy. Holland and Zeeland were technically independent counties in the Low Countries and were ruled by William, count of Hainault, a subject of the Holy Roman Empire. The two states were adjoining, Holland lying to the north of Zeeland, which was then a conglomeration of tiny islands (now much enlarged due to drainage and land reclamation schemes) in the Schelde estuary. The little principality was dwarfed and almost entirely encircled by its neighbours. To the south lay Flanders, which was ruled directly by the duke of Burgundy, whose only son, Philippe, count of Charolais, was his resident personal representative there. To the east lay Brabant, whose duke, Antoine, was the younger brother of John the Fearless. Since William himself was married to John and Antoine's eldest sister, Margaret of Burgundy, he was part of the family network and the region was

controlled by their threefold political alliance. The duke of Burgundy was unquestionably the dominant partner, summoning
William, Antoine and other petty rulers of the Low Countries to
assemblies over which he himself presided. Had John the Fearless forbidden William to allow English envoys to recruit ships
in his territories, there is no doubt that he would have obeyed.
That he therefore gave at least tacit approval must be inferred,
and, if he did so, it suggests that the French were correct in
assuming that secret alliances had been signed the previous
autumn between the English and the duke of Burgundy.[31]

The available records indicate that Clyderowe and Curteys
spent almost £5050 (over $3 million in modern money) hiring
ships in Holland and Zeeland. Although this is probably not the
complete sum, it allows us to make an educated guess about the
number of ships they were able to hire. If they paid the customary rates of 2s per quarter-ton, they must have secured some
12,625 tonnage of shipping; if all the vessels were the smallest
considered worth hiring (twenty tons), then this suggests that,
by 8 June, they had acquired around 631 ships for the king's
expedition. This exercise, and its resultant figure, is only of
value in that it bears out a report of the same day that seven
hundred ships were on their way to England from Holland.[32]
In view of the fact that medieval estimates of numbers are usually considered to be wildly exaggerated — and, indeed, often
are — this provides a salutary reminder that they can also sometimes be correct.

This was still not enough to fulfil the king's requirements. On
11 April he ordered that all English and foreign vessels of
twenty tons or more currently in English ports between the river
Thames and Newcastle-upon-Tyne were to be seized into the
king's hands, together with any others that arrived before 1 May.
The news caused consternation abroad. "We know that our
four merchant ships have not yet arrived . . ." the Venetian Antonio Morosini wrote in July, "and there can be no doubt that
they are in danger of falling into the king's hands, which is
greatly to be dreaded. May it please the eternal God that it may
not happen!" Successive intelligence reports received in Venice
that month indicated that Henry's fleet was first three hundred

strong, then six hundred and finally fourteen hundred "and more." English ships that were seized were sent to Southampton and foreign ones to Winchelsea, London or Sandwich. There, over the next three months, they were converted from carriers of merchandise into fighting ships and transports for the thousands of men, horses and pieces of equipment that would have to be carried across the Channel to France.[33]

As the summer of 1415 approached and, with it, the beginning of the campaigning season, the pace of military preparation increased steadily. On 20 April Nicholas Frost, the king's bowyer, was given powers throughout the entire kingdom to hire, at the king's wages, as many bow-makers and workmen, and purchase as many bow-staves, as were required. A fortnight later, Nicholas Mynot, "ffleccher," was similarly authorised to commission twelve other fletchers and take timber to make arrows and crossbow bolts, together with the feathers, wax and silk that were also necessary. One thousand lance shafts were ordered from John Wyddemere, a London joiner, at a cost of 6d each. Between 3 May and 4 June, the masters of the king's ships of the Tower were empowered to impress sailors for the expedition. On 16 May Robert Hunt, the sergeant of the wagons of the royal household, was given nationwide authority to acquire "sufficient carts and wagons" for the king's campaign, together with wood, iron, carpenters and workmen for making new ones, and "sufficient" horses, with "sufficient" men to lead and drive them.[34] (How Henry's servants must have dreaded the words "as many as required" and "sufficient" as they strove to assess the needs and fulfil the commands of such an exacting monarch!)

Orders now came thick and fast. To Stephen Ferrour, sergeant of the king's farriers, to procure farriers, iron, nails and horseshoes. To Simon Lewys and John Benet, masons, to hire for service on the expedition one hundred of the best and most able masons in London and the Home Counties, with their tools. To William Merssh and Nicholas Shokyngton, smiths, to hire forty smiths on the same terms. To Thomas Mathewe and William Gille, carpenters, to hire one hundred and twenty carpenters and turners, ditto. To John Southemede, "fare carter," to provide sixty-two wheeled carts, together with the horses and their harness.[35]

No detail was too small or unimportant for the king's all-seeing and ever-watchful eye. Anticipating the problem of feeding the great army about to gather at Southampton, he sent orders to the sheriffs of Kent, Oxfordshire, Wiltshire and Hampshire, that they were each to purchase "at our expense and at a reasonable price" two hundred cattle from within their counties and bring them to appointed places. A month later, the sheriffs of the two closest counties, Wiltshire and Hampshire, were each ordered to buy a further one hundred oxen, bullocks and cows. A further writ to the sheriff of Hampshire ordered him to proclaim that all the king's loyal subjects in Winchester, Southampton and all the other towns, markets and hamlets of the county should begin baking and brewing "against the coming of the king, his retinue and his subjects."[36]

Whether hiring carpenters or ordering bread and ale, the constant refrain of all Henry's commands was that nothing was to be taken from Church property or without paying a fair price. This was something that he insisted upon, as a monarch who prided himself on being just to all men, but it was not universal practice. Purveyors behaved notoriously badly, seizing goods without payment or, more commonly, requisitioning them at a low price and then selling them on at a higher one for their own profit. Faced with a purveyor, waving the king's writ and backed by a group of armed men, few peasants or small farmers would dare to challenge his right to seize their corn, peas and beans, drive off their cattle, pigs and sheep or take their carts and horses. Sometimes the goods would be paid for with a wooden tally, which was the medieval equivalent of a cheque. This was literally a stick, scored across with notches to indicate the sum owed and then split down the middle so that each party retained an identical copy. Unfortunately for the recipient, when the parties presented their tallies for payment in cash, they frequently turned out to be completely worthless.

The purchasing of live cattle, which could be driven to the point of embarkation, was an innovation that reduced the pressure on those living in the immediate neighbourhood to provide meat. More importantly, the king's insistence on fair and reasonable treatment was extended not just to his own officials but to anyone, of whatever rank, in his army. On 24 July the sheriff of Hampshire was ordered to proclaim that every lord, knight, esquire, valet "and all others whatsoever" going with the king was to provide himself with victuals and other necessaries for the next three months. In the same proclamation he was also to declare that any person who felt aggrieved or harassed by any captain or his soldiers should present himself for remedy before the senior officials of his treasury or household. Complete justice, the king promised, would be rendered on his arrival.[37] This was an innovation without parallel in Europe, where the abuses of the purveying system were accepted as a fact of life. It marked a new era in the relationship between the king and his subjects in England.

Henry's sense of justice demanded that these abuses should be reformed, but there was also a pragmatic benefit to be gained. He wanted and needed the goodwill of his subjects if he was to embark upon a war whose end could not be foreseen. For this reason, he also took care to ensure that every man, woman and child in the country knew why he was going to France. Every writ he issued to obtain provisions was to be read aloud in the county courts and in the marketplaces by the sheriff of the county to whom it was addressed. This was an opportunity to persuade his subjects of the legitimacy of his cause and the necessity for action. Each one was therefore prefaced with a phrase that was both an explanation and a rallying call: "Because, as you well know, we, with God's help, are about to go overseas to recover and regain the inheritances and just rights of our crown, which, as everyone agrees, have long been unjustly withheld. . . ."[38] This was a campaign that would involve all the king's subjects, not just those capable of bearing arms.

❖ CHAPTER SEVEN ❖

OF MONEY AND MEN

W hat will the wise prince . . . do when . . . he must under-take wars and fight battles?" Christine de Pizan asked in *The Book of Deeds of Arms and of Chivalry*. "First of all, he will consider how much strength he has or can obtain, how many men are available and how much money. For unless he is well supplied with these two basic elements, it is folly to wage war, for they are necessary to have above all else, especially money."[1]

Henry V's bitter experiences of campaigning on a shoestring in Wales had taught him the important lesson that successful warfare had to be properly financed. By the simple expedients of cutting back fraud and waste, restoring central control and auditing, reviewing rents on crown lands and keeping a close eye on expenditure, he had succeeded in improving the traditional crown revenues to the extent that, from some sources, he received more than double the income available to his father. Annuities, or pensions, which his father had cheerfully dished out like sweets to children to win favour, were cut back by half under Henry V — and those receiving them were now compelled to work for them by serving on the king's expeditions, on pain of losing them altogether.[2]

Now, in preparation for the Agincourt campaign, Henry ordered his treasurer, Thomas, earl of Arundel, to audit all the departments of state and to report back to him on what income he could expect and what debts he owed "so that before departing the king can make provision according to the burden of each charge; and thus the king's conscience will be clear and he can set forth as a well ordered christian prince and so better accomplish his voyage to the pleasure of God and comfort of his lieges."[3] These were not just fine words. Every single royal official, from the treasurer of England down to the humblest clerk in the exchequer, knew that the king himself was scrutinising their accounts. Despite all the other demands on his time, no detail was too small, no financial arrangement too complex, to escape his attention. The chance survival of a note by a clerk of the council reveals that even when Henry returned to France in the crisis after the disastrous defeat at Baugé in 1421, he still found time to go through the accounts of one of his officials, who had died four years earlier. Not only that, but he checked the mathematics, signed the accounts with his own hand, and made notes in the margin, indicating which items needed further inquiry from the exchequer auditors. Such personal and meticulous attention to detail was unprecedented and reflected both the energy and commitment that Henry brought to his role as king.[4]

As a result of all these measures, hard cash began to pour into the exchequer at levels undreamt of by Henry's predecessors. Even so, it was not enough to finance a major campaign outside the realm. For this, the king needed to tax his subjects, something he could not do without the approval of Parliament. The principle had been established in 1254 that a tax which fell on all the people of the realm had to have their common consent and could no longer be approved solely by an assembly of lords; in 1407 it was further accepted that only the House of Commons had the power to grant taxation. The representatives of "the commune of your land," as the Commons came to describe itself, were the knights of the shire and the burgesses of the towns who were elected in the shire and borough courts, two for each constituency. The lords spiritual and temporal were summoned individually and personally by the king himself. Both houses met separately and together in the king's palace of

Westminster, sometimes in the royal presence, and their meetings provided an opportunity to present petitions for the redress of grievances, to enact statutes, ratify treaties and confirm judgements (such as the condemnations of Cambridge, Scrope and Grey for treason) as well as to grant taxation.[5]

The forty years preceding Henry's reign had been marked by constant and sometimes bitter conflict between the king and Parliament. All this was to change under the new king. During his years as prince of Wales, Henry had established extremely good relations with the Commons, which were to serve him in good stead when he became king. Parliament met more frequently in his reign than in his father's, but its sessions were much shorter and, like the king himself, more businesslike and efficient. Working with and through its members, whose advice he actively and genuinely sought, Henry listened and responded to their concerns but also pre-empted their criticism by acting as a model king himself, prompt to do justice, financially efficient, administratively effective. As a result, Henry enjoyed the confidence of his parliaments to a degree that was almost unprecedented.[6]

The most significant result of this collaboration was the willingness of the Commons to grant Henry's requests for money. Taxation at this period was levied directly and indirectly. The direct taxes were called subsidies, and were levied on the value of movable goods at the customary rates of one-fifteenth in the countryside and one-tenth in the towns. Subsidies were payable by everyone, regardless of rank, and only those having movable goods worth less than 10s were exempt. As far as the towns and villages were concerned, a fixed sum was levied from each one and it was then up to the local assessors to decide what proportion each individual inhabitant should pay. The clergy were also liable to pay subsidies at the higher level of a tenth, but these were granted in their own assemblies, called convocations, which usually met at the same time as Parliament. There was a separate convocation for each see, presided over by the archbishops of Canterbury and York, and their grants tended to mirror those made by Parliament. Indirect taxes were principally levied on the export of English wool. English merchants were required to pay 43s 4d for each sack of wool or 240 fleeces, and 100s for each hide; foreign merchants paid proportionately more, at 50s and 106s 4d, respectively. Henry also obtained further taxes of 3s per tun of wine and 12d in the pound on all other merchandise entering or leaving the country, for the specific purpose of funding the safeguarding of the seas. Grants of this kind were usually awarded for a limited term of several years so that the king had to come back to Parliament to obtain their renewal. In the nine and a half years of Henry's reign, he received more than ten full "subsidies," all but two of them during the years of intensive war effort between 1414 and 1420. Taxation at these levels had not occurred since the beginning of Richard II's reign — and then it had caused the Peasants' Revolt. Henry's demands, by contrast, were met with scarcely a murmur of protest: as one historian has pointed out, he got more money with less trouble than any other king of England. By exercising his skills in political leadership, he was able to summon his parliaments in the knowledge that they would, by and large, do as he wished.[7]

Henry had been granted a full fifteenth and tenth in his first parliament, in 1413, but, in a move calculated to surprise and endear him to his subjects, had declined to ask for another at his next parliament in April 1414. This proved to be the lull before the storm because his third parliament, held in December of the same year, was asked to grant a double subsidy — not one, but two whole fifteenths and tenths. It fell to the king's half-uncle Henry Beaufort, bishop of Winchester, who, as chancellor, had to make the traditional opening address to the assembled Lords and Commons, to put forward a persuasive argument. A brilliant orator, he needed all his skills to win the day. Parliament had been called at the king's command, he declared, to advise how to recover the king's inheritance, which had long been unjustly detained by the enemy. There was a season for everything. Just as there was a time for a tree to seed, flower, fruit and die, so it was given to men that there should be times for peace, for war and for labour. The king, seeing that peace reigned in his kingdom and that his quarrel was just (both of which were necessary if he was to wage war overseas), had decided that, with God's assistance, the time was now ripe for putting his purpose into action. He therefore needed three things: the good and loyal counsel of his parliament, the strong and true assistance of his people and a heavy subsidy from his subjects — but, Beaufort added, somewhat lamely, victory would reduce the costs to his subjects and bring great honour.[8]

The double subsidy was duly granted, its approval by the Commons assisted by the fact that the speaker for this parliament was none other than Beaufort's cousin and Henry's trusted adjutant Thomas Chaucer. The southern and northern convocations also obliged with grants of two-tenths, having their own reasons to be grateful to Henry V for his stout defence of the Church in the face of the Lollard threat. Fortified with the knowledge that large sums of money would soon be flowing into his treasury, Henry was able to intensify his preparations for war.[9]

Generous though the subsidy grants were, the money could not be collected all at once. Half was to be paid by February 1415 but the second half was not due until a year later. This left Henry with the headache of finding ready cash to pay for his military expenditure in the meantime. There was only one way this could be done: he would have to borrow. Edward III had financed his French wars by loans from the Bardi and Peruzzi banking families of Florence — and had ruined them when he defaulted on their repayments. This was not an option open to Henry V. Instead, he looked to his own subjects to help him finance the forthcoming war.

On 10 March 1415, Henry summoned the mayor and aldermen of London to the Tower and informed them that it was his intention to cross the sea to reconquer the possessions of the crown and that he needed more money. Four days later, Henry Chichele, archbishop of Canterbury, Henry Beaufort, bishop of Winchester, the king's youngest brothers — John, duke of Bedford, and Humphrey, duke of Gloucester — and Edward, duke of York, met with the city dignitaries at the Guildhall to discuss the matter. London was incomparably the richest city in the kingdom, and, as an international centre of trade, its merchants had greater access to cash than those of most other towns and cities. This was particularly important at a time when most movable wealth, hereditary, ecclesiastical, aristocratic and mercantile, was tied up in goods, especially jewellery and plate, rather than hard cash. It was an indication of how much the king needed the London loan that the mayor was given the seat of honour, and was invited to sit with the archbishop on his right and the royal dukes on his left. This flattery produced the required result. On 16 June the city offered the king a loan of 10,000 marks (almost $4,450,000 today), receiving from him a gold collar called the "Pusan d'Or," weighing 56 ounces as security for its repayment.[10] The choice of this particular item was pregnant with meaning, for it was an "SS collar," which had been the livery of the Lancastrians since at least the time of John of Gaunt and was worn by their most important retainers as a symbol of loyalty and allegiance. It was so named because it consisted of a chain of some forty-one S-shaped links, which were made of gold, silver or pewter, according to the rank of the wearer. The "Pusan d'Or" was probably the king's own collar, since it was made of gold and richly decorated with jewelled and enamelled crowns and antelopes, the former suggesting royal status and the latter being one of Henry V's personal badges.

Though London was the first and the wealthiest city to be approached for a loan, it was by no means the only one. On 10 May Henry addressed what was, in effect, a begging letter to his "very dear, and loyal, and well beloved" subjects. It was written in French, which was still the language of choice for the English aristocracy, as it had been since the Norman Conquest, and under the signet, the most private and personal of the king's seals. Since it was dictated by Henry himself, it bore the unmistakable imprint of his character and, as such, it is a very revealing document indeed. The letter was frank and to the point; a persuasive appeal to the recipient's loyalty, backed up with just the tiniest hint of a threat. As an insight into Henry's methods of governing, it could not be bettered. It opened by explaining that he was now setting out on his voyage, that he had paid his men the first part of the wages which were due to them and that he had promised them the second on the point of embarkation.

The grants and loans he had received from his faithful subjects were not enough to enable him to fulfil that promise, "so that, for lack of this second payment, our said voyage is likely to be delayed, and the first payment, made by us, to be wasted, to the great injury of us, and of our whole realm, which God forbid." Each recipient was asked, "as you desire the success of our said voyage, and the common good of us and of our whole realm," to lend such a sum as the bearer of the letter would suggest and to send it "with all the haste that can be made." "And you ought to take this our prayer tenderly and effectively to heart," Henry added, "without failing us, or the confidence we have in you."[11]

Who could refuse such a very personal and direct appeal? Certainly not the towns, religious communities and individuals to whom the letter was addressed. Richard Courtenay, bishop of Norwich, as treasurer of the king's chamber, was the official charged with the overall responsibility for raising the money, probably because the chamber was responsible for the many personal items of jewellery and plate that the king had to pledge as security. Richard II's gold crown, for example, which was studded with 56 rubies, 40 sapphires, 8 diamonds and 7 large pearls, and valued at £800, was pawned for a loan of 1000 marks from the people of Norfolk, who contributed sums ranging from 500 marks from the mayor, sheriffs and citizens of Norwich down to 10 marks from a certain Nicholas Scounfet. A great tabernacle of gold, richly garnished with jewels, which had belonged to the duke of Burgundy, was similarly given as security for 860 marks loaned by a consortium of laymen and clergymen from Devon, including the dean and chapter of Exeter Cathedral, the mayors and citizens of Exeter and Plymouth, and the abbots and priors of Tavistock, Plympton, Launceston and Buckfast.[12]

The biggest loan of all, worth £10,936 3s 8d, came from Roger Salveyn, treasurer of Calais, who would have to wait more than six years for repayment in full. Other towns and cities gave what they could, the sums providing an interesting indication of their comparative wealth. Bristol, for instance, offered £582, Norwich £333 6s 8d, King's Lynn and Newcastle £216 13s 4d each, York £200, Boston £80, Beverley, Canterbury, Exeter, Northampton and Nottingham £66 13s 4d each, Bridgewater £50, Gloucester, Maidstone and Sudbury £40 each, Bury St Edmunds and Faversham £33 6s 8d, Plymouth £20 and Dartmouth £13 6s 8d. As with subsidies, where a loan came from a town or city, the level was fixed by discussion with the mayor and his officials, who then had to recoup the figure from the inhabitants. The records for a loan of £100 made by the city of Coventry in 1424 reveal that scarcely anyone was exempt and individuals had to pay sums ranging from £1 6s 8d down to the merest 10d (the equivalent of $27.77 today).[13]

It would be surprising if fund-raising on this scale did not meet with protest, particularly from townsmen who had already contributed the first of the two-tenths of the value of their movable goods through the double subsidy of 1414, and were now being asked to contribute to a further "voluntary" loan. They could not even look to the consoling prospect of receiving interest, since usury was strictly prohibited by the Church, and all loans between Christians had to be interest-free. The sum of £100 had been demanded from Salisbury but was reduced, after much hard bargaining, to two-thirds of that figure, which was to be raised from eighty-five of the leading citizens. Even so, it took the threat of the king's displeasure before the town finally handed over the money. Resentment in Salisbury apparently boiled over when Sir James Harington, bringing his retinue of Lancashire men-at-arms and archers to the muster at Southampton, attempted to cross the Avon by the Salisbury bridge and found himself embroiled in a full-scale affray with the townsfolk, in which four citizens were killed and fourteen thrown over the bridge into the river. In London, too, a grocer, a draper and a ward official were charged with having falsely accused an alderman of having levied a larger sum than was due from them for the city's loan to the king; they confessed their guilt and were sentenced to a year and a day in Newgate Prison, though this was remitted on payment of a bond for good behaviour.[14]

Wealthy individuals, many of whom had lent money to the crown before, were more prepared to come forward with substantial loans. London mercers (textile dealers) were foremost among these. John Hende, for instance, made the largest single loan of £4666 13s 4d (now worth almost $3.2 million) and Richard Whittington, known to generations of English school-children as Dick Whittington of pantomime fame, lent £700. Either a younger son or a member of a junior branch of a family of Gloucestershire gentry, Whittington had made his fortune by coming to London and setting up as a dealer in costly textiles. Having established himself as a supplier of cloth of gold and embroidered velvets worth well over £1000 annually to the royal household, he became an alderman of the city of London, and went on to serve three terms as mayor in 1397–8, 1406–7 and 1419–20, and also as a Member of Parliament in 1416. As mayor of the Staple at Calais, he was one of the wealthiest merchants in the country and could therefore afford to make regular loans to both Henry IV and Henry V, including one of £2000 to the latter soon after his accession.[15]

Not all merchants were as willing as Richard Whittington to bankroll the king and his forthcoming war. Resident foreign merchants, who had commercial interests in other countries, including France, were not at all happy at being asked to contribute to the war chest. Antonio Morosini, the Venetian chronicler, complained that many Lombard and Italian merchants were being seized, together with their goods, and were forced to pay the king huge sums to obtain their release. Discreditable though it seems, Morosini was right. On 25 May 1415 ten partners in Italian merchant houses were summoned before the privy council and, when they refused to make loans totalling £2000, were flung into the Fleet Prison — a nicely sardonic touch, since this was the jail for debtors.[16]

This sort of action probably had the desired effect, for, by the beginning of June, money from foreign merchants was rolling into the treasury: the Albertis and John Victor from Florence obliged with almost £800 and £266 13s 4d, respectively, Paul de Meulan from Lucca with £132 and Nicholas de Muleyn and his associates from Venice with £660. Perhaps as compensation for their harsh treatment, all were repaid in full within the year, though it was an indication of the strain on the king's finances that Laurence de Alberti had to accept a novel form of credit, being allowed to bring in five ships without having to pay any duty on their cargoes.[17]

The wealth of the Church was also placed at the king's disposal. It comes as no surprise to find that Henry Beaufort, bishop of Winchester, the wealthiest clergyman in England, lent his nephew almost £2630 in June and July alone, or that Henry Chichele, archbishop of Canterbury, and Philip Repingdon, bishop of Lincoln, should also have supported their monarch to the tune of £200 and £400, respectively. Abbots, priors and deans of cathedral chapters also had access to the funds of their communities — though quite where Friar Henry Cronnale, a member of a mendicant order dedicated to poverty, got the £200 he lent is a mystery. What is surprising is the number of relatively humble clergymen who, willingly or not, pledged quite substantial sums: thirteen parsons in the diocese of Durham alone each lent £20 ($13,330 today), as did William Shyrymton, rector of Holt-market, in Norfolk.[18]

The complex systems of accounting for this money, the deferral of some repayments (in some cases for many years) and the incomplete nature of the records mean that it is virtually impossible to determine exactly how much Henry managed to raise. The only chronicler to hazard a guess was the Burgundian Enguerrand de Monstrelet, writing thirty years afterwards, whose estimate of 500,000 gold nobles (the equivalent of $111 million today) was accepted by most subsequent chroniclers, English and French.[19] Convenient though this may be, all that can be said with any certainty is that it was a huge sum, and that it was enough not only to pay the army's wages but also to finance the campaign. Whatever else dictated Henry's military decisions on the Agincourt campaign, shortage of money was not one of them.

Despite the fact that England had no standing army in medieval times, which meant that every single serving soldier had to be individually recruited, raising sufficient men to fight under Henry's command was a much easier exercise than finding the cash to pay them. Indeed, in this respect, he had an embarrassment of riches, for he was unable to find places on board for all the men who mustered at Southampton. Even though he issued a last-minute repeat of the order to seize any ships left in the port of London and bring them "with all possible speed" to Southampton, he still had to leave some men behind.[20] The old feudal system of owing personal military service for a particular piece of land had long since broken down, though its influence remained. The king still expected his tenants-in-chief to accompany him to war and to bring with them a certain number of men, most of whom would inevitably be drawn from their own landholdings and areas of influence. Instead of being bound by ties of loyalty and obligation, however, these soldiers, from highest to lowest, were bound by written contracts of service, which were legally defined and enforceable by law. England had developed a particularly sophisticated system for raising armies by this method in response to the almost continuous demands of fighting the war in France under Edward III. It was based on the indenture, a single document that consisted of two identical copies of the contract, both signed, witnessed and, where relevant, sealed by the two parties. The document was then cut in two, not in a straight line, but in a wavy or indented one. Each party then took one of the copies. If any dispute arose about the terms and conditions of service, both parties had to produce their copies, which could then be placed together to ensure that the indents matched and that the two were genuinely parts of the original indenture. This simple but ingenious stratagem made it extremely difficult to produce a fake document, or for either party to defraud the other by making changes to his own copy.

There were two types of retaining indenture. One was drawn up to create a contract for service in peace and war, usually for life, the other for a specific military campaign and for a predetermined length of time. Many of the men who fought at Agincourt were there as life retainers of the king or other lord whom they served, and, just as they formed the core of his household in peace, so they were the basis of his military retinue in war. These men were the first Henry would call upon, issuing an order on 22 March 1415 that any knight, esquire, valet or anyone else who was in receipt of a royal fee, wage or annuity granted by Edward III, Richard II, the Black Prince, John of

Gaunt, Henry IV or himself was to present himself in London by 24 April at the latest.[21]

On 19 April the king entertained the members of his great council — all four royal dukes, together with nine earls, fifteen barons, both archbishops, eight bishops and several abbots of major houses — to breakfast at Westminster Palace and once again sought their approval for his war against France. Having noted that the king had followed their earlier advice to renew his diplomatic efforts and moderate his claims without success, the meeting duly gave the war its formal sanction and put in place the arrangements that would be necessary for its success-ful prosecution.[22]

Ten days later, a large number of temporary military inden-tures for the Agincourt campaign were signed at Westminster. A typical example was that of Thomas Chaucer, speaker of the House of Commons. In his indenture with the king, Chaucer contracted to serve in person for one year with a company of eleven men-at-arms and thirty-six archers (though, like many other captains, he actually mustered an extra archer when the campaign began).[23] "Men-at-arms" was a loose term that had come to replace "knights" as the standard description of the medieval fighting man. As it included every rank in society, from the king and royal dukes down to the humblest esquire who could afford to equip himself with the basics of horses, arms and armour, the indenture always indicated the status of the men-at-arms. In Chaucer's case, all his men-at-arms were esquires, including himself. His archers were to be mounted, as were those of most contingents, though some archers were recruited without horses and so presumably travelled, as they fought, on foot. In either case, the archers almost invariably outnumbered the men-at-arms by three to one, a proportion that was unusually high and unique to England.[24]

The wages for the campaign had been set by the king at the meeting of the great council. The rates were customary and var-ied according to where the campaign was to be fought. In this case, although the council had discussed an expedition "towards Harfleur and the region of Normandy," Henry was determined to maintain the military advantage by keeping the enemy guessing as to where he intended to attack. He could not hide the scale of his preparations, but his precise objective in France would remain a secret until after his fleet had sailed. The indentures therefore deliberately left the destination open: service would be required "in our duchy of Guyenne, or in our realm of France," commencing on the day of muster. Wages would be paid at the daily rate of 13s 4d for a duke, 6s 8d for an earl, 4s for a baron, 2s for a knight, 12d for an esquire and 6d for an archer, mounted or not. Every group of thirty men-at-arms was also entitled to a "regard," or bonus payment, of 100 marks, which was effectively a form of compensation for the cost of armour and loss of horses. If the expedition went to Aquitaine no bonus would be paid, but the wages of the esquires and archers would be increased to an annual rate of £26 13s 4d and £13 6s 8d, respectively.[25]

The wages offered for military service in France were proportionately better for those in the lower ranks than for those in the upper echelons of society. The aristocracy were expected to fight by virtue of their birth: the military profession was their calling and duty, and it was not anticipated that they could earn a living from their military wages alone. The same was true of knights, whose outlay in horses, arms and armour for the campaign would probably cost them more than they could expect from a year's income. (Forty pounds a year of landed or rental income was considered sufficient to support the status of knighthood in the medieval period, and this was also about the sum a knight could expect to earn from a year's military service at the king's wages.) For esquires and archers, who made up the backbone of the army, the financial attraction was much greater. An esquire earning £18 5s a year in war was likely to be better off than in peacetime: the London subsidy rolls for 1412 identify 42 citizens who claimed the rank of esquire, but only 12 of them enjoyed a rental income exceeding £15 per annum. An archer was even better off: on a daily wage of 6d, he would receive roughly £9 a year, without having to pay for his food and drink. In civilian life, even highly skilled workmen and craftsmen, such as carpenters, masons and plumbers, generally earned only between 3d and 5d a day, out of which they had to find their own subsistence.[26] The prospect of earning 6d a day was also attractive to those of higher social rank. Many of Henry V's archers were yeomen, farmers and minor landholders with incomes in the region of £5 a year, who could afford to equip themselves with a horse and basic armour; some were even younger brothers or sons of gentry whose family purse was not deep enough to provide the king's host with more than one man-at-arms. For them, military service in France offered the prospect of advancement, and a number of men who were initially recruited as archers would later be found serving as men-at-arms.[27]

The wages for the campaign were to be paid quarterly in advance: the first half of the first quarter was due on signing the indenture and the second on mustering with the correct number of men ready for embarkation. (Henry V was, as one might expect, an absolute stickler for this: every company was mustered regularly before, during and after the campaign, and wages were docked for every missing man.) If the campaign lasted less than a year, then wages were to be paid up to the point of embarkation for the homeward journey, plus eight days' travelling allowance. As we have already seen, the cash sums required to finance these payments were immense. The first quarter's wage bill for Chaucer's company alone — which was around the average size for a man of his standing — amounted to £156 7s 10½d (almost $104,650 in modern currency).[28] The aristocrats fielded much larger companies. Thomas, duke of Clarence, had the largest, with 240 men-at-arms, including himself, one earl, two barons, fourteen knights and 222 esquires, and 720 mounted archers; his brother Humphrey, duke of Gloucester, came second, with 200 men-at-arms and 600 mounted archers; Edward, duke of York, Thomas, earl of Dorset, and Thomas, earl of Arundel, each fielded 100 men-at-arms and 300 mounted archers.[29]

As security for the payment of the wages, Henry had to raid his treasure chests once more. Chaucer received jewels and plate to the nominal value of the second tranche due, which the king was obliged to redeem within nineteen months; if he did not do so, then, according to the terms of the indenture, Chaucer and his heirs were to be at liberty to keep, sell or otherwise dispose of the items as they wished, without fear of any impediment or retribution by the king. This was a standard term in all indentures, but it was not one that either party felt obliged to keep. Clarence, for instance, was given "the crown Henry" on condition that it was kept whole and undamaged: in fact, he could not afford to pay his own men and broke the crown up into several pieces, giving a large bejewelled fleur-de-lis and several pinnacles to various knights and esquires, none of which he was able to redeem in his own lifetime.[30] Edward, duke of York, and Thomas, earl of Salisbury, also received items of extraordinary workmanship and value: York was given a gold alms dish, "made like a ship, standing on a bear, garnished with nineteen balays [peach-coloured rubies], twelve great and fourteen other pearls, weighing 22 lbs 1½ oz," while Salisbury got "a large ship of silver over gilt, with twelve men-at-arms, fighting, on the deck, and at each end of the ship a castle, weighing 65 lbs 3 oz." The craftsmanship, for which English silversmiths and goldsmiths were famed throughout Europe, counted for nothing: it was the melted-down value of the precious metal, together with the jewels, that gave these objects their value.

Less important men, with smaller retinues, also found themselves in receipt of quite extraordinary items: Sir Thomas Hauley was given a sword garnished with ostrich feathers, which had belonged to the king when prince of Wales; Sir John Radclyff a bejewelled tablet of gold, containing a piece of Christ's seamless robe; and John Durwade, esquire, "a Tabernacle of gold, within which were an image of our Lady sitting on a green terrage, with the figures of Adam and Eve, and four angels at the four corners."[31]

The king's financial commitment to his men was not limited to paying their wages and the bonus; in every indenture he also undertook to pay the costs of shipping each company to and from France or Aquitaine, together with its horses, harness and supplies. As with the wages, there was a predetermined schedule listing how many horses each man was permitted to take according to his status. The three dukes, Clarence, Gloucester and York, were allowed fifty each, the earls twenty-four, each banneret or baron sixteen, each knight six, each esquire four and each archer one. Again, if we look at Chaucer's company of forty-eight men, he was expected to travel with a minimum of eighty-four horses at the king's expense; presumably, had he so wished, he could have taken more at his own cost. Clarence's company of 960, by comparison, was entitled to take 1798 horses.[32]

Why were so many horses needed? The army had to be capable of covering long distances at speed but every man-at-arms, even the esquire, was still expected to be able to fight on horseback as well as on foot. Warhorses were highly prized and ferociously expensive, since, like horses used in jousts or tournaments, they had to be intensively trained to act contrary to their natural instincts, so that they would run unswervingly towards opponents, obey commands in the heat of close fighting and remain unpanicked by the noise and press of battle. Though there were breeding programmes in England and Wales, the best horses were usually imported from Spain, Italy or the Low Countries and sold at the great international fairs of Champagne in France and at Smithfield in London.[33] Most medieval knights of the late fourteenth and early fifteenth centuries spent anything between £5 and £100 on their warhorse, £25 being an average sum. At the top end of this scale was the courser, standing some fourteen to fifteen hands high, and capable of carrying the weight of a man in a full suit of armour. The courser had both stamina and agility, so it was ideal for campaigning and was the preferred mount of those who could afford it. Those who could not had to make do with a cheaper rouncy; even this was of a better quality than the horse of a mounted archer, which was needed only for travelling, never for a fighting situation, and was usually worth a mere £1.[34]

The six horses that a knight was permitted to take to war at the king's expense would fall into three categories: his warhorse, which was probably a courser, and a substitute; a lighter saddle-horse, such as a palfrey, for riding when not in full armour, and one or two rouncies for his servants; and finally one or two packhorses to carry his baggage. The greater the status of the company leader, the more servants and baggage he would be taking with him. Even the humblest esquire, with his four horses, must have been expected to bring a warhorse, a palfrey, a rouncy and a packhorse, a retinue which presupposes that he had at least one or two servants to look after them. Some of these servants may have been archers, but others were undoubtedly just boys or non-combatants, who took no part in the fighting and therefore do not figure in either the indentures or the muster lists, though their presence is acknowledged in other sources.[35]

The final part of a military indenture, such as the one that Chaucer signed with Henry V, dealt with the important matter of prisoners and prizes. This could be an extremely contentious issue, not least because these winnings did not automatically belong to the person who captured them. Because all the soldiers in the army were paid wages, it was accepted that a proportion of their winnings should be given to their employers. The indenture therefore set out what had become, since the 1370s, the customary division of spoil. The king was to receive one-third of every indenting captain's personal winnings and one-third of a third of those of his retinue, providing that the value exceeded 10 marks (£6 13s 4d, or almost $4,444 at today's prices); anything worth less than that remained entirely the captor's own. In addition, if anyone, of whatever status, captured the king of France, or any of his sons, nephews, uncles, cousins, lieutenants or chieftains, or a king of another country, these prisoners were to be handed over to the king, who was to be the sole recipient of the full value of their ransoms. It was generally understood that compensation would be paid to the original captors, but this was not specified by the indenture, and the amount was left to the king's generosity.[36]

The king's copy of his indentures was preserved in the exchequer, where it was kept in a leather draw-string pouch with the name of the indenting captain on the outside. As the campaign progressed, all relevant documentation would be added to this bag, including the muster rolls and wage claims which enabled the exchequer clerks to work out how much money was owed to each company. By this means, the superb administrative machine of the exchequer, which had been honed by centuries of efficient tax collecting, gives us a unique and almost unprecedented level of insight into the fate of the usually nameless men-at-arms and archers whom chronicle sources ignore. The records of Sir Thomas Erpingham (Shakespeare's "good old knight"), for example, reveal that he contracted to serve with twenty men-at-arms, including himself, and sixty mounted archers; that two of his men-at-arms, Thomas Geney and John Calthorp, were knighted on landing at Chef-de-Caux but were invalided home from Harfleur and died in England; that another man-at-arms, John Aungers, died at Calais; that only two of his knights, Hamon le Straunge and Walter Gold-ingham, were present at the battle of Agincourt; that two archers, Henry Prom and Robert Beccles, died at Harfleur, and that another, John de Boterie, was invalided home during the siege; and finally that two more archers were casualties of the war, Richard Chapman dying on the march between Harfleur and Agincourt, and Stephen Geryng at the battle itself, significantly the only one of the entire company to lose his life there.[37]

Some 250 individual indentures for the Agincourt campaign have been identified, though this may be only a small proportion of the whole, since 632 pouches were purchased for the exchequer in 1416. Even so, 250 was an unprecedented number: nothing like it had been seen before the Agincourt campaign or would be again. Instead of subcontracting the task of providing the entire force to three or four aristocrats, as had always been done in the past, Henry V consciously sought to recruit as widely as possible for his army. A large number of the indentures were for numbers that seem barely worth the trouble of inscribing the parchment they were written on: the deliciously named Baldewin Bugge, for example, contracted to serve with just three archers, but his fellow esquires, John Topclyff, Robert Radclyf of Osbaldeston and William Lee, could only offer two. There are even instances of single archers, such as Richard Shore, John Wemme and Thomas Newman, signing contracts with the king as individuals, though the exchequer clerks' preference seems to have been that archers proffering their services should be dealt with in groups of at least four and usually twelve, if only for accounting purposes.[38]

Men such as these would normally have been subcontracted into the retinues of the great lords. William Bedyk, for instance, an esquire who could offer only himself and two archers, was signed up into the company of Thomas, earl of Salisbury, who had contracted to bring forty men-at-arms and eighty mounted archers. The terms of Bedyk's indenture precisely paralleled that between the earl and the king, even stating explicitly at one point that he was to be paid "in the same manner as our said Lord the King does to the said Earl for people of his condition." This was a necessary precaution, since it was not unknown for retinue leaders to make a profit out of their indentures: in 1380 Sir Hugh Hastings had received £45 3s for each man-at-arms in his company but paid them only £40, keeping the difference himself. Above and beyond his wages and shipping costs for his little group, Bedyk was to have free food and drink for himself and one valet, or servant, on both sides of the sea; in return he was obliged to give the customary one-third of all his winnings to the earl.[39]

Though drawing up royal indentures for such small numbers was time consuming and expensive, it had several advantages. It meant that the recruits had a much more direct personal link to the king than was usual and it encouraged their loyalty by suggesting that he valued their contribution, however small, to his war effort. It also meant that, unlike previous campaigns where soldiers would be recruited from within the areas of influence of the great lords who had signed the indentures, Henry V's army would be drawn from every quarter of the kingdom. As a consequence of this unprecedented level of national involvement, the campaign inspired an exceptional degree of pride and enthusiasm across the country, all of which was centred on the charismatic figure of the king himself.

CHAPTER EIGHT

THE ARMY GATHERS

On 16 June 1415 Henry V rode out of London on his way to Southampton, pausing only to attend services and make offerings at St Paul's and Southwark. He was accompanied by four members of the extended royal family, Edward, duke of York, Thomas Beaufort, earl of Dorset, Sir John Cornewaille and Sir John Holland, and the earls of Arundel, March and Oxford. The mayor, aldermen and some 340 citizens of London turned out to honour their king by riding some ten miles with him as far as Kingston, where they took their leave and wished him Godspeed on his voyage. According to his instructions, they then returned to the city, to remain there until his return from France.[1]

The very next day, a French embassy, led by a senior diplomat, Guillaume Boisratier, archbishop of Bourges, landed at Dover. Not realising that Henry had already left London, the ambassadors made their way to the city for an interview with the king. By the time Henry learnt of their arrival he was already at Winchester, some twelve or thirteen miles north of Southampton, where he had taken up residence in Wolvesey Castle. It was here that he summoned the Frenchmen to his presence for what he knew, but they did not, would be the final move in the diplomatic game.

Henry received them graciously but in his most regal manner: bare-headed, but dressed entirely in cloth of gold, and surrounded by members of his great council, including his three brothers. Once more the French declared their desire for a "true, complete and perfect peace" between the two realms and repeated their offer of an enlarged Aquitaine, marriage with Catherine of France and a dowry of eight hundred thousand francs, if only Henry would disband the army which, they knew, he was assembling at Southampton. After some days of inconsequential and half-hearted bargaining, the ambassadors were again summoned to the king's presence to hear his final answer from the mouth of his chancellor, Henry Beaufort, bishop of Winchester. The king and his great council, Beaufort declared, had decided that if the French did not give him Catherine and the duchies of Aquitaine, Normandy, Anjou and Touraine, together with the counties of Poitou, Maine and Ponthieu, "and all the other places which once belonged to his predecessors by right of inheritance, he would not put off his voyage . . . but with all his power he would destroy the realm and the king of France." At the conclusion of Beaufort's speech, Henry himself added that, with God's permission, he would indeed do as the bishop had said, "and this he promised the ambassadors, on the word of a king."

Realising that nothing they could say or do would deflect Henry from his purpose, the archbishop of Bourges permitted himself one last defiant speech, protesting that the French had made their generous offers, not through fear of the English, but for love of peace and to avoid the spilling of Christian blood. The king of France would drive the English from his realm and all his dominions. "You will either be taken prisoner there," he warned Henry, "or you will die there."[2]

Faced with the failure of their mission, there was nothing left for the French ambassadors to do but to return to Paris, where they reported Henry's intransigence and what they had been able to learn about the English preparations for war. Yet, even now, it seems that the French continued to underestimate the strength and scope of Henry's purpose. In this it appears that they were deliberately misled by the English. Richard Courtenay, bishop of Norwich, who was a close friend of the king and had been intimately involved in the negotiations, confided in Master Jean Fusoris, a canon of Notre Dame attached to the embassy, that he believed the marriage might have been arranged if only the ambassadors had come earlier, and declared that he had not yet given up all hope of a treaty. As late as August 1415 (after Henry had sailed for France), the Venetians were still getting reports that a settlement and peace were possible. The general expectation on the French side appears to have been that even if the invasion did go ahead, it would be a brief raid, like that of 1412, which would achieve nothing to justify its expense.[3]

The role that Fusoris played in the delegation was at best questionable and at worst treasonable. In all probability he was an English spy. Although a clergyman, he was better known to his contemporaries as an astrologer and maker of astrological instruments. He had pestered his way into being taken on the embassy by claiming that he was owed large sums by the bishop, whom he had met on the latter's two diplomatic missions to Paris in the autumn of 1414 and spring of 1415. Courtenay had then cultivated Fusoris, telling him that he shared his interest in astrology and buying books and instruments from him. He had also consulted him professionally, persuading Fusoris to use his almanacs and astrolabes to divine the omens for a marriage between Henry and Catherine and the likely success of his current embassy. Courtenay had also expressed concern about Henry V's long-term health and sought a horoscope reading, based on the king's nativity, to predict how long he would live.[4]

Bizarre though it seems to find a bishop consulting an astrologer, this was by no means unusual in France. In England, astrology as a means of predicting the future was regarded as both sorcery and the false prophecy condemned in the Bible. It had been further brought into disrepute by its association with Richard II, whose unusually continental tastes had included one for divination; predictions of his second coming had persuaded Henry IV to enact legislation against prophecy in 1402 and 1406. Charles V of France, on the other hand, had been a devotee of the arts of astrology and geomancy (an art similar to reading tea-leaves, but using a handful of earth), collecting an impressive library on all the occult sciences. His court astrologer was a former lecturer in astrology at the university of Bologna, Tommaso da Pizzano (now more familiar as the father of Christine de Pizan). Da Pizzano famously claimed that he had used his arts to drive the English out of France in the 1370s. He had done this by having five hollow human figures made out of lead under a propitious constellation, labelling each one with the name and astrological character of the king of England and his four captains, then filling them with earth taken from the middle and the four corners of France respectively. At the right astrological moment, he had buried each one, face downwards and with its hands positioned behind its back, in the place from which the earth had been taken, reciting incantations for the annihilation of the persons they represented and the expulsion of the English from France as he did so. The result was sensational, if not instantaneous, for "within a few months all the said companies had fled from the realm."[5]

Fusoris, probably unaware of the difference in attitude between the two countries, may have hoped to gain a post as court astrologer, or, at the very least, to sell some of his books and instruments to the English king. In either case, he was an easy target for a wily diplomat like Courtenay, who persuaded him that Henry V had a great interest in astrology and that he wished to meet him. Having strung Fusoris along for the entire length of the negotiations at Winchester — during which time the astrologer roused the suspicions of the official French envoys by failing to turn up for meals and by his frequent meetings and conversations with Englishmen — Courtenay finally introduced him to the king after mass, making a pointed speech about how the Frenchman, "thinking there would be a treaty of peace," had brought Henry gifts of astrolabes, charts and almanacs. If Fusoris had expected a fulsome welcome and expressions of gratitude or interest, he did not get them. Henry's response was a typically laconic "Thank you, Master John" in Latin, followed by a slightly less formal "many thanks" in French. He even refused to accept one of the treatises or a little book of astrological puzzles.[6]

In fact, Henry's interest in astrology was either minimal or, more likely, feigned as a cover for a public meeting with a man whose occupation had given him privileged access to and contacts within French royal circles, making him a potentially useful spy. At least two of the other envoys would testify at Fusoris's trial for treason that he had also had another meeting with the king, during which he was closeted away with him for a two full hours, but this Fusoris vigorously denied. Nevertheless, before he left, he paid yet another visit to Courtenay and was given £33 6s 8d, money that, he claimed, was due to him as payment for the bishop's outstanding debt, but which may have been for services rendered. Fusoris's considered opinion of Henry — which may be unreliable, as it was given in the courtroom during his trial — was that the king had the fine manner of a lord and great stateliness, but that he thought him more suited to the Church than to war. To his mind, Clarence cut an altogether more warlike figure.[7]

Henry, however, was about to reveal his martial side. Having nothing further to discuss with the French ambassadors, he abandoned them at Winchester and on the evening of 6 July 1415 rode off to join his army, which was now mustering around Southampton. He set up his headquarters at Portchester Castle, whose great keep and curtain walls, interspersed at regular intervals with round watch towers, had benefited from his recent modernisation programme. Standing on a headland in the natural harbour of Portsmouth Bay, directly opposite the sea entrance, the castle was conveniently placed for Henry to make regular forays to review the gathering troops and to keep an eye on the progress of the fleet building up in Southampton Water and the Solent. When the time came, it would also prove to be his ideal point of embarkation: from Portchester he could sail directly to the head of the fleet and lead it out to sea.

The final arrangements for the campaign were now in place. Henry's twenty-six-year-old younger brother, John, duke of Bedford, had been appointed to act, with the assistance of a small council, headed by the archbishop of Canterbury, the bishops of Winchester and Durham, and the earl of Westmorland, as king's lieutenant for England, Wales and Ireland during

Henry's absence. Sir John Tiptoft, a long-standing Lancastrian retainer and highly experienced royal and parliamentary administrator, had likewise been appointed seneschal of Aquitaine and departed with a substantial army for the duchy in June.[8]

Measures had also been taken for the defence of the kingdom in the absence of not just the king but so many of the fighting men upon whom it normally relied. Reinforcements had been sent to safeguard the Scottish, Welsh and Calais marches, and to join the fleet guarding the coast. As a matter of principle, those living in areas that were most likely to be attacked, such as the northernmost counties, had not been recruited for the campaign and had actually been ordered to remain at their posts. Robert Twyford, who attempted to join the king's own retinue, had his indentures cancelled because "it pleased [the king] that he should remain in the company of lord Grey, Warden of the East March of Scotland, for the reinforcement of the said marches." All military leave in Calais was cancelled for the duration of the king's expedition.[9]

Commissions had also been appointed in every county to identify each man capable of fighting and ensure that he was properly armed and equipped according to his status. As we have seen, all men aged between sixteen and sixty, irrespective of rank, were required by law to practise at the archery butts every Sunday and Holy Day after mass; those with lands or rents worth between £2 and £5 had also to provide themselves with a bow, arrows, sword and dagger, so that they were ready to serve whenever called upon to do so. Though many of these men were undoubtedly recruited into the king's army, those too young, old or incapacitated in some way would remain behind as the medieval equivalent of the Home Guard.[10]

It is a measure of the exceptional strain placed on the resources of manpower within the realm by the demands of the Agincourt campaign that this was not considered sufficient. It was to the Church that, once again, Henry looked to make up his shortfall. Contemporary legal opinion was divided many ways on the subject, but it was generally accepted that clergymen could defend themselves if they were attacked, and it was on this principle that commissions of the clergy for the defence of the realm could be justified. Henry therefore addressed a writ to the archbishops of Canterbury and York, and to all the bishops individually, demanding a muster of the clergy in every diocese with all possible haste. The array was to include anyone capable of bearing arms, irrespective of whether they were secular clergy, such as parish priests, or members of religious orders living in enclosed monastic houses. Even those who were officially exempt from such demands were to be called up and, for once, the liberties of the Church were not to be respected. Every single cleric was to be well and suitably armed, according to his status and his capabilities, and ready to resist "the malice, impudence and harassment of our enemies." Perhaps to sweeten the pill, the preamble to the writ hinted that the Church's own enemies, Lollards and heretics, rather than marauding Scots or Frenchmen, were the object of this extraordinary measure: it declared that the king was acting "for the defence of the realm and of our Mother Church of England and of the Catholic Faith."[11] The records for the eleven dioceses which still exist show that, between them, they mustered over 12,000 clergymen; the great diocese of Lincoln found 4500 suitable men in total, of whom 4000 were arrayed as archers, while even the comparatively tiny see of Bath and Wells produced sixty men-at-arms, 830 archers and ten mounted archers.[12] When the lost figures for the remaining eight dioceses are added to these, the Church must have fielded an extraordinary shadow army of tonsured and habit-clad monks, canons, friars, priests and chaplains, drawn from the sanctuary of monastery, cathedral and university cloister, parish churches and chantry chapels. What is more, it was a militia that substantially outnumbered the more conventional armed forces gathering in Southampton.

That army now numbered just over 12,000 fighting men drawn from almost every corner of the kingdom, including Aquitaine. (There were no Irish or Scottish contingents, despite the colourful captains Macmorris and Jamy, of Shakespearean fame.) This represented a tremendous effort on the part of the individual retinue leaders who, like the king himself, found the responsibility of raising, equipping and feeding their companies a severe financial strain. The accounts of the young John

Mowbray, for whom this was his first official outing in his military capacity as earl marshal, reveal that he spent more than £2000 (almost $1.6 million today) on his contribution to the war effort, even though he only received £1450 back from the king in wages for himself and his men.[13]

The earl had been one of the first to sign up for the campaign, indenting with the king on 29 April. By 1 July, when his accountants paid the quarter's wages to those who had signed indentures to serve with him, he had fifty-five men-at-arms, only two of whom were knights, and 147 archers. All of them were paid their wages for the whole of the first quarter (ninety-one days) in full and at the rate for going to France, even though the earl himself, in common with the rest of those who indented to serve the king directly, had only received half of the pay for the same period. His second payment was only due when he mustered his troops before the king's reviewers (on 1 July, which is why he had arranged to pay his men on that day), but the muster was postponed for a fortnight and the earl was left to bankroll the shortfall in the meantime.[14]

The earl's accounts reveal that he had to build up this large retinue out of very small units. The largest sub-retinue was raised by an esquire Perceval Lynlay, who brought five men-at-arms with him and a company of fifteen archers. Although two knights and five other esquires also produced comparatively large contingents, thirty esquires signed up as individual men-at-arms, each one bringing either two or three archers with him, and forty of the archers were also recruited on an individual basis. From their names, which sometimes occur elsewhere in the accounts in a professional capacity, one can guess that many of this last group were members of the earl's household: William Coke (the cook), Nicholas Armourer, William Sadelyler, John Foteman, John Fysshelake. One archer is even specifically referred to as a tentmaker.[15]

The accounts also include wages paid at military rates to a small group who were almost certainly non-combatants and therefore could not count towards the numbers of fighting men whom the earl had contracted to supply. The group included the earl's two heralds (each of whom had to provide himself with an archer), three minstrels and his trumpeter, "Thomas Trumpet," the last of whom was paid a flat rate of £10 a year. This raises the unanswerable question of just how many non-combatants accompanied the English army to France. The chancery rolls, which list those to whom royal letters of attorney and protection were granted for the campaign, record the professions of a small proportion of the applicants. These include men who were obviously not intended to fight: Thomas Baudewyn, rector of Swaby in Lincolnshire, who accompanied the duke of Clarence; John Hugge, a notary in the retinue of the Flemish knight Hertonk von Clux; and John Cook, one of the king's chaplains. Others may have been there in a purely professional capacity. The particular skills of William Merssh, the king's smith from the Tower of London, or John Persshall of London, a "bladesmith" in the retinue of Nicholas Merbury, were more valuable than a capacity to fight. Some of the more important grocers, fishmongers and merchants, many of whom were London citizens, may have been involved purely as suppliers to the various retinues. But what are we to make of the two tailors, the Norwich baker, the Coventry woolman, the Petworth butcher, the London drover and William Belle, a taverner in the duke of Clarence's retinue, the last of whose letters of protection were revoked in November "because he delays in London"?[16] Were they there to practise their trades or as soldiers? The latter would seem the most likely answer, although the two were not necessarily incompatible. Only one of the approximately five hundred men who received letters of protection or attorney described his occupation as "archer" and many of those paid as archers by the earl marshal were members of his household. An army of this size would inevitably have to draw heavily on the civilian population to supplement the ranks of professional soldiers.[17]

Just like the new king, the earl marshal found himself pouring considerable sums into the equipping of his retinue, purchasing bows, arrows, bow-strings and, perhaps surprisingly, even crossbow supplies, from a number of different fletchers and tradesmen. All were carefully boxed up for transportation in specially purchased chests, which were then covered with waxed cloths to protect them from water damage.[18] Though it seems to have been expected that retinue leaders like the earl would provide at least some military equipment for their archers, there was no similar obligation towards the men-at-arms. It was taken for granted that they would provide for themselves entirely, the bare minimum being a full suit of plate armour, weaponry and the four horses allowed by the terms of the indentures. The quality of all these might differ markedly according to income, but it was important to have the best affordable, since the owner's life might depend on it. Valuable weapons, particularly swords and daggers, might be passed from father to son or bequeathed to favoured retainers because their design did not change significantly and they could be refurbished. Lances were expendable, like arrows, but more adaptable. The wooden shafts needed to be long enough for use on horseback, but could also be cut down at short notice: the French men-at-arms at Agincourt would be ordered to shorten their lances when the decision was taken to fight on foot.[19] Perhaps the most significant new weapon in the armoury of the man-at-arms was the axe, or pollaxe, which had been developed in the late fourteenth century in response to the introduction of plate armour. Like the mace, which it replaced, the axe was designed with a hammer head to crush an opponent's armour with a swinging blow, but it also had a deadly spiked point that could be used in a stabbing action to puncture plate armour and drive between its vulnerable joints.[20]

Not every man-at-arms could afford to equip himself with the latest armour, but the earl marshal was determined to cut a fine figure for his first campaign. In June and July he managed to spend more than £70 (the equivalent of almost $48,300 today) on armour alone. Confounding modern misconceptions that a complete suit of armour could be bought off the peg, as it were, the earl went to considerable trouble to source each piece independently. One London armourer supplied him with a pair of plates, which encased his trunk, another made him two bascinets, or helmets, and a third provided the plate defences for his legs (*legharneys*) and his upper and lower arms (*vantbraces* and *rerebraces*), together with plate gauntlets and *sabatons*, which protected his feet. Another specialist, John Freynch of London, sold him a pair of gilded spurs and mended an old pair for him, charging him £1 3s 4d for the privilege. The job of adding the finishing details, such as the internal padding that prevented the plate pieces chafing and ensured a good fit, making a crest for one of the helmets and a ventail or neckpiece for a bascinet, or producing laces *(armyngpointes)* for the skilled and onerous task of securing each piece in its correct place, was left to the earl's own employee, the aptly named Nicholas Armourer. Nicholas was also responsible for repairing broken pieces and sometimes sourcing new ones: on 26 June, for example, he bought a pair of mail thigh defences made in Milan, the acknowledged centre of European armorial expertise. Mail, made of interlinking metal rings, provided a second line of defence under plate armour, particularly at vulnerable points, such as under the arms and at the joints, which were often exposed when moving. A further protective layer closest to the skin was provided by a thickly padded fabric garment, which cushioned the wearer from the weight of the blows falling on his armour. Materials for making a new *armyngdoublett* "for the lord for when he was about to cross over to French parts" duly appear in the earl marshal's accounts.[21]

Encased from head to foot in plate armour, with even his face hidden behind the visor of his helmet, the earl would have been unrecognisable among his peers. He therefore spent another small fortune on the blazonry or heraldry that would enable him and his company to be identified. A London embroiderer, John Hunt, was paid the vast sum of £40 for making and embroidering in silk and gold a surcoat, or short, tight-fitting tunic worn over the armour, for the earl and a matching trapper for his horse, both decorated with Mowbray's arms as earl marshal of England. So much work was involved in this that there was a risk that neither surcoat nor trapper would be ready in time for the campaign, prompting the earl to add a tip of 2s 8d "to hurry up" the process. A London painter was also employed to paint the earl's arms on trappers, pennons, standards, pavilions and forty-eight shields, the last probably being for decorative rather than military purposes, since shields were an unnecessary encumbrance to a man-at-arms clad head to toe in full plate armour.[22]

Though uniforms in the modern sense were unknown at this time, retainers of a great lord were accustomed to wear his livery, supplied at his cost, which included clothing in his chosen colours and badges bearing his arms or device. Sir John Fastolf, for instance, clad the men of his retinue in the distinctive red and white cloth manufactured by the tenants of his manor of Castle Combe in Wiltshire and the contingents of archers raised by the crown in Wales and Cheshire were clearly identifiable by their caps and tunics of green and white. John Mowbray also bought copious amounts of red, white, black and green cloth for members of his household (though his falconers were more appropriately dressed in russet) in the months leading up to the Agincourt campaign. He may even have provided them with their crosses of St George, which the king's ordinances compelled them to wear on their chests and backs while serving in the royal army.[23]

The earl's preparations extended to his own living accommodation. His pavilion would be equipped with every facility, including a new bed, mattress and bolster, a new seat for his latrine and an old pavilion pressed into service as his wardrobe. His cook busied himself purchasing cauldrons, cooking vessels and bottles, his carter repaired and put in order the wagons that would carry his luggage and his master of horses bought a new pavilion in London that had been specially adapted and fitted out to serve as a stableblock for the duration of the campaign.[24]

Given the scale of the earl's expenditure, and his limited income, it was not surprising that he soon ran out of money and was obliged to borrow from Thomas, earl of Arundel. He was by no means the only one who found himself in debt. John Cheyne, an esquire in the retinue of Sir John Cornewaille, wrote in desperation from Southampton on 12 July 1415. "I am hiere, and have been atte greet costages and dispens," he informed Sir John Pelham. He needed a "certain notable somme er[e] I go" and therefore sent his servant with "certein thynges of meyne" to pledge as security for a loan, which he offered to pay back at whatever terms Pelham suggested. Even so wealthy a magnate as Edward, duke of York, was obliged to mortgage some of his estates before he left England, so that he could meet the wage bill of his vast retinue.[25]

The earl marshal's company was typical of most of those now gathering at Southampton, but there were some notable exceptions. In certain instances, these reflected the conditions of the locality in which the men had been recruited. Jehan de Seintpee, unable to recruit archers in his native Aquitaine, brought 100 crossbowmen instead, eighty of them on foot.[26] John Merbury, the king's chamberlain of south Wales, brought 500 archers from Carmarthenshire, Cardiganshire and Brecknockshire, but only twenty men-at-arms, at least three of whom — Meredith ap Owen ap Griffith, Griffith Don and David ap Ieuan ap Trahaiarn — were former rebels who had made their peace with Henry V. They were to meet some of their compatriots, who had not, on the field of Agincourt, fighting for the French.

Some retinues were composed entirely of those with specialist skills. Sir John Greyndor, for instance, brought his own company of nine men-at-arms and thirty archers, but also recruited 120 Welsh miners, six of whom were masters of their craft and paid 12d a day, the rest receiving 6d a day for their services.[27] Mining was an essential part of siege-craft, as was the use of artillery. Henry had personally retained twenty-one master gunners and five gunners, each of whom had two "servants of guns," making a team of seventy-eight in all. The best artillery men in medieval times were said to come from Germany and the Low Countries, so it is interesting to see that most of the king's master gunners had names suggesting Dutch origin and that he paid the highest rates to obtain their services. Even the ordinary gunners received the same wages as a man-at-arms, but the master gunners were paid an extraordinary 20d a day, a differential that was reflected in the pay of their servants. Gerard Sprunk, the king's own gunner, by contrast, had only £10, out of which he had to pay four archers.[28]

In addition to the latest in cannonry, Henry also anticipated using the more traditional catapult assault weapons, such as trebuchets and mangonels, and had gone even further afield to find the best available. The mayor and municipal magistrates of Bordeaux were ordered to send him "two of the best engines, called brides, and a suitable and capable master and carpenter to operate them" for his campaign.[29] Henry also took belfries with him. These were two-storey towers on wheels, timber-framed and covered with ox-hides, which could be pushed right up to the besieged position, providing shelter for battering rams, attacking forces and ladders or bridges reaching across to the tops of walls. In order to be able to maintain and repair all these machines, Henry retained 124 carpenters, twenty-five cordwainers (leather-workers, whose numbers indicate that they were not solely employed making and mending shoes), six wheelwrights (who would also be needed to repair the wagons and carts accompanying the expedition) and 120 simple labourers.[30]

Henry's personal company, like that of the earl marshal, was an expanded version of his own household. John Waterton, the master of the king's horse, brought sixty grooms, a surveyor and a clerk of the stable, a clerk and twelve yeoman purveyors of oats for the horses, twelve smiths, nine saddlers and a couple of men whose sole responsibility seems to have been to be "the King's Guides by night." Altogether, Waterton appears to have had 233 royal horses in his care, though by the end of the campaign he had a mere ninety-eight, a salutary reminder that horses were no more immune to the impact of war than men. Six bow-makers, six fletchers, a bascinet or helmet specialist called Nicholas Brampton and a team of twelve armourers, led by "Albryght mayl maker," had responsibility for the armour and weapons of the king's household. John Conyn, "sergeant of our tents and pavilions," had four painters and twenty-eight servants to look after the royal pavilions.[31]

The king's kitchens, which were supervised by William Balne and his two under-clerks, boasted three yeomen and a clerk of the king's poultry, eight yeomen and a clerk of his bakehouse, three clerks of his spicery, a clerk of his table-linen and another for his hall, a clerk and fifteen assorted labourers for the scullery, plus 156 yeomen and servants not assigned to any particular department. Henry had his own carpenters and labourers "of the hall" and three pages "of his chamber" to act as messengers. His clerks of the marshalcy and the wardrobe, two almoners (responsible for administering the king's alms-giving) and William Kynwolmersh, the cofferer or treasurer of the royal household, also accompanied the king. Henry's piety was amply demonstrated by the size of the religious establishment he took with him. The most senior clerics were Master Jean de Bordiu, a Gascon doctor of law and former chancellor of Aquitaine, and Master Esmond Lacy, the dean of the king's chapel, but there were also three clerks, fifteen chaplains and fourteen monks, the last group having charge of the vestments and altar equipment. Among these clerics was the anonymous chaplain, author of a wonderfully vivid account of the campaign, the *Gesta Henrici Quinti*, who sat in the baggage train, quaking with fear and praying for victory, as the battle of Agincourt raged around him.[32]

No self-respecting medieval monarch or aristocrat ever went far without his band of minstrels, and Henry, a music lover, was no exception. Eighteen minstrels accompanied him to France, each earning 12d a day, the same rate of pay as a man-at-arms. Of these, at least three were trumpeters, three pipers and one a fiddler. Though the instruments of the rest are not specified, it would be normal for there also to be some clarion or wind players and at least one "nakerer," or drummer. (Medieval manuscripts and carvings often depict the nakerer with two small round drums, slung from a belt and carried at groin level, which perhaps explains the origin of the vulgar term "knackers" for testicles.)[33] Ensemble playing was in its infancy in this period, but the minstrels would play when marching, in the chapel and for recreational purposes: at the siege of Melun in 1420, Henry would have his "six or eight English clarions and divers other instruments" playing "melodiously for a good hour at sunset and at the daybreak." The trumpeters would also be used on formal occasions, such as to announce the king's arrival, when fanfares were required, or to attract public attention before proclamations. Most important of all, on military campaigns they were the medieval equivalent of the modern signal corps, enabling commands to be passed quickly and effectively down the line.[34]

Not all minstrels were musicians, however, and it would be a mistake to assume that all eighteen played instruments. The term had a much more general meaning in the medieval period and corresponds better to the modern definition of an entertainer. Some minstrels told or sang tales of chivalry; others danced, did acrobatics or played the fool. Henry II, in the twelfth century, had been so fond of the favourite party trick of one of his minstrels that he gave him a thirty-acre estate in Suffolk, on the sole condition that he and his heirs repeated it in the royal presence every Christmas. When one learns that the minstrel was known as Roland le Fartere and that the trick was to make a leap, a whistle and a fart, one can understand why his descendants had alienated the estate by the 1330s. Henry V's tastes were perhaps less crude, though he employed both a royal fool, William, and a tregatour, or conjuror, "Maister John Rykell," whose sleight of hand earned him immortality in the poet John Lydgate's *Daunce de Macabres*.[35]

There was something of a family tradition in minstrelsy, as Roland le Fartere's descendants learnt to their cost. Henry V's marshal of his minstrels, John Clyff, who signed the indenture with the king for service on the Agincourt campaign on behalf of his fellows, was the son or grandson of John of Gaunt's nakerer. Of the remainder whose surnames are not simply a description of the instrument they played, three were members of the Haliday family. Thomas and Walter, who were probably the sons of William Haliday, were among the group of named minstrels who received bequests of £5 each from Henry V's will and went on to serve his son. A Walter Haliday and a John Clyff, presumably of another generation, were still active in royal service (albeit the house of York, rather than Lancaster) under Edward IV, and in 1469 were granted a licence to establish a guild of royal minstrels.[36]

The same sort of family tradition affected the heraldic profession. This was not surprising, since heralds had begun life as minstrels, and only achieved their distinctive status as the knowledge required of them grew more specialised and technical. Hereditary badges had been used on the shields of knights and nobles since the twelfth century, developing into a unique heraldic device or blazon for each individual, which heralds were expected to recognise instantly. By the late fourteenth century, heralds had also established themselves as the rule-makers and judges of the chivalric world. As the acknowledged experts on the history and drawing up of blazonry, they were called upon to identify the arms of those fighting in joust, tournament and war, to judge cases of disputed arms and to confirm orders of social precedence. Their knowledge of chivalric conventions and rules of conduct also made them unrivalled masters of ceremony, whose responsibility it was to award the palm of honour to those who displayed outstanding combat prowess and to organise all the social ritual connected with knighthood, from tournament to coronation. Last, but not least, they had become the authors of chivalric record, drawing up reference books of English and continental coats of arms, preserving exceptionally fine examples of jousting challenges and chronicling deeds of chivalry. It was no accident that at least two of the eyewitness accounts of the battle of Agincourt were drawn up by heralds. "Yours is a fair office," the allegorical figure Dame Prudence declared in one of the popular literary debates regarding heralds written in about 1430, "for by your report men judge of worldly honour."[37]

In times of war, heralds had a very important role to play. It was their responsibility to record for posterity the granting of knighthoods in the field, to note the arms and names of those who fought well and, more macabrely, to identify and record the dead; they were sometimes even required to judge who had won the victory. They were also expected to act as messengers between the warring parties, delivering defiances, demanding surrenders and requesting truces or safe-conducts.[38] This duty had developed out of their original function of delivering jousting challenges, both nationally and internationally, often to hostile nations. Like knighthood, the possession of heraldic office was regarded as transcending national boundaries and allegiance, ensuring a herald diplomatic immunity and honourable treatment wherever he went in Europe.[39]

Every nobleman had his own herald, but by the fifteenth century a hierarchy had developed with the kings of arms at the top and pursuivants at the bottom. In England, the kings of arms were royal appointments and the realm was divided into four provinces. England itself had a northern and a southern province, presided over by Lancaster and Leicester kings of arms respectively; then there was also a king of arms for Ireland and for Aquitaine (Guyenne). Despite their names, all were based at court, and all were summoned to attend the king for the Agincourt campaign.[40]

The other essential profession represented in every major retinue was the medical one. The king himself took his personal physician, Master Nicholas Colnet, and twenty-three surgeons. There was an important distinction between the physician, who was at the top of the medical tree and responsible only for diagnosis and prescription, and the surgeon, who was less learned and more practical, carrying out operations, treating fractures and wounds and applying plasters and purges. Though there was much jostling for position between the two, they were united in their disdain for the barber-surgeons and unlicensed practitioners (usually women) whose ignorance, superstition and lack of skill they deplored. Nevertheless, women were practising as both physicians and surgeons. Westminster Abbey employed women in both capacities, even though it meant that they had to come within the precincts of the monastery and, inevitably, have close physical contact with the monks; they were well paid for their services, too, suggesting that they were effective.[41]

Most physicians were not only men but also university graduates who had studied for up to fourteen years to obtain a doctorate in medicine. For authority, they relied heavily on classical texts, such as those by Hippocrates and Galen, and for diagnosis, they looked mainly to the analysis of urine, whose colour was compared to a graduated chart that depicted every hue from white to red, including green. Nicholas Colnet was a fellow of Merton College, Oxford, who had entered royal service as a clerk and physician in 1411, but owed his advancement to Henry V. In August 1414, at the king's personal request, Colnet was granted a papal dispensation allowing him to remain a cleric in minor orders, so that his medical services to Henry were not interrupted by ecclesiastical promotion or transfer. He was one of the first to sign an indenture for service on the Agincourt campaign, for which he was to receive the same rate of pay as a man-at-arms, 12d a day, and to bring with him three archers.[42]

Henry V's personal surgeon, Thomas Morstede, was one of the most interesting men on the Agincourt campaign. Originally from Betchworth, near Dorking, in Surrey, by 1401 he had moved to London and was working there as a humble "leche." As a young surgeon, he may have been present when John Bradmore removed the arrow from Henry's face after the battle of Shrewsbury, an operation he was later able to describe in detail. Like Colnet, he owed his rapid rise to wealth and fame to royal patronage. In 1410 he was retained as the king's surgeon, on a salary of £40 a year, an office that was confirmed on Henry V's accession, on condition that the king had exclusive use of his services. At the same time, he was also appointed to the highly profitable post of examiner, or collector of customs, for all vessels passing through the port of London, the actual work being delegated to his deputies. Like Colnet, he signed an indenture for service on the Agincourt campaign on 29 April 1415, having successfully petitioned the king to be allowed to take twelve men of his profession and of his own choosing, together with three archers. Unusually, he was to have the same wages as Colnet, an indication not only of his abilities but also of the enhanced role he was likely to play in a war situation; the other surgeons were to receive 6d a day, in common with the archers.[43]

A second royal surgeon, William Bradwardyn, was also retained to serve on the Agincourt campaign with a team of nine surgeons under his command. Bradwardyn was older than Morstede, having served Richard II on his Irish expedition in 1394 and been retained by him for life in 1397. The change of regime had not affected his career, though he too seems to have found a patron in the prince of Wales, rather than Henry IV, who preferred foreign doctors.[44] Despite Bradwardyn's evident seniority, it was Morstede who was the chief surgeon in the king's army. He was clearly an open-minded, dynamic and ambitious man. Frustrated by the traditional rivalry between physicians and surgeons, and by the incompetence of so many of those in the medical profession, he initiated a project in 1423 to found the first English college of medicine. Its aims were to introduce better education and supervision for all those engaged in the medical profession, including the setting of common examinations, inspecting premises stocking medicines, regulating fees and providing free medical care to the poor. The college was to consist of two self-governing bodies, one for physicians and one for surgeons, under the joint leadership of an annually elected rector. Morstede himself was the first master of surgery to be appointed (Bradwardyn, significantly, was only a vice-master). The college collapsed a few years later under the stresses of the antipathy between the two professions, but Morstede did not give up his dream, and in 1435 he was the driving force behind the foundation of the Mystery, or Guild, of Surgeons, a professional body that survives to this day.[45]

Morstede's dedication to his profession prompted him to train dozens of apprentices, lend other surgeons books from his extensive library and make regular and generous charitable donations to prisoners and the poor. In 1431 he married a wealthy widow, who was the daughter of John Michell, a former alderman, sheriff and mayor of London; he served as sheriff of London himself in 1436 and, unusually for a surgeon at this time, was granted a coat of arms. By 1436 he was listed as the fourth wealthiest person in the city, having an annual income of £154 ($102,647 at today's values) from lands in London, Surrey, Essex, Suffolk and Lincolnshire. Possibly Morstede's greatest claim to fame, however, was that he wrote the *Fair Book of Surgery*, which became the standard surgical textbook of the fifteenth century.[46] Written in English, so that it was far more accessible than the Latin tracts and compendia then available, the *Fair Book of Surgery* drew on Morstede's decades of experience in Henry's wars and was illustrated with helpful examples of successful operations. It was an eminently pragmatic teaching manual, but it was also an unusually ethical work. Other treatises of this kind had often displayed an unhealthy degree of cynicism. Henri de Mondeville, for instance, recommended that surgeons should use magical cures, not because they worked, but "so that if they do effect a cure the surgeon will be credited with a marvellous piece of work, while if they do not he will not be accused of having omitted some vital step." Mondeville advised surgeons always to charge for medicine because the more expensive the cure, the more confidence the patient would have in it. He also suggested that all doctors should use big words and, if necessary, make up terms to impress their patients: "the ordinary man believes that pronouncements which he does not understand are more effective than those which he understands perfectly well." The more imposing the name of the condition, the more ill the patient felt himself to be: "give some awful names to the illnesses of ignorant peasants if you want to get any money out of them," he suggested.[47]

Morstede's attitude and approach were completely different. It was the duty of a surgeon, he wrote, to have a thorough understanding of "the principles of surgery, in theory and in practice, [and] . . . all things which are comprehended in anatomy." He should be well trained and experienced, with "small fingers and steadfast hands, not trembling, and clear of sight." Finally, he should be "well mannered . . . gracious to sick folk, and merciful to poor folk, and not too greedy but reasonable, to set his salary considering the labour of the cure, and the worthiness and the poverty of the patient, and not to meddle with no cures that he supposes are not capable of curing."[48]

With his emphasis on the importance of anatomy — including a cut-by-cut description of how to dissect a newly dead body, "as of them whose heads have been smitten off or hanged" — Morstede placed a premium on practical experience and observation over simple book-learning. In common with all other medieval practitioners, he might not have realised that the blood circulated continuously round the body, rather than dissipating into the flesh like sap into leaves, but he knew his internal organs, his bones, cartilage, veins and arteries, muscles, ligaments and sinews.[49]

Death in battle was a possibility that no one preparing to go to France could afford to ignore. Hamon le Straunge, a man-at-arms in the company of Sir Thomas Erpingham, thus made careful provision for his wife, Alienor, in the event of his death, setting his seal to his will on 10 June 1415. The king himself drew up his will on 24 July, leaving generous bequests, ranging from beds to horses, to his "most dear brother" Bedford and his "dearest brother" Gloucester, but nothing at all, not even a personal memento, to his brother Clarence, who would, nevertheless, inherit the kingdom. There were individual bequests, too, for "our most dear grandmother, the countess of Hereford," for the officers of his household and his chamber, his physician Nicholas Colnet, and his chaplains. Henry's two religious foundations, the Carthusian monastery at Sheen and the Bridgettine house at Syon, were to benefit from legacies of one thousand marks each. His body was to be buried in the church of Westminster Abbey, where a tomb was to be built, serviced by its own altar.[50]

As one would expect from so pious a king, Henry also made provision for his own soul, trusting for redemption in the intervention of the virgin Mary and a holy host of angels, saints and martyrs, including his own personal favourites, Edward the Confessor, St John of Bridlington and St Brigit of Sweden. Thirty poor men were to be fed and clothed for a year on condition that they daily repeated the prayer, "Mother of God, remember thy servant Henry who placed his whole trust in thee." In addition, twenty thousand masses were to be sung as soon as possible after his death, the title and number of each one being laid down with his usual meticulous attention to detail. Though it has been suggested that twenty thousand masses was an excessive number, reflecting a guilty conscience for embarking on an unjust war, such extravagance was by no means unusual in the medieval period. Piety rather than guilt dictated the scale. At the end of the will, which was written in Latin, Henry signed his initials and then added his own personal plea in English, "Jesu Mercy and Gramercy. Lady Marie help."[51]

Four days after making his will, Henry wrote for the final time to Charles VI of France. Ostensibly it was a last-ditch attempt to avert war: a personal appeal from one man to another, prompted by the dictates of conscience and, in particular, a wish to avoid bloodshed. Henry pleaded for a settlement of their quarrel and the restoration of peace between two great nations which were "once united, now divided." Charles should know, he declared, that "we call to witness in conscience the Supreme Judge, over whom neither entreaties nor bribes can prevail, that, in our sincere zeal for peace, we have tried every way possible to obtain peace. If we had not done so, we would have rashly given away the just title of our inheritance, to the eternal prejudice of posterity."[52]

For many modern commentators this letter is simply another example of Henry's hypocrisy: he was mouthing platitudes about peace and justice but, in reality, "whatever the cost, he wanted war."[53] Such an interpretation misses the point. It is true that the king had no intention of abandoning his campaign at this late stage and that this "last request" was pregnant with threat — it was written "at the very moment of making our crossing" and dated from "our town of Southampton on the sea shore" — making it clear that invasion was imminent. It is also true that he did not expect to extract any further concessions from the French that would be substantial enough to persuade him to call off the expedition. It is even true that the letter was a useful tool in the propaganda war because it could be copied and distributed to allies of both sides as evidence of the English willingness to compromise. (It was no accident that transcripts of it were to appear in many contemporary chronicles.)[54]

Nevertheless, this "last request" was not a cynical, empty gesture. Henry was, with his customary attention to detail, following precisely the code of conduct that governed the medieval laws of war. If Henry V's war to recover his rights in France was to be accepted as morally justified in the eyes of the world and, more importantly, of God, it was crucial that every step he took along the path was correct and followed the prescribed form. He had already consulted the "wise men" of his kingdom both in Parliament and in his great council. More recently, he had taken the second step of consulting impartial international opinion on the justice of his cause, ordering notarised transcripts to be made, under the seal of the archbishop of Canterbury, of the 1412 Treaty of Bourges, in which the Armagnac princes had recognised English sovereignty in Aquitaine. He had sent these copies to Constance (now in Switzerland), where the general council of the Church was in session, and to European princes, including the Holy Roman Emperor, "to this end: that all Christendom might know what great acts of injustice the French had inflicted on him, and that, as it were reluctantly and against his will, he was being compelled to raise his standards against rebels."[55]

The third and final step in this quasi-judicial process was to set out the case before the adversary himself and ask for the restitution of his rights. Henry's letter to Charles VI had taken precisely this form. In it he made a point of citing the twentieth chapter of the biblical book of Deuteronomy, which formed the basis of the medieval laws of war and commanded that "when you draw near to a city to fight against it, offer terms of peace to it."[56] It was a quotation that would appear repeatedly on Henry's lips and dictate his actions throughout the coming war with France.

There was now nothing left to be done except to begin the enterprise that had been so long in preparation. On 29 July Henry gave the order for everyone engaged in his service to embark upon the ships allocated to them and to be ready to sail by 1 August at the latest. The discovery of the Cambridge plot and the necessity of dealing with the culprits caused an unexpected delay, but six days later Henry left Portchester Castle on board a barge, which took him out into the deeper waters between Southampton and Portsmouth, where his flagship, the *Trinity Royal*, was waiting for him. As soon as he was on board, the signal was given for all the ships of the fleet in the various ports and harbours along the south coast to make haste to join him. All he needed was a favourable wind as he prepared to set sail for France.[57]

1. Henry V (1386–1422), a fifteenth-century portrait by an unknown artist.
(National Portrait Gallery/Bridgeman Art Library)

2. This manuscript illustration from Thomas Hoccleve's *The Regimen of Princes* (1411) depicts the poet kneeling to present his book to Henry, who was then prince of Wales. The book gave advice on how to educate a future king and was dedicated to the prince. This copy, dating from around 1413, belonged to John Mowbray, the earl marshal, who fought in the Agincourt campaign. *(British Library/Bridgeman Art Library)*

3. The coronation of Henry V (1413). A detail from one of the stone carvings in the chantry chapel housing his tomb in Westminster Abbey. Although Henry died in 1422, the chapel was built in 1438–50 according to the instructions he had left in the will he made in 1415 before setting out on the Agincourt campaign. *(Conway Library/Courtauld Institute of Art)*

4. Two German gunners prepare a cannon for firing in an illustration from a German master-gunner's book (1411). The man on the left holds the wooden bung which separated the powder chamber from the wider barrel; the gun-stone was then inserted into the barrel where it was held in place by wooden wedges until fired.
(Osterreichische Nationalbibliothek Bildarchiv)

5. A female blacksmith forging the nails for Christ's crucifixion (see p. 92), from a manuscript of *c.*1325–30. Margaret Merssh was employed in the king's forge at the Tower of London throughout Henry's reign.
(British Library)

7. A silver SS collar of the first half of the fifteenth century. The collar, made of interlinked S shapes, was worn by members of the house of Lancaster and their retinue. Henry V's personal SS collar, the Pusan d'Or, was pledged to the City of London as surety for repayment of its loan to him for the Agincourt campaign. *(Museum of London)*

8. The Dunstable swan jewel (*c.*1400), an exquisite example of the richest form of livery badge. The swan was the personal badge of Henry V. Measuring only 3.3 cm high and 2.5 cm wide but made of gold and covered with white enamel, this badge must have been worn by either a member of the royal family or an aristocrat closely associated with it. Cheaper versions, made from silver, gilded bronze or even lead, were worn by members of Henry's household. All those serving on the Agincourt campaign were required to wear the livery badge of their captain at all times for identification purposes. *(British Museum)*

6. Reliquary of the Order of St-Esprit, probably made in England in 1390–1410, and presented by Henry V's stepmother, Joan of Navarre, to her son, John, duke of Brittany, in 1412. Made of gold, and decorated with pearls, rubies, sapphires and enamelled figures representing God, the Virgin Mary, Christ and seven saints, this reliquary is typical of the sort of treasures that Henry V gave to his retinue captains in pledge for the payment of their wages for the Agincourt campaign. *(RMN/Jean-Gilles Berizzi)*

9. The herald William Bruges (c.1375–1450) served on the Agincourt campaign as Guyenne king of arms and in 1417 was made the first Garter king of arms. In this manuscript of c.1430, he is depicted kneeling before St George, the patron saint of the order, who bears the cross of St George on his shield and is flanked on either side by the Garter badge. Bruges wears a heraldic tabard of the royal arms and a crown to signify his office as the premier herald in England. *(British Library)*

10. The white leather bag containing Sir Thomas Erpingham's indenture to serve the king for the Agincourt campaign and his wage claims for his retinue. A bag like this was purchased for every retinue leader and kept in the exchequer so that the king's clerks could add to it all the documentation necessary to substantiate claims and authorise payments. *(National Archives)*

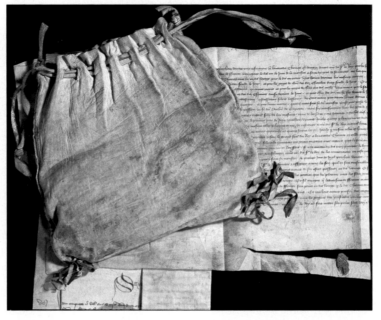

11. An early fifteenth-century manuscript illustration of a knight taking leave of his wife and child as he sets off for war. He is wearing "white harness," the full suit of plate armour, jointed for ease of movement at the knees and elbows, that was worn by all men-at-arms at Agincourt. Additional defences made of mail can be seen at his throat and at his groin, which were both vulnerable points. Some knights even took the precaution of having sacred symbols or Christian invocations, such as "IHS" or "Jesus of Nazareth" or *Ave Maria* incised into their armour as talismans. The horse is also prepared for war, bearing the knight's heraldic arms on its trapper and wearing a steel chanfrein or head protector. *(British Library)*

12. The duke of Bourbon sets sail for Barbary on crusade in 1390 in a scene similar to the launch of the Agincourt invasion fleet. Note the flat-bottomed rowing boat carrying the men-at-arms out to their ships in the foreground, the display of shields bearing the arms of those in the ships and the two trumpeters standing at the rear of the duke's vessel. *(British Library/Bridgeman Art Library)*

13. Richard Whittington, whose substantial loans to Henry V helped to finance the Agincourt campaign, on his deathbed in 1421. The priest administering the last rites has been joined by Whittington's three executors and the residents of the almshouses he had founded. In the background a physician examines a flask containing the dying man's urine. This picture introduces the 1442 English translation of the ordinances for the governance of Whittington's almshouses. *(Mercers Company Archives)*

14. The remarkable tomb effigy of Henry Chichele (1362–1443), who was appointed archbishop of Canterbury by Henry V in 1414. The tomb in Canterbury Cathedral shows him lying in state as convention demanded but counterpointed by a realistic image of his naked cadaver beneath. An inscription on the lower section states "I was born poor." *(Winchester Cathedral, Dean and Chapter)*

15. The Evesham Abbey world map. Commissioned in 1390 and amended in 1415, this *mappa mundi* portrays the world in terms of its biblical importance, rather than geographical accuracy. The Garden of Eden is at the top, with the Red Sea to its right and Jerusalem, with its towers, the focal point in the centre. English political influence is represented in the lower half of the map. The largest of the three islands at the bottom of the map represents England, with Wales and Ireland below it; the two smaller islands to its right are Scotland and, on the outside edge, the Isle of Man. *(The College of Arms)*

16. An artist's impression of the fortified medieval town and port of
Harfleur. The seaboard entrance to the harbour is between the two towers in
the foreground; this side of the town was blockaded by the English fleet.
The inhabitants of Harfleur had flooded the valley above the town, forcing
Henry to divide his forces. He took up his position before the Leure gate on
the extreme left of the picture and sent the duke of Clarence to lay siege to
the Rouen gate, on the opposite side of the town.
(Parcours du Patrimoine: www.nap.fr)

17. A fifteenth-century illustration of the siege of a walled town. On the left
is a belfry, a wooden tower on wheels, from which archers could shoot in
comparative safety. The belfry also provided cover for men-at-arms to get
close to the walls and make an assault by means of scaling ladders. In the
foreground are two cannon, one of which is lying on its cradle ready to fire.
The archer in the centre who is firing up at the besieged is protected by a
wooden palisade which has been erected for that purpose. *(British Library)*

18. The alabaster tomb effigy at Canterbury Cathedral of Thomas, duke of Clarence (1387–1421), the second of Henry IV's four sons, and his father's favourite. As befitted someone who was killed in battle, Clarence is depicted in full plate armour, over which he wears a surcoat of his arms and the Lancastrian SS collar. *(Angelo Hornak/Corbis)*

19. John, duke of Bedford (1389–1435), the third of Henry IV's sons, kneels before St George, who wears the Garter device on his cloak, in this illustration from a famous Book of Hours commissioned by the duke. Of all Henry V's brothers, Bedford was the closest to the king and was entrusted with the regency of England during the Agincourt campaign. *(British Library/ Bridgeman Art Library)*

20. Humphrey, duke of Gloucester (1390–1447), the youngest of Henry V's brothers. Like his brothers he had been knighted and made a member of the order of the Garter by his father, but the Agincourt campaign was his first experience of war and he was wounded at the battle. From a sixteenth-century copy of a contemporary drawing. *(British Library)*

21. The tomb effigy of Charles VI of France (1368–1422) in the abbey church of St Denis, near Paris. Known as Charles the Well-Beloved to his subjects, his long reign was marred by intermittent periods of madness during which he believed that he was made of glass. His inability to rule at such times led to the civil wars between Armagnacs and Burgundians that enabled Henry V to invade France. *(Basilique St-Denis, Paris/Bridgeman Art Library)*

22. A fifteenth-century portrait of John the Fearless, duke of Burgundy (1371–1419), leader of the Burgundian faction, whose ambition to control the throne of France led to the assassination of his rival Louis, duke of Orleans, and plunged France into civil war. His role during the Agincourt campaign was opaque: he was not present at the battle and used the English victory to launch his own attack on Paris. He was assassinated himself in 1419. *(Kunsthistorisches Museum, Vienna/Bridgeman Art Library)*

23. Fifteenth-century bowmen at a siege. The man in the centre is using a crossbow which he has to wind up, bracing his weapon by putting it on the ground and placing his foot on it. The bag at his waist is for his bolts, or quarrels, and the bracing mechanism. The two archers on either side of him are using longbows, and instead of using a quiver they have stuck their arrows into the ground in readiness for use. All three are lightly armed with kettle hats and padded body armour; the archer on the right also has a mail jacket while the crossbowman has plate pieces to protect his legs. *(Bibliothèque Nationale, Paris)*

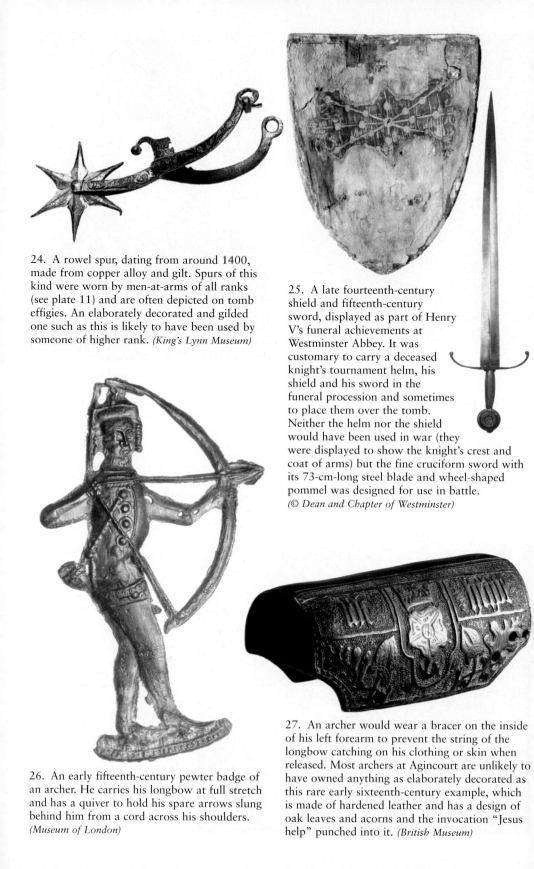

24. A rowel spur, dating from around 1400, made from copper alloy and gilt. Spurs of this kind were worn by men-at-arms of all ranks (see plate 11) and are often depicted on tomb effigies. An elaborately decorated and gilded one such as this is likely to have been used by someone of higher rank. *(King's Lynn Museum)*

25. A late fourteenth-century shield and fifteenth-century sword, displayed as part of Henry V's funeral achievements at Westminster Abbey. It was customary to carry a deceased knight's tournament helm, his shield and his sword in the funeral procession and sometimes to place them over the tomb. Neither the helm nor the shield would have been used in war (they were displayed to show the knight's crest and coat of arms) but the fine cruciform sword with its 73-cm-long steel blade and wheel-shaped pommel was designed for use in battle. *(© Dean and Chapter of Westminster)*

26. An early fifteenth-century pewter badge of an archer. He carries his longbow at full stretch and has a quiver to hold his spare arrows slung behind him from a cord across his shoulders. *(Museum of London)*

27. An archer would wear a bracer on the inside of his left forearm to prevent the string of the longbow catching on his clothing or skin when released. Most archers at Agincourt are unlikely to have owned anything as elaborately decorated as this rare early sixteenth-century example, which is made of hardened leather and has a design of oak leaves and acorns and the invocation "Jesus help" punched into it. *(British Museum)*

28. Two French men-at-arms captured at the battle of Agincourt are led away from the battlefield by an Englishman with the cross of St George on his chest; it is unclear whether he is meant to be a man-at-arms or an archer. The prisoners have their hands bound, though this was not normal practice in the field. From a highly stylised fifteenth-century illustration to Martial d'Auvergne's *Vigiles de Charles VII*. *(Bibliothèque Nationale, Paris/Bridgeman Art Library)*

29. An unusual depiction (*c*.1483) of the usual aftermath of a medieval battle, in this case the Swiss victory over the Burgundians at Morat in 1476. Corpses were normally stripped of their armour and clothing before burial in mass grave pits. Here, as at Agincourt, it is noticeable how many of the corpses have head and throat wounds.
(Burgerbibliothek Bern, MSS.h.h.XY)

30. A fifteenth-century manuscript of the words and music for the famous Agincourt carol, which was probably composed soon after the battle to celebrate the English victory. The chorus, however, firmly attributed the success to God. *(British Library)*

31. Enguerrand de Monstrelet (*c*.1390–1453), a nobleman from Picardy, who served as a soldier and administrator in the Burgundian administration of the region, writing his chronicle of France and England which includes one of the most important accounts of Agincourt. He presented his book to Philippe, duke of Burgundy, in 1447. This fifteenth-century illustration from a copy of the work, which he modelled on the works of Froissart, also includes a battle scene, though the armour and weaponry are not contemporary. *(Bibliothèque Nationale, Paris)*

32. A gold noble, worth 6s 4d, from the reign of Henry V. The coin depicts the king standing on-board ship. He is wearing his crown and armour and bearing a shield of his royal arms in his left hand and a sword in his right. The Latin legend round the coin reads "Henry by the grace of God king of England and France, lord of Ireland." *(British Library)*

33. Jean le Meingre, better known as Marshal Boucicaut (*c*.1366–1421), was one of the chivalric heroes of medieval France. This illustration from a Book of Hours commissioned by him depicts Boucicaut and his wife kneeling at their daily devotions. Boucicaut was captured at Agincourt and died while still a prisoner in England. *(Institut de France-Musée Jacquemart-André, Paris)*

34. Raoul, sire de Gaucourt (*c*.1370–1461), the defender of Harfleur who surrendered himself to Henry V after the battle of Agincourt and spent ten years as a prisoner in England. On his release he became a major figure in the reconquest of English-held lands in France. Here he is depicted in a fifteenth-century manuscript on the campaign of 1429 that led to the French recapture of the Dauphine. *(Bibliothèque Nationale, Paris)*

Es nouuelles Dalbÿon
Il vous en plaist escouta
mon frere & mon compaÿno

35. Charles, duke of Orleans (1394–1465) was not quite twenty-one when he was captured at the battle of Agincourt. He remained a prisoner in England for the next thirty-five years. This manuscript (c.1487) depicts the duke (wearing a white fur collar) during his confinement in the Tower of London. He is shown writing his poems, languishing at a window, greeting the bearer of his ransom and hiding away after his release. London Bridge, with its houses and shops, is in the background. *(British Library/Bridgeman Art Library)*

PART II

THE AGINCOURT CAMPAIGN

✤ CHAPTER NINE ✤

"FAIR STOOD THE WIND
FOR FRANCE"[1]

On Sunday, 11 August 1415, at about three o'clock in the afternoon, Henry V gave the signal that launched the invasion of France. Fifteen hundred ships — a fleet twelve times the size of the Spanish Armada[2] — now weighed anchor, hoisted sail and made their way into the Channel from the shelter of South-ampton Water and the Solent. Unlike the huge Spanish galleons of the sixteenth century, these were not purpose-built warships but a motley collection of privately owned merchant vessels: great ships that braved the Atlantic to bring wine from Aqui-taine and carry the highly prized heavy woollen broadcloth to the continent; smaller coastal traders importing salt from Bourgneuf Bay in Brittany and exporting salted herring from Yarmouth to the Low Countries and the Baltic; even river boats, the freight carriers of the inland waterways, supplying every-thing from stone and marble for building cathedrals to hides for making leather boots, gloves and saddles.[3] There were ships of every size and shape: cogs and carracks, galleys and balingers. Most were built in the distinctive northern style of clinker con-struction — their hulls composed of a series of overlapping planks from the keel upwards — with a single mast and one square or rectangular sail, but some were lighter Mediterranean

vessels, double-masted, with triangular sails and banks of oars-
men. Those ships that had been converted into fighting vessels
sported small wooden castles at both prow and stern; others
had been fitted with rows of stalls to carry horses, a small ship
like a cog having the capacity to carry only thirty, at a time
when transport for some twenty-five thousand was needed.[4]

Many of the ships had gaily painted hulls, carried rows of
white shields bearing the red cross of England along their sides,
and flew sails, pennons and banners decorated with heraldic
beasts and coats of arms. Some were privately owned by retinue
commanders, like the four carracks provided by Sir John Holland, but most were impressed, like the four vessels, two each
from Bayonne and Dartmouth, which conveyed the 180 men in
Sir Thomas Carew's company. Frustratingly, a number of men
who had mustered at Southampton had to be left behind for
lack of shipping, and approximately one hundred ships also
failed to join the fleet, either because they could not catch the
tide or because they were not ready to sail. Three more were lost
when they caught fire, a routine hazard of life on board ship,
which was probably an accident but may have been connected
with the Cambridge plot, since burning the fleet to prevent the
expedition sailing had been one of the options discussed by the
conspirators.[5]

At the head of the fleet, escorted by the admiral, Thomas
Beaufort, earl of Dorset, and a convoy of fifteen ships carrying
150 men-at-arms and 300 archers, sailed the *Trinity Royal*. At
540 tons, this was one of the largest ships in northern Europe.[6]
She had just returned to sea after a two-year refit and there was
now no mistaking whom she carried on board, or the purpose
of his voyage. The royal coat of arms, a shield quartered with
the three lions of England and the three fleurs-de-lis of France,
was painted on her sail. A golden crown adorned her top-castle
and a gilded sceptre, worked with three fleur-de-lis, decorated
the capstan. At the deckhead stood the carved wooden figure of
a crowned leopard, another heraldic beast associated with the
kings of England. Painted and gilded, it carried six shields, four
of which bore the king's arms within a collar of gold, and two

the arms of the patron saint of England, St George, within the Garter, the emblem of the English order of chivalry. At the mast and on the rear deck flew four of the banners that would also be carried at Agincourt: the royal arms; the arms of St George; the arms of Henry's royal ancestor, St Edward the Confessor; and the curious cipher representing the Trinity.[7]

This display of heraldry was not simply the unavoidable rag-bag of inheritance. It was deliberately chosen, a carefully thought-out piece of visual propaganda, whose meaning would be as clear to anyone connected with the profession of arms as that of the religious paintings and artefacts in medieval churches. Even the royal coat of arms made a provocative statement. The ancient arms of England, borne by every king since Richard the Lionheart in the twelfth century, had been three golden lions on a red background. This had changed only at the start of the Hundred Years War when Edward III made a symbolic statement of his claim to the throne of France by quartering them with the French royal arms, the golden fleurs-de-lis scattered on a blue background.[8] Edward III had also, at about the same time, unilaterally adopted St George as the patron saint of England. The significance of this gesture was that St George had previously been recognised throughout Europe and the Christian east as the patron saint of all knighthood. By making him exclusively English, Edward III identified himself and his country as the embodiment of the treasured chivalric values that the saint represented. The seemingly miraculous English victories at Crécy, in 1346, and Poitiers, a decade later, could therefore be seen as indisputable proof that the saint had withdrawn his favour from the French (with whom the very concept of chivalry had originated) and become a partisan of England.[9]

The Order of the Garter, founded by Edward III after Crécy and dedicated to St George, was a celebration of English military supremacy, and its twenty-six members were admired and envied throughout Europe. When Jehan Werchin, the young seneschal of Hainault who would later be killed at Agincourt, was seeking to establish a reputation for prowess in 1408, he did it by issuing a jousting challenge to the Knights of the Garter, whom he regarded, quite literally, as the heirs of the Arthurian Knights of the Round Table and therefore the champions of England. (His offer to fight them all at once brought a mild reproof from Henry IV, who said such a thing was unheard of in the ancient chronicles of the Round Table, and was therefore inappropriate; he should fight against a single representative.) Likewise, the greatest honour Henry V could bestow on Sigismund, the Holy Roman Emperor, whose alliance he was seeking in the war against France in 1416, was the Order of the Garter. The insignia and the ceremonies associated with the order were highly prized as the visible symbols of a knightly reputation won by outstanding courage and loyal service. It was no accident that Garter knights, such as Sir John Cornewaille (who had independently accepted another of the seneschal of Hainault's challenges to a feat of arms), were to play a prominent role in the Agincourt campaign, deliberately seeking out the most dangerous — and therefore the most honourable — exploits to perform.[10]

The heraldic displays on the *Trinity Royal* were visual assertions of Henry's royal status, his claim to the throne of France, and English military supremacy; the religious banners declared that this earthly army also enjoyed the patronage and protection of the heavenly hosts. At least three other ships, all members of Henry's embryonic royal navy, bore his personal devices painted on their sails: the *Katherine de la Tour* and the *Nicholas de la Tour* displayed an antelope and a swan respectively, and the third, an unnamed vessel, the ostrich feathers, which had been his badge as prince of Wales. Given the importance of these symbols, and the medieval weakness for anything that smacked of prophetic insight, the appearance of a flock of swans swimming through the fleet as it left the Isle of Wight was guaranteed to gladden every English heart as the perfect omen.[11]

Most of those on board had no idea whether they were heading straight across the Channel for France or taking the much longer sea voyage that would eventually bring them to Aquitaine. Speculation as to their ultimate destination must have intensified as they saw the white cliffs of the Normandy coastline looming. Would they land, as Clarence had done three years earlier, at St-Vaast-la-Hougue on the Cotentin peninsula? Or would they attack one of the prosperous seaports to the east — Boulogne, perhaps, or Dieppe or Fécamp?

Two days after they had put to sea, about five o'clock in the afternoon, the fleet sailed into the bay that lies at the mouth of the river Seine. There they dropped anchor in the lee of the Chef-de-Caux (now Cap de la Hève), the westernmost tip of the great chalk headland that is the Roman nose on the face of upper Normandy. It was not an obvious place for a landing, even though the cliffs here rose less steeply and were more accessible than their precipitous and crumbling neighbours on the Channel coast. The gentler wooded slopes of the southern shore of the bay were more vulnerable to invasion — which is why Constable d'Albret was lying in wait for them there with a force of fifteen hundred men.[12]

Henry V was almost certainly unaware of their presence, but he had chosen his landing site, in the small bay of Sainte Adresse, with care. Only a few miles away, hidden from view on the landward side by a wooded bluff, lay his objective: the royal town and port of Harfleur.

Henry's first action after dropping anchor was to unfurl the banner that was the signal to his captains to attend a meeting of the council on board the *Trinity Royal*. Knowing that his knights and esquires would be vying with each other to achieve the honour of being the first to set foot in France, he then gave orders that no one, on pain of death, was to land before he did and that everyone should prepare to disembark the following morning.[13] Discipline, strictly enforced, was to be the watchword of his entire campaign.

Under cover of darkness Henry sent a scouting party ashore to explore the lie of the land and find suitable quarters. The man chosen to lead this party, and the one to whom the glory of being the first to land in France was therefore given, was his twenty-year-old cousin Sir John Holland. That Henry should entrust him with such a mission was significant, for there were others, such as Clarence, Gloucester and Dorset, who had better claims in terms of both rank and military experience. It was an opportunity for Holland to prove his worth and finally step out of the shadow of his father's execution for treason by Henry IV. He seized it with both hands and despite his youth would serve with distinction on this campaign and become one of Henry V's most able and dependable commanders in France.

Though Holland was nominally in charge of the scouting party, Henry ensured that his lack of years and experience were offset by those chosen to accompany him. These were, or became over the course of the campaign, a tightly knit little group who, with Holland himself, would, time and again, be entrusted with actions requiring particular courage and military skill. Foremost among them was Holland's stepfather, Sir John Cornewaille, one of the most widely respected chivalric figures of the day, even though he was still in his mid-thirties. The son of a West Country knight and a niece of the duke of Brittany, he had first come to prominence in 1400, when he was imprisoned for marrying Henry IV's sister, Elizabeth of Lancaster (Holland's mother), without the king's permission. Even though she was some years older than he and already twice-widowed, it was said that the marriage was a love-match, and that she had fallen for him when she watched him defeat a French knight in a joust at York that year. Cornewaille certainly excelled at combats of this kind, and earned himself an international reputation for his success in them. In September 1406 he defeated some Scottish knights in jousts held in London, and in June 1409 he performed the feat of arms to which he had been challenged by Jehan Werchin, seneschal of Hainault. This latter event, which took place over a period of three days in Lille, was a single combat, fought *à outrance* — that is, with the normal weapons and armour of war, "which accomplishment is the greatest honour to which prowess and chivalry can aspire." Cornewaille distinguished himself, fighting several courses each with lance, sword, dagger and axe in turn, and at the end he was presented with a gold collar set with jewels by John the Fearless, duke of Burgundy, who had presided over the whole event. In 1412 he also fought a challenge at Smithfield in London against the Armagnac knight Tanneguy de Chastel, who had been captured in a Breton raid on the Devon coast in 1404.[14] Cornewaille's military career had been equally bold and idiosyncratic. Its highlights had included defeating a French assault on Blackpool, in Lancashire, in 1404; commanding an English mercenary troop of sixty men-at-arms and five hundred archers on behalf of the duke of Burgundy at the battle of Othée in 1408; and accompanying Thomas, duke of Clarence, as one of the leaders of the abortive invasion of France in 1412. He had indented to serve Henry V for the Agincourt campaign with a substantial company of thirty men-at-arms and ninety archers (the future earl, his stepson, could only afford to take twenty and sixty, respectively).[15]

William Porter was another member of the scouting party. A squire of the chamber for both Henry IV and Henry V, he had served on several important diplomatic missions for the latter, including being sent "on secret business" to King João of Portugal in 1413 and on Bishop Courtenay's embassy to Paris in the winter of 1414–15. He was clearly high in Henry V's favour. He received a personal legacy of a gold cup, a horse and £6 in cash in the king's will, was given some of the lands in the south-east of England confiscated from Henry, Lord Scrope, and in 1422 was appointed an executor and administrator of the king's revised will. Although he had indented to serve with a retinue of eight men-at-arms and twenty-four archers, he was nominally, at least, supposed to be in the company of Michael de la Pole, son and heir of the earl of Suffolk. Why he was picked for the scouting party is therefore unclear, but it may have been connected to the fact that he was John Cornewaille's brother-in-arms.[16] Porter and Cornewaille were real examples of what is often dismissed as simply a literary conceit. Like the most famous fictional pair of brothers-in-arms, Arcite and Palamon from Geoffrey Chaucer's *The Knight's Tale*, they had sworn a mutual oath to assist each other, "Til that the deethe departe shal us tweyne." Though brotherhood-in-arms had idealistic overtones, arising out of the concept that the oath had originally been administered while mingling the blood of the two parties, it was in practice a much more formal legal relationship, very similar to the system of retaining, except that it was made between equals, rather than lord and man. The agreement between Porter and Cornewaille has not survived, but one drawn up between two English esquires, Nicholas Molyneux and John Wynter, at Harfleur in 1421, is a model of its kind. It had been made, they declared, "to increase and augment the respect and brotherhood which has for long existed between the said Molyneux and Wynter, so that it may henceforth be even stronger and more enduring, the said persons have personally sworn to become brothers in arms; that is to say, that each shall be loyal to the other without fraud or deception." The principal heads of their agreement were that they should each be responsible for raising the first thousand pounds of the other's ransom, in the event of either of them being captured; that one would remain hostage for both and the other seek to raise their joint ransoms, if both were captured; that all profits of war they won between them should be sent to London for safekeeping, until they could be invested in the purchase of land in England; and that the survivor (having made provision for any widow and children of the deceased) should inherit the full value of all their joint winnings.[17]

The brotherhood-in-arms that existed between Cornewaille and Porter must have been particularly lucrative, given the former's military prowess and the latter's diplomatic and administrative skills. Little is known about Porter's financial affairs, but Cornewaille displayed a business acumen to rival his martial abilities. As early as 1404 he had purchased a Norman knight and some of the French prisoners captured in the raid on Dartmouth as an investment in their ransoms, something he would do again after Agincourt, when he bought a part share in the count of Vendôme from Henry V for 20,000 crowns. In 1412 the hostages kept as collateral for the payment of the 210,000 gold écus with which the Armagnacs bought off Clarence's English forces were placed in Cornewaille's hands, and a tenth of the entire sum was specifically allocated to him. It was said that he built his magnificent new home, Ampthill Castle in Bedfordshire, out of his profits of war, and his long and loyal service certainly earned him an elevation to the peerage. When he became Lord Fanhope in 1436, his annual income was said to be in excess of £800 (the equivalent of $533,232 today).[18] In fact, much of his fortune rested on his marriage, which brought him a vast income from lands and rents, especially after Parliament granted his wife her dower rights in her first husband's estates in 1404. He had to wait many years — twenty-eight in the case of the 1412 debt — to get the payments due to him for ransoms, during which time he had to keep his noble prisoners in the style to which they were accustomed.

The final member of the elite group that led the scouting party was another knight who would pay the ultimate price for his service in France. Sir Gilbert Umfraville was a nephew of the Sir Robert Umfraville who had played such an opaque role in relation to the Scottish invasion that was part of the Cambridge plot. Sir Gilbert's loyalty was beyond question: like Porter, he had been a knight of the chamber since the beginning of Henry V's reign. Like Cornewaille, he indented to serve with a substantial retinue of thirty men-at-arms and ninety archers, suggesting he had a considerable fortune at his disposal. With his fellow Garter knight Cornewaille, he would be entrusted with the joint leadership of the first battalion on the march from Harfleur to Agincourt.[19]

The scouting party that slipped ashore before dawn on Wednesday, 14 August 1415, was entrusted with several tasks, the two most important being to discover what resistance might be expected and to identify the best route to Harfleur. It is inconceivable that spies had not already provided the king with much of his geographical information before he set sail, but the medieval world lacked the main resource of modern travellers, friendly or hostile: the map, as we know it today, simply did not exist. Medieval *mappae mundi*, or world maps, like the famous late thirteenth-century one at Hereford Cathedral, were intended to be only a symbolic representation of the known inhabited world. The comparative sizes and distances between places did not reflect geographical fact, or even the state of current knowledge, but rather their importance historically and, especially, in relation to Christianity. Maps were oriented towards the east (hence the word "oriented"), rather than the north as they are today, and Jerusalem, as the most important city in Christ's life and death, lay at their centre. The scientific world was aware that a fourth, antipodean continent existed, besides Asia, Europe and Africa, but the Church resisted the idea and had burnt two university professors from Padua and Bologna in the early fourteenth century for insisting that it was true. The idea that people in the Middle Ages believed that the world was flat or disc shaped, and that they might fall off if they went to its edge, is a modern myth based on a misunderstanding of the concept of the *mappa mundi*. Observers seeing the shape of the shadow of the earth during a lunar eclipse, or watching a ship's hull disappear before its masts as it sailed over the horizon, had been aware of the curvature of the earth's surface since classical times, and this knowledge had not been lost. By the fifteenth century, astronomical studies had reinforced this to the point that it was simply taken for granted that the world was spherical. Texts of every kind compared the earth to an apple or an egg, and medieval illustrations often depicted Christ holding the world — as an orb or a sphere — in his hands.[20]

A *mappa mundi* was of no use to anyone wanting to plan a journey. Established routes were therefore of prime importance. Crusaders and pilgrims, for instance, relied on being given an itinerary to follow: when they reached a named place en route, they would ask for directions to the next on the list. (That was the main reason why so many of them passed through Venice, rather than other Mediterranean ports, on their way to the Holy Land.) This sort of information was obviously not available to an invading army: military objectives were not the same as holy places. Merchants, who were the most regular travellers of the Middle Ages, together with diplomats, similarly relied on established trade routes and, wherever possible, preferred to journey by sea or river rather than over land. For this purpose, they had developed rudimentary navigational charts as early as the thirteenth century. Within two hundred years, the Italians, who had a virtual monopoly on producing them, had mapped out the coastline of most of Europe and the Mediterranean in a form that would be more recognisable to modern eyes than that of the *mappa mundi*. Unfortunately, again, for the potential invader, the interiors of the countries remained a blank: large cities and commercial centres were named, but only as a list of names along the nearest coastline and without reference to their distance from it. Other than giving a general indication of which country to aim for, if one wished to go to a particular place, these maps were also useless for military purposes.[21]

What was an invading army to do? Spies would, no doubt, have provided the groundwork and merchants from England and her allies visiting the busy port of Harfleur would have been able to give details of the layout of the city and its neighbourhood. For the rest, they would have to rely on what intelligence could be gleaned from the investigations of scouting parties and the interrogation, by force, bribery or persuasion, of local people. The choice of landing site at Chef-de-Caux does not seem to suggest any sophisticated prior intelligence; even the French admitted that it could easily have been defended and an English landing prevented. As with all this stretch of Normandy coastline, the shore was a mass of shingle, cast up into a bank by the action of the tides. According to Henry V's chaplain, who is our main eyewitness of the campaign, it was also strewn with large boulders, which were a major hazard to the barges and skiffs ferrying the troops, horses and supplies from the ships. On the landward side of this shingle ridge, the French had prepared a set of shoreline defences, consisting of thick earthen walls, "furnished with angles and ramparts . . . after the manner of the walls of a tower or castle," and a series of water-filled ditches, between which "the earth was left intact for the breadth of a cubit, permitting only one man at a time to enter or leave between them." Beyond the man-made ditches, there was the natural hazard of tidal salt-water marshes to negotiate, again along treacherous narrow paths, which left the invaders seriously exposed to danger.[22]

It should have been easy for the French to prevent the landing. Even though not a hand was raised against them, it still took the English three days to disembark, during which time they were at their weakest and constantly vulnerable to attack. The French also had the advantage of an inexhaustible supply of ready ammunition, in the form of the stones from the beach and riverbed. "However," the chaplain remarked, "as a result of their slackness, folly, or, at any rate, lack of foresight, the place was left completely undefended by men when, as far as one could judge, the resistance of a few, had they but had manly hearts, would have kept us at bay certainly for a long time and perhaps indefinitely."[23]

The mortifying failure of the French to offer even a token resistance seemed inexplicable, even to their compatriots. An invasion had been expected since the failure to agree terms during Bishop Courtenay's embassy to Paris. In April 1415 a great council of the realm had been called, which had decided that, due to Charles VI's incapacity, the eighteen-year-old dauphin, Louis de Guienne, should be appointed captain-general with authority to organise resistance. Men-at-arms throughout France were to be put on alert so that they were ready to resist the English, garrisons in towns and castles near the sea were to be reinforced and money was to be made available for war. As a result of these decisions, Robin de Hellande, the *bailli* of Rouen, was one of many royal officials who received orders to prepare against an English landing. The Caux region, including Harfleur, fell within his bailiwick, and the defences erected along the shore at Sainte Adresse were his responsibility, whether or not they had been built directly under his personal supervision.[24]

After the return to Paris of the archbishop of Bourges and his fellow ambassadors from their abortive mission to Winchester, preparations had been stepped up another gear. On 28 July Charles d'Albret, the constable of France, and Marshal Boucicaut were appointed king's lieutenant and captain-general respectively, and dispatched to Normandy, each at the head of an army fifteen hundred strong. Not knowing where the English would strike, they had divided their forces, d'Albret setting up his headquarters at Honfleur, the greatest fortified town on the southern shore of the Seine estuary, and Boucicault at Caudebec, a town some twenty-five miles away as the crow flies on the north bank of the Seine, which guarded the first river crossing. Between them, they were within striking distance of most of Normandy. The defence of Ponthieu and Artois was delegated by d'Albret to a nobleman of that region, David, sire de Rambures, who was also a councillor and chamberlain of Charles

VI, captain of Boulogne and master of the crossbowmen of France.[25]

It was fishermen from Boulogne who first raised the alarm that the English fleet had set sail and was heading for France. The town officials promptly sent a messenger, Jacques Rolequin "the younger," to forewarn other likely targets on the coast, the town of Etaples, at the mouth of the river Canche, and le Crotoy and St Valery, the twin guardians on either shore of the bay of the Somme. On his return, Rolequin did not have time to draw breath before being posted further afield, this time to Abbeville, Dieppe and Honfleur, with the latest news that the fleet had now entered the Seine. Though it took him a lengthy ten days to complete this second mission, it is clear that other messengers were also plying the roads with news of the progress of the English invasion.[26] As a result of this network of communication, all the coastal towns of the region were in a state of constant alert and prepared for attack.

This explains the evident effort that had gone into building the physical defences at Chef-de-Caux, but it does not explain why they were unmanned. It is possible that there had been so many false alarms that the locals did not expect a genuine one, but even so the landing would have been observed. The monks at the priory of Graville, perched high on an eminence above the bay, had a bird's-eye view of the entire operation and cannot have failed to send messengers over the hill to Harfleur. (The square Norman tower and the soaring walls of Graville's abbey church of Sainte Honorine would also have made it an obvious landmark from the sea.) Even Constable d'Albret, on the opposite shore at Honfleur, must have seen the fleet at anchor and realised what was happening. Why, then, did no one attempt to resist the landing? The simple answer is that it was impractical. It would have taken the constable's army the best part of two days to get to Sainte Adresse by land, by which time it would be too late. The only chance of fighting off the invasion would have been as the disembarkation began — and at that point it would have been all too easy for Henry to divert his fleet elsewhere, including Honfleur, which was only some five miles away across the bay. The little garrison of Harfleur could have taken a stand but, in doing so, it would have had to abandon the defence of the town, leaving it vulnerable to attack from those still on board ship in the bay. From a purely pragmatic military point of view, it was better to retreat behind the walls of the great fortified towns, which could only fall to a lengthy siege, than to risk everything in open combat.

Despite the fact that this sort of defensive strategy had been standard policy throughout the Hundred Years War, there were, inevitably, rumours of treason. The monk of St Denis, a contemporary chronicler of these events, claimed that the local inhabitants would undoubtedly have risen to the occasion, as they had done many times before, if they had not believed that the noblemen of the area, who had rallied to the standard of Constable d'Albret, would do the job for them. "I ought to say, without embarrassment, because it is the truth," the monk wrote, "that the constable compromised himself on this occasion in the eyes of wise and thoughtful men." At a later council of war, the bastard brother of the duke of Bourbon, "a man in the springtime of early youth, but bold and rash in character," dared to say what many others thought, and accused d'Albret of treason in failing to prevent the landing. It was said that, as a member of the diplomatic embassy to England earlier that year, the constable had promised Henry V that he would not oppose him and, therefore, although he was not far away when the English descended, this was the reason for his inaction. Worse still, he was accused of having, in the French king's name, ordered the local men-at-arms who came to him seeking leadership to return to their homes and not to resist the invasion. The story was patently untrue — d'Albret had not been on a diplomatic mission to England since 1413 — but even his advocates could only offer the lame excuse that he had given these orders because he underestimated the strength of the English army.[27] The truth was that it was impossible for him to guard the entire length of the Channel coast and, having expected the invasion to take place on the southern shore of the Seine, d'Albret was in the wrong place when it came and too far away to rectify his mistake. This error, right at the beginning of the campaign, would have terrible consequences, seriously compromising both his authority and his ability to persuade the other army leaders to any future course of action.

By Saturday 17 August, Henry had completed the disembarkation of his troops and supplies without incident. According to one source, when the king himself came ashore, shortly after dawn on the first day, he fell on his knees and prayed that God would give him justice against his enemies. As was customary on such occasions, he took the opportunity to bestow knighthoods on several esquires, including Sir John Cornewaille's brother-in-arms, William Porter, and Thomas Geney and John Calthorpe, who were both in the retinue of Sir Thomas Erpingham, the steward of the king's household. The king himself took up residence at the ancient priory of Graville, on the hillside overlooking the landing site, from which vantage point he could watch the progress of the disembarkation. His brothers found quarters nearby, but the rest of the army had to find lodgings where they could, in the "hamlets, closes, and orchards" on the steep slopes of the little valley behind the shore.[28]

After the long wait in Southampton and the days of close confinement on board ship, there was inevitably a strong temptation to run riot and, especially, to loot the farms and houses in the vicinity. Several places had already been burnt before Henry reined in his troops by issuing a set of ordinances that were to be the code of conduct for the campaign. The ordinances have not survived, but were neatly summarised by Henry's chaplain. On pain of death there was to be no more arson; churches, sacred buildings and their property were to be preserved intact; and finally, "no one should lay hands upon a woman or on a priest or servant of a church, unless he happened to be armed, offered violence, or attacked anyone."[29]

The issuing of ordinances of this kind was a customary practice, dating back at least to Edward III's reign. They were a vital means of controlling an army, especially one raised by indenture. Every army raised by this method was effectively a new creation, so it was essential to reissue new ordinances each time an indentured group was gathered together. By the fifteenth century there was a standard format: the ordinances Richard II issued at Durham in 1385, on his way to invade Scotland, were substantially the same as those Henry V himself would draw up at the siege of Mantes in July 1419, or those proclaimed by the earl of Leicester for his soldiers in the Low Countries in 1584. The ordinances always opened with the statement "that all manner of persons, of what nation, estate or condition they be, shall be obedient to our lord the king, to his constable and marshal, under penalty of everything they can forfeit in body or goods." In addition to the clauses mentioned by our chronicler, the English chaplain, a whole series of clauses dealt with internal army discipline, insisting that every man should remain in the company to which he belonged and wear the badge of his captain; everyone in the army, regardless of rank, was also to wear "a large sign of the arms of St George before, and another behind upon peril that if he be hurt or slain in default thereof, he who shall hurt or slay him shall suffer no penalty for it." (The obverse of this was that if an enemy was captured wearing the St George's cross, his life was forfeit.) Unauthorised battle-cries, such as "montez" (to horse) or "havoc" (break ranks and seize booty, hence Shakespeare's famous line, "Cry, 'Havoc!' and let slip the dogs of war"), were prohibited by threat of summary execution, since they could shatter discipline and imperil the whole army.[30] All gains of war were to be divided three ways, one-third going to the king, one to the captain, and one to the captor. This was to hold good even if the captor was a person serving without pay in the army. The precise etiquette of taking a prisoner was also laid down: a captor should take his prisoner's parole (an admission of surrender and oath not to escape) and with it a tangible piece of evidence, such as a glove or bascinet, as pledge and proof. The captor was then under a duty to protect his prisoner's life; if he left him alone and undefended, another captor could take him and was then entitled to his ransom. Finally, every prisoner had to be presented as soon as possible to the captor's captain, who then had to pass him on to his superiors for interrogation. Once this had taken place, the prisoner's safekeeping was again entrusted to the captor and his captain, though he could not be released, even to seek money for his ransom, without a written pass, authorising his departure and providing him with the king's protection against arrest or harm. This could only be obtained from Henry himself, or the constable or marshal acting in his name, and it was to be observed on pain of death. All disputes between individuals or companies were to be dealt with by the constable or marshal, as were all breaches of the ordinances.[31]

There was nothing new in the ordinances of 1415, but, as Henry V had demonstrated so often before, he was able to take a customary practice and give it new life and vigour by effective enforcement. The unusual discipline of the English army was something even its enemies commended. The monk of St Denis reported that the English regarded it as an almost unpardonable crime to have prostitutes in their camp and behaved more considerately towards the French than vice versa; they observed the rules of military discipline strictly, he noted, and obeyed the orders of their king to the letter. This discipline unquestionably derived from Henry himself. To maintain his claim that his invasion was a just one, he needed to ensure that his soldiers observed the customary laws of war. This was not simply altruism of the sort advocated by Christine de Pizan, who had declared that it was "dangerous in time of war for an army to be more driven by greed for pillage than by the intention to preserve the righteousness of their cause or the honour of chivalry or to gain praise." It was also a pragmatic recognition that a disciplined army was stronger and more efficient, while a local populace that was not maltreated would be less likely to respond with violence or sabotage.[32]

Henry's ordinances can be seen working in practice, albeit slowly and creakily, in the case of one of the first French prisoners to fall into English hands. Raoul le Gay, a twenty-eight-year-old priest, was captured on 16 August, while the disembarkation was still taking place. Le Gay was trying to follow his employer, a rich burgess, who lived in the suburbs of Harfleur and had fled to Rouen on learning of the English landing, when he was captured by a group of seven scouts or foragers, who spoke no French and evidently thought they had caught a spy. They deprived him of his tunic, knife and purse, tied his hands behind his back and demanded a ransom of one hundred francs, which he could not pay. After a couple of days, he was taken before their superior officer, an elderly knight, who asked him the name of the commander at Harfleur, which he claimed not to know, and then lost interest in him. His plight was noticed by a young Englishman, who spoke to him in Latin, suggesting that he probably realised that le Gay was a priest, despite the fact that he was dressed in secular clothing and wore a cap hiding his tonsure. He ordered him to be taken before the earl of Dorset, who questioned him in French and detained him for a further seven days.

On the tenth day of his captivity, he was brought before Henry V, who, alone among all his officers, enquired whether this priest had been captured in arms. Having discovered that he had not and that his capture was therefore in contravention of the ordinances, Henry still did not let him go, suggesting that he too thought le Gay was a spy. The priest was therefore handed into the custody of Richard Courtenay, bishop of Norwich, who offered to release him on condition that he carried a letter to none other than the astrologer Jean Fusoris in Paris. The letter was highly compromising, referring in what was obviously code to certain "pumpkins, melons, almonds and other fruits," which Fusoris was to obtain from the prior of the Celestines in Paris, and send back to Courtenay, who would pay him for them. Fusoris was told that in his reply he was not to mention his own or Courtenay's name, for the matter was a secret from everyone except Henry, "who is most discreet, as you know." Le Gay was also entrusted with a verbal message, to tell Fusoris that the king of England had landed with fifty thousand men, four thousand barrels of wheat, four thousand casks of wine, twelve large guns and sufficient material to sustain a six-month siege of Harfleur. He was to ask Fusoris whether Charles VI was in one of his mad phases and would oppose the English, if the dauphin, the duke of Burgundy or any other lords would be with him, and, if so, with how many men.

Courtenay gave le Gay a safe-conduct allowing him to pass through English lines and a purse, containing the letters and twenty gold crowns, which he hid beneath his shirt. On 29 August he was released, having spent thirteen days in English custody. Lacking the courage to make his way to Paris, he fled back to Montivilliers, where, until only a few months previously, he had been the chaplain of the abbess. Instead of going straight to the convent or to the local authorities with the information he had gained, he skulked about the town until he was denounced by a Benedictine monk from Honfleur, who had also been an English prisoner and knew that le Gay was carrying enemy letters. Le Gay confessed, pleading that he had not intended to deliver them, but both he and Fusoris were arrested and imprisoned, and the latter was put on trial for high treason before the Parlement of Paris. Le Gay's protestations of innocence were eventually accepted, but it was almost a year before Fusoris was able to exchange his Parisian prison cell for house arrest and the rural banishment that was to last until the end of his days.[33]

By the standards of the day, le Gay had been treated comparatively well while he was a prisoner in English hands. He complained that he had been kept short of food and drink (he did not like English beer) and held for too long, but he had not been physically or verbally abused and he had been released without having to pay a ransom. Given the magnitude of the military operation taking place, delays in his being referred up the chain of command were inevitable, especially as he could not, or would not, impart any useful information.

On Saturday 17 August, the day after le Gay's capture, the slow process of unloading everything needed for the campaign from the ships was completed. Having issued his ordinances, Henry now ordered his forces to take up the places allocated to them in the customary three "battles," or divisions, known as the van (because they generally went "avaunt" or before), the centre and the rear. Taking his own place at the head of the centre, he gave the command to move off and the vast cavalcade of men, horses, cannon, siege engines and wagons began the ascent that would lead them over the hill from Graville to Harfleur.[34] One can only begin to imagine the terror that must have struck the hearts of the people of the town when they looked up and saw that seemingly numberless host, its banners fluttering in the breeze and armour glinting in the sun, massing on the crest of the hill and poised, like some great hawk, ready to fall upon its prey below. The king of England, who had failed to obtain his "just rights and inheritances" through diplomacy, had come to claim them by the sword. The war was about to begin in earnest.

❖ CHAPTER TEN ❖

HARFLEUR

Visiting Harfleur today, it is almost impossible to believe that this quiet little backwater was once one of the most important ports in northern Europe. Virtually nothing remains of the town Henry V saw on that August day in 1415; it is now merely a suburb of Le Havre, the port founded by François I in 1517 when Harfleur's own waters silted up. The great walls that were once its pride and glory have been replaced by a labyrinthine road system of flyovers and roundabouts that are almost as impenetrable as its medieval fortifications. The salt marshes on its seaward side have became a vast industrial wasteland of smoking chimneys, oil terminals and container ports; the valley above the town, through which the river Lézarde flowed to join the Seine, is now an industrial estate and retail park linking it to Montivilliers. The lazy loops of the river itself were "redressed" by French engineers in the 1830s and replaced with rectilinear canals and quays; the fortifications that made the harbour one of the wonders of medieval Europe were demolished in the nine-teenth century and the harbour itself filled in. Even the great church of St Martin, rebuilt in celebration after the English were expelled in 1435, with a delicate spire that can still be seen for miles around, is a sad and decaying historic monument for which the key literally cannot be found.[1]

And yet the heart of the town remains defiantly picturesque: a medieval jewel lost in the swamp of Le Havre. Though Henry V's own guns destroyed almost every building within the walls, much of the rebuilding that took place in the fifteenth century remains. Half-timbered houses crowd the narrow cobbled streets and little squares that still echo to the sound of footsteps; the more important public buildings, including the library and priory museum, though heavily restored, sport militaristic towers; and here and there, half hidden in the undergrowth, one can still find impressive vestiges of the massive walls and gates.

French contemporaries were justifiably proud of the medieval town of Harfleur. For the monk of St Denis, sheltered in his convent outside Paris, it was "the most admirable port in Normandy, sending out ships to all corners of the world and bringing back every type of foreign merchandise to provision and enrich the whole kingdom." Enguerrand de Monstrelet, a military man, recognised its strategic importance. For him, as for Henry V, it was "the key to the sea of all Normandy."[2] Lying on the north bank of the tidal Seine estuary, Harfleur controlled the access to France's most important inland waterway. Some forty miles up river, travelling as the crow flies, lay the ancient city of Rouen, where the first dukes of Normandy were buried in the tenth century and the Capetian kings of France established their royal naval yard in 1294. Around eighty miles further up river lay Paris itself, capital city, royal residence and administrative centre, with the Seine flowing through its heart. If the English could capture Harfleur, they could establish a stranglehold on military and commercial traffic using the Seine and block one of the main arteries of France.

There was a second strategic purpose to be achieved in capturing the town. Of all the places on the northern coast of France, Harfleur posed the greatest threat to English interests. In recent years it had become the base of choice for attacking the south coast of England: Don Pero Niño, the "unconquered knight," had retreated to its safety with his prisoners and plunder after raiding the coast of Cornwall in 1400, and Louis d'Orléans had gathered an invasion fleet there in 1404. French troops sent to aid Owain Glyn Dŵr's revolt in Wales and the Scots in their campaigns against the English had all sailed from Harfleur. In England the town had also acquired the reputation of being a nest of pirates: many of the attacks on merchant shipping in the Channel had been carried out by French and Italian vessels which took refuge within its harbour and found a ready market for their prizes there.[3] For all these reasons, Henry V had identified Harfleur as the target for his invasion. Its capture would serve a dual purpose, increasing the safety and security of English shipping and establishing another bridgehead, like Calais, for any future campaign in France.

Harfleur's strategic importance had ensured that it enjoyed the best protection that medieval military might could devise.[4] Great stone walls, some two and a half miles in circumference and fortified at intervals with twenty-four watch towers, encircled the whole town and its famous harbour. These were relatively modern fortifications, built between 1344 and 1361, and the plan was polygonal, with semicircular flanking towers at each angle, which were harder to demolish by cannonade or undermining than traditional square towers. The walls themselves were thicker at their base than at the top, sloping outwards so as to deflect shots from guns and catapults back into the enemy, and the many towers provided vantage points from which flanking fire could be rained on anyone approaching the walls. There were only three gates, guarding the entrances into the town from Montivilliers to the north, Rouen to the southeast and Leure to the south-west. A remnant of one of the towers at the Rouen gate, which also commanded the harbour, or *clos-aux-galées* as it was known to the French, is the sole survivor today. Though a ruin, its former might is still readily apparent in the depth of its great stone walls, strengthened by arches inside, the absence of any flat external surface and the many small embrasures, at varying heights, for crossbows and guns. Each of the three gates was protected by a bastion (a fortification projecting beyond the line of the walls), a portcullis and a drawbridge over a water-filled moat; these permanent defences had also been strengthened against missile attack by thick tree trunks, driven into the ground and lashed together on the outside, and earth and timber shoring up the walls on the inside.

The defence of Harfleur had been entrusted by Charles VI to Jean, sire d'Estouteville, who held the honorary office of grand butler of France. He had with him a garrison of some one hundred men-at-arms, which, even with civilian assistance, was not a large enough force to be able to offer any prolonged resistance to a determined English assault. Nevertheless, all the natural advantages of the site had been exploited to the full. The town lay about a mile from the Seine, at the head of the tributary valley of the river Lézarde. The southern approach was protected by the ebb and flow of the Seine tides over treacherous salt marshes. The waters of the Lézarde, which entered Harfleur midway between the gates of Leure and Montivilliers, had been partially diverted along a series of ditches and culverts to create a great moat which encircled more than half the town, from the north-east to the south-west, and defended it against attack from the upper reaches of the valley. Controlled by sluices, the river waters powered two mills for grinding corn, which lay just within the walls, and then flowed down a series of culverts through the middle of the town before broadening out to form the harbour and joining the Seine. The great advantage of these sluices from a defence point of view was that they could be closed completely. When this happened, the Lézarde was effectively dammed at its entrance to the town and therefore burst its banks, flooding the entire valley bottom to the depth of a man's thighs. Forewarned that the English were landing close by, the men of Harfleur broke all the bridges across the river and closed the sluices, creating a vast lake to protect the northern side of the town.[5]

The *clos-aux-galées* was probably even more strongly fortified than the town. It was created in the 1360s by constructing a massive wall, more than six and a half feet thick and standing fifty feet high above ground and thirty-six feet below, around a loop in the Lézarde to the south of the town. This was then flooded to create a twelve-acre harbour that was both commercial port and royal military arsenal. Protected to the north by

the town walls and on either side by its own higher wall, sur-
mounted by defensive turrets, its seaward entrance was guarded
by two massive towers, with chains strung between them to prevent unauthorised access. When the English invasion threatened, the French had taken emergency measures to provide
additional defences, planting great sharpened stakes around the
entrance and under the walls facing the sea, so that, when the
tide was up and enemy ships could sail right up to the walls to
launch an attack, they ran the risk of being driven onto the
stakes and foundering.[6]

The story of the siege of Harfleur might have been very different had it not been for the courage and resourcefulness of one
man. Raoul, sire de Gaucourt, was a French version of Sir John
Cornewaille, and, like him, a medieval chivalric hero whom the
modern world has forgotten. He came from a noble Picard family with a long and distinguished record of service to the crown.
Like his father before him, he was deeply attached to the Armagnac cause and had strong personal connections with Charles
d'Orléans, Charles d'Albret and Marshal Boucicaut. More
importantly, de Gaucourt was a man who aspired to live out the
knightly ideal. He was knighted on the field of Nicopolis as a
twenty-six-year-old crusader against the Turks, and, with Boucicaut, was captured and put to ransom in that disastrous
battle. In 1400 he was one of the fourteen founding members of
Boucicaut's short-lived knightly Order of the White Lady on a
Green Shield, who swore "to guard and defend the honour,
estate, goods, reputation and praise of all ladies and maidens of
noble line" and to fight *à outrance* against their oppressors.
Nine years later, when Boucicaut was governor of Genoa, de
Gaucourt led a small French army to his assistance. The two
men campaigned together in Italy throughout the summer of
1409, besieging and capturing Milan, and when Boucicaut
made his triumphal entry into the city, de Gaucourt was at his
side. In the armed struggle between the Armagnacs and the Burgundians, de Gaucourt distinguished himself in 1411 by capturing the bridge of St Cloud on behalf of Charles d'Orléans, but
was later defeated in battle at the same place by a combined

English and Burgundian force. As the chamberlain of Charles d'Orléans, he played a prominent role in the negotiations that led to the withdrawal of the duke of Clarence's army from France in 1412 and served as captain of several Armagnac castles.[7]

On 1 January 1415, de Gaucourt was one of sixteen knights and esquires who were chosen by Jean, duke of Bourbon, to be the founding members of another new order of chivalry, the Order of the *Fer du Prisonnier*, or Prisoner's Shackle. Like Boucicaut's order, the duke of Bourbon's was intended to uphold the honour of women of good birth: the golden shackle, with its chain, being a symbolic representation of the bonds of love, which fettered the knight to his mistress, rather than a reference to criminal activity. In accordance with the order's constitution, de Gaucourt swore to wear a golden shackle and chain on his left leg every Sunday for two years, "in the expectation that, within that period, we may find an equal number of knights and esquires, of worth and ability, all of them men without reproach, who will wish to fight us all together on foot to the end, each to be armed with what armour he will, together with a lance, axe, sword and dagger at least, and with clubs of whatever length he may choose." The arms of all the members of the order were to be hung in a chapel where, throughout the two years, a candle would burn, day and night, within another golden shackle used as a candlestick, before an image of Our Lady of Paris. If the challenge was accomplished, then the candle was to be endowed in perpetuity, together with daily masses, and each member would donate to the chapel his shackle and a picture of himself in the arms he wore that day. Anyone who forgot to wear the shackle on the designated Sundays had to pay a fine of four hundred shillings to charity for each offence.[8]

De Gaucourt's membership of this order raises the interesting possibility that he was wearing his golden shackle on Sunday 18 August, as he performed the far more serious challenge of leading three hundred men-at-arms to the relief of Harfleur. Constable d'Albret and Marshal Boucicaut had not been entirely idle during the English landing. As soon as it became clear that Harfleur was Henry V's objective, they sent a stream of

supplies, including weapons, cannon and ammunition, to reinforce the town. They must also have decided that they needed
an experienced and trustworthy knight to take charge of the
defences, which is why Raoul de Gaucourt was chosen for the
task. Whether he came from Honfleur or Caudebec, the only
route he could take into the town was through the Rouen gate
on the eastern side. Time was of the essence. He had to get there
before the English. His arrival, only the day after Henry laid
siege to the western side of Harfleur, is an indication of the desperate pace of his dash across Normandy. Fortunately for his
mission, the flooded fields that denied him access to Harfleur
from the Montivilliers road also protected him, for the moment,
from the English troops encamped on the hillside before the
Leure gate. They could only watch helplessly as de Gaucourt
coolly rode unopposed down the other side of the valley and
into the town.[9] It was not often that Henry V was outmanoeuvred and, as de Gaucourt was to discover to his cost, the king
was not a man to forgive or forget such actions.

Henry's inability to prevent de Gaucourt and his men getting
into Harfleur demonstrated that it was imperative that no further reinforcements should reach the town by the Rouen road.
He now entrusted this important task to his brother the duke of
Clarence, whom the chaplain described as "a knight no less
renowned for the practice of war than for personal courage." In
this instance, he proved himself worthy of both Henry's confidence and the chaplain's praise. Under cover of night, he led a
large force of men and an artillery train on a difficult ten-mile
detour that took them above, up and around the flooded Lézarde valley. During their march they even managed to intercept
more reinforcements arriving from Rouen and captured "certain carts and wagons belonging to the enemy, with a great
quantity of guns and powder-barrels and missiles and catapults." At dawn the following day, to the consternation of the
besieged, Clarence and his men appeared on the opposite hillside above the town, facing Henry and his troops.[10]

While all these preparations were being made to lay siege to
Harfleur by land, the seaward side was not neglected. Most of
the merchant ships that had transported the army to France

were allowed to go home after completing their disembarkation, though some returned again, bearing further supplies and
reinforcements, including the men who had been left behind
when the fleet first sailed.[11] The fighting ships and the royal fleet
were not released from service but moved in to blockade
Harfleur, barring all access from the Seine or the sea; a number
of small boats, carried overland and taking up position on the
flooded Lézarde, did the same from the north. Trapped between
the two armies to west and east, and blockaded by water to
north and south, Harfleur was now completely encircled.

Before the great guns began their bombardment, Henry,
punctilious as ever, gave the people of the town one last chance
to surrender. He sent one of his heralds to proclaim that in
accordance with the twentieth chapter of the book of Deuteronomy (which Henry had already quoted to Charles VI in his letter of 28 July), he offered them peace — if they would open
their gates to him freely and without coercion, and, "as was
their duty," restore to him the town, "which was a noble and
hereditary portion of his crown of England and of his duchy of
Normandy."[12] If this offer was refused and Harfleur was captured by force, Deuteronomy authorised Henry to exact a
terrible vengeance: "you shall put all its males to the sword, but
the women and the little ones, the cattle, and every thing else in
the city, all its spoil, you shall take as booty for yourselves; and
you shall enjoy the spoil of your enemies, which the Lord your
God has given you." Though de Gaucourt and d'Estouteville
knew as well as Henry what the consequences of their refusal to
surrender would be, their duty and honour would not allow
them to do anything other than reject his offer out of hand, and
defy him to do his worst.[13]

The siege that followed was literally a textbook one, based
principally on the ancient classical treatise on military tactics by
Vegetius, *De Rei Militari*, which dated from the fourth century
but had been translated and glossed by every medieval writer on
the subject, including the fourteenth-century Egidius Romanus,
known to the English as Master Giles, and Henry V's own contemporaries, Christine de Pizan and Thomas Hoccleve. Following standard military practice, Henry ordered that the suburbs

of Harfleur should be burnt and cleared, so that he could bring his cannon and siege engines within range of the walls. As the chaplain proudly pointed out, the king "did not allow his eyelids to close in sleep," but laboured day and night to get his artillery in position. Many "great engines" to assault the town were constructed on site, as were "cunning instruments" for the protection of his own forces. Hordes of carpenters were employed in erecting huge wooden screens to protect the guns and catapults from enemy assault: an ingenious pulley-based device, operated from behind, allowed the gun crews to raise the base of the screen to set the gun's projectory and fire it. The gunners themselves were protected by trenches built either side of their cannon and by ramparts, hastily constructed from the excavated earth thrown over bundles of sticks.[14]

Once the assault on Harfleur began, it was devastating. For days on end, the seventy-eight gunners kept up an incessant bombardment; they worked in shifts, as soon as one team tired, another immediately taking its place, so that there was no respite for the besieged during the hours of daylight. The English cannon and catapults were trained on the main points of resistance — the bastion guarding the Leure gate, the towers and the walls — and as the ten thousand gun-stones they had brought with them did their deadly work, the fortifications of Harfleur gradually crumbled. The noise was terrible: the explosion of cannon-fire, the thud of gun-stones crashing into their targets, the splintering of timber defences and the rumble of falling masonry. One of the cannons, the monk of St Denis was told, was the biggest anyone had ever seen before. When it was fired, it discharged huge blocks as big as millstones with so much black smoke and such a terrifying report "that they seemed to issue forth from the fires of hell."[15]

In the face of this overwhelming assault, de Gaucourt and his men fought back with courage and determination, keeping up a retaliatory bombardment using guns, catapults, and crossbows as long as the bastion, towers and walls remained defensible. (One English man-at-arms, Thomas Hostell, was "smitten with a springolt [that is, a crossbow bolt] through the head, losing one eye and having his cheek bone broken," though this injury did not prevent him from continuing to fight.)[16] When it was no longer possible to defend the broken remnants of fortifications, the French doggedly fought on, "from inside the ruins also, from behind screens, and through shattered openings in the walls, and from other places where shelter would not have been thought possible."[17]

At night, when the guns were silent, the siege engines still and the English slept, there was no rest for the besieged, who laboured to repair their defences as best they could. Under de Gaucourt's direction, and presumably with the aid of the civilian population, the crumbling walls were shored up with timber props, bundles of sticks and tubs packed with earth, dung, sand or stones. The lanes and streets inside the walls were also covered with a thick layer of clay, earth and dung to soften the impact of gun-stones falling or shattering inside the town and causing death or injury to the besieged. There was neither time nor energy to spare for repairing the civilian buildings, which suffered terribly under the bombardment. The parish church, St Martin's, lost both its steeple and its bells. Many "really fine buildings," as the chaplain noted with regret, even those almost in the middle of the town, were completely destroyed or so badly damaged that they were on the point of collapse.

While the artillery wreaked its devastation from the air, Henry's Welsh miners were hard at work burrowing under the fortifications of Harfleur. The greatest efforts were made on the Rouen side of the town, where Clarence was in command, because at this point there was no moat to be crossed. Here the walls were protected only by a double ditch, the depth of the inner one being an unknown quantity, as no spy or scout had been able to get close enough to investigate.[18]

Military mining had been introduced to Europe from the east during the Crusades in the thirteenth century. It involved digging a tunnel, or a web of tunnels, under the weakest point of a fortification, which was usually a corner or a gatehouse. The walls and roof of the tunnels, like those in a conventional mine, would be shored up with timber props which, at the right moment, would be set alight to make the tunnel collapse. Unlike a conventional mine, where those digging for coal or metal ores had to follow a seam and could work on their hands and knees if necessary, military mines had to be large enough to be able to bring down tons of masonry. This meant that they were usually wide and tall enough to take at least a man standing upright, and in some cases must have resulted in the creation of a vast underground chamber.

The most effective way of preventing a successful mining operation was for the besieged to counter-mine, or dig their own tunnels beneath and into the enemy mines to make them collapse before they reached the walls. Where the sheer weight of earth failed to do this, brushwood and incendiary devices were dropped or thrown in to set the props alight, smoke out the miners and bring down the tunnels. (Christine de Pizan even recommended placing large tubs of boiling water or urine at the entrance to the mine, which could be emptied on the unfortunate miners to scald or maim them.[19]) Occasionally, mine and counter-mine would meet, providing the opportunity for a curious subterranean version of the feat of arms, which, given the difficulties to be overcome, was highly prized by chivalrous knights and esquires as a demonstration of exceptional personal valour. In the narrow and gloomy confines of the mine, lit only by the flickering flames of torches, two men-at-arms would fight with whatever weapons they had to hand — swords, daggers, axes and maces — until one of them conceded defeat or an impasse was reached. One cannot imagine men of the calibre of Sir John Cornewaille and Raoul de Gaucourt neglecting such an opportunity to distinguish themselves, and the chroniclers report that there were daily encounters in the mine: "And who most manly fought in the same, supposed himselfe to have achieved greate victorie. And so that mine that was begun for the sudden invasion of the Towne was changed into the exercise of knightlie acts." So dangerous and prestigious was such combat held to be that those who fought an encounter of this kind were judged to share a special bond and could become brothers-in-arms, even though they came from opposing sides. The most spectacular instance on record took place during the long siege of Melun in 1420, when Henry V himself is said to have fought the captain of the garrison, the sire de Barbazan, on horseback within the mines. When Melun finally fell, Henry announced his intention to execute Barbazan as a rebel. Barbazan responded by invoking the law of arms, claiming that they were brothers-in-arms because they had fought together in the mine, and that his life should therefore be spared. Henry accepted the validity of this claim and did indeed refrain from executing him.[20]

Despite the English efforts, the French successfully thwarted every attempt to undermine their walls. Henry V had ordered a "sow" to be made, this being a protective mobile shelter under which the miners could take cover as they did their work. All the military textbooks recommended that mining should be conducted out of sight of the enemy, but this was impossible at Harfleur because of the lie of the land. As soon as the French saw that the sow was in place and that a mine was in progress, they took retaliatory measures, digging counter-mines and employing "other technical skills" that were evidently superior to those of the less experienced Welsh miners. Two attempts to undermine the walls were foiled and a third failed to achieve its objective. The only compensation for this lack of success was that the operation had been a useful diversion and forced the French to divide their forces in the town's defence.[21]

Clarence was also forced to abandon his attempt to fill in the ditches below the Rouen gate walls. For this purpose, he had been gathering bundles of wood and piling them up in front of the ditches. He then discovered that the French had also been busy, stockpiling barrels of flammable powders, oils and fats on the walls. They were only waiting for the English to begin crossing the ditches before setting fire to the barrels and flinging them onto the ready-made bonfires below so as to burn Clarence's men alive. But this threat did not prevent his men from taking possession of the outer ditch. Having advanced to this new position, Clarence appointed masters-of-works to supervise the digging of a trench, a section of which every man-at-arms and archer in his force was assigned to complete. The excavated soil thrown up on the front facing the enemy was further fortified with a palisade made of tree trunks and stakes, from behind which the gunners and archers could operate in comparative safety. Shielded behind their new defences, the English were now in range and able to drive the defenders off the walls with a barrage of missiles and gun-stones.[22]

Although these operations were all carried out under Clarence's orders, the king himself was in direct control and issuing the commands that his brother obeyed. It was a situation fraught with difficulties, not least because every message carried between the two divisions of the army had to be taken either by boat across the flooded Lézarde valley or by land on the long detour round the valley head. This was a problem that demanded an urgent solution and Henry had applied himself to finding one. According to Master Jean de Bordiu, one of the most senior clerks in the royal household, "Our king cut off the water supply before Montivilliers, which they had retained so that it could not run into the sea." Though this rather mysterious phrase is open to interpretation, it suggests that Henry dammed the Lézarde higher up the valley, closer to Montivilliers, which was less than three miles away from Harfleur. This would have had two effects. First, it would have deprived the people of Harfleur of their main supply of fresh water, which was a priority of any besieging army hoping to make life on the inside increasingly wretched. Second, it must also have led to the draining of the flooded fields above the town. No chronicler mentions such engineering works, or, indeed, that the flood waters created by closing the sluices at Harfleur gradually evaporated or drained away during the course of the siege, but it is difficult to find any other explanation for de Bordiu's explicit statement.[23]

Henry was indefatigable in his personal supervision of the siege. No one, not even his brother, knew when or where he would appear next. "The Kinge daylie and nightlie in his owne person visited and searched the watches, orders, and stacions of everie part of his hoast, and whome he founde dilligent he praised and thanked, and the negligent he corrected and chasticed." Jehan Waurin, the fifteen-year-old illegitimate son of the seneschal of Flanders, believed that "King Henry, who was very cunning, often went around the town in disguise to identify the weakest and most suitable place by which he could take it."[24] Whether true or not, the circulation of such stories was a tribute to the power of the king's character and a highly effective way of keeping his men up to the mark. (They also would inspire Shakespeare's "little touch of Harry in the night" scene.) This was increasingly important as the siege entered its third week and the battering inflicted on Harfleur had not yet forced its surrender.

Henry, however, was convinced that its fall was imminent. On 3 September Master Jean de Bordiu, who was well placed to know the king's plans, wrote to the citizens of his native Bordeaux in English Aquitaine:

> Please know that the town of Harfleur, with the aid of the Holy Spirit, will be in the king's hands before 8 days at most. For now it is well and truly breached on the landward side and on two flanks, and everything destroyed inside . . . And when he has taken it, I have heard it is not his intention to enter the town but to stay in the field. In a short while after the capture of the town, he intends to go to Montivilliers, and thence to Dieppe, afterwards to Rouen, and then to Paris.[25]

On the same day, Henry himself also wrote to Bordeaux, cheerfully informing the citizens that "ourselves and all those of our company [are] in good health and disposition."

> For this, in all humility, we give thanks to our lord God the Almighty, hoping that, by His grace, He will give us, in pursuit of our right, the fulfilment of our desire and undertaking, to His pleasure, and for the honour and comfort of us and you, and of all our other faithful lieges and subjects. To this end we shall do our duty, so that, with God's help, our enemies will be henceforward less powerful to cause you trouble and harm than they have been in the past.[26]

Henry had underestimated the determination and ingenuity of de Gaucourt and his men. Harfleur would not fall in eight days, but in eighteen. And those ten extra days were to wreak havoc in the English army and force the king to change his plans.

The problem was dysentery, the scourge of every army on campaign, which was known to the English as "the bloody flux" because its main symptom is bloody diarrhoea. Epidemic dysentery[27] is almost always caused by an extremely virulent bacterium, *Shigella dysenteriae* type 1, which is spread through human faeces. This is usually the result of food or water coming into contact with infected faeces, but so few bacteria are needed to cause infection that it can be spread from one person's hands to another's. Up to a third of the population in an epidemic area can be infected and though some recover without treatment within seven days, between 10 and 20 per cent die, usually within thirteen days of the onset of symptoms, from complications including persistent diarrhoea, septicaemia and kidney failure.

All the conditions for an outbreak were present at Harfleur, both within the beleaguered town and in the besieging armies. The weather was hot and humid and the salt marshes and standing water of the flooded fields in the valley bottom were breeding grounds for bacteria and insects. If Henry had indeed succeeded in damming the higher reaches of the Lézarde, this may well have contributed to the problem by reducing the amount of running fresh water available to his own men. The marshy nature of the land also made it more difficult safely to dispose of not only human and animal faeces but also detritus, such as animal carcasses, which was the inevitable consequence of feeding so many troops. Trenches were dug for privies and burial pits for other waste, but these could not be sealed and the problem of sanitation would only increase the longer the siege went on. Nor should it be forgotten that the many thousands of horses in the army, each needing to drink four gallons a day, would probably have contributed to the contamination of the water; we know that many of them, too, died of murrain, an infectious disease.[28]

The physicians and surgeons in the king's army were not unaware of the dangers of diseases associated with campaigning. The king's personal physician, Nicholas Colnet, possessed a copy of Bernard Gordon's influential and popular treatise, *Lilium Medicinae*, which set out the following highly relevant and practical advice:

> But if the physician is in an army, then the King's tent and the tents of the physicians and surgeons should be on higher ground,

facing a favourable wind; on no account should the tent be at a lower level where all the refuse gathers. Good fresh air, without any stench of corpses or any other things, should be chosen. In summer, the tent should face south and the physicians should carefully take into account everything that might bring sickness on the army and eliminate it as far as possible; such things are heat, rain, rotting corpses, diseases, nuts, cabbages, trees, plants, reptiles, swamps, and such like.

In accordance with this advice, the king and his brother had pitched their tents on the hillsides above Harfleur.[29] What neither they nor anyone else in the army could do, even if they had understood how the disease was transmitted, was avoid all contact with those who were infected.

Contemporary chroniclers, unaware of the true cause of the epidemic, blamed either a lack of supplies or, paradoxically, English greed, which (they claimed) led the men to gorge themselves on unripe fruit and the shellfish that were plentiful and readily available in the salt marshes between Harfleur and the Seine estuary.[30] (In the medieval mind, the seemingly inexplicable could always be explained by sin.) In fact, such a diet was irrelevant to the spread of dysentery, and the charge that the English were short of victuals is not borne out by the evidence. Apart from what each man had brought with him, which, according to the order of 24 July, was to be enough for three months, they were in receipt of a constant supply of fish (fresh and salted), wheat, beef, wine, ale and other foodstuffs from England and possibly Aquitaine. The earl marshal hired his own ships to bring regular supplies of corn, flour, beer, wine and even a barrel of salmon across from England to Harfleur, suggesting that other retinue leaders did likewise. In addition to the ships plying the Channel, foraging patrols throughout the Chef-de-Caux brought in large quantities of fresh food on a regular basis, particularly corn, which could be ground into flour for bread. The king's stores at Harfleur issued the archers of Sir James Harington's retinue alone with 428 pounds of flour, 2576 pounds of beef and 4545 gallons of wine, which does not sug-

gest straitened circumstances.[31] Maintaining supplies at an
appropriate level was a matter of such importance that even the
king concerned himself with it. When Henry wrote to his subjects in Bordeaux at the beginning of September, he urged them
to send him "as quickly as possible" and "without failing in any
way" as much wine and other victuals as they could provide,
reassuring them at the same time that "those who bring it to
us . . . will receive full satisfaction in payment." Master Jean de
Bordiu's cover letter interpreted this as being a request for
between five hundred and seven hundred tuns of wine, but he
added two other comments which are perhaps indicative of a
sense that the unexpected length of the siege was beginning to
cause concern. "Although at present the fields are providing an
adequate supply of corn, this cannot, however, meet the future
requirements of the great army which is with him, and which
increases every day." Perhaps more significantly, he also noted
that "my lord of Dorset . . . who is second in command" and
his men "are loudly complaining that there is no way of paying." It was probably no great encouragement to the merchants
of Bordeaux to learn that the king had "great confidence" that
the earl would find a way to pay, but Henry's irritatingly blithe
certainty was, as usual, underpinned by his practical arrangements, for he was at that very moment in the process of securing
loans from Richard Whittington and others "for the maintenance of our siege of Harfleur."[32]

Exactly when the first cases of dysentery appeared in the
English army (or in Harfleur) is not recorded. The presence of
the disease only comes to the chroniclers' attention on 15 September, when its most prominent victim died. Richard Courtenay, bishop of Norwich, was a man who, despite his profession,
had put his extraordinary abilities wholly at the service of his
king rather than his God. A doctor of civil and canon law, twice
elected chancellor of the University of Oxford, of which he was
a generous and learned patron, diplomat, financier and a constant companion and advisor to Henry V, the only thing he had
never found time to do was to visit his diocese, where John Leicester, archbishop of Smyrna, lived in his palace and performed his

ecclesiastical duties for him. For the English chaplain (who was unaware of the bishop's spying activities), Courtenay was "a man of noble birth, imposing stature, and superior intelligence, distinguished no less for his gifts of great eloquence and learning than for other noble endowments of nature, . . . regarded as agreeable above all others to members of the king's retinue and councils." He was also, the chaplain said, "the most loving and dearest" of the king's friends, which is perhaps a more remarkable epitaph, since there were few men who could claim such a relationship with Henry V. That it was justified is indicated by the fact that the king himself attended his deathbed, bathed his feet for him and closed Courtenay's eyes when he died. Courtenay was just thirty-five years old. His body was sent back to England where, on the king's personal command, he was buried among the royal tombs behind the high altar in Westminster Abbey.[33]

Three days later, on 18 September, the king lost another devoted servant to the same disease. Michael de la Pole, earl of Suffolk, "a knight of the most excellent and kindly reputation," was fifty-four years old, had accompanied Henry's father on crusade to Prussia, and after he became king served him in all his expeditions "by See and by Lande." The war in France which brought about his premature end would also claim the lives of four of his five sons. His eldest son Michael, who was not yet twenty-one and was also in the army at Harfleur, was killed at Agincourt. Joan of Arc proved to be the nemesis of the rest. Alexander met his death at the battle of Jargeau on 12 June 1429, and in the same battle his three remaining brothers were taken prisoner; two of them, John and Thomas, died in captivity. The de la Poles paid a high price for their loyalty to the Lancastrian kings of England.[34]

On 15 September, the same day that Richard Courtenay died, a second serious setback occurred. Either because Courtenay's death had distracted them or, more likely, because they had simply relaxed their guard after almost a month of siege, the men besieging the Leure gate fell victim to a surprise attack by the French. Remarkably, those responsible for this dereliction of duty included Sir John Holland, Sir John Cornewaille and his

brother-in-arms Sir William Porter, who had all shared the privilege of being the first to land at Chef-de-Caux. Seizing the
moment, the French made a desperate sally out of the gate and
managed to set fire to the English defences before being driven
back with heavy losses. (It is tempting to think that Raoul de
Gaucourt was behind this doomed but gallant gesture, not least
because it took place on a Sunday, the day when he wore his
golden prisoner's shackle and chivalric deeds were uppermost in
his mind.) Though the attack had inflicted only minor damage
in military terms, it was a significant morale-booster for the
beleaguered garrison, who taunted their foes as being only half-
awake, lazy and failing to keep a better watch.[35]

There could be only one response to such insults. The following morning, Holland and Cornewaille began an all-out assault
on the gate. Arrows, wrapped in tow, dipped in pitch and set
alight, were rained upon the fortified position to drive those
guarding it away and wreak further destruction. Under cover of
night, at Henry V's command, the ditch separating the English
from the gate had been filled with bundles of sticks, so that they
could now cross over, torch the gun-shattered remnants of the
outer walls and attack the French defenders. Holland's standard
was carried into the centre of the bastion and his men streamed
in after it. The French put up a fierce resistance in the hand-to-
hand fighting that followed, but eventually, exhausted by their
futile attempts to put out the flames, surrounded by smoke and
conflagration and overwhelmed by sheer force of numbers, they
were forced to abandon their position and retreat behind the
town walls. Even now they did not give up their efforts, but
swiftly blocked the entrance behind them with timber, stone,
earth and dung, so that the English, having gained the bastion,
were still unable to enter the town. It took them several days to
extinguish the flames, but the remains of the shattered fortification continued to smoke for another fortnight.[36]

Evidently hoping that this success would have broken the
spirit of the French, Henry sent a herald into Harfleur the next
morning, 17 September, with a safe-conduct for de Gaucourt
and a group of representatives of the town council, so that they
could come into the English camp to discuss terms. Henry was

at his most charming and persuasive: he greeted them in person and advised them, in his kindliest manner, to surrender the town. He reminded them that Harfleur was part of the duchy of Normandy, which had belonged to the English crown by right since ancient times, and of the fate that would befall them if they continued to resist him. De Gaucourt was exhausted, half-starved, suffering from dysentery himself and staring death in the face, but he still had his pride and his sense of duty. He refused to surrender. Defiantly, he informed Henry that he had not received his office as captain of the town from him and did not recognise his authority: he knew that the king of France would not allow the siege of Harfleur to continue much longer and that any day he would arrive at the head of his army to drive the English away.[37]

It is impossible to know whether de Gaucourt believed these proud words himself. He may have had a blindly optimistic faith that his king would not allow such an important place as Harfleur to fall without striking a blow in its defence. On the other hand, a man of his military experience must have known that, in tactical terms, it was probably better to allow Harfleur to fall and recapture it after the English had left, rather than risk everything on the unpredictable outcome of a pitched battle.

Cut off from the outside world by the besieging armies, it must have been difficult for de Gaucourt to get any intelligence, let alone up to date information, about what efforts were being made on his behalf. Constable d'Albret and Marshal Boucicaut had now, apparently, united their forces at Rouen. There they had spent huge sums purchasing a small boat, filling it with food and other necessaries and entrusting it to one Jehan Lescot, a local mariner, with instructions that he should take it to the relief of Harfleur. Astonishingly, Lescot (who may have been a pirate and was highly paid for his services) succeeded in getting through the English blockade not once, but twice, for de Gaucourt later arranged for him to escape in secret from the town, so that he could report back to d'Albret on conditions there. D'Albret also sent Robin de Hellande, the *bailli* of Rouen, to Paris, entrusted with verbal messages to the king, dauphin and council "touching the descent and arrival of the English and the provisions that ought to be made against them, for the salvation of the said town of Harfleur and of the countryside around it."[38]

De Gaucourt may also have been aware that in addition to d'Albret and Boucicaut, some of the local nobility — among them the young seneschal of Hainault, who had once been so eager to test his valour against Englishmen in jousting challenges — had raised their own troops to resist the English. Frustrated by the failure of any officially organised resistance, they had determined to take matters into their own hands, continually harrying the English troops, especially those camped with Clarence before the Rouen gate, and attacking any small groups of Englishmen they found scouting or foraging away from the army. One force of some five hundred or six hundred local knights, led by the sire de Lille Adam and Jacques de Brimeu, decided to make a grand gesture. The plan was that a small party would ride within sight of the enemy camp so that the English would raise the alarm and then give chase on horseback, leaving their archers behind. When they had been drawn sufficiently far away from the main army, they would be ambushed and slaughtered by de Lille Adam and de Brimeu. Unfortunately for the French, de Lille Adam made his move too early and was seen by the English men-at-arms. Realising it was a trap, they immediately abandoned the chase and returned to the safety of their camp. The disaster was compounded by the capture of both de Lille Adam and Brimeu.[39]

While the local nobility did what they could to resist and harry the English invaders, the princes of the blood royal seemed incapable of decisive action. It was not until 28 August, a week and a half after the siege of Harfleur had begun, that the king's council at last issued the general call to arms in defence of the country, which it was the duty of every man capable of bearing weapons to obey. The king's letters authorising the proclamation of the summons in every town and at every public meeting were sent out to the *baillis* and seneschals of each district with instructions that the muster should take place at

Rouen. Letters were also sent directly to towns such as Verdun, Tournai and Amiens, which had their own city militias, ordering them to send assistance to Harfleur. Fifty crossbowmen did indeed belatedly leave Tournai on 17 September, but they did not get as far as Harfleur and returned home two months later, never having encountered the English at all. On 1 September embassies were sent to both Charles d'Orléans and John the Fearless, duke of Burgundy, requesting them to send five hundred men-at-arms each. It was a measure of how deep the rift between them remained, despite the peace that had been celebrated only a few months previously, that both dukes were asked not to come in person with their troops.[40]

On 1 September the dauphin set out with his household from Paris, arriving a couple of days later at Vernon, just over halfway to Rouen, where he remained for the rest of the month. Charles VI himself was not capable of leading his army into war, but on 10 September he made a personal pilgrimage to the great royal abbey of St Denis and there collected the sacred oriflamme from the high altar. It was then entrusted to Guillaume Martel, sire de Bacqueville, who took the customary oath as its bearer, before setting off to join the king's army gathering at Rouen. A citizen of Paris was sufficiently stirred by these events to note the preparations and departures in his journal. It was perhaps indicative of the general mood in Paris that it was not the plight of his fellows in far-off Harfleur which stirred his indignation, but the tax imposed to finance the campaign. It was, he complained, the heaviest ever seen.[41]

As the situation in Harfleur became increasingly desperate, de Gaucourt sent message after message to the dauphin, pleading for assistance. "Your humble subjects, so closely besieged and reduced to great distress by the English, beg your highness that you will make haste to send them help to raise the siege, so that they are not compelled to surrender this most renowned and valuable port and thus bring shame on the majesty of the king." The dauphin was either embarrassed by these pleas, or simply indifferent to them, for the messengers found it almost impossible to gain admittance to his presence. When they did, they were fobbed off with assurances that "our father the king will deal with these things at an opportune moment." All they could do was report back that a vast army, forty thousand strong, it was claimed, was gathering at Rouen.[42] What they could not do was say whether it would arrive in time to save the courageous defenders of Harfleur, or merely to avenge them.

✤ CHAPTER ELEVEN ✤

"OUR TOWN OF HARFLEUR"

Raoul de Gaucourt's defiant refusal to surrender Harfleur merely hardened Henry V's resolve. In the words of the chaplain, he decided "to proceed to sterner measures against this stiff-necked people whom neither persuasive kindliness nor destructive harshness could make more amenable." That very evening, Henry sent his trumpeters throughout the camp to proclaim that the final assault would begin the next morning and that every sailor in the fleet, as well as every soldier in the army, should make his preparations. At the same time, he ordered an even heavier bombardment than usual, to prevent the French from sleeping and make them easier to defeat the following day.[1]

This prompt reaction to the rejection of the king's terms finally brought Harfleur to its knees. De Gaucourt, d'Estouteville and the military contingent may not have wished to surrender, but the citizens could not take any more. Terrified at the prospect of the town being taken by force, with all the terrible reprisals authorised by Deuteronomy, the town council determined to offer a conditional surrender. Before dawn broke on Wednesday 18 September, the day for which the final assault had been planned, a group of fourteen burgesses carried a message to the duke of Clarence, offering to render the town into his hands if they had received no aid from their king by Sunday 22 September.[2]

There is something of a mystery about this surrender. The English chaplain, who was an eyewitness, merely noted that the besieged entered into negotiations with the king, and does not mention the role of the duke of Clarence or the burgesses. Thomas Walsingham, the author of the *St Albans Chronicle*, written in the early 1420s, describes the offer being made to Clarence, but attributes it to a single herald commissioned by de Gaucourt and the other lords in the garrison. The monk of St Denis, writing between 1415 and 1422, ascribes the agreement of terms entirely to the intervention of the duke of Clarence.[3] But why should the offer to capitulate have been made to Clarence, when the king himself was present at the siege and he alone could authorise the cessation of the fighting? The monk hinted that it may have been because Clarence was perceived as a more sympathetic figure: it was widely known in France that he had favoured the Armagnac cause during his father's lifetime. But in fact there was probably a very different explanation. Several French sources imply that treachery was at work. The chronicler of Ruisseauville, near Agincourt, reported that "it was commonly said that Clignet de Brabant [an Armagnac leader and sometime admiral of France] and the sire de Gaucourt with the constable of France had sold it." This can be dismissed as malicious gossip, like the rumours that Charles d'Albret had treasonably entered into an agreement with Henry V not to resist the English landing.[4] But the monk of St Denis had learnt, from de Gaucourt and d'Estouteville, that the English actually began their 18 September assault "on the south side" and that the besieged resisted them bravely for three full hours, until those "on the other side" of the town opened the gate to the enemy. If this version of events is true, it would explain why the offer to surrender was made to Clarence, instead of to Henry himself, as would have been more appropriate and usual. The gate "on the south side," where the assault was launched, was the Leure gate, where both de Gaucourt and Henry himself were based. The gate "on the other side," from which the delegation issued to offer terms, was the Rouen gate, where Clarence was in command. The fact that the assault "on the south side" continued for three hours could therefore be explained by the length of time it must have taken to get the message to Clarence and from him to the king.[5]

Additional support for this interpretation of events comes from the letter that the king himself wrote to the mayor and aldermen of London on the day of the formal handing over of Harfleur.

> . . . it was our full purpose to make assault upon the town on Wednesday the 18th day of this month of September; but those within the town had perceived it, and made great instance, with means which they had not employed theretofore, to have conference with us. And to avoid the effusion of human blood on the one side and on the other, we inclined to their offer, and thereupon we made answer unto them, and sent to them the last conclusion of our will; to the which they agreed, and for the same we do render thanks unto God, for we thought that they would not have so readily assented to the said conclusion. And on the same Wednesday there came by our command out of the said town the Sieurs de Gaucourt, d'Estouteville, Hankevile [that is, de Hacqueville], and other lords and knights, who had the governance of the town, and delivered hostages; and all those . . . were sworn upon the body of Our Saviour that they would make unto us full deliverance of our said town . . .[6]

The very fact that the king commanded de Gaucourt to come out of the town suggests that the latter had not initiated the submission. Indeed, it seems likely that he had no prior knowledge of the burgesses' intention to surrender, despite being captain of the town, and therefore the one who should ultimately have been responsible for making the decision. Nevertheless, treachery is perhaps too strong a term to describe the action of the civilian population. They had fought long and bravely, and endured great hardship for almost five weeks; they had lost their houses, their livelihoods and, in many cases, their lives. They had no wish to see their wives and daughters raped or their menfolk murdered by a horde of Englishmen salivating at the thought of plunder. Unlike de Gaucourt and the rest of the military garrison, they were not accustomed to putting their lives on the line, and they did not have to pay lip-service to romantic chivalric notions of glory and honour. There was nothing to say that they, too, had a duty to fight to the death.

Even if de Gaucourt had wanted to fight on to the bitter end, the town council's decision to surrender forced his hand. He could not continue to hold Harfleur if he did not have the support of those within its walls. He had lost as many as a third of his own men; those who remained were exhausted, famished and sick.[7] Henry had made it clear from the outset that he regarded the defenders of Harfleur as rebels against his authority, rather than loyal subjects of another country resisting a foreign invasion. Like the Burgundian captain of Soissons, Enguerrand de Bournonville, who had been executed by their own Armagnac forces the previous year, they could expect no mercy:[8] the laws of war authorised them to be treated as traitors, and their lives and everything they owned would automatically be forfeit. Knowing all this, de Gaucourt had to weigh in the balance the damage to his personal reputation and the possibility that he and the other military leaders faced the gallows against the universal bloodbath that would be the inevitable consequence of further futile resistance. However unwillingly, de Gaucourt decided to submit.

With d'Estouteville and Guillaume de Léon, sire de Hacqueville, de Gaucourt entered into negotiations with the king's representatives, agreeing to terms which, after a fashion, allowed him to salvage something of his honour. There was to be a truce on both sides until one o'clock on Sunday 22 September. Harfleur was to be allowed to send one last request for help to the king or the dauphin, but if the appointed time had elapsed without either of them coming to lift the siege by force of arms, then the town, its people and all their possessions would be unconditionally surrendered to the king's mercy. In that event, at least the burden of responsibility for the surrender would not fall entirely on de Gaucourt's shoulders.

Later that same day a solemn procession made its way to the foot of the walls. At its head was Benedict Nicholls, bishop of Bangor in Wales, who was carrying the Eucharist, accompanied by all the royal chaplains, including our chronicler, wearing their ecclesiastical robes. The earl of Dorset, Lord Fitzhugh and Sir Thomas Erpingham followed, carrying the indentures in which the terms were set out. As they reached the foot of the walls, the bishop cried out, "Fear not! The king of England has not come to lay waste to your lands. We are good Christians and Harfleur is not Soissons!" As Henry had commanded, the representatives of the town and garrison, led by de Gaucourt, then emerged, and both parties swore on the Eucharist to observe the articles of the agreement and signed the indentures. Twenty-four French hostages "from the more noble and important among them," including d'Estouteville, were handed over as pledges and a safe-conduct was given to the sire de Hacqueville, and twelve of his entourage, to allow them to go to seek help for Harfleur. The king absented himself from all these proceedings and did not even appear when the hostages were brought to his tent, though he allowed them to dine there and ordered that they were to be treated honourably until de Hacqueville returned.[9]

For the next few days an eerie silence reigned over Harfleur; the deadly hail of missiles had ceased, the cannon were silent, the catapults still. Even now, however, there could be no real relaxation for de Gaucourt and his men. According to the terms of the truce, they could not fight and they could not repair their shattered fortifications, but they had to prepare themselves for the possibility of further military action. They may have tried to snatch some rest, but how could they sleep when their fate stood on a knife's edge? Would the blood-red oriflamme suddenly appear on the horizon, heralding the approach of a relieving army? Would there be battle? Or would they have to face the shame of surrender, imprisonment in a foreign country, even execution?

The man who carried all the hopes of Harfleur with him made his way as swiftly as he could to Vernon, where the dauphin was still in residence. There de Haccqueville made an emotional plea for aid, with the added poignancy that, this time, there was no doubt as to the fate that awaited Harfleur. The dauphin's response was brief and to the point. The king's army was not yet fully assembled and it was not ready to give such help so quickly.

And so de Hacqueville had to return, empty-handed and with a heavy heart, to tell de Gaucourt that his mission had failed and that the gallant defence of Harfleur had all been in vain.[10]

The sense of shock and shame that the surrender of Harfleur to the English inspired throughout France was so great that those who knew nothing of the circumstances were quick to blame and condemn de Gaucourt and his men for their failure to preserve the town. Only the monk of St Denis sprang to their defence, with an impassioned and sympathetic paean of praise.

> It ought to be remembered how often they repeatedly made daring sorties against the enemy, and how with their utmost strength they drove back every attempt to gain entry into the town through underground mines dug out in secret. Without any doubt, these men were worthy of the highest praise for their endurance of every adversity: even as the roofs of the buildings were crashing in around them, they remained continuously in arms, sustained by the most meagre rations and spending their nights without sleep, so that they were prepared to repel any sudden assaults.[11]

At the appointed hour, one o'clock, on Sunday 22 September, Henry V seated himself on a throne draped with cloth of gold, under a pavilion of the same material, on the hillside above the Leure gate. A great number of his magnates and nobles, all clad in their richest finery, took their places around him, and at his right hand stood Sir Gilbert Umfraville, holding aloft the king's great helm with its golden crown. A route, lined with armed soldiers to hold back the crowds of Englishmen gathered to watch the spectacle, had been marked out between the pavilion and the town gate for the representatives of Harfleur to make their approach to the king. On the hour, the gate opened and de Gaucourt emerged at the head of a small procession of between thirty and forty knights and leading burgesses. To add to their humiliation, they had been forced to leave their horses, weapons, armour and all their goods in the town, so they had to climb the hill on foot, clad only in their shirts and hose. According to Adam of Usk, they were also obliged to wear a hangman's noose about their necks, the traditional symbol of the fact that their lives were now in the king's hands.[12]

When they reached the royal throne — a process that must have taken some time, since the hillside was steep and many of them, including de Gaucourt himself, were seriously ill — they all fell on their knees and de Gaucourt presented the keys of the town to the king with these words: "Most victorious Prince, behold here the keyes of this Towne, which after our promise I yealde unto you with the Towne, my selfe, and my companie." Henry did not deign to touch the keys himself, but ordered John Mowbray, the earl marshal, to take them. He then addressed de Gaucourt, promising him that "although he and his company had, in God's despite and contrary to all justice, retained against him a town which, being a noble portion of his inheritance, belonged to him, nevertheless, because they had submitted themselves to his mercy, even though tardily, they should not depart entirely without mercy, although he said he might wish to modify this after careful consideration." The king then ordered that de Gaucourt's party and the hostages who had been handed over earlier as guarantors for the truce should be taken to his tents, where all sixty-six were to be fed "with some magnificence," before being distributed as prisoners among his men.[13]

Immediately after de Gaucourt had formally surrendered the keys of Harfleur, his standard and those of his companions and of France, which had flown over the gates of the town throughout the siege, were taken down. In their place, the standards of St George and of the king were raised, no doubt to the cheers of the watching English army. Henry then handed over the keys to the earl of Dorset, whom he had appointed warden and captain of Harfleur.

As was so often the case with Henry V, everything about the formal surrender of Harfleur was designed to achieve a particular purpose. The ritual humiliation of his French prisoners — denied even the ordinary trappings of their rank as they were forced to take the long walk through the victorious army — was intended to serve as an example to any other town or garrison that dared to resist him. The splendid spectacle of the king, enthroned in majesty on high and surrounded by the chivalry of his realm, reinforced the message of his speech. He had enforced his just claims by the sword and had won Harfleur because his cause was righteous; the French had lost it because they had acted contrary to God's will and to justice. Even his offer of leniency, hedged about as it was by the suggestion that it might be withdrawn "after careful consideration," was a powerful demonstration that mercy could not be expected, but was the prerogative of the king alone to grant.

It had not originally been Henry's intention to enter Harfleur himself. He had expected to be able to continue in the field and carry his campaign further into France, but the unexpected duration of the siege and the epidemic of dysentery sweeping through his army forced him to rethink his decision. It was typical of the man that, after all the regal pomp and splendour of the ceremonial around the surrender, he now chose to forgo the customary triumphal entry into the conquered town. The day after the formal surrender, he rode as far as the gates, dismounted, removed his shoes and, like a penitent or pilgrim, made his way barefoot to the ruined parish church of St Martin, where he gave devout thanks to God for his victory.[14]

Having toured the town and seen at first hand the devastation that his bombardments had caused, Henry turned his attention to the civilian population. All those in holy orders were allowed to go free and unmolested. Those burgesses who were prepared to swear an oath of allegiance to him were allowed to keep their possessions, though, like the French inhabitants of Calais, they were not permitted to retain ownership of any residential or commercial property within Harfleur or their rights as citizens to self-government, tax exemptions and trading privileges. The town's charters and the title deeds of its inhabitants were all publicly burnt in the marketplace as a symbolic demonstration of the introduction of the new regime. Those of the richer burgesses who would not accept the king's terms, of whom there were at least 221, were imprisoned until they paid their ransoms, some of them subsequently being sent to Calais to await transportation to England.

The poorer inhabitants and those who were sick, together with the women and children of every rank, were all expelled from the town. Though this might seem an excessively harsh measure, contemporaries accustomed to the brutality of medieval warfare regarded it as unexpectedly lenient. Each one was given a small sum of money to purchase food on the journey and, "taking pity on their sex," the women were allowed to take as much of their property as they could carry. Some two thousand people were expelled from Harfleur in this way, "amid much lamentation, grief, and tears for the loss of their customary although unlawful habitation." Aware that they were vulnerable to the depredations of his own troops, Henry provided an armed guard to escort them beyond the limits of his army to Lillebonne, fourteen miles away, where Marshal Boucicaut was waiting to send them by boat down the Seine to the safety of Rouen. "And thus, by the true judgement of God," the chaplain noted, "they were proved sojourners where they had thought themselves inhabitants."[15]

Henry was equally merciful to those who least expected it. Around 260 French men-at-arms had survived the siege, many of them gentlemen of noble Norman or Picard families, whose ransoms would be of considerable value. Instead of committing them to prison or sending them to England, Henry released them on parole. The reasons for this act of clemency were both pragmatic and humanitarian. "As the greater part of us were extremely sick," de Gaucourt later recalled, "the King of England granted us indulgence, upon our swearing, promising, and sealing an obligation that we would all find our way to Calais, and appear before him on the approaching day of St Martin." It was a calculated risk to release them, but with so many of Henry's own troops about to be invalided home, he could not spare the men to look after such a large number of diseased prisoners. He needed as many able-bodied men as possible to defend Harfleur against any attempt to retake it. Alternatively, if he took the prisoners with him to Calais, they would be a major encumbrance, slowing him down and requiring constant guard and medical attention. On 27 September, after five days in custody, and having sworn to abide by the conditions set down in writing by the king's negotiators, including the fact that they were to surrender themselves as his prisoners at Calais on or by 11 November, they were allowed to return home.[16]

The king had not yet finished with Raoul de Gaucourt, however, who had one more task to perform before he, too, obtained his temporary release. As the former captain of the captured town, he was required to carry a message from Henry V to his master, the dauphin. The message was a challenge to fight a single combat that would decide the future of France. Written as a letter under the privy seal, from "our town of Harfleur," the challenge opened with the words, "Henry, by the grace of God, king of France and of England, and lord of Ireland, to the high and powerful prince, the dauphin of Guienne, our cousin, eldest son of the most powerful prince, our cousin and adversary of France." Out of reverence to God and to avoid the effusion of human blood, Henry went on, he had many times and in many ways sought to obtain peace.

> And considering also that the result of our wars is the death of men, the destruction of countryside, the lamentation of women and children, and so many evils generally, that every good Christian ought to grieve for it and take compassion, especially we whom this matter touches most nearly, and ought to make every effort and diligently seek to find all the ways that man can devise to avoid these said evils and disadvantages, so that we gain the favour of God and the praise of the world.

As Charles VI, to whom the challenge ought to have been sent, was not capable of answering it, Henry proposed to the dauphin that the quarrel should be put to a trial by battle "between our person and yours." Whoever won would have the crown of France on the death of Charles VI. A verbal message must have accompanied this letter, for the dauphin was informed that Henry would wait for an answer at Harfleur for eight days, after which time the offer would lapse.[17]

Henry's challenge has been much derided by historians as bombastic, ridiculous, frivolous and obsolete. In fact, it was none of these things. Trial by battle had an ancient and venerable tradition: for centuries it had been part of the judicial process in cases where neither side in a dispute could offer evidential proof to allow a jury or court to decide their case. When it was one man's word against another's, then the only way to settle the quarrel was to offer it for divine judgement. God would not permit an injustice to be perpetrated, the argument went, so the victory would fall to whichever party had right on his side — the reason why trial by battle was also known in medieval times as the *judicium dei*, or the judgement of God, a concept that had particular appeal for a king as deeply pious and absolutely convinced of the justice of his cause as Henry V. Henry's own family had a long history of involvement in judicial combats. His great-grandfathers Edward III and Henry, duke of Lancaster, had both issued and received challenges to settle the wars in France by this method. His great-uncle, Thomas of Woodstock, duke of Gloucester, was responsible, as constable of England, for drawing up the standard set of rules governing such combats. His own father, when duke of Hereford, had been on the brink of fighting a judicial duel against Thomas Mowbray, duke of Norfolk, in 1398, when Richard II forbade it and banished him from the realm.[18] Though the practice became increasingly rare, the right to trial by battle was not legally abolished in England until 1819.

Because the trial by battle was fought within lists and under strict rules, it has often been confused with tournaments and jousts, which explains why some historians have been so contemptuous of Henry V's challenge to the dauphin. Challenges to perform feats of arms, such as those which passed between the seneschal of Hainault and Sir John Cornewaille, were highly regarded in chivalric circles because mere participation bestowed honour on those involved, whatever the outcome. Even if these were fought *à outrance*, with the ordinary weapons and armour of war, the objective was not to kill the opponent, only to prove one's own courage and skill. Trial by battle, on the other hand, was emphatically not a chivalric game: it was a legally binding judgement. A defeated participant, if he was not killed in the course of the combat, could be removed from the lists and executed as a convicted criminal. Those who took part in judicial duels did so reluctantly and because their reputation had been impugned; failure meant death but also dishonour.

Henry V's challenge was not an empty gesture, but a deadly

serious undertaking. If he could prove his claims to France in single combat, instead of with an army, then he would save lives on both sides. If the dauphin had accepted the challenge, there is no question but that Henry would have fought in person — and won. If he did not, then Henry could still circulate copies of his challenge to all his friends and potential allies as proof of his wish to be reasonable and of his determination to avoid bloodshed at all costs.[19] Once again, Henry had demonstrated his mastery of the art of propaganda, wrongfooting the dauphin and claiming the moral high ground. The sin in prolonging the war would fall upon the dauphin's head and his reputation would be tainted with the charge of personal cowardice.

On 27 September de Gaucourt set off to deliver the letter of challenge to the dauphin, who was still lingering at Vernon, some twenty-eight miles south of Rouen and approximately sixty-eight miles upriver from Harfleur. He was accompanied on this mission by William Bruges, Guyenne king of arms, which begs the question why de Gaucourt was sent at all. Delivering a challenge was one of the principal duties of a herald. Bruges was highly experienced and had no need of any escort or assistance. That de Gaucourt was forced to accompany him can only be attributable to Henry's desire to confront the dauphin with the consequences of his own inaction. He would hear at first hand and from one of his own loyal lieutenants — now an English prisoner — that Harfleur was in enemy hands. Henry may also have hoped that de Gaucourt would be able to persuade the dauphin to accept the challenge, or at least to make some conciliatory gesture to buy himself peace.[20]

De Gaucourt and Guyenne were kept waiting for an interview with the dauphin, and neither of them had returned to Harfleur by the time the eight days Henry had set as the limit for a response had elapsed. (By contrast, de Hacqueville had managed to get to and from Vernon within three days.)[21] The challenge placed the dauphin in a dilemma. He had no intention of accepting it, but he could not turn it down without appearing a coward. Unable to commit himself to either of these courses, he hid his head in the sand and left the challenge unanswered.[22]

One can imagine that a knight as committed to the chivalric ideal as de Gaucourt would be unimpressed by this demonstration of the dauphin's singular lack of courtly qualities. It must have been humiliating to compare the shortcomings of his own leader with the exemplary behaviour of Henry V.

Having delivered his message, de Gaucourt was at least spared the necessity of taking back the dauphin's reply. Prohibited from taking any further part in military action against his captors, there was nothing else he could do except retreat to his sickbed until he was required to surrender himself at Calais. For him, the war was over.

Henry, in the meantime, had not been idle as he waited at Harfleur for the dauphin's reply. On the day of the formal surrender, as we have seen, he had written to the mayor and aldermen of London to inform them that, "by the good diligence of our faithful lieges at this time in our company, and the strength and position of our cannon, and other our ordnance," he had succeeded in bringing about the town's capitulation. The expulsion of its inhabitants had prepared the way for its repopulation with English settlers, the intention being to create a second Calais. On 5 October proclamations were made in London and other large towns throughout England, offering free houses and special privileges to any of the king's subjects who were prepared to take up residence in Harfleur. The objective was to find merchants, victuallers and tradesmen, so that the town could become both self-reliant and part of the trading nexus linking London with the continent through Calais and Bayonne. Among those who were granted property in the town were the king's clerk Master Jean de Bordiu, who was presented to the parish church of Harfleur, and Richard Bokelond, a London merchant, who was given an inn in the town called "the Peacock" as a reward for assisting the king during the siege with two of his ships.[23]

Urgent orders were also given to reprovision the town. On 4 October a messenger was sent "with the greatest speed" bearing a commission under the king's great seal to the constable of Dover Castle and the warden of the Cinque Ports, which ordered them to go in person to all the neighbouring ports on the south coast of England "where fishermen commonly reside and dwell, and strongly enjoin and command all and singular the fishermen . . . without delay to proceed to the town of Harfleu [*sic*] with their boats and other vessels, and with their nets, tackle, and other things, necessary to fish upon the Norman coast, near the town aforesaid, for support of the King's army there." Two days later John Fysshere of Henley was ordered to take supplies of wheat to Harfleur at the king's cost, and six days after that John Laweney, a London grocer, was similarly ordered to send "provisions, arms and necessary stuff." To ensure that stocks remained plentiful, orders were issued prohibiting anyone in England from "taking over any wheat or grain to any foreign parts except the towns of Calais or Harflewe in Normandy without the special command of the king." Those shipping supplies to Calais and Harfleur were also compelled to provide proof of delivery, so that they could not fraudulently divert their cargoes elsewhere.[24] Reginald Curteys, the former supplier of Calais who, earlier in the year, had been entrusted with the task of hiring ships in Holland and Zeeland for the invasion, was appointed as the official victualler of Harfleur, and stocking the garrison and town thereafter became his responsibility. After their enforced weeks of military service, many of the ships that had served to carry troops and supplies during the siege were now free to return to their original purpose. Two of the king's own vessels, the *Katherine de la Tour*, which had sailed with the fleet, and the newly commissioned *Holy Ghost*, which had not been ready in time for the invasion, were kept busy plying the cross-Channel trade, bringing beer and wine to the garrison.[25]

The biggest problem facing Henry at this point was not so much supplies as men. Dysentery continued to make huge inroads into his army, greatly reducing the numbers of those fit to fight. Even after the siege had ended, his men were still dying at an alarming rate and many more were incapacitated by sickness. Their presence in the army being both a hindrance and an unwarranted drain on precious resources, Henry took the decision to send them home. This in itself was a major logistical problem. There were literally thousands of sick and dying. Each retinue captain was therefore required to muster his men and certify the names of those who were unable to continue in active service to the king and his clerks. The sick were then separated out from those who were still fit and well, and given the royal licence to return home. Some of the ships that had blockaded Harfleur from the sea were entrusted with the task of transporting these men back to England, and the evacuation began within a week of the town's surrender. The English chaplain estimated that some five thousand of Henry's men were invalided home from Harfleur. Though he was usually well informed about such things, this figure may be an exaggeration. Lists of the sick who received licence to return home have survived, but they are incomplete. Even so, they record 1693 individual names, including three of the king's young earls, Thomas, earl of Arundel, John Mowbray, the earl marshal, and Edmund, earl of March.[26] Arundel was one of the king's closest associates, having served him in peace and war for the previous ten years, and been treasurer of England since Henry's accession. He was now mortally sick and, although he returned to England on 28 September, he never recovered. He died at home at Arundel Castle on 13 October, his thirty-fourth birthday. (As he died childless, his great estates, which had made him one of the richest men in the country, were divided between his three sisters and his title passed to his second cousin.) Mowbray and March were more fortunate. Both recovered, the former with the aid of numerous remedies for the pestilence, the flux and vomiting, purchased at great expense from a London grocer.[27] Arundel cannot have been the only man to have died in England of dysentery contracted during the siege, but it is impossible to discover the fate of the vast majority of the rest, particularly those of low rank. Once their names had appeared on their licences to return home, they disappeared into oblivion as far as records are concerned.

It is equally difficult to establish how many died of the disease at Harfleur. In addition to Richard Courtenay, bishop of Norwich, and Michael, earl of Suffolk, the names of at least eight knights who brought their own retinues are known: William Beaumond from Devonshire, Roger Trumpington from Cambridgeshire, Edward Burnell from Norfolk, John Marland from Somerset, John Southworth, Hugh Standish and William Botiller from Lancashire and John Phelip from Worcestershire.[28] Sir John Phelip, too, had been a close associate of the king. He had been a member of Henry's household when he was prince of Wales and was one of the select few chosen to be made a Knight of the Bath at his coronation in 1413. He had taken a leading role in the earl of Arundel's expedition to France in 1411 and was in the Anglo-Burgundian force that defeated the Armagnacs at St Cloud; for the Agincourt campaign he had brought a substantial retinue of thirty men-at-arms and ninety foot archers. Phelip, who was a nephew of Sir Thomas Erpingham, the steward of the king's household, was married to Alice Chaucer, the only child of Thomas and granddaughter of the poet, though she was only eleven years old when she was widowed. Phelip himself was thirty-one when he died. His body was taken back to England and interred at Kidderminster under the proud, if ungainly, Latin epitaph: "Henry V loved this man as a friend; John was bold and strong and fought well at Harfleur."[29]

Few names of the less eminent victims of dysentery have survived — and these only because their deaths were recorded on the muster rolls so that the exchequer did not have to continue paying their wages. The exchequer clerks attempted to make a distinction between those who "died" of the disease and those who were "killed" as a result of enemy action, though it is unclear how reliable their efforts were; combined with the incomplete nature of the records themselves, this makes it difficult to reach any firm conclusions as to how many died. Monstrelet hazarded a guess at two thousand, a figure that was taken up and repeated as fact by other chroniclers. This may be accurate. If modern rates of mortality among untreated victims of dysentery are taken as a guide, it is likely that Henry lost between 10 and 20 per cent of his army, which translates as something in the region of 1200–2400 men. Whatever the actual numbers, the chroniclers on both sides of the conflict were all united in one belief: more men died from disease at Harfleur than from the fighting throughout the campaign.[30]

Occasionally we get a glimpse of the scale of the loss in terms of death and sickness to individual companies. Arundel's retinue, as one might expect, given the contagious nature of the disease, was badly hit. Out of a total of 100 men-at-arms, two died at Harfleur and twelve (or possibly eighteen) were invalided home; of the original 300 archers who also accompanied him, thirteen died and a further sixty-nine were sent home sick, together with three of his minstrels. In other words, almost exactly a quarter of his retinue were casualties of the siege. Mowbray's company was even harder hit: death and sickness reduced it by almost a third. Of the fifty men-at-arms he brought with him, three died during the siege and thirteen, including the earl himself, were sent home ill; of his 150 archers, as many as forty-seven were invalided back to England. Similarly, John, Lord Harington, who had brought a retinue of thirty men-at-arms and ninety archers, had to return home sick from Harfleur himself on 5 October, together with ten of his men-at-arms and twenty of his archers. The effect on smaller retinues was equally devastating. Sir Ralph Shirley also lost a third of his men: he had originally mustered only six men-at-arms and eighteen archers; three of the former, including himself, and six of the latter were invalided home. Sir Rowland Lenthalle, a Herefordshire knight, brought a retinue of twelve men-at-arms, of whom two died at Harfleur and three more were sent home sick; his thirty-six archers fared much better, with only two of them dying during the siege. Thomas Chaucer, as we have seen, brought twelve men-at-arms and thirty-seven archers; two of the former died of dysentery at Harfleur and Chaucer himself was invalided home, but all of his archers survived unscathed. Dysentery was not, as one might have expected, a disease that always afflicted the lowest ranks hardest.[31]

If such figures can be taken as a general trend — and there must have been retinues that suffered both more and less — then we can assume that, in total, the king lost between a quarter and a third of his men to dysentery as a result of the siege. There were other casualties, including, of course, those who were killed in action, and those like Nicholas Seymour, brother of the lord of Castle Cary, who was captured at Harfleur and was still believed to be alive and a prisoner in France at the end of December. Additionally, as the chaplain pointed out, there were those who, to the king's great indignation, "out of sheer cowardice, leaving or rather deserting their king in the field, had stealthily slipped away to England beforehand."[32]

The need to garrison Harfleur was a further drain on manpower. Having gained the town at such cost, it was critically important that it should stay in English hands. It was therefore necessary to ensure that it was adequately manned to prevent its recapture the moment the main English army departed. Henry decided that the earl of Dorset should have a force of 300 men-at-arms and 900 archers to safeguard its defences — a garrison that was almost two and a half times the size of that at Calais. How the men were chosen is not known, but it is likely that it was on a volunteer basis. This is suggested by the fact that, rather than simply assigning certain whole retinues to the task, which would probably have been the simplest method, men were drawn, apparently indiscriminately in terms of numbers, from a variety of different companies: Michael de la Pole, whose father died during the siege, provided two men-at-arms and five archers, and Thomas, Lord Camoys, a single man-at-arms, for example, while eight of the fifty Lancashire archers brought by Sir Richard Kyghley were also selected.[33] A muster roll for the winter of 1415–16 reveals that the 300 men-at-arms included four barons, the lords Hastings, Grey, Bourchier and Clinton, and twenty-two knights (Sir Thomas Erpingham and Sir John Fastolf among them). This was an unusually high proportion of senior members of the nobility, reflecting the importance Henry attached to keeping the town, but also providing the earl of Dorset with a ready-made council of experienced and reliable soldiers and administrators in the event of an emergency. For some of them, this appointment proved to be a turning point in their careers. Fastolf, for example, saw the focus of his activity shift from England to France. Within a few months he had acquired the life grant of a manor and lordship near Harfleur that had belonged to Guy Malet, sire de Graville, and his profits of war would be so great that he was able to spend the next thirty years investing £460 annually (over $305,900 at today's values) in the purchase of lands in England and France.[34]

The English garrison was to benefit from the protection of a small fleet that was ordered to patrol and guard the coastline close to Harfleur. A number of cannon were also installed in the town, together with eighteen gunners to operate them. Additionally, forty-two carpenters and twenty masons were to remain behind to restore the broken fortifications of the walls and towers. It was not until December that additional masons and tilers were to be recruited for the restoration of the houses and other buildings within the town. The cost would be phenomenal. Their wage bill, claimed by Harfleur's new treasurer for the first five months alone, amounted to just over £4892 (more than $3,250,000 at today's values), and that did not include exceptional sums such as the £800 paid to one Thomas Henlemsted, a "dyker" from Southwark, for removing a mound and making a ditch outside the town walls.[35]

Once the arrangements for the security of Harfleur had been completed, Henry had several choices before him. He could return to England with a short but successful campaign behind him having established a bridgehead for any future attempt to reconquer his heritage in Normandy. He could follow in his brother Clarence's footsteps, and make a *chevauchée*, or armed raid, plundering and burning his way down through the south and west of France to his duchy of Aquitaine. He could extend his area of conquest by besieging another neighbouring town, such as Montivilliers, or Fécamp or Dieppe, which were both further up the coast towards Calais, or even Rouen, which would take him a major step further inland up the Seine.

There were good reasons why Henry adopted none of these alternatives. A five-week campaign, even one that resulted in the capture of a place as important as Harfleur, was not enough to justify the expense, effort and time he had put into the preparations. Nor would it do anything to advance his claim to the crown of France. If he were to force any greater concessions from the French, or, indeed, keep the support of his own people for further campaigns, then he needed to make a grander gesture.

A *chevauchée* to Bordeaux had its attractions: plenty of plunder on the journey for his men, a safe haven at the end, a chance to visit his duchy and perhaps carry out a campaign in the region. Indeed, Master Jean de Bordiu, in his letter of 3 September to the duchy, had stated categorically that it was the king's "intention" to go to Bordeaux "before he returns to England."[36] On the other hand, this was written when the fall of Harfleur was expected imminently and before dysentery had made its appearance in his army. It was a month further into the campaigning season before Henry was ready to set off and Bordeaux was over 350 miles away — a very long way to travel for a depleted army that was not in the best of health. The lateness of the season, combined with his reduced numbers and the uncertain state of health of his men, made another siege out of the question, so the guns and siege engines were either put into Harfleur or shipped back to England.

Although rumours were rife all over Europe about the king's intentions, Henry had already made up his mind what he was going to do. The great army he had assembled at Southampton was now reduced to a mere shadow of its former self. Excluding those in the garrison at Harfleur, he probably had only nine hundred men-at-arms and five thousand archers able to draw sword or fit to fight, as the chaplain put it. Even with this comparatively small number, he did not have enough shipping available to him at Harfleur to send them home directly, since he had dismissed most of his invasion fleet before the town capitulated.[37] Nor did he have enough victuals to enable them all to remain indefinitely in the town.

Henry had arranged to meet his prisoners at Calais on 11 November and it was to Calais that he intended to go. He could have travelled there easily and safely by sea. Instead, he chose to follow in his great-grandfather's footsteps, and march through what he claimed were "his" duchy of Normandy and "his" county of Ponthieu to "his" town of Calais. He even intended to cross the Somme at the same place, in the full knowledge that it was on a similar expedition, in 1346, that Edward III had won a famous victory over the French at Crécy. Although he would follow a route close to the coastline, it would inevitably bring him within easy striking distance of the French army at Rouen. He probably calculated that his diplomatic efforts of the previous year would ensure that neither John the Fearless, duke of Burgundy, nor Jean, duke of Brittany, would move against him. In that case, the "French" army would actually be a much smaller and weaker Armagnac army. He had failed to draw the dauphin into battle at Harfleur or to give him trial by battle in person. Perhaps this deliberate act of provocation would finally rouse him to action.

CHAPTER TWELVE

THE MARCH TO CALAIS

Henry's decision to march his army overland to Calais was a calculated risk. It was also very much a personal one. A large majority of his council advised against it, fearing that the dwindling English forces would be an easy prey for the French multitudes that had been gathering at Rouen for over a month.[1] In the meetings that took place after the fall of Harfleur, Clarence argued that the English should return home immediately by sea as being "the next and surest way": they had lost too many men, both to the sickness and death wrought by dysentery and to manning the garrison, to run the risk of a journey to Calais overland, "and most especiallie considering the greate and infinite multitude of theire enemies, which then were assembled to prevent and hinder the King's passage by land, whereof by theire espies they had knowledge." In anyone else's mouth this would have appeared sound enough reasoning — and there were plenty of others who shared his view — but coming from Clarence this reluctance to engage with the enemy was open to sinister interpretation. His well-known sympathy for the Armagnac cause cast a shadow of suspicion, long and dark, over his motives, his advice, his actions.

Clarence could not have openly defied his brother by refusing to go — that would have been an act of high treason — but he was reckless enough to make his feelings known. If he was not prepared to run the risk of the march to Calais, thus causing a very dangerous confrontation with the king, or would only go with a bad grace that might affect the morale of the men and provide a focus for discontent, then it was in everyone's interest that an honourable exit should be found for him. Clarence's name duly appeared on the rolls of the sick and at the beginning of October he received his licence to leave the army and return home. Though it is true that his retinue had been severely affected by dysentery, Clarence's own actions do not suggest a man suffering from a debilitating disease. Instead of going straight home, he took ship for Calais, where his arrival with "such a great number of men" caused panic in neighbouring Boulogne, which immediately sent off a messenger to Abbeville to inform Constable d'Albret. Fears that Clarence was about to launch a second invasion from Calais were unfounded, but the author of *The First English Life*, who did not know that Clarence was supposed to be ill, assumed that he had been sent back to England to take charge of the fleet, perhaps because the admiral, the earl of Dorset, had been left to captain Harfleur.[2]

Though he lacked his brother's intellectual qualities, Clarence was still every inch the soldier. As noted earlier, Jean Fusoris had contrasted Clarence's martial character with that of Henry V, whom he thought more suited for the Church than for war. This opinion must have struck a chord with many of the other royal councillors who advised against the proposal to march to Calais. In response to their protestations about the inequality of the size of the respective armies, Henry serenely countered by "relying on divine grace and the justice of his cause, piously reflecting that victory consists not in a multitude but with Him for Whom it is not impossible to enclose the many in the hand of the few and Who bestows victory upon whom He wills, whether they be many or few."[3] It was an argument that Henry had advanced before,[4] and, in an age of faith, it was unanswerable. What is more, it was not simply unthinking piety. Henry was well aware that every military treatise since classical times had expounded the view that a small, well-trained army could defeat a larger one. Christine de Pizan, for instance, discussed the subject at length in *The Book of Deeds of Arms and of Chivalry.*

> One finds that many armies have been thrown into disarray by their own greater number rather than by enemy forces. And why is this so? Certainly there are good reasons, for a great multitude is more difficult to maintain in good order and is often in trouble because it requires more provisions, is more quarrelsome, and is subject to more delays on the roads . . . For this reason . . . the ancients who had mastered such things useful in battle, knowing the perils from experience, placed a higher value on an army well taught and well led than a great multitude.[5]

As Vegetius himself had said, rather more succinctly: "Bravery is of more value than numbers."[6]

Orders were issued for those selected for the march to equip themselves with enough provisions to last for eight days. It has often been suggested that this was a serious miscalculation and that Henry had been overly optimistic about the length of time it would take to get to Calais. In the light of hindsight, this was clearly the case. On the other hand, without the benefit of that future knowledge, Henry and his advisors had to plan reasonably and appropriately. It was important for the men to have enough supplies to get them to Calais, but they also needed to be able to travel lightly and not be weighed down with unnecessary baggage.

The eight-day figure was not simply plucked out of the air. Despite the fact that he had no maps to calculate his route, Henry knew he would need to cover an average of just under nineteen miles per day, which was perfectly reasonable given that nineteen miles was the acknowledged medieval standard for travelling by land. The ever-reliable Vegetius had stated that an army marching on foot should be able to cover at least twenty miles in only five hours in summertime; had Henry been able to achieve this, his eight days would have taken him well beyond Calais. The English army was disciplined and mostly mounted, but it was not a Roman legion accustomed to long route marches, and it could travel only as fast as its slowest members. Even so, given a longer travelling day, it should have been able to cover the same distance within the eight days for which supplies were allotted, especially as it would be possible to supplement these rations along the way.[7]

Before the march began, Henry once more issued a set of ordinances in accordance with customary practice and the laws of war. It was going to be of the utmost importance that his small army stayed together and that neither individuals nor companies were tempted to stray by the prospect of plunder, prisoners or even chivalric dreams of a heroic encounter with the enemy. Henry was determined to maintain order among his own men, but also that this would not be a traditional *chevauchée*. His objectives were to challenge the French military and to get to Calais: he did not wish to despoil, massacre or exploit the civilian population. The presence of his army, sweeping through northern France, would be enough to strike terror into the hearts of those living there. With an eye to the longer term, it was important that he did not alienate those whom he hoped and believed would be his future subjects. He therefore decreed that, on pain of death, there should be no burning or laying waste of property or land, that nothing should be taken "except food and what was necessary for the march" and that no "rebels" were to be captured, unless they were offering resistance.[8]

There is some confusion as to when the army actually set off from Harfleur. Contemporary English sources, who were best placed to know, variously date it to 6, 7, 8 or 9 October. The exchequer accounts paying the wages of the men who went on the march would seem to provide conclusive evidence that it was 6 October, "on which day they left the town of Harfleur with the lord king heading for the battle of Agincourt." Most of the wage accounts for those who remained in the garrison also run from 6 October, though some begin two days later. Of the three English chroniclers writing before 1422, Thomas Walsingham avoids giving any date at all, Thomas Elmham plumps for 9 October, which was the feast of St Denis, and the chaplain — the only one actually present on the march — miscalculated his dates and gave two conflicting ones.[9]

The reason for this confusion is that there was no single universal system of dating in medieval times. There were only two constants. The first was the Julian calendar, introduced by Julius Caesar in 45 BC. It divided the year into twelve months and 365 days, with an extra day at the end of February every fourth year to catch up the discrepancy between the arithmetically calculated year and the solar year as observed by astronomers. The second constant, the "year of grace," was introduced in AD 535 by the Church in Rome. This drew a definitive line between the pagan and Christian eras, dividing them into years reckoned before the incarnation (BC — Before Christ) and after it (AD — *Anno Domini* — the Year of Our Lord). The English, led by the example of the Venerable Bede, had adopted this system by the eighth century; by the fifteenth century it had spread across all of western Europe, except Portugal, which until 1420 clung to 38 BC as the beginning of its era.[10]

Though the introduction of the "year of grace" or AD system brought some measure of uniformity and certainty to the chronologies of western Europe, it had one basic flaw. No particular date was designated for the start of the year. There were, therefore, any number of conflicting dates. Some were logical, like Christmas Day, the day celebrated as Christ's birth, or Lady Day, otherwise known as the Feast of the Annunciation, which fell on 25 March and was the day that the angel informed Mary that she was to have a child. Others were totally illogical, such as Easter Day, which varied from year to year. Throughout the Middle Ages, the Church, which preferred to start the year with one of its major Christian festivals, successfully opposed attempts to revert to the pagan Roman practice of beginning the year on 1 January. Even though the spread of Protestantism in the sixteenth century gave it renewed credibility, it was not formally adopted in England as New Year's Day until 1 January 1752.[11]

To complicate matters still further, there were other ways of calculating the year. In the Middle Ages each new year began according to the local customary practice or the particular allegiance of the person computing it. In England, the financial and legal years were divided into terms, Michaelmas, Hilary, Easter and Trinity, the new year beginning with Michaelmas on

6 October. These cut across the most popular form of reckoning, which was the regnal year, dating from the start of a new king's reign. Regnal years were used by those in the employment of popes and bishops, kings and princes, and therefore, of necessity, varied from region to region. The regnal year of Henry V, for example, began on 21 March 1413, the first full day after his father's death.[12]

Throw into this equation the fact that most dates were not given as simple consecutive numbers and that there was an uneasy mismatch between the Christian and Julian calendars, which were both in use at the same time, and one can begin to see why historians and chronologers in the Middle Ages sometimes made mistakes. In the Christian calendar, dates were referred to as the names of Church festivals and saints' days, including not only the day itself but the day before (*pridie* and *vigilia*) and "the day after" (*crastinum*). In the Julian calendar, every month was unequally divided into the periods of calends, nones and ides, within which the days were counted in numerically descending order. According to this system, our 25 October was thus the eighth day before the calends of November, whereas 30 October was only the third.

A medieval writer wishing to give the date of the battle of Agincourt would have several options before him. Chivalric authors tended to go for the easy option: Monstrelet, for example, simply called it "Friday, the xxvth day of the month of October, one thousand four hundred and fifteen."[13] Ecclesiastical writers, including chroniclers and clerks in the royal administration, perhaps because they were more numerate and more obligated to abide by Church practices, used the more complicated systems. A Church-trained English and French chronicler would have described the same event in different terms. Neither would have referred to it as being fought on 25 October, but on the Feast of St Crispin and St Crispinian. The Englishman might have placed it "in the third year of our lord king Henry the fifth of that name after the conquest." His French counterpart, writing in the name of Charles VI, would have described it as being "on the Feast of St Crispin and St Crispinian, in the thirty-fifth year of our reign." That was why every medieval chronicler and clerk had to have a set of chronological tables to hand whenever computing a date.

It was not even easy to tell exactly what time it was. Although it was generally accepted that there were twenty-four hours in a day, how these hours were measured varied. There were three systems in use in the early fifteenth century. One was the early medieval custom of splitting the day into two periods, from sunrise to sunset, and sunset to sunrise, each of which was artificially subdivided into twelve unequal hours. In winter, the daylight hours would be shorter and the night-time ones longer, a situation that reversed in summer. The second method also varied according to the season, and was determined by the seven canonical hours that marked the principal daily services in the church; they began with Prime at daybreak and ended with Vespers as darkness fell. The advantage of this system was that, although it varied from place to place because it depended on the time that the sun rose and the hours were again of uneven length, the services were marked by the ringing of bells in monasteries and parish churches, which were audible to the people living around them. Like the schoolbells and factory horns of the modern world, these determined the length of the working day for the vast majority of people.[14]

The third method of telling the time, which was only reluctantly adopted in some monastic houses, was entirely divorced from the seasons. Mechanical clocks divided the day into twenty-four hours of equal length and measured from midnight to midnight. Sundials and hourglasses, filled with water or sand, had been in use for centuries, but the new clocks were made out of precision-crafted moving parts of iron. The earliest recorded example in England was made in 1283 by the canons of Dunstable Priory, but the oldest surviving one, in Salisbury Cathedral, dates from a century later. Many of these clocks were works of remarkable craftsmanship: in 1322 the priory of Norwich Cathedral had one with a large astronomical dial and automata, including fifty-nine images and a procession of monks. By the fifteenth century, mechanical clocks dictated the time in most Benedictine houses and were displayed on churches and other buildings for the benefit of the wider population.[15]

Our poor chaplain, trying to work out the date of the king's departure from Harfleur, had to struggle with all the conflicting elements of the medieval calendar. In his praiseworthy efforts to be precise, he merely muddied the waters. They had set off, he decided, "on Tuesday, the day before the feast of St Denys, on the nones of October." The feast of St Denis was 9 October, and in 1415 it fell on a Wednesday, so the day before would indeed have been a Tuesday. Unfortunately, the nones of October, according to the classical Roman calendar, were on 7 October. It is likely that this was just a slip of the pen, or of the finger as he cross-checked his chronological tables.[16]

What is more difficult to explain is why the chaplain thought they left Harfleur on Tuesday 8 October, when the exchequer records explicitly state that it was on Sunday 6 October. There is no obvious answer to this question, but it is likely that the exchequer arbitrarily selected 6 October for reasons of administrative convenience, that being the first day of the new financial quarter for the campaign. All that can be said for certain is that the chaplain was there in person and that, in view of his profession, he would surely have known if they had set off on a Sunday. On this admittedly slim basis for a decision, we shall follow the chaplain, but bearing in mind that he may have been a couple of days out on his reckoning.[17]

On Tuesday 8 October, therefore, the king, with his nine hundred men-at-arms, five thousand archers and numberless assorted civilians, including the royal surgeons, minstrels, heralds and chaplains, set out from Harfleur by the Montivilliers road. As was the customary practice, the army had been divided into the three battles, or divisions, in which it would fight. The honour of leading the vanguard, or first division, fell once more to the indomitable Sir John Cornewaille and Sir Gilbert Umfraville. The main body of the army was led by the king himself, with some of his younger and less experienced noblemen, including his twenty-four-year-old brother Humphrey, duke of Gloucester, twenty-year-old Sir John Holland, who had distinguished himself at the landing and during the siege in the company of his stepfather, and John, Lord de Roos, who had inherited his father's estates the previous year and was still only eighteen or nineteen. The leadership of the rearguard, like that of the vanguard, was entrusted to seasoned campaigners, in this case the veteran Edward, duke of York, and Richard de Vere, earl of Oxford.[18]

Within the three divisions, it is likely that the men were still grouped according to the retinues into which they had originally been recruited. There was, in other words, no separating out of the men-at-arms from the archers, even though the latter now outnumbered the former by more than five to one, instead of the usual ratio of three to one favored by the English. What must have taken place, however, was a considerable amount of reorganisation. Many retinues, including Clarence's, which, with almost a thousand men, had been the single largest company at the beginning of the campaign, had lost their leaders. Many more had seen their numbers reduced by as much as a third. In order to maintain the command structure and discipline, it was important that new leaders should be appointed. In some cases this meant that someone from within the retinue took over, as Sir Thomas Rokeby did when the earl marshal was invalided home. In others, particularly where large numbers of archers were involved, the men would be reassigned to other retinues to restore their numbers to a fighting unit.[19]

Given the distance that the army had to travel and the possibility that it would soon have to face battle, it is likely that most if not all the men were mounted. There were plenty of surplus horses at Harfleur, for the priority had been to ship home the men who were sick, rather than their mounts. Together with all the spare horses that everyone above the rank of archer was permitted to take, and the packhorses required to carry the baggage, there must have been a minimum of twelve thousand horses in the column, and it may well have been double that figure.[20] Though the horses were essential for the army's speed and mobility, their presence in such large numbers meant that it would be difficult to keep them all adequately fed and watered on the journey.

The English could not, and did not, expect their march to be unopposed. On 7 October William Bardolf, the acting lieutenant of Calais, wrote to John, duke of Bedford, Henry's lieutenant in

England, warning him that he had heard reports from both France and Flanders that "without fail" the king would have battle against his adversaries within fifteen days at the latest. Around five thousand Frenchmen had already assembled and "a notable knight," with a force of five hundred men, had also been posted to the defence of the French frontier against the Calais marches. A reluctant bearer of bad tidings, Bardolf excused himself by explaining that "I thought I ought to tell you this."[21]

Bardolf's reports were entirely accurate. Ever since 2 August, when the truces between England and France in this area had elapsed, the Calais garrison had launched a number of diversionary raids to distract the French away from Harfleur during the invasion and siege. David, sire de Rambures, grand-master of the crossbowmen of France and captain of Boulogne, had been sent to defend the area from the depredations of the garrison. Despite anguished messages from the townsmen of Boulogne, who sought him out at Fécamp and Rouen, it was not until Harfleur was on the very point of surrender that de Rambures at last obtained permission to send the sire de Laurois, commander of Ardres, with a force of five hundred men, to garrison Boulogne.[22] The arrival of de Laurois and his men was a serious setback to Henry's plans. He had intended that a three-hundred-strong force from Calais should be sent to Blanche Taque to secure the river crossing of the Somme in readiness for his own arrival. The heightened state of security around the Pas-de-Calais would now make it nearly impossible for this expeditionary force to reach the Somme. When it eventually set out, it was ambushed and overwhelmed by a band of Picards, who killed some of the men and took the rest prisoner, intending to hold them to ransom. The failure of this venture would have important consequences for the English army's attempts to cross the Somme, the single greatest barrier between them and the safety of Calais.[23]

While Henry was besieging Harfleur, Charles d'Albret and Marshal Boucicaut had anticipated his next move by destroying bridges and breaking causeways across all the major rivers and reinforcing and resupplying the towns and castle garrisons

throughout Normandy and Picardy. The preparations at Boulogne, which was close to the Pas-de-Calais and therefore faced
a double threat of a combined assault from the king in the
south-west and the Calais garrison in the north-east, were typical. Strict orders had been given as early as 15 September that
the nightly watches were to be augmented with dogs and
lanterns set beyond the moat; during the day, watchmen were
also to be stationed on the hills above the town, to give early
notice of an English approach. The embrasures in the town
walls and towers were widened to facilitate crossbow fire, miners were hired and the suburbs were cleared away in anticipation of a siege. David, sire de Rambures, provided a "long
bombarde" which was mounted on the walls and the town's
own cannon was brought up from the guildhall. Gunners were
brought in to man the artillery and supplies of saltpetre and the
other ingredients required for making gunpowder were bought
from St Omer.[24]

There was little that could be done to protect the country
people, but this was an area that had been invaded and had suffered the depredations of war so many times that its inhabitants
had long ago learnt that their safety depended on their ability to
disappear into local forests and caves. In some instances, caves
provided a remarkably sophisticated refuge. At Naours,[25] just
to the north of Amiens, subterranean chalk quarries had been
artificially enlarged and used as places of safety for centuries.
Working along the seams of chalk, which were sandwiched
between layers of impenetrable silex, an underground city had
been created which was capable of sheltering up to two thousand people at once, together with their sheep, cattle, horses
and mules. Twenty-eight galleries led to three hundred chambers, each one large enough to house a family of eight, and to a
number of public rooms, including a chapel, a law court and a
jail. Excavated at three different levels, between 100 and 140
feet below ground, the cave system was naturally dry, enjoyed a
constant temperature of 48 degrees Fahrenheit and had access
to the river for water. Six chimneys provided ventilation and
enabled food to be cooked. So that the smoke did not betray
the presence of the people hiding below, the outlets were over

130 feet away and two of the chimneys vented into the local millers' houses on top of the hill, giving the impression that the smoke came from their own domestic fireplaces. Any intruders who stumbled upon the entrances found themselves lost in a maze of narrow winding corridors, or ambushed when bending double below doorways deliberately set too low.

So well hidden and secure was this underground city that it was in constant use from Roman times until the end of the seventeenth century. Rediscovered in 1887, after a lapse of almost two hundred years, it found a new lease of life in the bloodbath of the twentieth century, serving as the headquarters of English, Canadian and Australian troops in the First World War and of Rommel in the Second. Nevertheless, early fifteenth-century graffiti and coins dating from the reign of Charles VI, which were discovered in the lowest-level chambers and galleries, indicate that the people of the Naours district also fled there in response to Henry V's invasions of Normandy.

The news that Henry was making preparations for his army to march towards Calais was already known as far afield as Boulogne on 6 October, but it was 11 October before the men of that town knew for certain that he had indeed left Harfleur and was heading for Blanche Taque. From the moment of its departure the progress of the English army was observed and the vital information relayed by couriers on horseback to Constable d'Albret and Marshal Boucicaut at Abbeville. It says much for their military leadership and organisation that the English would not take a single town or castle by surprise.

The English army was only two miles outside Harfleur when it came under attack for the first time. As it passed within half a mile of Montivilliers, Colard, sire de Villequier, and twenty-five crossbowmen launched an ambush. It was easily beaten off, but not without casualties: Geoffrey Blake was killed and an esquire, two archers and three cordwainers (leather-workers) were captured.[26] From Montivilliers, the English made their way northwards and slightly eastwards across the Caux plateau towards the town of Fécamp on the Norman coast. This was not the most direct route, but, in the absence of maps and in hostile country, the coastline was the best possible visual guide to enable them to get to Calais and they would stay within a couple of miles of it for as long as possible.

Fécamp, like Montivilliers, was a small town dominated then, as now, by a huge eleventh-century abbey church with the distinctive squat and square Norman tower at its centre. Both had strong links with the English monarchy and with Henry V's own claims to the duchy of Normandy. William the Conqueror's father had rebuilt the abbey of Montivilliers after its destruction by the Vikings and had installed his sister as abbess: the Conqueror himself had celebrated his victory at the battle of Hastings in the abbey church at Fécamp. According to at least one chronicler, Henry had expressed a great desire "to see those lands, whereof he ought to be Lord" and he was now about to get his wish.[27]

The energetic David, sire de Rambures, had anticipated Henry's descent on Fécamp and got there before him. Five years earlier, the town had been the victim of an English sea-raid in which some four hundred houses were burnt and half the population driven out. Perhaps as a result of this attack, the castle was in a state of disrepair, so de Rambures placed military necessity before piety and put a large garrison into the famous abbey: the church, with its rough-hewn exterior walls and great flying buttresses, surrounded by the high walls and towers of the monastery, was just as defensible as any military fortification. And the abbot of Fécamp was likely to have been sympathetic, since he was the brother of Jean, sire d'Estouteville, who had led the defence of Harfleur with Raoul de Gaucourt; in September he had made his own preparations for an English offensive by drawing up an inventory of all the abbey's goods. His efforts were in vain, for Henry V had no intention of engaging in either a siege or an assault. When he made his appearance before the town on 9 October, he merely skirted round it and continued on the road eastwards towards Dieppe. Once again, however, the French garrison was able to pick off a few English stragglers, capturing a man-at-arms, William Bramshulf, and two archers, Edward Legh and John de Rede.[28]

On Friday 11 October the English arrived on the outskirts of Dieppe. They had now travelled some fifty-five miles in three days, and were almost exactly on target for achieving their goal of reaching Calais within eight days. Only five weeks earlier, Master Jean de Bordiu had reported to his native Aquitaine that Dieppe was the next major town on the king's list, scheduled for conquest after the fall of Harfleur.[29] Now, however, Henry gave the place a wide berth and headed inland along the south bank of the river Arques to find a crossing. Four miles away, in the shadow of a spectacular twelfth-century fortress that commanded the length and breadth of the wide valley at the confluence of the tributary rivers Béthune and Varenne, lay the small town of Arques and its bridges. The garrison here had taken the precaution of barricading the narrow bridges, but had not actually destroyed them, so they were still usable.

The presence of such a powerful castle was an indication of the strategic importance of the place and should have deterred any attack. Yet Henry, an experienced soldier and master tactician, had no qualms about forcing a passage under the nose of the garrison. He knew that, although the castle itself was virtually impregnable, the town was its weak point. Unlike the great merchant towns of Normandy and Picardy — Harfleur, Dieppe, Abbeville, Amiens, Péronne, Boulogne — Arques had neither walls nor ramparts to defend itself. If the castle garrison was outnumbered or outmanoeuvred, it could retreat behind the safety of its curtain walls or into its keep: though room might be found for the civilian population, their property was at the mercy of marauders.

It was absolutely necessary that the army should cross the river, so this time Henry V did not shirk a conflict. He ordered his men to take up their battle positions in full view of the castle and made himself conspicuous by appearing in the front ranks. (His banners and coat of arms blazoned across his chest would have marked him out, even if he had not been wearing his helm with its crown.) The garrison made a half-hearted attempt at defiance, lobbing a few gun-stones to prevent him coming any closer, but without inflicting any damage. The news of what had happened to Harfleur had already spread right across the duchy of Normandy and the garrison at Arques had no wish to become martyrs to the king of England's cause. When he sent a deputation to its defenders, threatening to burn the town and the surrounding countryside if they did not permit him free passage, they gave up all pretence of resistance and quickly came to terms. That same day, they handed over the hostages and the bread and wine for his troops which he had demanded as the price of sparing the locality, removed the tree trunks barricading the bridges and the entrance to the town, and allowed the king and his army to pass through to the other side without any impediment.[30]

What happened at Arques was to become the pattern for the remainder of Henry's campaign. He would carefully avoid the major walled towns, but the presence of a castle, no matter how intimidating or well garrisoned, would not deflect him from his planned route.

On 12 October, having spent the night in the fields near Arques, the English recommenced their journey up the coast, making their way towards Eu, "the last town in Normandy." As their scouts approached, some of the garrison sallied out to meet them. What followed was a chivalric encounter worthy of the pages of Froissart. Among the Frenchmen was "a very valiant man-at-arms," the appropriately named Lancelot Pières, who was anxious to demonstrate his prowess against the invaders. He therefore couched his lance under his arm as a sign of challenge, which was accepted by one of the English knights or esquires, who responded by doing the same. The two men charged towards each other, but before Pières could get his blow in, he was himself hit in the stomach with the steel blade of his opponent's lance, which slid between the plates of his armour. Knowing that he was mortally wounded, he did not flinch, but revenged his own death by killing his opponent. Those who were witnesses to this deadly joust of war observed that the two men had clashed with such force that their lances had passed right through each other's body. This exploit won Lancelot Pières a small place in the annals of French chivalry, though his equally deserving opponent died anonymously, and therefore, on his terms, in vain. After this individual encounter, the English scouts succeeded in driving the rest of those involved in the sortie back into the town, inflicting further deaths and injuries, but also incurring some wounds themselves.[31]

Fighting a scouting party was one thing, but when the massed ranks of the main body of the English army advanced towards Eu, the garrison prudently decided to remain behind its great walls. After his success at Arques, Henry determined to try the same tactic again. As his men settled down for the night in the neighbouring towns and villages, he sent messengers to Eu, demanding specified quantities of food and wine in return for not laying waste to the entire district. This had the desired effect. Hostages were handed over, bread and wine were rapidly produced and the troops in the garrison sat on their hands as the English prepared to move off the next day.[32]

So far, the march to Calais had proceeded exactly according to plan. Although the French chroniclers rehearsed the customary chorus that the English had wantonly burnt and destroyed everything in their path[33] (as would have happened on a traditional *chevauchée*), this was patently not the case. The mere threat had been sufficient to bring the indigenous population to heel. The French had behaved as they always did when faced with an English *chevauchée*, retreating behind their fortifications and offering the line of least resistance, in order to get the enemy to move on and out of their neighbourhood as rapidly as possible.

But of course this was no ordinary *chevauchée*. Its objective was to provoke a pitched battle, and some of the prisoners who had been taken along the way now reported that a great French army was poised to fight within the next two days. "But there were different opinions amongst us as to when battle would be joined," the chaplain commented. Some thought that the Armagnac leaders would not dare to leave Rouen and march against them, for fear that the duke of Burgundy would seize the opportunity either to attack them from behind or to return in triumph to Paris. Others believed that whatever their differences in the past, the dukes of Burgundy and Orléans would unite in the face of the English challenge.[34] Although the Peace of Arras had been agreed between the Armagnacs and Burgundians in September 1414, and had been formally concluded and celebrated in Paris in February 1415, John the Fearless had not been happy with its terms. Though it was supposed to offer an amnesty to all involved in the partisan fighting, a royal ordinance of 2 February had unilaterally excluded five hundred of his own Parisian supporters, the Cabochiens, who had been exiled from Paris in 1413. When the duke learnt that his own ambassadors had accepted this, he was furious and reprimanded them severely. The Armagnacs in the dauphin's entourage "are only trying by all the means that they can think of and imagine to bring about the total destruction of us and of ours," he raged; "we inform you that the things that have been done are and will be displeasing to us . . . and we do not want you to proceed with them in any way whatsoever. And if, which God forbid, [the dauphin] . . . remains and persists absolutely in this purpose and there is no possibility of another arrangement honourable for us and ours, we would like you to depart and take leave of him."[35] While the other French princes and their partisans up and down the country took their oaths to abide by the terms of the treaty, the duke of Burgundy remained aloof, insisting that the five hundred Cabochiens should be included in the general amnesty before he would swear himself. It was not until 30 July, only a few days before the English invasion began, that he finally submitted. Even then, he did so conditionally, having a formal document drawn up in secret by papal notaries in which it was stated that his oath was dependent on the dauphin pardoning all his supporters, including the Cabochiens. In the letters he sent to the dauphin, recording his oath, he also included a clause implying that he would only regard it as valid if the Armagnac princes implemented their part of the treaty.[36]

Throughout August, while the English besieged Harfleur, the duke and the dauphin were locked in a dispute about the wording of the oath. The dauphin demanded that it should be unconditional; the duke insisted that all his supporters should be pardoned. The deadlock might have remained unresolved, had it not been for the presence of Henry V and his army in Normandy. The Armagnacs already had their suspicions that the duke was in league with the invaders, but they could not afford to drive him openly into the arms of the English. On 31 August the dauphin finally gave way and issued a royal amnesty to all but forty-five of the Cabochiens. The duke responded by reissuing his letters in September, with the offending contingency clause removed. Nevertheless, he continued to press for the pardon to be extended to the last forty-five throughout the autumn — and also continued to harbour the exiles in his own lands. To outward appearances, the Peace of Arras had at last been formally ratified by all parties, but no one who knew anything of the duke believed that he was fully committed to it.[37]

And of course there were persistent rumours that John the Fearless was in league with the English. Although the offensive and defensive alliance he had suggested to Henry V the previous summer had not come to anything, it seems likely that the duke had indeed made a secret pact with the king that he would not resist an English invasion of France. As we have seen, English envoys were allowed to recruit ships for the campaign in Holland and Zeeland, areas that were within the Burgundian sphere of influence.[38] Contingents of English mercenaries, said to be archers, were present in the Burgundian garrisons of both Soissons and Arras when they were besieged by the Armagnacs in 1414. With typical medieval xenophobia, the English archers at Soissons were accused of betraying the town to the Armagnacs by opening one of the gates, and forty of them were later hanged, though this was more likely to be because they were English and mercenaries, rather than for any betrayal, real or imagined.[39]

In addition to this circumstantial evidence, there is no doubt that the duke of Burgundy was in contact with the English throughout the summer and autumn of 1415. In July Burgundian ambassadors spent sixteen days in England, negotiating an alliance at the very time when the final embassy of the Armagnac archbishop of Bourges failed to secure peace: members of his party observed a herald in the Burgundian livery among the crowds at Winchester as they left. (Another Burgundian herald, the future chronicler Jean le Févre, was to accompany the English army throughout the Agincourt campaign.) On 10 August, the day before the invasion fleet sailed, in what must have been one of his last acts before leaving, Henry appointed

Master Philip Morgan, a highly skilled lawyer, to make final arrangements for an alliance with the duke. Morgan left London on 19 August and did not return until 19 December; the exchequer accounts refer to him as an "ambassador on secret business to the duke of Burgundy" and he was evidently successful for "letters of peace with the duke of Burgundy sealed with his own seal" were deposited in the exchequer on 10 October, fifteen days before Agincourt.[40]

John the Fearless had not gone to the assistance of Henry V at Harfleur, as some Armagnacs had suspected he would. Yet rumours were rife throughout Europe that, while the dauphin and the Armagnacs were preoccupied in resisting the English, the duke intended to raise his own force and march on Paris. As we have just seen, there were those in the English army who believed this would happen as soon as the dauphin moved from Rouen to engage them in battle. In Paris itself, where the duke had always enjoyed great popular support, the citizens were in a state of high excitement anticipating his return. The wife of one of the exiled Cabochiens received a letter from her husband the very week that Harfleur fell, telling her to get twenty crowns and meet him at a certain town on 20 October because the duke of Burgundy would be there with a large army. Not having the money herself, she borrowed it from a relative, who promptly informed the authorities. Terrified of another bloody revolt, they did not wait for the king's order but immediately changed all the city's officers, barricaded the gates and made preparations for a siege. Though this proved to be a false alarm, it was a credible enough threat to be reported as a fact in Venice that the duke had indeed entered Paris again.[41]

In this highly charged and deeply distrustful atmosphere, it was not surprising that the dauphin and his advisors had tried to persuade the dukes of Burgundy and Orléans to send their men to the muster at Rouen, but to remain at home themselves. John the Fearless penned a caustic reply. It was addressed to the king rather than the dauphin, and though it was couched in the deferential terms due from a faithful subject, it was pregnant with menace. Despite his deep loyalty to the crown, the duke declared he could not forget the insult proffered to him by asking him to remain at home when every other prince of the blood had been summoned to the assistance of France. His honour, which he valued more than anything else on earth, was impugned by this request. Nevertheless, it was the duty of all good friends and subjects to lend a hand in this crisis, so he intended to save the kingdom from its peril and uphold his own position as the premier duke of France by sending far more than the five hundred men-at-arms and three hundred archers who had been requested. The letter was accompanied by two others, written in a similar vein, by the duke's leading vassals.[42]

In the meantime, the duke had also written to all his subjects, in Picardy and elsewhere, ordering them to make themselves ready to accompany him when he sent for them, but also specifically forbidding them from going "at the command of any other lord, whoever he might be."[43] This order could be interpreted two ways. Either it was intended to ensure that, if those of the Burgundian allegiance did go to war, it was only under his personal command or, alternatively, that they did not go to war at all. If the duke really had made a non-interference pact with Henry V, then he needed to prevent his own men from rising in defence of their homeland. Whatever the reason, his order put the nobility of Picardy in an impossible situation. They would have to choose between obeying their king or their duke.

Since they had failed to respond to the issuing of the general call to arms, a number of nobles from Picardy received personally addressed royal commands to come with all their forces to assist the dauphin, on pain of incurring the king's indignation.[44] When this, too, failed to bring them to heel, the royal orders were reissued on 20 September in terms that left their recipients in no doubt that they had incurred the king's grave displeasure. "Through the negligence and delays you and others have made in executing our orders and for lack of help and aid, our noble and good and loyal subjects within the town of Harfleur, despite making a very great and notable defence, have been compelled to render the town by violence, because they could no longer resist the oppression and force of our enemies." The blame for the fall of Harfleur was thus placed squarely on the shoulders of the local nobility, despite the rather poignant fact that the town

had not yet formally surrendered and its defenders were still forlornly waiting the answer to their final plea for aid.

The new order commanded, "on the faith and loyalty that
you owe us and on pain of all that you can forfeit," that proclamations were to be made everywhere and "so often that no one
can pretend ignorance"; anyone who refused to go to the
dauphin immediately, armed and ready to fight, should be
imprisoned, have their goods seized and have men billeted upon
them at their expense. Any town which could spare any
"engines, cannon and artillery" was to send them also, without
delay.[45] The fall of Harfleur did what the English invasion had
failed to do: it galvanised French officialdom into action. Men
who had been torn between their loyalty to the king and to the
duke now rose in defence of their homeland. As the English
made their way across Normandy into Picardy, the great French
army rumoured to be gathering at Rouen became a reality.

CHAPTER THIRTEEN

CROSSING THE SOMME

Henry had intended to cross the Somme in exactly the same place as had his great-grandfather, Edward III, in 1346, on the campaign that culminated in the spectacular English victory at Crécy. The old Roman ford at Blanche Taque lay between the mouth of the river and the town of Abbeville, nine miles inland. The waters here were tidal, but the great advantage was that the ford itself was wide enough for twelve men to cross at one time. Unfortunately for the English, the French knew their history too and had anticipated that their opponents would take this route. Two days before the English reached Blanche Taque, the news that they were heading there had already spread as far north as Boulogne, and preparations for their reception were well advanced.[1]

On Sunday 13 October, when Henry's army was still some six miles away from Blanche Taque, the men of the vanguard captured a French prisoner, who was brought before Sir John Cornewaille for interrogation. He turned out to be a Gascon gentleman in the service of Charles d'Albret, whom he had left earlier that day at Abbeville. Further questioning revealed that d'Albret had a force of six thousand men with him and was waiting to obstruct their passage; what is more, the ford itself had been barricaded with sharpened stakes to make it impassable.[2]

The prisoner was hastily brought before the king himself and reinterrogated, but he stuck stubbornly to his story and even pledged his life on its truth. Convinced of his honesty, Henry called an immediate halt to the march and summoned his barons to an urgently convened council meeting. After two hours of debate, the decision was taken to abandon the attempt to cross at Blanche Taque. They would have to find a safer, unguarded crossing further upstream. If necessary they would have to go to the very head of the river, which was said to be sixty miles away.

This was the first major setback of the entire campaign, and morale among the rank and file, which had been high as they marched unopposed through Normandy and into Picardy, now began to falter. Ever since they had left Fécamp they had seen tantalising glimpses of the long vista of white cliffs lining the Norman coast as far as Cap Gris-Nez, knowing that the safety of Calais was a mere thirteen miles beyond that point. Never was the old adage "so near, yet so far" so true. Now, instead of the swift, straight road to their destination, they faced a long and uncertain journey, in the knowledge that their rations could not last out and that battle was becoming increasingly likely. It is not difficult to imagine the despair that the sight of the bay of the Somme must have instilled in the English. It was not just its width (more than a mile across at its narrowest point between le Crotoy and St Valery), but the vast and desolate expanse of marshland stretching as far as the eye could see to the west, north and east. As they were about to discover, these marshes were as impenetrable a barrier as the river itself.[3]

There was no point in lingering at Blanche Taque, so Henry gave the order to move and the army set off again, turning east and taking the south bank of the Somme towards Abbeville. In preparation for their approach, this ancient capital of Ponthieu, which had already twice suffered English occupation, in 1340 and 1369, had powerfully reinforced its defences: 12 cannon, almost 2200 gun-stones and vast quantities of gunpowder had been installed, together with a large contingent from the army gathering at Rouen. This was no simple garrison like that at Harfleur. Some of the greatest names in France were now stationed at Abbeville, headed by Constable d'Albret, Marshal

Boucicaut, the count of Vendôme, who was grand-master of the king's household, Jacques de Châtillon, sire de Dampierre, who was the admiral of France, Arthur, count of Richemont, who was the duke of Brittany's brother, and Jean, duke of Alençon. Fore-warned of this by their Gascon prisoner, the English duly main-tained a respectful distance, skirting round Abbeville and settling for the night at Bailleul-en-Vimeu three miles to the south.[4]

Next morning, they changed tack, cutting north-eastwards in the hope of using the bridge at Pont Rémy. There they not only found that the bridge and the various causeways across the Somme had been dismantled by the local garrison, but, for the first time, they saw a sizeable force of Frenchmen gathered on the opposite bank. Though the English did not know it, they were facing a company led by the father and brothers of Raoul de Gaucourt, and in their eagerness to avenge the shame inflicted on him they were drawn up in full battle order, "as if prepared to engage us there and then." Even the chaplain, who was timid by nature, could see that this was merely posturing: "the fact that the river at that point had a broad marsh on both sides prevented either of us from coming any closer, so that not one of us, even had he sworn to do so, could have inflicted injury on the other."[5]

There now began a deadly game of cat and mouse. As the English pushed on further and further into the interior of France, searching with increasing desperation for somewhere to cross the river, they were shadowed on the opposite bank by a French force, led by Boucicaut and d'Albret, which was deter-mined to prevent their passage. "At that time we thought of nothing else but this," the chaplain wrote:

> that, after the eight days assigned for the march had expired and our provisions had run out, the enemy, craftily hastening on ahead and laying waste the countryside in advance, would impose on us, hungry as we should be, a really dire need of food, and at the head of the river, if God did not provide otherwise, would, with their great and countless host and the engines of war and devices available to them, overwhelm us, so very few as we were and made faint by great weariness and weak from lack of food.

On 15 October — the eighth day of their march and the day that they should have reached Calais — the English were almost thirty-five miles away from their planned coastal route and every step was taking them further away from their destination. Tired, hungry and dispirited, the English could only pray that the Blessed Virgin and St George, under whose banners and protection they marched, would intercede for them with the Supreme Judge, and deliver them from the swords of their enemy. Dreams of achieving glory, conquest, plunder had all been forgotten. Only one hope remained: that they would eventually get safely to Calais.[6] That day they made another detour to avoid the great Burgundian city of Amiens, capital of Picardy, with its network of little canals and its garden suburbs set in the midst of fens. Did Henry V recall, as he observed the soaring white walls and pinnacles of its glorious thirteenth-century cathedral, that his own great-grandfather, Edward III, had once done homage for Aquitaine to Philippe VI of France in that very place? If he did, the irony that it was the same unresolved quarrel that had brought him to Amiens eighty-six years later cannot have escaped him.

The following day, they pushed on as far as the little town or village of Boves, almost five miles south-east of the centre of Amiens. The town, with its all-important bridges over the river Avre, a tributary of the Somme, lay at the foot of a chalk cliff that was crowned by the white walls of a great twelfth-century castle belonging to Ferri, count of Vaudémont, a younger son of the duke of Lorraine. Although he was a Burgundian by allegiance, he was one of the local nobility who had belatedly responded to the king's summons to arms and, with a force of three hundred men, was now stationed with Boucicaut's army on the other side of the Somme.[7]

Boves was small enough for Henry V to be able to hold it to ransom, as he had done the towns of Arques and Eu; again, there was a military imperative to do so, as he needed to cross the Avre over the town bridges. Once more he sent his messengers to a parley and it would appear that, whatever the loyalties of Ferri de Vaudémont, the captain he had left in charge of the castle garrison was more favourably inclined to the English than his master. Not only did he agree to ransom the village and its surrounding vineyards from burning by meeting the usual demands for bread and wine, he even allowed the army to be billeted within the village overnight.

The garrison was only able to provide eight baskets of bread to feed the six thousand, though the baskets were large enough to need two men to carry each one. There had been a plentiful harvest of grapes, however, so the place was overflowing with wine. The English would not have been human if they had been able to resist such a temptation. They made straight for the winepresses and the barrels full of new vintage, and started to help themselves to this unexpected bounty. While some of his commanders regarded this behaviour with indulgence, believing it to be a much-deserved reward after all their labours and privations, the king eventually called a halt. When someone asked him why, and remarked that the men were only trying to refill their bottles, Henry replied that he did not mind the bottles, but that most of the men were making bottles out of their own stomachs, which did concern him. In the heart of hostile territory and living daily, if not hourly, under the threat of attack, he could not afford to have his army incapacitated through drink. They were vulnerable enough as it was.[8]

Before they left Boves, the following day, Thursday 17 October, Henry had a further conversation with the captain of the castle. Two of his men-at-arms were now so sick that they were unable to continue on the journey. Henry did not wish simply to abandon them to their fate and the captain courteously agreed that he would take them in and look after them. Having handed over two horses in lieu of payment, Henry gathered the rest of his army together, and once more took to the road.[9]

After crossing the Avre at Boves, the English returned to the banks of the Somme to resume their search for an unguarded bridge or ford. It was a forlorn hope. Boucicaut and d'Albret were patrolling the opposite bank and every town and castle was on a state of high alert. As the English passed by the walled town of Corbie, about ten miles east of the centre of Amiens, the garrison made a sortie and in the skirmish that followed, the standard of Aquitaine, which was carried by Hugh Stafford,

Lord Bourchier, was captured. This was the greatest disgrace that could befall any standard-bearer, whose chivalric duty it was to die in its defence. Fortunately, one of his kinsmen, a young esquire called John Bromley, who was a groom of the king's chamber, came to Bourchier's assistance, recovered the standard and succeeded in driving the French back towards Corbie, killing two of them and capturing two men-at-arms.[10]

This minor success was not enough to gain the bridge over the Somme, which was too well guarded to force a crossing, but the capture of the men-at-arms proved to be a significant stroke of luck: when they were interrogated, they disclosed that the French commanders had taken prudent measures against the huge numbers of archers they knew were in the king's host. They had assigned "many hundreds" of men-at-arms to special squadrons and mounted them on heavily armoured horses; their specific task was to ride down the English archers, breaking up their formations and reducing the effectiveness of their massed fire-power. On learning this, Henry issued a proclamation throughout the army that every archer was immediately to make himself a six-foot-long wooden stake, sharpened at both ends, and carry it with him. As soon as the French drew near to engage them in battle, the archers were to take up their stations in staggered rows, so that the man on the row behind stood between the two in front of him. Each archer was then to drive one end of his stake into the ground in front of him in such a fashion that the other end was above waist-height and pointing towards the enemy. When the French cavalry caught sight of the stakes as they charged, they would either be forced to withdraw or run the risk of being impaled.[11]

This was not a new tactic. The "hedgehog" had been a standard defensive manoeuvre for European infantrymen fighting against cavalry since at least the beginning of the fourteenth century, though they used their steel-tipped pikes, rather than improvised wooden stakes, to create the bristling hedgehog effect. The first recorded example of wooden stakes being used specifically to protect archers, however, was comparatively recent and it was an eastern innovation. In 1396 a force of French and Burgundian crusaders had come to grief against the invading

Ottoman Turks at the battle of Nicopolis in what is now Bulgaria. The Turks had hidden their foot archers in a dip in the landscape and behind a screen of lightly armed cavalry. Tempted by what appeared to be an outnumbered and outarmed force, the crusaders had charged the Turkish cavalry, whose ranks gave way to reveal a field of stakes behind which the archers had taken cover. Unable to check their charge, the crusaders were easily overwhelmed and slaughtered. Three of the veterans of this battle, who were captured and later ransomed, were none other than the leader of the crusade, John the Fearless, the future duke of Burgundy, who was then count of Nevers, Raoul de Gaucourt, the defender of Harfleur, and Marshal Boucicaut, who was now jointly commanding the forces opposing Henry V.[12] So many of the leading nobility of France were killed or captured at Nicopolis that news of the disaster and how it had occurred spread swiftly throughout Europe. Whether the idea of improvising stakes to protect the English archers was Henry's own or came from Edward, duke of York, as some chroniclers suggest, its genius lay not in complete innovation, but in marrying two established but different precedents: the Turkish use of stakes to protect their archers and the tightly packed formation of the European pikemen.

The French prisoners captured at Corbie may have given Henry other information just as important as that which prompted the adoption of stakes to protect the archers. Some time before he left Corbie, the king learnt that the French army patrolling the crossings from the opposite bank of the Somme was heading for Péronne, a fortified town at the top of a lazy loop in the river. It was therefore extremely unlikely that he would be able to find an unguarded passage anywhere between Corbie and Péronne; even if he did, the French would be swiftly upon him, either attacking him at his weakest as he crossed, or forcing him on to the defensive once he had. The choice of battlefield would be theirs.

It was at this point that Henry took another calculated gamble. In all probability, he was going to have to follow the river all the way to its source before he could turn north and west again towards Calais. Instead of continuing to follow the Somme in all its meanderings, he therefore decided to cut directly across the open country between Corbie and Nesle. Though he risked missing a potentially viable crossing, he would reduce his journey by at least ten miles and bypass the French troops waiting at Péronne. What is more, by doing the unexpected, he stood a chance of catching the French unawares and finding an unguarded crossing further upstream, especially as he would disappear from their sight for perhaps twenty-four hours.

The English army therefore turned south-east and started the long climb up to the Santerre plateau. For many miles now, the journey had become increasingly arduous. The gentle undulations of the Caux peninsula and the flat, featureless landscape of the lower reaches of the Somme had given way to heavily wooded hills and the long, steep ridges that are now associated with the battlefields and trenches of the First World War. The easier terrain of the wide and flat Somme valley was still inaccessible: recent October rains had swollen the river and made the marshes even more treacherous, forcing the army to take the higher, harder ground. As the English reached the plateau above Corbie there was a dramatic change in landscape. A vast expanse of seemingly endless plain now stretched out before them. There were no landmarks to guide them, except the shimmering white walls of Amiens Cathedral rising ghost-like in the distance behind them, and the occasional spire of a village church or a clump of woodland silhouetted against the horizon. For the ordinary rank and file, totally reliant on the king and his officers for leadership in this alien and hostile country, which was so unlike anything they had ever seen at home, it must have been a bewildering and frightening experience. It was also a test of their faith in that leadership.

By the evening of Thursday 17 October, the English army had pushed on another twelve or so miles from Corbie and was encamped between the hamlets of Harbonnières and Vauvillers.[13] One of the most famous incidents of the Agincourt campaign now occurred. That morning, in the fields outside Corbie, an English soldier had been brought before the king, charged with the offence of stealing from one of the village churches a pyx, the box which contained the consecrated bread from the Eucharist.

There had not been time to deal with him then, but now he was put on trial. The pyx, which he had hidden in his sleeve, was produced. The chaplain, who knew about such things, remarked that it was only made of cheap copper-gilt, although the thief had probably mistaken it for gold. It was a mistake that was to cost him his life. He was found guilty of acting "in God's despite and contrary to royal decree" and, at the king's orders, was promptly hanged from a tree in full view of his fellows.[14] Significantly, it is the only recorded example of anyone breaking the king's ordinances throughout the entire campaign.

For the last few days of the march, the increasingly weary English had covered only thirteen or fourteen miles a day. Encumbered with their stakes, progress was inevitably slower, but they were also tired and hungry, reduced to drinking water and eking out their last rations of dried meat with hazelnuts gathered from the hedgerows. By the evening of Friday 18 October, they had reached the neighbourhood of Nesle and decided to camp for the night in the small hamlets scattered outside its fortified walls. Henry sent in his customary message but, for the first time, met with defiance. The townspeople not only refused to supply bread and wine but draped red cloth over their walls, a mysterious gesture whose origin is as unclear as its meaning is obvious. Such an insult could not be allowed to go unpunished and Henry ordered that all the hamlets in the vicinity of Nesle should be burnt to the ground the following morning.[15]

Before first light, the Virgin and St George answered the prayers of the English with the news that a suitable crossing of the Somme had been found only three miles to the north-east of Nesle. It is unclear how this information came to Henry V. It is possible that the English scouts uncovered its existence on one of their forays but, given the timing, it was more probably one of the villagers who decided to reveal its whereabouts in the hope of saving his home and livelihood from the flames.[16] Mounted patrols were immediately dispatched to test the passage and find out the depth of the water and the speed of the current. What they found was not ideal, but it was possible.

There were actually two crossings, both fords, less than two miles apart, at the neighbouring villages of Béthencourt-sur-

Somme and Voyennes. They were approached by long, narrow causeways that the French, under instruction from the ubiquitous Boucicaut and d'Albret, had broken up in the middle "in such a way that it was scarcely possible, and then only with difficulty, to ride across the broken parts in single file." At their deepest points, the waters of the fords came slightly higher than a horse's belly, but a marsh a mile wide had to be negotiated before reaching the Somme. These disadvantages were outweighed by the fact that the crossings were unguarded. The men of St Quentin, who had been entrusted with the task, had been caught by surprise. What is more, there was no sign of the French army that had dogged their footsteps for so long. The gamble of the short-cut had paid off.[17]

Early on the morning of Saturday 19 October, under the watchful eye of Sir John Cornewaille and Sir Gilbert Umfraville, the archers of the vanguard began to make their way in single file and on foot across the broken causeways, holding their bows and quivers full of arrows aloft to keep them dry. After they had scrambled onto the opposite bank and taken up a position to protect the rest, Cornewaille, Umfraville and their standard-bearers went over, followed by the men-at-arms, also in single file and on foot. Only when they were all safely across were their horses sent over to join them.

While the vanguard was completing this difficult and dangerous manoeuvre, the rest of the English army was busy pulling down the nearest houses and taking away any ladders, doors and shutters they could find. Once a secure bridgehead had been established on the other side of the Somme, providing covering fire if required, they set to work repairing and rebuilding the gaps in the broken causeways with the wood they had found, together with bundles of sticks, straw and any other materials they could lay their hands on. By one o'clock in the afternoon, the causeways were passable by three men riding abreast, and the full-scale operation of crossing the Somme began. Although it was not ideal that the army should be divided and separated by a distance of almost two miles, it was imperative that the crossing be effected as quickly as possible. The king therefore ordered that the slower baggage should cross by one causeway,

probably that at Béthencourt where the lie of the land was flat-
ter, and his fighting men by the other.[18]

There was an obvious danger that so many men trying to use
so narrow a causeway could result in chaos: they were tightly
packed together, eager to get across and, if they came under fire
from the enemy, might panic in the crush. Foreseeing these dangers, the king stationed himself on one side of the entrance to
the ford and a couple of hand-picked men on the other to maintain discipline. His stern presence proved sufficient to quell any
unruliness before it began and both the main body of the army
and the rearguard reached the opposite bank of the Somme
without loss or major incident. Nevertheless, it was after nightfall before the operation was complete and the last men and
horses came safely ashore.[19]

It was impossible for such a huge logistical exercise to take
place without attracting attention from the enemy. According to
the chaplain, even before a hundred men had waded across the
river, small groups of French cavalry began to emerge from the
hamlets on the northern side. They sent their swifter outriders
on ahead to assess the situation, while the rest made belated
attempts to join together into an opposing force. Before they
could do this effectively, they were attacked by the mounted
patrols of the vanguard, adding to their confusion. By the time
they had gathered in sufficient numbers to risk an approach, the
English bridgehead was secure and men were pouring across the
river to reinforce it. "For this reason," the chaplain remarked
with obvious satisfaction, "the French, taking up a position at a
distance and having estimated our capacity to stand firm and
their own incapacity to resist, abandoned the place and van-
ished from our sight."[20]

The English spent a cheerful night lodging in and around the
hamlets of Athies and Monchy-Lagache, their spirits raised by
the boldness and efficiency with which they had so unexpectedly accomplished the river crossing. "We thought it a matter of
great rejoicing on our part," the chaplain wrote, "that we had
shortened our march by, as many reckoned, about an eight days'
journey. And we were of the firm hope that the enemy army, the

army which was said to be waiting for us at the head of the river, would be disinclined to follow after us to do battle."[21]

These hopes were dealt a blow the following morning, Sunday 20 October, when three heralds arrived in the camp with a message from the dukes of Orléans and Bourbon and Constable d'Albret. Though the French cavalry had failed to prevent the English crossing the Somme, they had evidently succeeded in getting information through to their masters very quickly. The letters that the heralds now delivered to Henry were couched in the courtly terms of a jousting challenge. Orléans, Bourbon and d'Albret well knew, they said,

> that ever since he had left his own realm, his desire had been to have a battle against the French. And so, they, being three princes born of the blood royal of France, were ready to relieve him and fulfil his desire and perform that which he sought; and, if he would care to name a place and a date where he would wish to fight them, they would be happy to meet him there; representatives of each side would choose and notify [the actual site] so that it did not offer any physical advantage to one or the other party, provided that this had the approval of the king, their sovereign lord.[22]

To modern eyes it seems strange, absurd even, for an invaded nation to give away the critically important military advantages of choosing their own time and place to give battle, especially to a vulnerable enemy that had been forced far from its path and was short of men and supplies. But like Henry V's challenge to the dauphin, this was an honoured chivalric custom of the time. Similarly, the fact that the terminology was interchangeable with that of a challenge to perform a joust or feat of arms — even to the point of referring to Henry's *"désir"* to do battle and the French princes' wish to relieve him of it — did not mean that this was a game or insincere posturing. The Frenchmen were quite serious.

More interesting than the challenge itself is the fact that it was issued in the names of the dukes of Orléans and Bourbon and the constable of France. All three men enjoyed eminent chivalric reputations. Charles d'Orléans, who had defied the royal command to send his troops but remain at home himself, was now twenty years old, a jouster of note, as well as a talented writer of courtly love poems. Jean, duke of Bourbon, was thirty-four or thirty-five, and, like d'Orléans, had acquired considerable military experience in the recent wars: only a few months previously, he had demonstrated his devotion to knightly ideals by founding the Order of the *Fer du Prisonnier*, of which Raoul de Gaucourt was a member.[23] Charles d'Albret, at forty-six, was the oldest of the challengers. As discussed earlier, by virtue of his office as constable of France he was a veteran military commander, but in his younger days he had also been an ardent jouster and in 1400 he was one of the founding members of Boucicaut's Order of the White Lady on the Green Shield.[24]

That men of this calibre should have issued a challenge to battle is not surprising, but the responsibility for doing so should actually have belonged to the dauphin, who was not only a higher representative of the French royal house but also the king's formally constituted captain-general. The fact that the three men issued the challenge in his place might almost be seen as a public reproach to the dauphin, not only for failing to do so himself, but also for his craven dereliction of chivalric duty in not responding to Henry's personal challenge to individual combat. That duty his commanders had now taken upon themselves, in order to uphold the honour of France.

Henry's response to the challenge was everything that the dauphin's was not. He did not keep the heralds waiting but received them "ceremoniously and honourably," reading their letters "with great joy" and rewarding them with generous gifts. Although he did not entrust them with a reply, he did send two of his own heralds to the French princes to tell them that "since leaving the town of Harfleur, he had striven and was striving daily to reach his realm of England, and not hiding himself away in walled towns or fortresses. So, if the three princes of France wished to fight him, it was not necessary to pick a day nor a place; for every day they could find him in the open fields without any difficulty."[25] It was a lesson in the art of the courte-

ous and bold response which the dauphin had singularly failed
to learn.

As a result of the visit by the French heralds, Henry had to
anticipate that he might be forced to a battle as early as the next
day. His men had been travelling in battledress — suits of
armour for the men-at-arms and padded jerkins and kettle hats
for the archers — ever since they left Harfleur. He now gave
orders that all those entitled to wear coats of arms should put
them on before they left their lodgings the next day, this being a
symbol to a potential opponent that they were armed, ready to
fight and would not retreat. As he had done at Harfleur, he also
made it his own task to go round the army, inspecting their
preparations, praising where he found things in good order and
offering encouragement to those who needed it.[26]

On Monday 21 October, the English army set out from
Athies and Monchy-Lagache, fully expecting at any moment to
find the armed might of France blocking the way to Calais. Tension was high, especially as their route took them uncomfort-
ably close to Péronne. The town was heavily fortified and
enclosed within a deep narrow moat and massive red-brick
walls; at its centre lay a formidable castle with huge round stone
towers, built by Philip Auguste at the end of the twelfth century,
punctuating its ancient red-brick curtain walls. It was here that
Boucicaut and d'Albret had stationed themselves after following
the English from Abbeville.

There was a nervous moment when, as the English skirted the
town's walls at a safe distance to their left, a party of French
cavalry made a sudden sortie, perhaps in the hope of acting as a
decoy to draw them within range of their artillery. Such was the
discipline imposed on the English army that they did not
respond to this temptation, and a small force of their own
mounted men was able to put the French to flight, though not
without loss: a man-at-arms from the earl of Suffolk's retinue
was captured.

A mile beyond Péronne Henry's troops came across a sight
that struck dread into their hearts. The muddy roads were heavily rutted and churned up, indicating that many thousands of

Frenchmen had passed that way before them. The message was clear: Constable d'Albret and Marshal Boucicaut had not remained walled up in Péronne but had gone ahead to choose the site for battle. The poor timorous chaplain was quite overcome by this sight. "And the rest of us in the army (for I will say nothing of those in command), fearing battle to be imminent, raised our hearts and eyes to heaven, crying out, with voices expressing our inmost thoughts, that God would have pity on us and, of His ineffable goodness, turn away from us the violence of the French."[27]

For three whole days the English continued their march towards Calais, striking out in a north-westerly direction[28] to compensate for the long detour they had been forced to make to cross the Somme. Throughout that time, they never caught a glimpse of the enemy. Despite their lack of food and drink, the increasingly hilly terrain and the unrelenting rain and bitter winds that now made every step an effort, they plodded doggedly onwards, crossing the river Ancre at Miraumont on Tuesday 22 October, turning northwards at Beauquesne, bypassing the town of Doullens the next day (no doubt sending the country people scurrying into the sanctuary of the underground city of nearby Naours as they did so) and crossing the river Grouches beneath the walls of the count of St Pol's great castle at Lucheux. That night they camped out in several hamlets between Bonnières and Frévent, the latter having been taken by the vanguard, in preparation for crossing the river Canche the following morning. The king, however, accidentally rode past the village selected by his scouts for his own lodgings. Even though he was within a bowshot of the place, he refused to turn back. He was wearing his coat of arms and to retreat, even for such an innocuous reason, would be to dishonour them.[29]

On the next day, Thursday 24 October, after the English had made their way west of the town of St Pol, and were descending the steep valley down to the next river crossing at Blangy, the scouts and mounted patrols brought news to the king that he, probably alone of all his men, had been longing to hear. A French army, many thousands strong, was only three miles away on the other side of the river. A battle was now inevitable, and if the

English were not to be caught at a disadvantage, it was imperative that they should cross the river Ternoise as quickly as possible. Six knights from the vanguard were sent ahead to find out
whether the ford at Blangy was guarded, and when they reported that it was not, Henry gave orders to proceed with all
possible haste.

Having crossed the river, the English had to negotiate the
steep hillside facing them. This, too, they achieved without
significant incident, but as they emerged over the crest of the
hill and onto the plateau before them, the view was dreadful:
massed ranks of the French army, marching in battle order with
pennons flying, were streaming out of the valley to their right
and taking up their position "like a countless swarm of locusts"
in a broad field half a mile in front of them. The road to Calais
was blocked. "Their numbers," the chaplain noted grimly,
"[were] so great as not to be even comparable with ours." This
was not just the relatively small group that had shadowed their
footsteps from Abbeville along the banks of the Somme. That
army had now been joined by the belatedly mobilised force of
the general call to arms, the fruit of the seed that had been growing for so many weeks at Rouen.[30]

Yet it was not quite the full military might of France.
Although many of his subjects had eventually responded to
Charles VI's summons, John the Fearless was still several hundred miles away in Burgundy, as he had been since at least the
beginning of September. His imminent arrival in Flanders had
long been expected. His son Philippe, count of Charolais, had
written to the Flemish town of Lille on 10 October, for instance,
stating categorically that "my father has recently informed me
of his departure with all his power to advance against the
English in the service of the king." Whether the count knew it or
not, this was simply untrue. The letter was merely a sop thrown
to the unfortunate inhabitants of Lille (who stood in the way of
the English march from Harfleur to Calais), in an attempt to
persuade them that their duke had not altogether abandoned
them to their fate. Two days later, John the Fearless sent an
embassy to Charles VI, again announcing his mobilisation and
impending arrival. Instead, he simply remained in Burgundy, in

the company of Henry V's secret envoy, Philip Morgan, waiting to see what would happen and hoping to seize his chance to march on Paris.[31] Burgundian chroniclers, especially those writing during the literary golden age of Philippe's reign, had the unenviable task of explaining away the absence of both father and son from Agincourt. Most got round the charges of treachery by declaring that John the Fearless had been "forbidden to come,"[32] while his nineteen-year-old son, "who desired with all his heart to be present, in person, at the battle," had had to be physically restrained from joining the French army. His father had ordered that he was not to go, they said, and charged three knights, the sires de Chanteville, de Roubaix and de Laviéville, with the responsibility of ensuring that he did not. "I have heard it said of the comte de Charrollois," le Févre reported, "that even when he reached the age of sixty-seven, he still regretted that he had not had the good fortune to be at the battle, whether he had died or lived."[33] It was certainly a useful gloss to put on an otherwise inexcusably shameful dereliction of duty.

While Philip Morgan, the English secret envoy, ensured that the duke of Burgundy kept to the terms of his non-interference agreement with Henry V, others were playing a similar role with the duke of Brittany. On 28 July, shortly before he sailed for France, Henry had appointed Master John Hovyngham and Simon Flete to conduct "secret business" with the duke, and truces between England and Brittany were proclaimed during the first week of the siege of Harfleur. On 23 August Hovyngham and Flete left London for Brittany and, like Morgan, did not return until December.[34] The coincidence of these two missions to Henry's only French allies during his invasion of their realm is too striking to be ignored. Though Hovyngham and Flete were ultimately successful in trying to persuade the duke of Brittany to remain neutral, they had the more difficult task because he had less to gain than John the Fearless. (His ambitions were limited to increasing the independence of his duchy, rather than controlling the crown of France.)[35]

Two other French dukes were also absent from the battle: Jean, duke of Berry, and Louis, duke of Anjou, both of whom remained at Rouen and did not advance with the rest of the

French army to Amiens. The duke of Berry was seventy-five and his advanced age was sufficient to excuse him an active role in the fighting, but as the uncle of Charles VI, his seniority gave him unusual authority among his warring nephews and great-nephews and would surely have been useful in the councils on the field of battle. Louis d'Anjou had no such excuse, though no one seems to have blamed him in the same way that they later did the dukes of Burgundy and Brittany. Perhaps that was because Berry and Anjou were intended to remain at Rouen as a form of rearguard. They had a small force with them and their presence might have been sufficient to prevent the English retreating, if confronted by the larger army further north. The more likely reason appears to be that they were there simply to protect Charles VI and the dauphin. The royal council that met at Rouen and decided to give battle to the English had also determined that neither the king nor his eldest son was to be there. The duke of Berry, remembering the fate of his father, Jean II, who had been captured by the English at the battle of Poitiers in 1356 and spent many years in prison in England, had argued strongly against giving battle at all. He was, according to his own herald, furious with the dukes of Orléans and Bourbon and Charles d'Albret for issuing their challenge to Henry V and refused to allow the king to leave Rouen. "He said it would be better to lose the battle only, rather than both king and battle."[36]

Given that it was obvious that Charles VI's mental state would render him a liability on the battlefield, the eighteen-year-old heir to the throne should have been the natural choice to lead the army, even if in name only. Henry V had, after all, been actively fighting campaigns in Wales since his early teens and had taken part in a pitched battle before his seventeenth birthday. But Louis de Guienne was not an inspirational figure, least of all one that the peers of France could look to for leadership. "He had a pleasant face," the registrar of the Paris Parlement observed, "was tall enough, but fat in his body, heavy and slow, and not at all agile." The reason for the dauphin's portly frame, according to the monk of St Denis, was the fact that he was indolent and not much given to the practice of arms. He loved to wear jewels and rich clothes, did not mix in a friendly fashion with other lords, unlike his father, and was not affable even to those of his own household. He would not brook any criticism, despite his many faults, which included turning night into day by dining at three or four in the afternoon when he awoke, supping at midnight and falling into bed at dawn. Those who knew him said that if he had lived much longer, he would have surpassed all other contemporary princes in the extraordinary extravagance of his clothes, in the excessive number of his horses and his retinue, and in his showy generosity to the Church. In summary, he was the absolute antithesis of Henry V and not someone to whom the other princes of the blood would willingly defer.[37]

Even if the dauphin had been of a more martial nature, there were two other reasons that might have explained the decision to keep him away from the battle. The first was entirely practical: the personal risk was too high. Christine de Pizan accepted that "there is no doubt that knights and men-at-arms and the whole army would have greater courage in fighting, seeing their lord in his place, ready to live and die with them," but even she argued that it was better for him to be absent, because "no one can foresee to which side God will give the good fortune of victory." If a king or prince was killed, taken prisoner or fled, it was a loss and dishonour not just to himself, but to all his subjects and his country.[38]

The second reason for keeping the dauphin safely at Rouen with his father was that the Armagnacs in the royal council had no wish to take either of them into the lion's den. For them, the lion was not Henry V but John the Fearless, and once Henry V had crossed the Somme and continued his journey to Calais, he was marching into the heart of Burgundian territory. Everyone knew that the duke had been recruiting an army and his arrival at its head was still expected on a daily basis. Many believed that he was in alliance with the English and feared that he would join forces with them, especially if tempted by the prospect of crushing an Armagnac army, led by the king of France and his own son-in-law, the dauphin. This spectre was made more serious by the prospect that any conflict would take place in the duke's lands, which were still smarting from the brutal Armagnac campaign of the previous year. No one knew what might happen. If left in the comparative safety of Rouen, the king and dauphin could swiftly return down the Seine to Paris in the event of an Anglo-Burgundian partnership taking to the field.

So it happened that the thousands of Frenchmen who had willingly answered the call to arms in defence of their country found themselves in an army which, despite its overwhelming superiority in both numbers and armament, lacked the one thing that was absolutely essential. It had no commander. And it was about to face an enemy whose sole advantage was that it was supremely well led.

CHAPTER FOURTEEN

THE EVE OF BATTLE

As soon as Henry V saw the French taking up their stations, he "very calmly and quite heedless of danger" ordered all his men to dismount and drew them up into battle formation, "as if they were to go immediately into action." Every leader was given his allotted place and instructions, and the king himself went through the ranks encouraging the men. "He exhorted them to prepare for battle, animating their hearts by his intrepid demeanour, and his consoling expressions." His priests were also busy, hearing the confessions of men who thought they were about to die. "And there you could see the English, thinking that they would have battle that day, displaying great piety, falling to their knees, raising their hands towards heaven, offering their prayers to God that He would take them into his safekeeping." Le Févre de St Rémy, the Burgundian herald who wrote this, evidently did not expect his readers to believe him, for he added the defiant rider that it was true: "I was there and saw these things with my own eyes." Two Welshmen, Thomas Bassegle of Cardiff and John William ap Howell, were later arrested at Sawston in Cambridgeshire, by the servants of Sir Edmund de la Pole "while on pilgrimage to Walsingham in fulfilment of vows made on the battlefield."[1] They cannot have been the only ones to have sworn to undertake a pilgrimage if they lived through that day.

The chaplain also observed and, indeed, ministered to this unusual demonstration of religious devotion. "And amongst other things which I noted as said at that time," the chaplain reported,

> a certain knight, Sir Walter Hungerford, expressed a desire to the king's face that he might have had, added to the little company he already had with him, ten thousand of the best archers in England who would have been only too glad to be there. "That is a foolish way to talk," the king said to him, "because, by the God in Heaven upon Whose grace I have relied and in Whom is my firm hope of victory, I would not, even if I could, have a single man more than I do. For these I have here with me are God's people, whom He deigns to let me have at this time. Do you not believe," he asked, "that the Almighty, with these His humble few, is able to overcome the opposing arrogance of the French who boast of their great number and their own strength?"[2]

The two opposing forces were now drawn up, facing each other, on what would become the battlefield of Agincourt. Visiting the site today, it is easy to pick out the principal features that are described by eyewitnesses of the battle. The main road to Calais still runs straight across the plateau from the direction of the river crossing at Blangy, bisecting the flat arable fields that form a triangle between the three small villages of Azincourt, to the north-west, Tramecourt to the north-east and Maisoncelle to the south. The villages are all less than a mile from each other and each one still has its parish church, its cluster of traditional Artois cottages and farmhouses in varying degrees of dilapidation, and its surrounding patch of woodland. A Calvary by the roadside near the Tramecourt crossroads marks the burial ground of the French. The great castle of Azincourt which gave the battle its name has long since disappeared, and a local farmer, with a complete absence of historical empathy, cultivates corn so tall that it dwarfs the pedestrian and obscures the view across the battlefield. Otherwise, it would be easy to fall into the mistake of believing that the field of Agincourt has remained unchanged since that fateful day in 1415. It is an error that has seduced many historians as well as casual visitors to the site.[3] Yet the oldest of the three village churches dates from the second half of the sixteenth century; the Calvary was not erected until the nineteenth century and may, or may not, mark the site of the French grave pits; and hidden in the woodlands of Tramecourt is a magnificent eighteenth-century red-brick chateau with a tree-lined approach which has transformed its environs. Most important of all, the woods which six hundred years ago played such a crucial part in limiting the field of action are gone. Though many trees remain on the periphery, these are of relatively recent growth and cannot be taken as the literal boundaries of the original site or even as the direct descendants of the fifteenth-century woodland. Until detailed aerial and archaeological surveys are carried out, it will not be possible even to attempt a definitive description of the battlefield as it was on 24 and 25 October 1415.

Contrary to popular belief, there was no immediate rush to battle. This was partly because it took some time for both sides to settle into their final positions. According to the English chaplain, the only eyewitness who records the first contacts between the two armies, the French arrived first and initially took up a position parallel to the Calais road in a broad field rather more than half a mile away from the English as they emerged over the crest of the hill from Blangy: "and there was only a very little valley between us and them," the chaplain glumly observed. When Henry drew up his battle lines to face them, the French realised how small his army was and

> withdrew to a field, at the far side of a certain wood which was close at hand to our left between us and them, where lay our road to Calais. And our king, on the assumption that by so doing they would either circle round the wood, in order that way to make a surprise attack upon him, or else would circle round the somewhat more distant woodlands in the neighbourhood and so surround us on every side, immediately moved his lines again, always positioning them so that they faced the enemy.[4]

The French had now selected a strong defensive position in the open fields between Azincourt and Tramecourt. They had several miles of comparatively flat open countryside behind them, but the land fell away sharply all round the rest of the plateau in front of them, and the woods that surrounded both villages protected their flanks.[5] If the English wished to continue their journey to Calais, there was only one way open to them. They had no option but to mount a full frontal assault.

Given their superior numbers, why did the French not attack there and then, sweeping the English off the plateau and into the Ternoise valley? Both sides were ready for battle, their men-at-arms fully armed, wearing their coats of arms and flying their banners. But Constable d'Albret[6] and Marshal Boucicaut were too experienced to fall into the trap of rushing headlong into battle: indeed, they had argued strongly in the royal council that there should be no confrontation at all with the English. Henry should be allowed to complete his *chevauchée* to Calais unimpeded. Once he returned to England, Harfleur could be besieged and retaken, and the English adventure would have achieved nothing.[7]

Overruled on the actual decision of whether to give battle by the more hot-headed members of the council, d'Albret and Boucicaut were not going to make the mistake of underestimating their opponents in the field. Having shadowed the English for so long as they sought to cross the Somme, they knew that they were determined, resourceful and dangerous. "For it has often been noted that a small number of desperate men will conquer a large and powerful army," Christine de Pizan had written, "because they would rather die fighting than fall into the cruel hands of the enemy, so there is great peril in fighting such people as these, as their strength is doubled." Faced with imminent battle, she advised that a wise commander would not hasten to attack until he had discovered all he could about the state of his opponents:

> how great their will to fight, and if they have adequate food or not, for hunger fights from within and can conquer without the use of arms. So he will take counsel with his advisers to decide if

it is better to have the battle sooner or later, or if he should wait until attacked. For if he should discover that the enemy is suffering from hunger, or that it is badly paid, whereby the men are falling away little by little and abandoning their commander because they are malcontent, or that there are men present who are spoiled by the ease of courtly life with its luxuries, or even that there are men who can no longer endure the rigors of the field and the hard military life, but rather long for repose, men who will not be in a hurry to engage in battle — then he will remain quiet as if he were not paying attention, and as quietly as he can he will set out to bar the ways of escape. Thus he will surprise the enemy if it is at all possible.[8]

Boucicaut and d'Albret knew that they had nothing to lose by playing a waiting game. Every passing hour not only brought them more reinforcements but further frayed the already taut nerves of the English, who were tired, hungry and desperate.

As the darkness of a late October evening closed in, it became apparent to both sides that there would be no battle that day. The French were so confident that their superior strength and numbers would deter any prospect of an attack that they broke ranks and began to seek quarters for the night in Azincourt and Tramecourt. The English, still fearing a sudden assault, kept up their battle order as the light failed, continuing to stand rigidly in arms until it became so dark that they could no longer see the enemy. Only then were they allowed to stand down and seek whatever shelter they could find for the night. The two armies were so close that they could hear the voices of the French as they prepared their own camps for the night, "each one of them calling out, as usual, for his fellow, servant, and comrade."

When some of the English took this as a signal that they could do the same, Henry moved swiftly to stamp out such indiscipline, ordering that silence should be kept throughout the whole army on pain of forfeiture of horse and harness, if the offender was a gentleman, or of losing his right ear if he came from the lower ranks. The imposition of absolute silence was not simply an act of brutal repression, but was intended to make it more difficult for the enemy to carry out any surprise raids during the night. With so many French knights and esquires eager to avenge the loss of Harfleur and to prove their prowess in a daring encounter, the English could not afford to let down their guard. The wisdom of this was proved when a large party of French men-at-arms and bowmen, under the leadership of Arthur, count of Richemont, approached close enough to the English camp for there to be an exchange of fire. Though they quickly retreated back to their own lines, they may have succeeded in taking some prisoners, for the English exchequer accounts record that seven archers from Lancashire were captured on this day.[9]

Not surprisingly, the unnatural stillness of the English camp had an unnerving effect on both sides. The French began to suspect that their opponents were intending to slip away secretly during the night, so they lit fires and set heavily manned watches across the roads and fields to prevent them escaping. The English could not indulge in any camaraderie to keep up their spirits and, obliged to speak in whispers themselves, became acutely aware of the cheerful noises emanating from the French camp, in which there was no shortage of food or wine. Where their lines were closest, near Tramecourt, they could even see the faces of their foes in the firelight and hear their conversations. The chaplain, wandering through the army and administering what spiritual comfort he could, heard rumours that the French "thought themselves so sure of us that that night they cast dice for our king and his nobles." The king himself gave short shrift to such ideas: no one in England would ever have to pay a penny towards his ransom, he declared, as he intended either to win the coming battle or die in the attempt.[10]

Lodgings had been found for the king and some of his closest circle in the village of Maisoncelle, but before Henry retired for the night, he gave orders that all the French prisoners in the army, whatever their rank, were to be released. As at Harfleur, this was done to avoid having to commit some of his precious resources to their safekeeping and to maximise the number of men at his disposal. Again, too, the arrangement was conditional and sworn on oath. If he should win the next day's battle, the prisoners were bound to give themselves up to him; if he should lose, then they could consider themselves released from their parole and entirely at liberty.[11]

There was little rest and less sleep for anyone in the English army that night. Only the fortunate few had a roof over their heads and most of the army were camped out in the open, lying on the ground and sheltering as best they could under hedges and in the orchards and gardens of Maisoncelle. The English had endured days on end of "filthy, wet and windy weather." Now, throughout the long hours of darkness, it rained, not just incessantly, but in torrents.[12] Despite the dozens of watch fires burning round the edges of the camp, it was impossible to get warm or dry. The heavy woollen cloaks of even the wealthiest could not have been proof against such weather and must have become saturated as the night progressed.

Weapons and armour must also have suffered. Rust was one of the greatest problems that anyone wearing armour faced. In normal circumstances, it could be kept at bay if the armour were turned in a barrel of sand and regularly polished and oiled, though strenuous activity could still leave a knight's face streaked with rust from his helmet.[13] On an enforced three-week route march, when armour had to be worn constantly, whatever the weather, it was inevitable that rusting would take place, seizing up the joints and blunting the edges of weapons. The archers, too, must have struggled to keep their bows, arrows and bow-strings dry, even though their very lives depended on it. In the numbing cold and wet of that night and early dawn, frozen hands and fingers would have fumbled with awkward laces and buckles, and struggled with recalcitrant and corroding pieces of metal. Armourers, fletchers and bowyers must have been as much in demand as priests, as the tattered remnants of the English army sought to prepare their bodies as well as their souls against the coming fight.

Although Henry had the advantage of a roof over his head, he did not waste the night in sleep. In order to make appropriate decisions, he needed to have the best possible information about the place where the battle would be fought. Around midnight, therefore, he sent a hand-picked group of knights (Sir John

Cornewaille and his band, perhaps) to scout out the battlefield by moonlight. When they returned, their report enabled him to determine his final battle plan.[14] It was obvious that they were hopelessly outnumbered and that the French had many thousands more men-at-arms. Given this advantage, it was likely that they would attack first, for which he had to be prepared.

Though conventional military wisdom had it that the three divisions of Henry's army should stand one behind the other in a solid block, this formation was really intended for an army primarily composed of heavy infantry. The English numbers were so small in any case that, had they adopted this arrangement, they would have presented such a narrow front to an infinitely more numerous enemy that they ran the risk of being surrounded and overwhelmed. The alternative was to draw up the three battalions side by side to present an elongated but shallow front. The layout of the battlefield lent itself to this option because both flanks of the army would be protected from attack by the woods and hedges around Maisoncelle and Tramecourt, which would obstruct a massed charge by cavalry or infantry.

As the scouts had also discovered, the heavy rain that had created such miserable conditions for the men camping out overnight had created an unexpected opportunity. The fields where the battle was to take place had been newly ploughed and sown with winter cereals. The soil was not the fine, light loam of the vineyards of France, but the thick, heavy clay of the Somme, with its extraordinary capacity to retain water. Even before it became trampled and churned up by the feet of countless men and horses, it was already turning into a mud-bath. As Henry was quick to appreciate, this would slow down any attack by cavalry or infantry, creating easier targets for his archers. Unlike the men-at-arms, whether mounted or on foot, who had to cross the battlefield to fight at close quarters, the archers would be able to begin their deadly hail of arrows long before they themselves were in range of the lances, swords and axes of the men-at-arms.

Much ink and bile has been spilt in the argument as to how exactly Henry disposed his archers for the battle. The chaplain (who knew his Vegetius and was not a complete military novice) was quite clear on the point: "in view of his want of numbers, he drew up only a single line of battle, placing his vanguard . . . as a wing on the right and the rearguard . . . as a wing on the left; and he positioned 'wedges' of his archers in between each 'battle' and had them drive in their stakes in front of them, as previously arranged in case of a cavalry charge." Whatever the shape of the "wedges" — and the Latin word used by the chaplain in its classical form did literally mean a wedge — the chaplain is clear that archers were placed between the three battalions of men-at-arms. However, in his account of the course of the battle, he is equally clear that there were also archers positioned on the wings, describing how "the French cavalry posted on the flanks made charges against those of our archers who were on both sides of our army" and then "rode through between the archers and the woodlands."[15]

This confusion is not entirely cleared up by the evidence of the second eyewitness in the English ranks, the equally well-informed herald Jean le Févre, who simply states of the king that "he only made one battle, and all the men-at-arms were in the middle of his battle, and all the banners were very close to each other. On both sides of the men-at-arms were the archers . . ."[16] Le Févre's seems to be the more logical version. The chaplain's five thousand archers, if divided into only two groups and placed between the three divisions of men-at-arms, would have left the infantry separated from each other by a considerable distance, a major weakness when each infantry division can only have been three hundred men strong. Le Févre's account is also borne out, as we shall see, by the battle plans drawn up by the French, which aimed to destroy the English archers on the wings.[17]

Though our two eyewitnesses differ over where the archers were placed, they both agree that all three battles or divisions were placed side by side in a single line. It is a measure of how short of men-at-arms Henry was that he could not even afford to keep a reserve, as was standard practice. In doing this, he was taking a major risk. The archers would not be able to keep the advancing French back forever and at some point it would become necessary for the infantry to hold the line without the support of a reserve. The choice of leader for each battle was therefore a matter of critical importance, especially as the king intended to fight in person and therefore could not observe the course of battle and direct his troops from a vantage point, as Edward III had done at Crécy. There was never any question but that the king himself would be in overall charge and that he would continue to command the main battle, which would hold the centre of the field, but the leadership of both the vanguard and the rearguard would be changed. Sir John Cornewaille and Sir Gilbert Umfraville, who had led the van throughout the march from Harfleur, were now replaced by Edward, duke of York. According to at least one sixteenth-century source, the duke had begged the king for this honour on bended knee, but his age, military experience and rank, and the fact that he was the most senior member of the Order of the Garter present, were all more powerful arguments in his favour. The command of the rearguard, which the duke now relinquished, was given to Thomas, Lord Camoys, another veteran soldier, who had fought in Henry IV's wars against the Scots, Welsh and French.[18]

The decisions regarding the deployment of troops in the French army were not made so easily. The task should naturally have fallen to the king or his captain-general, but neither Charles VI nor the dauphin was there. In the absence also of the dukes of Berry, Burgundy, Brittany and Anjou, there was no senior prince of the blood royal to whom command naturally fell. Only Charles d'Orléans could lay claim to any right of precedence, but he was just twenty years old and had no experience of full-scale battle. By rights, the decision should have devolved from the king to his officers, but neither Constable d'Albret nor Marshal Boucicaut had been given any additional delegated powers that would enable him to overrule the princes and assume uncontested control. What is more, both men had served professionally under Charles d'Orléans' father, Louis, making it more difficult for them to assert their authority over his son.

It is so often assumed that the French rushed unthinkingly into battle that it comes as something of a surprise to learn that a detailed strategy had been worked out in advance. As soon as a decision to fight had been taken by the royal council at Rouen, a battle plan had been drafted, based on the traditional three divisions. The van was to be commanded by the duke of Bourbon, Marshal Boucicaut and Guichard Dauphin, who was the grand-master of the king's household; the main battle by Constable d'Albret and the dukes of Orléans, Alençon and Brittany; and the rearguard by the duke of Bar and the counts of Nevers, Charolais and Vaudémont. The two wings were to be commanded by Arthur, count of Richemont, and Tanneguy du Chastel, *prévôt* of Paris. Additionally, a hand-picked body of elite cavalry riding heavily armoured horses, whose specific task was to break the English archers by charging them down, was to be led by Clignet de Brabant, who was one of the two admirals of France, and the chivalrous youth Jehan Werchin, seneschal of Hainault. As Juvénal des Ursins, the French chronicler who reported this arrangement, remarked with justified bitterness, "nothing came of all this organisation."[19]

A revised French plan[20] seems to have been drawn up a few days before Agincourt, probably at the time when the dukes of Orléans and Bourbon and Charles d'Albret sent Henry V their challenge to battle, since it was designed for the much smaller force that was stalking the English along the banks of the Somme. The new plan envisaged only two battles, a vanguard led by Boucicaut and d'Albret and, behind it, the main body of the army, commanded by Jean, duke of Alençon, and Charles d'Artois, count of Eu. Instead of having a rearguard, there were to be two smaller wings on either side of the main battle, that on the right commanded by Arthur, count of Richemont, as in the original plan, and that on the left by Louis de Bourbon, count of Vendôme, brother of the duke of Bourbon. Each of these divisions was to be entirely composed of men-at-arms fighting on foot. All the "*gens de traict*," the miscellaneous bowmen, including both archers and crossbowmen, were to be placed in two companies, one in front of each of the two wings. Additionally, to the rear of the army, there were to be two cavalry forces. The first, composed of a thousand men-at-arms and half their valets, mounted on their masters' best horses, was to be led by David, sire de Rambures,[21] and its specific task was to make a flanking attack to "fall upon the archers, and use their force to break them." The second, commanded by Louis de Bourdon,[22] was made up of only two hundred men-at-arms and the other half of the valets mounted on their masters' less good horses. It was to go behind the English forces and attack the baggage train, the object being to seize the horses of the dismounted men-at-arms to prevent either a rally or flight in the event of defeat.

As soon as de Rambures ordered his cavalry to attack the English archers, the French bowmen were to begin their volleys, the infantry divisions to march on the enemy, and de Bourdon to launch his raid on the English rear. The aim was to deliver a combined assault so devastating that the English would be overwhelmed and unable to recover. The plan even took into account the changing conditions of the battlefield, allowing the vanguard and main battle to combine into a single division if the English did not divide their own forces, and giving the cavalry units considerable freedom in the way they carried out their tasks so that they could seize any opportunities that arose on the day.[23]

Having given such thought to tactics, it is inconceivable that the French did not give equal time and energy to preparing a strategy for the actual combat that they knew would take place the next day. Some further revision was necessary — as it always is on battle's eve — and they did try to take into account the conditions of the site and the fact that the size of their army had increased by possibly as much as a factor of ten. Unlike the English army, where contemporary administrative records support the chroniclers' assessment of its size as being in the region of six thousand fighting men, no such evidence exists for the French. It is therefore impossible to give even an estimated number with any certainty.[24] The commonest figure given by English chroniclers writing during Henry V's lifetime is 60,000, but rising as high as 150,000 in some sources. The French, with an equally pardonable desire to tweak the figures to their own advantage, give anything between 8000 and 50,000.[25] The three eyewitnesses also vary wildly in their estimates. The English chaplain states that "by their own reckoning" the French numbered

60,000, though he does not give his authority. Jean le Févre de St Remy, the Burgundian herald in the English army, suggests 50,000 and Jehan Waurin, a Burgundian in the French army, 36,000, based on his assertion that the French were six times more numerous than the English. Waurin's figure seems the most likely, if only because he gives it substance by listing the number of men assigned to each position: 8000 men-at-arms, 4000 archers and 1500 crossbowmen in the vanguard, a similar number in the main battle, two wings of 600 and 800 mounted men-at-arms and "the residue of the host" in the rearguard.[26]

Despite its prestigious absentees, the list of the nobility in the French army on the eve of Agincourt reads like a roll-call of the chivalry of France. There were four royal dukes, Orléans, Alençon, Bourbon and Bar (the duke of Brabant would arrive the next morning), the counts of Vendôme, Eu, Richemont, Nevers, Vaudémont, Blammont, Salm, Grandpré, Roussy, Dammartin, Marle and Fauquembergue, and innumerable lords. All the great military officials of France were also there: Constable d'Albret and Marshal Boucicaut; both the admirals, Clignet de Brabant and Jacques de Châtillon; the master of the crossbowmen, David de Rambures; and the grand-master of the king's household, Guichard Dauphin. Every *bailli* from the northern provinces had come, each with his assembled host, together with all the militias, crossbowmen and gunners who could be spared from their towns.

It has sometimes been suggested that the French had too many men and that this was the cause of their defeat. This was not the greatest dilemma facing their strategists, but rather that so many of those men wanted to play a leading role in crushing the English. Which prince of the blood royal would willingly command the rearguard when he had the opportunity to win fame and glory in the vanguard? What is more, it is easy to understand why those who had been assigned a particularly honourable role in previous plans resented what might appear to be a demotion in the latest version. There were not just personal tensions between the princes, but political and territorial ones. Why should Arthur, count of Richemont, and his five hundred Bretons accept a role on the wing, for instance, when he was the younger brother of the duke of Brittany and sole representative of the duchy? Should he not have a place in the vanguard? And what of Philippe, count of Nevers, whom the first plan had relegated to the rearguard? The youngest brother of John the Fearless, had he not defied his sibling to be present and should this not be rewarded? Marshal Boucicaut had knighted him earlier that very evening — was he not to be allowed to win his spurs by taking his place in the front line? On the other hand, one can well imagine that dyed-in-the-wool Armagnacs, like Charles d'Albret, Guichard Dauphin and, of course, Charles d'Orléans himself, would not want to see a party of Bretons or Burgundians in pole positions. Might they not, at a crucial moment, desert to their English allies?

Although it is by no means absolutely clear what battle order was finally agreed — which in itself is an indication of the competing claims and resulting confusion — it seems that the basic plan was similar to that decided upon a few days earlier. Again there would be two main divisions, a vanguard and a main battle, composed of men-at-arms fighting on foot and flanked by men-at-arms on both wings. And once more there was to be a cavalry force entrusted with the specific task of riding down the English archers in the opening moments of the battle. The only major changes were that the bowmen, who had previously been deployed in front of the wings, were now placed behind them, effectively curtailing any role they might play in the battle. This time, too, there was to be a proper rearguard, which was to be mounted and was to include those men-at-arms judged to be less proficient horsemen than those chosen for the elite company, as well as the valets of the great lords fighting on foot in the main body of the army.[27]

After much argument and many expressions of bad feeling, with every leader of consequence insisting that it was his right to lead the vanguard, they came to a conclusion that was fair but foolish. They would all take their places in the front lines. The vanguard would consist of Constable d'Albret, Marshal Boucicaut and all the other royal officers (except Clignet de Brabant), the dukes of Orléans and Bourbon, the counts of Eu and Richemont (the latter winning his promotion from the infantry wing on the former plan), and Philippe d'Auxy, sire de Dampierre, who was the *bailli* of Amiens. The command of the main battle was to belong to the dukes of Alençon and Bar, who were to be accompanied by the counts of Nevers, Marle, Vaudémont, Blammont, Salm, Grandpré and Roussy. The counts of Dammartin and Fauquembergue were to share the leadership of the rearguard, together with the sire de Laurois, captain of Ardres, who had brought the men from the borders of Boulogne to the battle. The unfortunate result of these arrangements was noted by Pierre Fenin, a chronicler from Artois who was writing in the 1430s: "all the princes were placed in the vanguard, leaving their own people without leaders."[28]

There is some confusion in the chronicles as to the composition and function of the two wings at each end of the vanguard. Most are agreed that one wing (the herald of the duke of Berry says it was the left) was once more to be entrusted to the command of the count of Vendôme, whose company consisted of six hundred officers of the royal household. These included Charles d'Ivry, the grand-master of the waters and forests of France, who had been one of the ambassadors to England earlier in the summer, Guillaume Martel, sire de Bacqueville, the bearer of the oriflamme, Gui, sire de la Roche-Guyon, the dauphin's chamberlain, "and all the chamberlains, esquires of the stables, buttery, pantry and other officers of the king." If neither the king nor the dauphin was to be present, at least both men would be represented by their loyal servants. It is nowhere explicitly stated that Vendôme's wing was mounted and the probability remains that it fought on foot, as originally planned.[29]

Greater confusion surrounds the other French wing. Berry herald tells us that it was also composed of six hundred men-at-arms and was again led by Arthur, count of Richemont, as in both previous battle plans. The monk of St Denis, on the other hand, attributes its command to Guichard Dauphin. Most sources place both men firmly in the vanguard, so it may be that this wing was at one of its extremities and absorbed into the larger force. In either case the company must have fought on foot.[30]

All the chronicles were agreed that there was also an elite

force of between eight and twelve hundred mounted men-at-arms, who had been specifically chosen from among the best horsemen in the army to ride down and destroy the enemy archers. There is also unanimity in ascribing its leadership to Clignet de Brabant, who had been the first choice of the royal council at Rouen for that role. His second-in-command this time was not the seneschal of Hainault, but Louis de Bourdon, who had been promoted from his previous position leading the attack on the English baggage train. The two men were both experienced Armagnac captains, had often worked together and, in doing so, had acquired a certain notoriety: in 1413 they were accused of pillaging the countryside around Paris at the head of groups of armed men and were ordered to desist and return home immediately. Clearly skilled and professional soldiers, their role during the battle of Agincourt would do nothing to improve their chivalric reputations.[31]

The likelihood would seem to be that, as originally envisaged in the earlier plans, the cavalry force was stationed somewhere towards the rear of the French lines. When the signal to attack was given, the company would divide along pre-allocated lines to ride round the infantry and launch itself on the archers on both English wings. And, as we have seen, it was the French expectation that this action would begin the battle.

One of the strengths of the English army was that everyone lived and fought within the company and under the leadership of the man who had raised the retinue. By the time it came to battle, they had bonded into tightly knit units, and there was a sense of esprit de corps that gave them a fighting edge. Every soldier knew his place within his own retinue and within the chain of command that led directly to the king himself.

The French had no such formal structure. Though there were groups who fought together as a unit, like the men of the royal household or the town militias, most of the petty nobility were both independent and independently minded. Even members of the same family did not necessarily fight side by side: Jean, sire de Longueval, for instance, fought in the main battle in the company of Robert, count of Marle, but his brother Alain in the vanguard, in the company of Jehan, sire de Waurin, the father of our chronicler.[32] The situation was further complicated by the continuous stream of new reinforcements arriving even during the course of the battle, risking a chain of command so stretched that it might break under the pressure.

The elite cavalry squadron had commandeered somewhere in the region of a thousand men-at-arms "supplied by men [taken from] all the companies."[33] Inevitably, those chosen for such roles would be the more experienced and best-equipped men-at-arms, who were most likely to be the career soldiers of the petty nobility. The rearguard became the dumping ground — le Févre refers to "all the surplus soldiers" being placed there — which probably contributed to the lack of leadership, the confusion and the irresolution that afflicted this division of the French army during the course of the battle.[34]

Indeed, it seems that the French had such a "surplus of soldiers" that they actually sent some away before the battle began. The monk of St Denis reports a highly partisan story that the citizens of Paris had offered to send six thousand men, fully armed, to join the royal army, with the proviso that they should be placed in the front rank if it came to battle. (If such an offer was really made, it is unlikely that it came with a condition of this kind.) Nevertheless, it was rejected with disdain: "the help of mechanics and artisans must surely be of little value," one Jean Beaumont is supposed to have said, "for we shall outnumber the English three to one."[35] The monk used this dubious anecdote as an excuse for some pious reflections on the pride of the French nobility, who deemed it unworthy to accept the help of plebeians and had forgotten the lessons of Courtrai, Poitiers and Nicopolis. If the story is true, it is more likely that the rejection of the Parisian citizens was due to fear that they would simply march straight to the assistance of the duke of Burgundy, rather than against the English.

Nevertheless, there is other evidence to suggest that "plebeian forces" were indeed rejected or deserted before battle began. Four thousand of the best crossbowmen, according to the monk, who ought to have begun the assault on the English, could not be found at their post at the moment they were needed, having been sent away, they claimed, because the nobles said that they were not needed. One might be inclined to suspect this story too, except that the four thousand archers and fifteen hundred crossbowmen who were, according to Waurin, assigned to the vanguard were nowhere in evidence during the battle. Waurin's own explanation for their absence echoes that of the monk: there was not room on the narrow battlefield between the woods of Azincourt and Tramecourt for anyone other than the men-at-arms, so the bowmen could not be used. Indeed, fifty crossbowmen, who left Tournai in response to the royal summons to assist Harfleur on 17 September, returned home on 18 November without having reached Harfleur or been at the battle of Agincourt.[36]

The heavy rains that had fallen almost the whole night through finally gave way to the chill and damp of a pale and watery dawn. It was the morning of 25 October 1415, a day celebrated in the Church calendar as the feast of Saints Crispin and Crispinian, the patron saints of shoemakers, saddlers and tanners. Though it is unlikely that anyone in the French army felt that this was an inauspicious day to commit to battle, with hindsight the chroniclers collectively shook their heads and groaned.

Legend had it that Crispin and Crispinian were two brothers from Rome who came to France as Christian missionaries at the turn of the third century and settled at Soissons. There they had plied their trade as shoemakers until they were martyred for their faith on the orders of Emperor Maximilian. As was so often the way with medieval stories of martyrdom, the brothers miraculously survived several gruesome attempts to put them to death: the torturer's tools would not hurt them, the river Aisne would not drown them and the oil would not burn them. In the end, the executioner had to resort to the more prosaic but successful method of beheading them. The previous year, in May 1414, an Armagnac force had been responsible for the brutal sacking of their home town of Soissons and the execution of its highly regarded captain, Enguerrand de Bournonville, by Jean, duke of Bourbon, who was now one of the leaders of the vanguard at Agincourt.[37] The cobbler-martyrs of Soissons were about to get their own revenge in spectacular style.

As soon as first light dawned, the French arrayed themselves in their companies and took up their allotted positions on the battlefield. "The number of them was really terrifying," the chaplain observed, and the vanguard "with its forest of spears and the great number of helmets gleaming in between them and of cavalry on the flanks . . . was at a rough guess thirty times more than all our men put together." (The chaplain's thirty was probably a scribal error for three, which still made the French vanguard eighteen thousand strong. Though this, too, was an exaggeration, he was certainly right that the French van alone outnumbered the entire English army.) "Compared with our men," he added gloomily, even the rearguard "were a multitude hardly to be counted."[38]

Henry V had been up before dawn, calmly preparing his own soul before he organised his army to face their foes. Leaving off his helm, he had put on all his other armour, which, unlike his men's rusting pieces, was "very bright," and, over this, a splendid surcoat emblazoned with the combined arms of England and France. Thus arrayed for the battle that was to decide the fate of his claim to France, he had made his way to his makeshift chapel to hear lauds, the first service of the day, followed by the customary three masses with which he always began each day. Having given God his due, he then made ready for the field. He put on his royal helm, a bascinet bearing a rich crown of gold, which was studded with jewels like an imperial coronet and, even more provocatively, was adorned with fleur-de-lis in reference to Henry's claim to the throne of France. With that curious mix of regality and humility that he had made peculiarly his own, he did not then mount a great dashing charger, but a small grey horse, which he rode quietly and without the use of spurs to the battlefield. There he rode hither and thither, without the customary use of trumpets to announce his presence, drawing his men together and deploying them as he saw fit.[39]

Every single Englishman, including the king himself, was to fight on foot. All their horses, the baggage, the pages of the knights and squires who were too young to fight, and those who were too sick to raise a weapon in their own defence, were sent behind the lines and committed to the safekeeping of one gentleman, commanding a company of ten men-at-arms and twenty archers.[40] Everyone else who was capable of wielding a bow or a sword was deployed according to the battle plan that the king had devised. Unlike the French force, where there were said to be so many banners that some of them had to be taken down and put away because they were causing an obstruction, the English ones were few and could be easily identified. The king's own bodyguard boasted the four banners that had flown on his flagship as he invaded France: his personal arms and those of St George, Edward the Confessor and the Trinity.[41]

Scattered among the thin line of men-at-arms could also be seen the banners of Henry's brother Humphrey, duke of Gloucester, their uncle Edward, duke of York, the earls of March, Huntingdon, Oxford and Suffolk, and those of Sir Gilbert Umfraville, Sir John Roos and Sir John Cornewaille. The archers, now outnumbering their own men-at-arms by five to one, had taken up their positions on the wings and between the battles, hammering their stakes into the muddy ground with leaden mallets that were to prove almost as deadly weapons as their bows.[42]

As he had done on the previous afternoon when battle was expected, Henry rode up and down his lines, exhorting and encouraging his men to do their best. He did not shrink from addressing the disquiet that some of them must have felt about the justice of the cause in which they were offering their lives, because he knew that this was not simply a moral difficulty, but one that went to the heart of each man's personal hope of eternal salvation. The laws of war stated that "if the quarrel is unjust, he that exposes himself in it condemns his soul; and if he dies in such a state, he will go the way of perdition."[43] Henry had come to France to recover his rightful inheritance, he reminded them, and his cause and quarrel were good and just. In that quarrel they could therefore fight with a clear conscience and in the certainty of salvation. Then he appealed directly to their sense of patriotism. They should remember that they had been born in the realm of England, where their fathers and mothers, wives and children, were living and waiting for them. For their sakes, they ought to do their best to return covered in glory and praise. The kings of England had inflicted many great defeats on the French in the past; today, every man should play his part in defending the king's person and the honour of the crown of England. Finally, he told them that the French had boasted that they would cut off two fingers from the right hand of every English archer, so that none of them would ever draw a longbow again. This was a pardonable untruth. Henry's men knew as well as he did that the French would simply kill anyone not wearing the coat of arms that identified the bearer as being of noble birth and therefore able to afford a ransom. The archers therefore faced certain death if they were defeated. The threat of being mutilated, however, and in a way which implicitly recognised the importance of the archer's skill, was an insult not to be borne. The very idea was enough to inflame the righteous indignation of the troops, and Henry's inspirational speech had the desired effect. A great cry went up from the ranks, "Sire, we pray to God that He may grant you long life and victory over our enemies!"[44]

There was now one last thing Henry had to do if he was to keep his own conscience clear and maintain his reputation for justice in the eyes of the world. He had to make one last effort to avoid battle. He therefore sent heralds to demand a parley and appointed several trusted envoys to meet the French representatives in the centre of the battlefield, in full view of the opposing forces. Though we do not know the names of the Englishmen involved, those of the French have been recorded and, apart from Guichard Dauphin, the grand-master of the king's household, they were a distinctly provocative choice. Each one had a personal reason to seek vengeance against the English in battle. Colart d'Estouteville, sire de Torcy, for example, was brother to Jean, the defender of Harfleur, who was on parole as the king of England's prisoner. Jean Malet, sire de Graville, also had a personal grudge against Henry V: he had lost lands round Harfleur worth five hundred livres due to the English invasion and occupation.

The most controversial choice, however, was Jacques de Créquy, sire de Heilly, marshal of Guienne, the only Burgundian in this group of Armagnacs. It was not his political allegiance that made him so contentious but the fact that he was an

English prisoner who had broken his parole. In the summer of 1413 the earl of Dorset, who was then Henry's lieutenant in Aquitaine, had embarked on an aggressive campaign of reconquest over the northern borders of the duchy. As marshal of Guienne, de Heilly had been sent from Paris at the head of a small army "to fall upon the English and drive them out of the country." Instead, he was ambushed, his men were slaughtered and he himself was one of those captured and sent back to England as the earl's prisoner. When news of the fall of Harfleur reached him, he could no longer bear his enforced captivity and, with a group of other prisoners, succeeded in breaking out of Wisbech Castle, where he was being held, and escaped back to France.[45]

While de Heilly had indeed broken his chivalric oath, he had done it for patriotic reasons and he now used this opportunity to attempt to clear the slur on his reputation. "Noble Kinge, it hath often been shewed unto me, and also to others of our realme, that I should fly from you shamefully and otherwise then a knight shoulde doe," he is alleged to have said to Henry, "which report I am here readie to prove untrue. And if there be any man of your host brave enough to reproach me with it, lett him prepare him to a single battaile. And I shall prove it upon him before thy Majestie, that wrongefullie that report hath been imagined and furnished of me." This demand was given short shrift by the king, who had more important things on his mind than watching a single combat to redeem de Heilly's honour. "No battaile shall be here foughten at this time for this cause," he replied, sternly ordering de Heilly to return to his company and prepare for real battle. "And we trust in God," he added, "that like as you havinge no regard to the order of honour of knighthood, escaped from us, so this day ye shall either be taken and brought to us againe, or else by the sworde you shall finish your life."[46]

As Jean le Févre freely admitted, apart from the airing of de Heilly's personal grievance, no one knew what the English and French negotiators discussed or what offers were made. The French chroniclers would later claim that Henry had realised that he was hopelessly outnumbered and could not win the battle, so he therefore offered to give back Harfleur (Calais, too, according to some sources), free all his prisoners and pay damages, if only he were to be allowed a free passage home with his men.[47] This flies in the face of common sense. Henry would hardly have come so far only to give up more than he had gained, simply to escape with his life; his absolute and unshakeable belief in his cause would not have allowed him to do it. Le Févre's own version is more plausible, even though he freely admits it was based on hearsay.

> The French offered, as I have heard said, that if he would renounce his pretended title to the crown of France, and never take it up again, and return the town of Harfleur which he had recently captured, the king [Charles VI] would be content to allow him to keep Aquitaine and that which he held from the ancient conquest of Picardy [Calais]. The king of England, or his people, replied that, if the king of France would give up to him the duchy of Aquitaine and five named cities which belonged to, and ought to be part of, the duchy, together with the county of Ponthieu and Madam Catherine, the daughter of the king of France, in marriage . . . and 800,000 *écus* for her jewels and clothing, he would be content to renounce his title to the crown of France and return the town of Harfleur.[48]

Whatever offers were really made, and by whichever side, the negotiations were brief and were rejected by both parties. All the formalities required by the law of arms and the demands of justice had now been met. Only one recourse was left. There would indeed be a trial by battle, not one between de Heilly and his accuser, nor even one between Henry V and the dauphin, but one between the assembled might of the two greatest military nations in Europe. Their disputed claims were about to be put to the judgement of God.

CHAPTER FIFTEEN

"FELAS, LETS GO!"

And then there was stalemate. "Everywhere and on all occasions that foot soldiers march against their enemy face to face," the military textbooks stated, "those who march lose and those who remain standing still and holding firm win."[1] So each side waited in vain for the other to make the first move. Neither did. As the minutes ticked by and turned into hours, it became a test of nerve and discipline. Who would crack first?

The contrast between the appearance of the two armies could not have been starker. On one side stood row upon numberless row of motionless French men-at-arms, clad from head to foot in burnished armour, armed with swords and lances shortened for fighting on foot, and with brightly coloured pennons and banners waving over their heads. Behind them and on the wings were those crossbowmen and archers whose services had been retained, together with the guns, catapults and other engines of war which had been brought from nearby towns, all waiting to discharge their shots on the enemy. The only movement was at the rear of the army, where the restive horses were literally chafing at the bit in the cold and damp of the late autumn morning and had to be exercised by the mounted men-at-arms and their valets. Well fed, well armed, secure in their superior numbers, this was an army brimming with confidence and eager to crush the tantalisingly small force that had had the temerity to invade France and capture one of its finest towns.

On the other side were the English, an equally fearsome sight, but for different reasons. These were trapped and desperate men, who knew that only a miracle could save them from death, and were therefore determined to sell themselves dearly. For almost three weeks they had marched across hostile enemy territory, their supplies of food and drink dwindling away to nothing, unable to wash or shave, their armour tarnished and their surcoats and banners grimy and tattered by the constant exposure to the elements. Some, it was said, were even barefoot, having completely worn out their shoes during the trek. Stomachs and bowels, already churning with dysentery and starvation, were now turned to water by fear. Many of the archers were reduced to cutting off their soiled breeches and undergarments in an attempt to allow nature to take its course more easily — an option not available to the men-at-arms, encased in their padded steel plate armour. Grim though the sight of them must have been, the smell was probably worse.[2]

In the end, it was the nerve of the English that broke first. After perhaps several hours of this motionless confrontation, Henry realised that the French were not going to make the first assault, as he had expected, and that they would continue to stand astride his route for as long as it took: they did not need to attack because fear and starvation would do their work in destroying his army for them. Indeed, one of the arguments put forward in the royal council at Rouen when deciding what battle plan to adopt had been that the mere sight of so many French princes in the front ranks of the army would be sufficient to strike such terror into the hearts of the English that they would simply run away. This was clearly what the French were still expecting to happen.[3]

Aware that the longer the impasse continued, the more his men's morale would ebb away, Henry decided that he would have to tear up the rule-book and make the first move. He ordered the baggage, the horses, the royal chaplains and all those who had been left behind in and around Maisoncelle to move forward to the rear of the army, so that they would not be left isolated and at risk of pillagers when the fighting began. Once most of the baggage train had taken up their new position, all the priests in the army were now commanded to employ themselves in prayer on its behalf: "then, indeed, and for as long as the conflict lasted," wrote our timorous chaplain, in perhaps one of the most evocative and human moments of the entire campaign,

> I, who am now writing this and was then sitting on a horse among the baggage at the rear of the battle, and the other priests present did humble our souls before God and . . . said in our hearts: "Remember us, O Lord, our enemies are gathered together and boast themselves in their excellence. Destroy their strength and scatter them, that they may understand, because there is none other that fighteth for us but only Thou, our God." And also, in fear and trembling, with our eyes raised to heaven we cried out that God would have compassion upon us and upon the crown of England . . .[4]

With the words of his priests ringing in his ears, the king gave the order for the army to prepare to advance. Every man, regardless of rank, now knelt at his command, kissed the ground and took a morsel of the earth from beneath his feet and placed it in his mouth. This extraordinary ritual was conducted with all the solemnity of a genuine Church sacrament. It combined elements of both the Last Supper and its commemoration, the Eucharist, in which the Christian receives the bread in remembrance that Christ the Redeemer died for him, but also of the committal words of the burial service, "earth to earth, ashes to ashes, dust to dust." Physical death and spiritual salvation were thus represented in the single act.[5]

The vitally important command of the archers had been given to one of the most experienced of all Henry's military officers, the steward of the royal household, Sir Thomas Erpingham, a fifty-eight-year-old Norfolk gentleman who had begun his own military career at the age of eleven, serving with the Black Prince in Aquitaine. In 1380, at the age of twenty-three and already a knight, he had become a retainer of John of Gaunt, fighting for the rest of the decade in French and Spanish campaigns to establish Gaunt's claim to the crown of Castile and León. He had accompanied Gaunt's son, the future Henry IV, on crusade in Prussia in 1390–1 and again, in 1393, on crusade to the Holy Land. In 1398–9 he had shared Henry's exile and played a significant part in his triumphant return by commanding the ambush that captured Richard II, whom he then kept a prisoner in the Tower. As a reward for organising Richard's deposition, he was made constable of Dover and warden of the Cinque Ports, carried Henry's sword before him at the coronation and, in 1401, was made a Knight of the Garter. Henry V had appointed him his household steward on his accession and made him a witness to his will, as well as entrusting him with the negotiations for the surrender of Harfleur.[6]

It was Sir Thomas Erpingham who now had the responsibility of ensuring that the deployment of the archers was not jeopardised by Henry's decision to move all his battle lines forward. The king was taking an enormous risk, particularly with regard to his archers. They had first to pull out their stakes, which was in itself a difficult task, since they had been hammered into the muddy earth at sufficient depth to resist the weight of a charging horse. Because of the angle at which the stakes had to project towards the enemy, the archers would not have been able to pull them out from behind, but would have had to go round in front of them, exposing themselves to enemy action while they did so. This dangerous manoeuvre had to be repeated once they had taken up their new positions as the archers would have had to stand with their backs to the enemy — this time within their artillery range — to hammer in the stakes again.

This was the obvious moment for the French to launch an attack, when the archers were at their most vulnerable, preoccupied with their tasks and unprotected by their stakes. Yet the cavalry corps designated for the task did not even attempt to mount a charge and the crossbowmen and gunners failed to shoot. Instead, the whole French army seems to have stood and watched as Henry ordered his banners forward with the cry, "In the name of Almyghti God, and of Saint George, Avaunt baner! and Saint George this day thyn helpe!" (or, depending on the source, possibly the more prosaic "Felas, lets go!"). His troops roared out their battle-cries, his musicians sounded their trumpets and drums and the whole army advanced in battle formation towards the French lines. Incredible though it seems, the English were allowed to take up their new position and replant the archers' stakes without any opposition. They were now within longbow shot of the enemy.[7]

Where was the French cavalry at this crucial moment? The answer is unclear. Chronicle accounts of the battle are confused, sometimes contradictory and often dictated by nationalist pride or party politics. The Breton Guillaume Gruel claimed that there were large numbers of "Lombards and Gascons" among the cavalry and accused these "foreigners" of fleeing at the first fusillade from the English archers. Others, such as the monk of St Denis and Gilles le Bouvier, laid the blame squarely at the door of the Armagnacs Clignet de Brabant and Louis de Bourdon, who were in command of the elite cavalry corps. The only thing most French chroniclers agreed on was that at the moment when they should have launched their cavalry charges against the English archers many of the mounted men-at-arms were not at their stations and were simply not to be found. Gilles le Bouvier, for example, asserts that they simply did not expect the English to attack, so some of them had wandered off to warm themselves and others were walking or feeding their horses.[8]

In other words, it was a classic case of being caught by surprise. And in this instance the sheer size of the French army was a major impediment to effective action. If the cavalry were at the rear, and not on the wing, they could not have observed the English advance and reacted promptly. Instead, valuable time would have been lost in relaying the information down the line and then in attempting to rally and mobilise their scattered forces. By the time sufficient mounted men-at-arms had gathered to launch a cavalry charge, it was too late. The English had taken up their new position and were now not only firmly entrenched behind their stakes again, but, having advanced into the narrower gap between the woodlands of Azincourt and Tramecourt, were protected on their flanks.[9] It would now be impossible for the French to carry out their planned manoeuvre of riding round in a semicircular pincer movement to attack the English archers from the sides. Instead, they would have to do exactly what they had been trying to avoid: launch a frontal assault straight into the firing line of the archers.

Anywhere between 800 and 1200 mounted men-at-arms should have rallied to the standards of Clignet de Brabant and Louis de Bourdon; perhaps as few as 420 did so. It was a catastrophic diminution in numbers because the effectiveness of a cavalry charge depended on the weight behind it. Not only did the French not have enough mounted men to ride down the massed ranks of English archers; they were also unable to maintain the serried ranks that were the other component of a successful all-out strike. This was the result not just of a lack of discipline — a charge the chroniclers were quick to throw at them — but more of the state of the battlefield. Henry's wisdom in sending out scouts in the middle of the night to test the ground now paid dividends. As the French cavalry discovered to their cost, the heavy rain had turned the newly ploughed fields into a quagmire of thick mud and surface water, slowing down their horses and causing them to slip, stumble and even fall. In such conditions it was difficult, if not impossible, to maintain a united front for what was supposed to be an irresistible onslaught.[10]

In the event, therefore, only 120 men-at-arms charged from one side of the French vanguard and 300 from the other towards the archers on each wing of the English army. Because their own lines were much broader than those of the English and the woods on either flank effectively channelled them inwards, the French were forced onto a converging trajectory over the battlefield. The men-at-arms of the vanguard, who had begun their own advance immediately after the cavalry set off, therefore found themselves in increasing difficulty as they got closer to the enemy because they were compelled to cover more of the same ground that the cavalry had already ridden over. The combined weight of heavily armed men-at-arms, charging on armoured horses, had churned up the already wet and muddy ground to such a depth that those on foot now found themselves floundering in mud up to their knees. The problem was exacerbated for each row of densely packed men-at-arms following in the foot-steps of the men in front. Dragged down by the weight of their own armour, their plate-clad feet slipping as they tried to keep their balance on the uneven, treacherous ground, and struggling against the suction of the mud at every step, it is not surprising that they too were unable to maintain the good order in which they had set out.

As the French cavalry bore down on the English archers, answering the English battle-cries with their own "Montjoie! Montjoie!," Sir Thomas Erpingham, who had dismounted and joined the king on foot in the front of the main battle, threw his baton of office into the air as a signal to fire and shouted the command "Now strike!"[11] Five thousand archers then raised their longbows and loosed a volley of arrows so dense, so fast and so furious that the sky literally darkened over as though a cloud had passed before the face of the sun. One can imagine how the English stood listening to the reverberations from the bow-strings and the whistling of the flights as they sped through the air, followed, after a few heart-stopping moments, by the thud of bodkin arrowheads striking through plate-metal armour and tearing into flesh, and the screams of the wounded and dying. The terrified horses, maddened by the pain of the arrows, plunged, reared and fell, throwing off their riders beneath their flailing hooves and into the suffocating mud. Those horses that got as far as the front line were either impaled on the stakes or wheeled round to avoid them and fled out of control: a very few managed to escape into the neighbouring woodland, but most were either struck down by the deadly hail of arrows or gal-loped back — straight into their own advancing front lines, scattering them and trampling them down in their headlong flight.[12]

Three of the cavalry leaders were themselves killed in this first assault. Robert de Chalus, Ponchon de la Tour and Guillaume de Saveuses all suffered the same fate: their horses were brought down by the stakes, causing them to fall among the English archers, who promptly dispatched them.[13] Tensions within the leadership of the cavalry unit might have contributed to its ig-nominious performance. Guillaume de Saveuses, "a very valiant knight," had ridden ahead of his companions, expecting them to follow. They did not. It may have been that they were deterred by the hail of arrows and the stakes, but it may also have been because de Saveuses and his two brothers Hector and Philippe were prominent Burgundians in a primarily Armagnac force. Hector had been a notorious captain of a gang of men-at-arms who had plundered and terrorised large areas of Picardy; captured by the Armagnacs while supposedly on a pilgrimage to Paris, he had escaped execution only through the intervention of the countess of Hainault and two Armagnacs whom his brother Philippe had captured in retaliation and forced to intercede on his behalf.[14]

One can well imagine that there was no sympathy, very little trust and probably some rivalry between men such as the de Saveuses brothers and their fellow captains who were loyal to the Armagnac cause. The relationship with their nominal leader Clignet de Brabant, in particular, was fraught with difficulties. De Brabant was an Armagnac through and through, a chamberlain of Charles d'Orléans and a renowned jouster, who had chivalrously dropped his own lance in a feat of arms against a Portuguese knight earlier in the year because his opponent's visor had flown open. Like the de Saveuses brothers, he had a reputation for roaming the countryside round Paris at the head of an armed band, terrorising the inhabitants and laying waste their lands. Though he did this in pursuit of the Armagnac cause, he had his own personal reasons for loathing the Burgundians, who, four years earlier, had executed his brother as a rebel after besieging and capturing the town of Moismes, of which he was captain.[15]

There were also private quarrels between the leaders of this group, as well as the more obvious political ones. Not many years earlier, Geffroi de Boucicaut and Jean Malet, sire de Graville, had had a very public falling-out. They had both fallen in love with the same woman, Charlotte de la Cochette, a maiden in the queen's household. De Boucicaut, a younger brother of the more famous marshal, had struck de Graville in a jealous rage and de Graville had sworn to exact his revenge before the year was out. At around eight o'clock on the evening of the last day of the year, he had therefore set upon de Boucicaut in the streets of Paris and given him a severe beating. Neither de Boucicaut nor de Graville forgot or forgave the insult he had received, and the whole shabby episode was gleefully immortalised by the chroniclers, the tabloid journalists of the time.[16]

However great the horsemanship skills or the superiority of their armour that had led to the selection of the men-at-arms for the prestigious cavalry force, these were probably not enough to outweigh the political and personal rivalries between their leaders. Why should a de Saveuses take orders from de Brabant? Why should de Brabant risk his own life to come to the aid of Guillaume de Saveuses? Why should de Boucicaut fight side by side with the man who had humiliated him so publicly? However much they hated the English, these men hated one another even more.

What is most striking about the leaders of the cavalry corps is not so much their failure to achieve their military objective in the battle, but the fact that they almost all escaped with their lives. Clignet de Brabant, Louis de Bourdon, Hector and Philippe de Saveuses, Geffroi de Boucicaut, Jean Malet, sire de Graville, Georges, sire de la Trémouille (another unsavoury character who, some years later, dragged the sire de Giac naked from his bed, drowned him and married his widow),[17] Jean d'Angennes, Alleaume de Gapannes, Ferry de Mailly,[18] all survived and evaded capture. This made them unique among the companies who fought for France that day and lends weight to the contemporary complaint that, after their abortive attempt to destroy the English archers, they made no further effort to rejoin their compatriots in the fight.[19] In the words of Gilles le Bouvier, apart from the handful who were killed, "all the rest failed to do their duty, for they fled shamefully, and never struck a blow against the English." As a herald, and a recorder of such things, he duly noted the names of each of these leaders on a roll-call of eternal dishonour.[20]

The failure of the cavalry attack had far more serious consequences for the Frenchmen following in its wake than for those actually taking part in it. As they toiled through the churned-up mud and tried to avoid being trampled by the fleeing horses, they were completely at the mercy of the English archers, who bombarded them with volley after deadly volley. Arrows flew so thick and fast that the French were convinced that Henry had planted a secret ambuscade of two hundred selected archers in the woods of Tramecourt to attack them from the flanks as well. (The story was repeated by several chroniclers, but flatly denied by le Févre de St Remy: "I have heard it said and certified as the truth by an honourable man who, on that day, was with and in the company of the king of England, as I was, that he did no such thing.")[21]

The accepted tactical response to a bombardment of this kind was to return similar fire. This the French were unable to do. Most of their own crossbowmen and archers were at the rear of their ranks and therefore unable to get a clear sight line at the enemy or, indeed, to inflict a comparable mass volley without injuring or killing their own men, who stood between them and their targets. Those on the flanks were in a better position to do so, but they could not maintain the speed or fire-power of the English longbows. The French artillery — consisting of catapults and some cannon — made a desultory attempt to launch a bombardment but, from fear of the English arrows, they were over-hasty in taking their aim, did little damage and, as the chaplain related with evident satisfaction, beat a hasty retreat. They succeeded in inflicting some casualties, for the exchequer records note that Roger Hunt, an archer in the retinue of the Lancashire knight Sir James Harington, had the misfortune "to be killed at the battle of Agincourt *cum uno gune* [with a gun]."[22]

As the English arrows rained down on them, the men-at-arms of the French vanguard, closely followed by those in the main body of the army, continued their inexorable march towards the enemy. Those without shields (which were not commonly used at the time) were forced to lower the visors of their bascinets to protect their eyes and faces from the lethal hail falling upon them. Even this was not sufficient to defend them completely, for eye-slits and ventilation holes were vulnerable to the narrow points of bodkin arrowheads, so they had to lower their heads as well.[23]

With visor down, the bascinet was like a diver's helmet, but without the manufactured air supply: it plunged the wearer into a disorientating and isolating artificial darkness. Vision was restricted either to a single slit, half an inch wide, which gave a narrow but unimpeded horizontal line of sight, or to a slightly wider opening of similar length, but with vertical bars to protect the aperture from a sword stroke, which created several blind spots. Though the visor projected outwards, like a pig's snout, and was punctuated with holes to allow the wearer to breathe, the circulation of air was very restricted and, in the throes of exertion, a panting man-at-arms must have felt almost suffocated by the lack of oxygen. If he dared, or was desperate enough, to raise his visor, he risked receiving an arrow in the face, just as Henry V himself had done at the battle of Shrewsbury.[24]

Ironically, had the men-at-arms been professional or lower-class infantrymen, such as the citizen militias of the neighbouring towns in Flanders and Picardy, they might have suffered less. The lighter, more flexible equipment of the ordinary infantryman, combining pieces of plate with mail and *cuir bouilli*, or boiled leather, made them more vulnerable to English longbow arrows, but enabled them to move faster and with greater freedom. The French nobility, clad head to toe in "white harness," or suits of plate armour, were literally bogged down by the treacherous terrain. In other circumstances the weight of their armour — between fifty and sixty pounds — would have been as irrelevant as carrying his full kit is to a modern soldier: Boucicaut could not only vault onto his horse but also climb up the underside of a ladder in full armour. The French were not vainglorious amateurs playing at war, as they are so often portrayed. They were hardened veterans who had spent their lives in arms: on crusade, fighting in Italy, Spain and Portugal and, most recently, in their own civil wars. They were as used to wearing their armour as their civilian clothes.

At Agincourt, however, the quagmire created by the hooves of the hundreds of horses that had charged over the newly ploughed, rain-soaked earth was literally a death trap for those wearing white harness. Sweating and overheated in the confines of their close-fitting metal prisons, the French men-at-arms were exhausted by the sheer labour of having to put one foot in front of the other as they struggled to extract feet, shins, sometimes even knees from the heavy, cloying mud. The heavy plate armour that marked them out as gentlemen of rank and wealth, and in other circumstances would have made them virtually invincible, had now become their greatest liability.

With heads lowered and unable to see properly where they were going, the French men-at-arms, many of them already wounded by the arrows hurtling down upon them, stumbled and slipped across the battlefield. As they struggled to maintain the solidity of their ranks, they had also to contend with the obstacles in their path: the fallen men and horses of the abortive cavalry strike, some dead, others dying or wounded; the frantic chargers that had escaped the slaughter, some of them riderless and fleeing out of control straight at them; the bodies of their own comrades who had fallen in the mud and were unable to get to their feet again in the crush of men pushing on them from behind.

It says something for the determination and discipline of the French that they overcame these difficulties to close with the enemy lines in such weight and numbers that the English were driven back six or twelve feet with the first shock. At the sight of this setback, the chaplain and the "clerical militia" in the baggage train all "fell upon our faces in prayer before the great mercy-seat of God, crying out aloud in bitterness of spirit that God might even yet remember us and the crown of England and, by the grace of His supreme bounty, deliver us from this iron furnace and the terrible death which menaced us."[25]

Despite being hopelessly outnumbered (and despite the disheartening wails of the terrified clergy behind them), the thin line of men-at-arms miraculously did not break under the French onslaught. Not only did they hold their own, but they recovered quickly and began to push forward again to regain their lost ground. While they closed with the enemy in fierce hand-to-hand fighting, the archers kept up a constant volley of arrows which, in these close quarters, were even more deadly than before, piercing visors and slicing through steel plate as if it were made of cloth. When the arrows ran out — as they must have done fairly quickly — the archers cast aside their long-bows and took up their swords, daggers and the lead mallets that they had used to hammer in their stakes. Running out from behind their barricade, they attacked with all the fury of men who knew they could expect no mercy for themselves. Striking down the men-at-arms with their mallets, they plunged their swords and daggers through the visors of the fallen.[26]

The battle was now at its height. The chaplain could only marvel at the transformation in the English. "For the Almighty and Merciful God . . . did, as soon as the lines of battle had so come to grips and the fighting had begun, increase the strength of our men which dire want of food had previously weakened and wasted, took away from them their fear, and gave them dauntless hearts. Nor, it seemed to our older men, had English-men ever fallen upon their enemies more boldly and fearlessly or with a better will." The situation was so desperate that there was no time to take prisoners: every French man-at-arms, "without distinction of person," was slaughtered where he fell.[27]

And they were falling in their hundreds, brought down not just by English weapons but also by their own weight of num-bers. Their ranks were so densely packed, and the men-at-arms so hemmed in on all sides, that they found it difficult to wield their weapons effectively. Worse still, when those in the front ranks recoiled in the face of the English rally, they came up against those behind them, who were striving to engage with the enemy. These men too were being pressed forward by the ranks behind them, who could not see what was happening at the front. So great was the pressure of the impetus forward from so many thousands of men that those in the front lines, caught between that and an immovable enemy, were simply over-whelmed, pushed over and crushed underfoot

In the chaos and confusion, the living fell among the dead. Great piles of bodies began to build up in front of the standards indicating the presence of Henry V, the duke of York and Lord Camoys, which were the main focus of the French attack. Many of the wounded and those who simply lost their footing in the crush were suffocated under the weight of their compatriots or, unable to remove their helms, drowned in the mud. The ragged archers ran hither and thither, administering the *coup de grâce* to the stricken and helpless. Others, arming themselves with the weapons of the fallen, joined their men-at-arms in clambering on top of the heaps of slain to butcher the hordes of Frenchmen below, who continued to advance relentlessly into the jaws of death.[28]

The English did not have it all their own way. Had the men-at-arms not recovered so quickly from the first assault and held their line, the English position would have collapsed immediately, with disastrous consequences. And for some considerable time afterwards there was a real danger that the French would overwhelm them with sheer numbers. There were desperate moments, too, in the hand-to-hand fighting. Every French man-at-arms worth his salt wanted the honour of striking a blow against the king of England and, in the grand chivalric tradition, a group of eighteen Burgundian esquires in the company of Jehan, sire de Croy, formed themselves into an impromptu brotherhood before the battle and swore to strike the crown — with its provocative fleur-de-lis — from the king's head, or die in the attempt. "As they did," le Févre reported drily — all eighteen, to a man, were killed (as were the sire de Croy and his two sons), though not before one of them had got close enough to Henry to sever one of the fleur-de-lis from his crown.[29] In what may have been part of the same incident, Henry's brother Humphrey, duke of Gloucester, was wounded by a sword-thrust in the groin and fell at his brother's feet. Careless of his own safety, the king stood astride his body and fought off his attackers until his brother could safely be carried away out of the mêlée.[30]

For three long hours the slaughter continued, as the English hacked and stabbed their way through the vanguard and the main body of the French army. At the end of that time, the flower of French chivalry lay dead on the field. The oriflamme, the sacred banner of France round which they had rallied, was also lost in the battle, probably trampled underfoot when its bearer fell; it was never recovered. The English now felt secure enough to begin searching through the mounds of dead and wounded to take prisoners for ransom. In this way, some of the grandees of France fell into the hands of the ordinary English-men whom they had so foolishly despised. The duke of Bourbon was captured by Ralph Fowne, a man-at-arms in the retinue of Sir Ralph Shirley, and Marshal Boucicaut by a humble esquire named William Wolf. Arthur, count of Richemont, brother of the duke of Brittany and younger son of Henry V's stepmother, was discovered alive, with minor wounds, under the corpses of two or three knights; their blood had so drenched his surcoat that his coat of arms was barely recognisable. Charles d'Orléans was found by English archers in similar circumstances.[31]

At this moment, when victory seemed assured and the En-glish were preoccupied with taking as many prisoners as pos-sible, a cry went up that the French had rallied and were about to launch another attack. In this crisis, Henry gave the only order possible. His men were physically and emotionally ex-hausted after three hours' intense fighting, they were about to face an assault by an unknown quantity of fresh troops and they had in their midst large numbers of the enemy who, although they were prisoners, could not be relied upon to remain inert and neutral during renewed fighting. He therefore commanded his men to kill all except their most eminent prisoners, "lest they should involve us in utter disaster in the fighting that would ensue," as the chaplain explained.[32]

In humanitarian terms, Henry's decision was indefensible: to order the killing of wounded and unarmed prisoners in such a cold and calculated way violated every principle of decency and Christian morality. In chivalric terms, it was also reprehensible. "It is against right and gentility to slay the one who gives him-self up," Christine de Pizan had written a few years earlier. The law of arms stated that a man who surrendered should be treated with mercy, "this is to say that his life should be spared, and, more important, the master [that is, the captor] is obliged to defend his prisoner against anyone else who would harm him." On this reading, not only the king but the men to whom the prisoners had surrendered were in breach of their chivalric obligations. In military terms, however, Henry's decision was entirely justified. The safety of his own men was his overriding priority. Even Christine de Pizan had admitted that a prince had the right to execute an opponent who had been captured and handed to him if he was convinced that great harm would befall himself and his people if he allowed him to go free.[33] The prisoners might have had their bascinets removed on capture and be unarmed, but the battlefield was littered with the armour and weapons of the fallen, and it would not have required much ingenuity or energy for the French to re-equip themselves while their captors were preoccupied in fighting off a renewed attack. And to be attacked on two fronts at once would spell death to the little English force.

It is impossible to know how many French prisoners were killed as a result of Henry's order, not least because we have no idea how many had been taken at this stage of the battle. The eyewitness accounts of how the executions were carried out are contradictory, which adds to our difficulty because they also imply a lengthy process that cannot have been practical in the crisis of the moment. The chaplain says that all the prisoners, "save for the dukes of Orléans and Bourbon, certain other illustrious men who were in the king's 'battle,' and a very few others, were killed by the swords either of their captors or of others following after."[34] Who decided which prisoners were sufficiently illustrious to be spared? How were they and the "very few others" separated from the rest condemned to die?

Our other eyewitness, le Févre de St Remy, says that when the order was given, those who had taken prisoners did not wish to kill them — a reluctance that he, rather uncharitably, attributes to a desire not to lose their ransoms, rather than to any sense of chivalric duty towards the captives themselves. Faced with this insubordination, the king was compelled to appoint a single esquire and two hundred archers to perform the mass execution. "So the said esquire fulfilled the king's command; which was a very pitiable thing. For, in cold blood, all the French nobility were there killed, and their heads and faces were cut off; which was a shocking thing to see."[35] Again, this raises the question of how quickly a body of two hundred archers could be raised to carry out the slaughter and how they could be spared from the imminent battle. If there were perhaps several thousand prisoners, as some modern commentators have suggested,[36] then how long must it have taken to behead them all? And if there were so many, why did they not resist when they had nothing to lose?

On this particular occasion we have a third eyewitness who sheds a rather more chilling light on the killings. Ghillebert de Lannoy's military career had begun in 1399, when he had taken part in a French raid on the Isle of Wight, followed by another in 1400 on Falmouth. From 1403 to 1408 he had been in the service of Jehan Werchin, the seneschal of Hainault, accompanying him on crusade to the east, to a tournament in Valencia and to war against the Moors in Spain. Though he had fought in the duke of Burgundy's campaigns of 1408 and 1412, he had also rejoined the Spanish campaign, and fought in the Prussian crusades, where, after being seriously wounded at the siege of Massow, he received the order of knighthood. He had just returned from a period of captivity in England, where he had been imprisoned while on a pilgrimage to the throne of St Patrick, and had obtained his release by paying a ransom to which the duke of Burgundy contributed.[37]

It was now his misfortune to be captured a second time. Though he has nothing whatsoever to say about the battle — which he calls the battle of "Rousseauville" — he records that he was wounded in the knee and in the head and lay with the dead until he was found by those seeking prisoners, captured and held under guard for a short time, before being taken to a nearby house with ten or twelve other prisoners, "all of them helpless." When the cry went up that everyone should kill their prisoners, "to have it done as quickly as possible, fire was tossed into the house where we were helpless. But, by the grace of God, I dragged myself outside and away from the flames on all fours. . . ." Unable to go any further, he was recaptured yet again when the English returned, and, recognised by his coat of arms as being of value, was sold to that canny collector of ransoms Sir John Cornewaille.[38]

Ghillebert de Lannoy does not divulge the fate of his fellow-internees, though one assumes they perished in the flames. The casual brutality of his account has a far more authentic ring to it than those of either the chaplain or le Févre de St Remy and it would have been a faster and more efficient method of disposing of large numbers of prisoners. Even so, one must doubt how many could have been killed by this means, since not all prisoners had been removed from the field, and some must have been slaughtered where they stood, as the other eyewitnesses testify. Yet to claim, as some modern historians have done,[39] that this mass execution was the reason why so many French nobles perished at Agincourt ignores the fact that victory could not have been achieved by such a small army without extraordinarily high levels of casualties among their opponents during the course of the battle, as indeed contemporary chroniclers so graphically describe taking place. The decision to kill the prisoners was undeniably ruthless. Yet if Henry had spared them and they had launched a second front, the outcome of the day would have been very different and Henry himself would be accused of destroying his own men through faint-heartedness or misplaced charity. Significantly, not one of his contemporaries, even among the French, criticised his decision.[40]

Was there any real need to kill the prisoners at all? Some historians, following the monk of St Denis, have claimed that there was no genuine threat of a renewed French attack, and that the whole terrible episode was based on a panicked response to a false alarm. Ghillebert de Lannoy, on the other hand, thought a rally by Antoine, duke of Brabant, prompted the order.[41] This is a possibility, as the duke arrived on the battlefield very late in the day. Like his older brother John the Fearless, Antoine had not joined the other French princes for the muster at Rouen. Instead, he had held aloof until the English crossed the Somme and it became clear that battle was imminent. At that point his loyalty to his country proved stronger than his loyalty to his brother. On 23 October he began a headlong dash across his duchy, posting from Brussels by day and night at such a pace that not all his men could keep up with him. By the morning of 25 October, he was at Pernes, midway between Béthune and St Pol, hearing mass before resuming his journey. Just as the host was being elevated, he was brought news that the battle would take place before midday. With some fifteen miles still to go, he and his household leapt on their horses and rode like furies to

Agincourt, arriving to find the battle already in progress. In his haste, the duke had not had time to put on his full armour or his surcoat bearing his coat of arms. He therefore borrowed the armour of his chamberlain, and tearing two pennons bearing his arms off his trumpets, he put one round his neck as a makeshift blazon and the other on a lance to serve as his banner. He then plunged into the battle, followed by his men, and was promptly cut down and slain, his unorthodox coat of arms having failed to protect him.[42]

Throughout it all, the French mounted rearguard had apparently stood idly by. Contemporary chroniclers blamed this on the absence of their commanders, who had left them to join those fighting on foot, so that there was no one to lead them into battle or give them the order to advance.[43] In fairness, it has to be said that there was little that they could have done. Their intended role had been to pursue and cut down the English as they fled, after the cavalry, vanguard and main body of the army had broken their lines. When this did not happen, they could not intervene effectively because their route to the enemy was blocked by their own men-at-arms. It was not until their own forces had been massacred or retreated in confusion that any sort of cavalry attack was possible — and by then it was a forlorn hope.

Those in charge of the rearguard, the counts of Dammartin and Fauquembergue and the sire de Laurois, had struggled to keep their men together and in order once it became clear that the battle was going against them. Although they were unable to prevent many of them fleeing, they now, finally, rallied a significant number and, with banners and ensigns flying, they made as if to mount a charge. Whether or not they were joined by Clignet de Brabant himself, this motley band of French, Bretons, Gascons and Poitevins united in one last brave effort to save the honour of France. It was doomed to failure. Like those before them, they were met with a hail of arrows and fell with their comrades on the field. All their leaders, except the count of Dammartin and Clignet de Brabant, were killed. The nobility and self-sacrifice they had shown earned them nothing but contempt from their compatriots, who laid the blame for Henry's order to kill the prisoners squarely at the door of "this cursed company of Frenchmen."[44]

The finger of blame was also pointed at a third group of people. In the final stages of the battle, while the English were occupied elsewhere, the alarm was raised that they were being attacked from the rear. Had this been true the English would have been caught between two fronts and in mortal danger, again giving sufficient reason to order the killing of the prisoners. In fact, though there was indeed an attack, it was not upon the army itself, but upon the baggage train. Contemporary chroniclers accused local men of carrying out the robbery and suggest that it was a spur of the moment affair, prompted by the rich pickings available. Three Burgundians, Ysembart d'Azincourt, Robinet de Bournonville and Rifflart de Plamasse, accompanied by a small number of men-at-arms and about six hundred peasants or "people of low estate" from the Hesdin area, were said to be responsible.[45]

It is possible that this was part of the official French battle plan. An attack on "the varlets and their carts" behind English lines had been envisaged in Marshal Boucicaut's earlier plan and a company of several hundred mounted men, under the command of Louis de Bourdon, had been appointed to carry it out.[46] On the day of battle, de Bourdon was reassigned to more important duties, but this does not necessarily mean that the idea was abandoned, especially as there was no shortage of men in the French ranks. What more natural than that the task should be given to local men, who knew the lie of the land intimately and could secretly work their way around the English lines?

The English chaplain, however, suggests that it was an altogether more opportunistic affair, with plunder as its sole objective. He was best placed to know, since he was himself in the baggage train, and had noted that "French pillagers were watching it from almost every side, intending to make an attack upon it immediately they saw both armies engage." According to him, the attack occurred not in the final stages of the battle but as soon as the fighting began and while the baggage train was still being brought up from its original position in and around Maisoncelle. The pillagers "fell upon the tail end of it, where, owing to the negligence of the royal servants, the king's baggage was." This seems a more likely scenario, especially as John Hargrove, a servant of the king's pantry, later received a royal pardon for losing the king's plate and jewels at Agincourt.[47]

Whenever the raid took place, it was successful beyond the dreams of the perpetrators. They acquired £219 16s in cash, jewels (including a gem-studded gold cross worth more than £2166 and a piece of the True Cross), the king's crown, his state sword and the seals of the English chancery. The sword, which rapidly acquired the reputation of having once belonged to King Arthur, was later presented by Ysembart d'Azincourt and Robinet de Bournonville to Philippe, count of Charolais, in the hope that it might persuade him to intercede for them if their theft incurred any repercussions. It was a fruitless gesture. Once the rumour had gained ground that it was their actions which had prompted the killing of the French prisoners, Philippe was forced to give up the sword to his father, John the Fearless, who had the two men arrested and imprisoned. If nothing else, they were convenient scapegoats and punishing them would appease not only the outcry in France but the duke of Burgundy's English ally.[48]

Back on the battlefield, it soon became clear that the attempt to rally the French had failed. With their leaders dead and the king of England advancing menacingly towards them, the last remnants of the rearguard realised that further resistance was futile. Those who still had their horses gave themselves up to flight, abandoning those on foot to their fate and the possession of the field to the English. Though it was obvious that victory was his, Henry had one last formality to observe. Before the battle began, he had ordered that his heralds "should diligently attend only to their own duties" and should not take up arms themselves. As le Févre de St Remy explains, the English heralds had then joined their French counterparts to watch the course of the combat together.[49] By reason of their office, they stood above partisan loyalties and were there as impartial international observers. As if they were attending a joust or tournament, it was their role to record valiant deeds and, ultimately, to award the palm of victory.

It was for this reason that Henry V now summoned them to his presence. He formally requested Montjoie king of arms, the senior herald of France, to tell him whether the victory had fallen to the king of England or to the king of France. In acknowledging that God had indeed given victory to Henry, Montjoie was thus forced to admit that the king of England had won his trial by battle and that he had proved that his cause was just. Afterwards, Henry asked him the name of the castle that stood close to the battlefield and was informed that it was called Azincourt. "And because, said the king, all battles ought to bear the name of the nearest fortress, village or town to the place where they were fought, this battle will now and for ever be known as the battle of Azincourt."[50]

PART III

THE AFTERMATH
OF BATTLE

✤ CHAPTER SIXTEEN ✤

THE ROLL OF THE DEAD

The sheer scale of the French defeat was genuinely humbling, even frightening. Thousands of Frenchmen lay dead on the field of Agincourt. The exact number is impossible to gauge because contemporary chronicle sources vary wildly and there are no comprehensive official administrative records to draw upon. Thomas Walsingham, for instance, gives the very precise figure of 3069 knights and esquires, plus almost a hundred barons, but admits that the number of common people was not counted by the heralds. The chaplain counted ninety-eight men above the rank of banneret, "whose names are set down in a volume of record," which was probably the same source used by Walsingham. He also says that the French lost a further fifteen hundred and more knights "according to their own estimate," and between four and five thousand other gentlemen, "almost the whole nobility among the soldiery of France." On the other hand, the Venetian Antonio Morosini, quoting a letter written at Paris on 30 October, five days after the battle, when no one yet knew for sure what the losses had been, lists (inaccurately) the names of twenty-six barons killed and thirteen taken prisoner, and puts the final number of dead at between ten and twelve thousand, though it is not clear whether this includes commoners.[1]

What is beyond dispute is not so much the precise magnitude of the French losses, but the fact that the corresponding figures for the English dead were, by any standard, infinitesimally small. Only two magnates lost their lives: Edward, duke of York, and Michael de la Pole, the young earl of Suffolk, whose father had died of dysentery at Harfleur a few weeks earlier. Most chroniclers suggest that somewhere in the region of thirty others were killed, together with some four or five gentlemen, of whom only two are usually named, Sir Richard Kyghley and Daffyd ap Llewelyn. These figures are, as we shall see, a serious underestimate of the true total, though it seems unlikely that the real number was as high as the 1600 "men of all ranks" cited by le Févre,[2] if only because this would have been over a quarter of the entire English army and not even the most ardent propagandist could have claimed that such a loss was insignificant.

The most interesting of all the English dead was Edward, duke of York, a man who has been much maligned by posterity. A first cousin of both Richard II and Henry IV, he has been characterised as "unstable and treacherous,"[3] a label that could just as easily be applied to every prominent figure who lived through the troubled reign of Richard II and survived the usurpation and change of dynasty. It was the duke's misfortune to have had to walk a fine political line and to be the victim of both Ricardian and Tudor propagandists (including Shakespeare). A particular favourite of Richard II, he had played a leading role in the arrest of the Appellants and had appealed them for treason in his role as constable of England. On the other hand, he became uncomfortable with Richard's increasingly despotic behaviour, balked at his decision to exile the future Henry IV and in the end deserted to the latter during the usurpation, as did all but a very few die-hard loyalists.

Although he was implicated by association in both the murder of the Appellant duke of Gloucester and the anti-Lancastrian plots of his sister and brother, his own complicity was never proved. He spent seventeen weeks imprisoned at Pevensey Castle after his sister's plot was discovered, but he was treated with a kindliness that casts doubt on his guilt and which he remembered many years later with a legacy of twenty pounds to his former jailer in his will. Though some of his lands remained forfeit to the crown, he won back his former posts and served Henry IV with distinction in Aquitaine and Wales; as a result of his role in the Welsh wars, he earned the friendship of the prince of Wales, who personally stood guarantor for his loyalty in Parliament in 1407 and appointed him to positions of trust in his own reign.[4]

Like many of those in Henry V's inner circles, including the king himself, Edward was deeply religious and imbued with that particular form of self-abasing piety which was the acceptable, mainstream version of Lollardy. When he made his will, during the siege of Harfleur, he called himself "of all sinners the most wicked and guilty" and requested that, if he died away from home, his corpse was to be taken back with the minimum of ceremony by two of his chaplains, six of his esquires and six of his valets. Six candles only were to burn round his bier and he was to be buried in the collegiate church of St Mary and All Saints, which he had founded at Fotheringhay, in Northamptonshire, three years earlier.[5]

Like many of his contemporaries, he was a man of literary tastes, who was familiar with, and able to quote from, the works of Geoffrey Chaucer. What makes him exceptional is that he was also the author of a treatise on hunting, which he wrote and dedicated to Henry V when the latter was prince of Wales. In his prologue he described it as a "simple memorial,"[6] but it is an extraordinary book in many ways. The duke, like most medieval noblemen, was passionate about hunting. For him it was not simply a pleasant pastime, nor even just a practical way of providing fresh meat for the table. It was a battle of wits and skill against a respected quarry, a question of intimate knowledge of habits, habitation and lie of the land, all governed by strictly enforced rules of conduct and etiquette to prevent the killing of breeding animals and those that were too young or inedible, but also to ensure that no part of a carcass was wasted.

Unusually, since the book was designed for the use of the aristocracy, it was not written in French, the language of chivalry, but in English. Much of it is a translation of a famous hunting treatise by Gaston Phoebus, count of Foix, who died in 1391, appropriately enough of a stroke sustained on the hunting field. But the duke of York was no mere translator. He was also Henry IV's official master of hart-hounds[7] and he knew his sport inside out. He therefore drew heavily on his own knowledge to add information that was peculiar to England, and to embellish his original with comments based on his own experience. *The Master of Game* is an unrivalled source of practical information about the medieval practice of hunting, from the basics of choosing the right dog for the right task, through to the highly prized art of correctly dismembering a carcass. It is not a dull scholarly treatise, but a celebration of one man's passion, written with a lyricism to rival that of Chaucer. For the duke, no pleasure on earth could rival that of hunting. It was a foretaste of paradise. "Now shall I prove how hunters live in this world more joyfully than any other men," he had written.

> For when the hunter riseth in the morning, and he sees a sweet and fair morn and clear weather and bright, and he heareth the song of the small birds, the which sing so sweetly with great melody and full of love, each in its own language in the best wise that it can . . . And when the sun is arisen, he shall see fresh dew upon the small twigs and grasses, and the sun by his virtue shall make them shine. And that is great joy and liking to the hunter's heart . . . And when he hath well eaten and drunk he shall be glad and well, and well at his ease. And then shall he take the air in the evening of the night, for the great heat that he hath had, . . . and lie in his bed in fair fresh clothes, and shall sleep well and steadfastly all the night without any evil thoughts of any sins, wherefore I say that hunters go into Paradise when they die, and live in this world more joyfully than any other men.
> . . . Men desire in this world to live long in health and in joy, and after death the health of the soul. And hunters have all these things. Therefore be ye all hunters and ye shall do as wise men.[8]

The manner of the duke's death is not recorded by contemporaries, but it is suggestive that there was a remarkably high casualty rate among his own retinue. (The legend that he was fat, and was therefore trampled underfoot and suffocated, is a late Tudor invention, though it is still repeated unquestioningly by modern historians.[9]) The duke had originally indented to serve with 100 men-at-arms and 300 archers, though he ended up taking 340 archers (and had to mortgage his estates to pay their wages before he sailed from Southampton).[10] By 6 October, when the exchequer records for the second financial quarter began, two days before the departure from Harfleur, his numbers had been reduced to eighty men-at-arms and 296 archers (four of the latter had been struck off because they could not fire the required minimum ten aimed arrows per minute). During the march he lost three more men-at-arms and three more archers, so his entire company at the battle consisted of 370 men. The records of those who reshipped home from Calais reveal that only 283 of them survived the battle: eighty-six of his esquires and archers — almost a quarter of those present — died at Agincourt with him.[11]

This high casualty rate tallies with what we know of the course of the fighting. The duke was commanding the English vanguard, which formed the right wing at the battle, and was therefore the recipient of the assault by the French left wing, led by the count of Vendôme, which also suffered very heavy losses.[12] The chaplain tells us that the fighting was hardest and the piles of bodies highest round the standards of the three English divisions, so this too suggests that the duke and his men were among those who bore the brunt of the French assault. The information that has survived about other English retinues indicates that the duke's losses at Agincourt were exceptionally high.[13]

Sir Richard Kyghley, a Lancashire knight and friend of Sir William Botiller, who had died at Harfleur, had a personal retinue of six men-at-arms and eighteen archers. Sir Richard himself was killed at the battle, with four of his archers, William de Holland, John Greenbogh, Robert de Bradshaw and Gilbert Howson. Although we do not know where or how Kyghley died in the battle, it is interesting to speculate that he may have been in charge of the Lancashire archers and that they may have been on the English right wing, flanking the duke of York's company. The Lancashire contingents certainly seem to have suffered heavier losses than any other retinue, apart from the duke of York's, suggesting that they too were in the midst of the fiercest fighting on that wing.[14]

The other men-at-arms killed at Agincourt whose names have been preserved were also a close-knit group from a single region.[15] Daffyd ap Llewelyn, known to his contemporaries as Davy Gam, has acquired semi-legendary status as the Welshman who was the inspiration for Shakespeare's Fluellen (a corruption of Llewelyn). He was also said to have been the subject of a verse by the rebel princeling Owain Glyn Dŵr, describing him as a short, red-haired man with a squint ("Gam" being a Welsh nickname for squinting). Llewelyn had always been a loyal Lancastrian. His lands, which he held from Henry IV, first as earl of Hereford then as king, were principally in Brecon. During the Welsh revolt, his loyalty made him a target for rebels, and in 1412 he had been betrayed into the hands of Owain Glyn Dŵr and held captive until he was eventually ransomed.[16]

Although he brought a retinue of only three archers to the Agincourt campaign, Llewelyn was knighted on the field, only to fall in the battle. With him died his two sons-in-law Watkin Lloyd and Roger Vaughan, the former of whom had been recruited by John Merbury, the chamberlain of south Wales, as one of a company of nine men-at-arms, fourteen mounted archers and 146 foot archers from Brecon. Vaughan's widow, Gwladis, married as her second husband William Thomas of Raglan, who was also a veteran of Agincourt, and, like her father, was said to have been knighted on the field.[17]

Though the picture is inevitably flawed because the available records are incomplete, one can identify at least 112 men from the English side who were killed in the battle, a figure that excludes those who later died of their wounds. Of these, almost exactly two-thirds were archers, whose names have survived only in exchequer records and would not have been recorded by any contemporary chronicler. When we turn to the French side, there are no equivalent administrative records to give us even a hint of the numbers of non-noble men who died. What we do have are lists of men whose names have been recorded only because they were entitled to bear a coat of arms. These lists were usually compiled by heralds, but even they were unable to be comprehensive. This was sometimes because local knowledge was lacking: a Breton chronicler, such as Alain Bouchart, was able to add the names of several Breton knights whom the Armagnac and Burgundian sources had failed to identify. (Bouchart also noted that all three hundred Breton archers, under the command of Jean de Chateaugiron, sire de Combour, "except for very few," were killed in the battle with him.)[18]

The main reason the lists of French dead are incomplete is that they were simply so numerous. The final toll included three dukes (Alençon, Bar and Brabant), at least eight counts (Blamont, Fauquembergue, Grandpré, Marle, Nevers, Roucy, Vaucourt and Vaudémont) and one viscount (Pulsaye, younger brother of the duke of Bar), which is suggestive.[19] Even the usually indefatigable Monstrelet, who devoted a whole chapter to recording those killed or taken prisoner, managed to record more than three hundred names of the dead before admitting "and many others I omit for the sake of brevity and also because one cannot know how to record them all, because there were too many of them."[20] The fact that the French dead also included an archbishop is shocking. Jean Montaigu, archbishop of Sens, was no ordinary priest. His role in the French army was not the diplomatic or pastoral one of his English colleagues, the bishops of Norwich and Bangor. Nor was he even a clergyman called up to defend his country in the extremes of danger, like those arrayed in England earlier in the summer. He was a member of a rare and dying breed, the militant priest, who was equally at home wielding a sword as a censer. As bishop of Chartres, he had been a member of Charles VI's romance-inspired Court of Love, set up in 1400 to "prosecute" offences against chivalrous behaviour towards ladies.[21] In 1405 his Armagnac loyalties procured him the position of chancellor of France, but he fled when his brother Jehan de Montaigu, grandmaster of the royal household, was executed by the Parisian mob in 1409. He was briefly captured at Amiens, wearing a helmet and body armour, only to resurface in 1411, commanding four hundred knights in defence of St Denis against the English and Burgundians at St Cloud. According to the monk of St Denis, who evidently rather admired this muscular Christian, he died at Agincourt "striking blows on every side with the strength of a Hector." Jean Juvénal des Ursins was less complimentary: the archbishop's death was "not much grieved over," he noted, "as it was not his office."[22]

There are three things that immediately strike even the most casual reader of the roll-call of French dead. The first is the apparently frivolous fact that so many bore the names of heroes of chivalric romances. There are a host of Lancelots, several Hectors, Yvains and Floridases, a Gawain, a Perceval, a Palamedes, a Tristan and an Arthur.[23] Even though the English and French shared the same culture and literature, this is a peculiarly French phenomenon. Romance names were simply not, as a rule, bestowed on the sons of England; "Tristan Anderton, esquire" is a very lonely example among the solid phalanxes of Johns, Williams, Roberts, Thomases, Henrys and Nicholases, which form the bulk of the 430 names listed in the king's retinue.[24] That they were so popular with the French nobility is an indication of the especial devotion to Arthurian romance and its courtly values and aspirations which still endured in the birthplace of chivalry.

The second striking feature of the list of dead is that it reads like a gazetteer of the towns and villages in the vicinity of Agincourt. To take just a few examples at random, Renaud, sire d'Azincourt, and his son Wallerand; Jean and Renaud de Tramecourt; Colart de la Porte, sire de Béalencourt; Raoul, sire de Créquy, and his son Philippe; Mathieu and Jean de Humières (the seigneur de Humières was captured); Alain de Wandonne; Colart and Jean de Sempy; Eustache and Jean d'Ambrines; Jehan de Bailleul.[25] These men, and those like them from the wider area, were the petty nobility upon whom depended the administration of the military, financial, judicial and other public affairs of not just the locality but the whole kingdom. The *baillis* of Amiens, Caen, Evreux, Macon, Meaux, Rouen, Senlis, Sens and Vermandois were all killed, many of them with their sons, and some of them with all the men they had brought from their *bailliage*, or so the citizen of Paris noted in his journal.[26] These men were the landowners, castellans and managers of estates, around whom the economy revolved: of necessity, since they had to be capable of fighting, they were in the prime of life and therefore at their most active. Agincourt cut a great swath through the natural leaders of French society in Artois, Ponthieu, Normandy, Picardy. And there was no one to replace them.

This pattern was repeated on a national scale, with the significant difference that there were plenty of men waiting to step into dead men's shoes — especially from the Burgundian faction. Most of the important royal officers of state died or were captured at Agincourt. Inevitably, the military contingent was particularly hard hit. In addition to the constable Charles d'Albret, France lost her admiral, Jacques de Châtillon, and her grand-master of the crossbowmen, David de Rambures. Her *prévôt* of the marshals, Galois de Fougières, who is still remembered as the inspiration for the foundation of the French *gendarmerie*, was also killed; his body was found on the battlefield and buried in the nave of the abbey church at Auchy, but was exhumed at the request of the Gendarmerie Nationale in 1936 and reburied in the mausoleum of Versailles-Le Chesney.[27] Marshal Boucicaut was captured and would die in an English prison.[28]

The king's household officers were also cut down in huge numbers. Among the casualties were two of its most senior members, Guichard Dauphin, the grand-master of the household, and Guillaume de Martel, sire de Bacqueville, bearer of the oriflamme, and two of the latter's sons. As the monk of St Denis lamented, Dauphin (a nephew of Charles d'Albret) and de Bacqueville were not young hot-heads, but "veteran knights, renowned for their high birth and military experience, who had guided the kingdom with their wise counsel"; their deaths were among those most to be regretted because although they had argued against giving battle, they chose to fight in the mêlée, whatever the outcome, rather than retreat with dishonour.[29] Louis de Bourbon, count of Vendôme, and Charles d'Ivry, the former ambassadors to England, were both taken prisoner, though the latter was reported dead, with his eldest son, another Charles d'Ivry, who had indeed met his end in the battle.[30]

As is already apparent from the examples of local men who

died at Agincourt, the third most striking aspect of the French list of the dead is that so many of them came not just from the same class but from the same families. From the greatest to the least, almost every family in the north of France with any pretension to nobility of birth lost at least one relative, and in some particularly tragic cases whole families were wiped out. Even the king of France himself was not exempt. Charles VI lost seven of his closest blood relatives in the battle: Jean, duke of Alençon; Edouard, duke of Bar, his brother, Jean de Bar, viscount of Pulsaye, and their nephew, Robert, count of Marle; Charles d'Albret; and finally, perhaps most ironically, both the younger brothers of John the Fearless, Antoine, duke of Brabant, and Philippe, count of Nevers.[31]

Time and again, the roll-call records brothers or fathers and sons who died together on the field of Agincourt. There are so many examples of these that to list them would be overwhelming, but it is worth pointing out that it is not unusual to find two or even three brothers who lost their lives in the battle. Jehan de Noyelle, a chamberlain of the duke of Burgundy, was killed there with his brothers Pierre and Lancelot, as were Oudart, sire de Renty, and his brothers Foulques and Jean; three brothers of Regnault de Chartres, the archbishop of Reims and chancellor of France, were also among the dead.[32] Worse still, Enguerrand de Gribauval and Marie Quiéret lost all four of their sons at Agincourt, and were left with only their daughter, Jeanne, as the sole survivor and heiress to the family estates near Abbeville. It is likely that this was not the end of their suffering, for the Quiérets also lost several other members of their family, including Hutin de Quiéret, who was killed, and Bohort Quiéret, sire de Heuchin, and Pierre Quiéret, sire de Ramecourt, who were both captured. A fourth Quiéret, Jean, escaped with his life.[33]

A similar tale of unimaginable loss was sustained by David de Rambures, master of the crossbowmen of France, who came from an ancient family of Ponthieu, which traced its ancestry back to a knight who had been on the First Crusade at the end of the eleventh century. A Burgundian by allegiance, he had been a member of the king's council since 1402 and helped to negotiate the Leulinghen truces with England in 1413. As we have seen, he had also been very active in securing local defences in preparation for the English invasion. In 1412 he had embarked on a grand scheme to build a chateau de Rambures, which was to be the future family seat for himself and his heirs. The building work had to be temporarily suspended when de Rambures was summoned to help organise resistance to the English; it would be another half-century before it recommenced. Not only was David de Rambures himself killed at Agincourt, but three of his five sons, Jean, Hue and Philippe; a fourth son, another Jean, was a clergyman and therefore did not take part in the battle. The eldest son, André, survived but lost his inheritance, which was confiscated during the English conquest of Normandy, and it was not until after their withdrawal in 1450 that the family recovered the fledgling chateau and their lands. Like the de Gribauvals, the de Rambures brothers also lost members of their mother's family, including Philippe d'Auxy, sire de Dampierre, and his son.[34]

Terrible though it must have been to lose two generations of a single family, there were those unfortunate enough to lose three. Robert, sire de Boissay, was one of the grand old men of French chivalry. He had been a companion of Bertrand du Guesclin, the simple Breton squire who rose to be constable of France and became a national hero for leading the French recovery after the defeat at Poitiers, and he was at du Guesclin's side when the great man died during the siege of Châteauneuf-de-Randon in 1380. Nine years later, he was one of twenty-two knights who jousted at St Denis before the king, whose councillor and chamberlain he later became. Such was his reputation that, when he was arrested in 1404 and charged with various crimes committed in connection with a conflict of authority between the *prévôt* of Paris and the grand-master of the king's household, he was entirely cleared of any wrongdoing: "the said Boissay, whose nobility is known to all, who has served the king so well, and who is wise, rich and an outstanding knight, so steadfast, . . . never accused or convicted of any crime."[35]

Inevitably, de Boissay became caught up in the political struggle between the Armagnacs and Burgundians; he and his sons were among those Armagnacs who were violently seized from the dauphin's household by the Cabochiens and thrown into prison during the revolt of 1413. Despite his advanced age, Robert de Boissay took up arms once again to resist the English invasion. He was killed at Agincourt, together with his two grandsons Colart and Charles. His son-in-law Thibaut de Chantemerle was captured at the battle and apparently never returned home,[36] dying while still a prisoner in England. Like the de Rambures family, the de Boissays were dispossessed during Henry V's conquest of Normandy, and it was many years later before another grandson Laurent de Boissay was able to regain the family lordship of Mesnières.[37]

Such stories could be told many times over, but one more is worth relating, if only because it gives us a rare glimpse of one of the women who lost so much in the battle. Perrette de la Rivière was the fourth child of Bureau de la Rivière, the friend and confidant of Charles V. Her two brothers Charles and Jacques both attached themselves to the Armagnac cause; Jacques, who was chamberlain to the dauphin, was arrested and imprisoned during the Cabochien revolt of 1413. A report that he had committed suicide in prison was circulated, but in fact he was murdered by the new Burgundian captain of Paris, who hung his body on a scaffold and put his decapitated head on public display. Perrette's sister Jeanne, a celebrated beauty, married Jacques de Châtillon, the Armagnac admiral of France, and in 1409 Perrette herself married another Armagnac, Gui de la Roche-Guyon, a chamberlain of Charles VI, whose hereditary right it was to bear in battle the "Draco normannicus," the dragon standard of the dukes of Normandy.[38]

At the battle of Agincourt, Perrette's husband and her brothers-in-law Philippe de la Roche-Guyon and Jacques de Châtillon were all killed. Gui had been one of the leaders of the left wing, under the count of Vendôme, which suffered particularly heavy casualties. As bearer of the "Draco normannicus" it was his proud duty never to retreat before the English and it was understood that he would die in its defence. Jacques de Châtillon, who, with Raoul de Gaucourt, had been one of the founder members of the Order of the Prisoner's Shackle, had taken his place as admiral of France in the vanguard and died there.[39] Perrette's brother, Charles de la Rivière, count of Dammartin, survived the carnage but there was little consolation in his escape: as one of the leaders of the rearguard, he was accused of having fled the field without ever having raised his sword.[40]

Bereft of almost all the adult males in her family, Perrette had now to take charge of her husband's estates and bring up her four infants on her own. In her husband's place, she became *châtelaine* of La Roche-Guyon, "the most inaccessible and the most impregnable of the castles of Normandy." When Henry V invaded Normandy a second time, in 1417, one of the first places he occupied was Roncheville, which had belonged to the Roche-Guyons for half a century. As the other castles and towns of the duchy fell to him, La Roche-Guyon stood firm, Perrette having taken the precaution of restocking the fortress with men, arms and supplies. After the fall of Rouen in January 1419, Henry V could no longer afford to leave La Roche-Guyon in enemy hands and sent Richard Beauchamp, earl of Warwick, to capture it.

Despite being one of Henry's most able captains, the earl met with such decided resistance that he was unable to make any headway. Gui le Bouteiller, the turncoat captain of Rouen and "a person full of experience and resourcefulness," then advised him to mine the fortress walls from the caves that riddled the neighbourhood. Having held out for several months, Perrette was forced to capitulate to save the lives of her garrison. According to the monk of St Denis, Gui le Bouteiller had his eyes on both the castle and its *châtelaine*: as a reward for his advice, Henry V granted him the castle and its dependencies in perpetuity for himself and his heirs, and gave his permission for him to marry Perrette. But both men had underestimated the courage and obstinacy of the lady herself. She flatly refused to marry le Bouteiller, not just because she considered him "a disloyal traitor" for taking the oath of allegiance to Henry V after the fall of Rouen, but because she had no intention of disinheriting her two sons by Gui de la Roche-Guyon, the elder of whom was not yet eight years old.

On 2 June 1419 she and her children, with all their moveable goods, left La Roche-Guyon under the king's safe-conduct, and were brought before him at Mantes. Henry offered to pardon her rebellion against him, if she accepted Gui le Bouteiller as her husband and took the oath of allegiance to him as "the legitimate heir to the throne of France." Once again, Perrette refused, declaring that ruin was less odious to her than marriage with "the most vile of traitors" and that she recognised only the dauphin as the true heir of France. Unusually, Henry V allowed this defiance to go unpunished and gave the redoubtable Perrette and her brood permission to leave Normandy unmolested and go wherever they pleased.[41]

In a macabre way, Perrette de la Rivière was more fortunate than some of the other women who lost husbands, fathers, sons and brothers in the battle. At least she knew they were dead, for the bodies of Gui de la Roche-Guyon and Jacques de Châtillon were among the very few to be identified by their servants and recovered from the field.[42] For many women there was no such certainty, and for months afterwards they were left in limbo, not knowing the fate of their loved ones or whether they themselves were wives or widows. The emotional distress this caused was exacerbated by the financial problems that the complex situation created.

The sisters of Charles, sire de Noviant, for example, knew that he was killed in the battle because his body was found, but the fate of Jean, his brother and heir, was still not known at the beginning of December. No ransom demand had been received, but the possibility remained that he was still alive and a prisoner somewhere in England. Until Jean's death was also confirmed, his sisters could not legally inherit the family estates. Though they were granted permission to administer and enjoy the use of them, they could not make any permanent settlement or disposal, and even the most basic transaction was complicated by the inability to pinpoint legal ownership. Ysabeau la Mareschalle, Charles's childless widow, even had to look to her sisters-in-law to pay her widow's dower.[43]

Worse still was the case of the unfortunate Jeanne de Gaillouvel, wife of Pierre de Hellenvillier, the *bailli* of Evreux, in Normandy. As late as 9 May 1416, almost six months after the battle, she had not yet discovered what had happened to her husband and she and her seven children were in severe financial straits. Pierre de Hellenvillier had held many of his lands, lordships and revenues in chief from the king, but the royal officials had taken them back into the king's hands, saying that her husband must be dead. Jeanne had clung to the belief that her husband was still alive and made diligent efforts to learn news of him. "She heard some say that her husband was a prisoner of a knight of England called Cornwall, by which she hopes at the blessing of the Lord to have good and certain news soon, hopefully that her husband is living rather than dead." It would, she pleaded, "be a very hard, costly and damaging thing," if she were to be deprived of so much of her husband's income on the mere assumption that he was dead. Jeanne's request to be allowed to keep the revenues until she had certain news of her husband's fate was temporarily granted, but it seems likely that it was a lost cause. Sir John Cornewaille was indeed an indefatigable collector of ransomable prisoners, but the name of Pierre de Hellenvillier does not occur among them. He probably lay where he had fallen, unrecognised on the field of Agincourt.[44]

The problem of identifying the dead was made more difficult than it might have been by the fact that the bodies were systematically plundered. The English, as was their right as victors, had stripped the corpses of any valuables, including armour, jewellery and clothing. These were legitimate prizes of war, some of which would be kept — particularly the weapons and armour, which would replace those lost or damaged by the men-at-arms — but most of which would be sold for profit. There was so much to be taken that Henry, ever conscious of the possibility of a French rally, or an ambush on the road, became concerned that his men were overburdening themselves and gave orders that no one was to acquire more than he needed for himself.[45]

Once the English had finished, the corpses were despoiled for a second time by the local people, who literally stripped them stark naked. "None of them, however, illustrious or distinguished, possessed at our departure any more covering, save only to conceal his nature, than that with which Nature had endowed him when first he saw the light," the chaplain noted.[46]

This was more than just a conventional pious platitude about all men being equal under the skin. Without their banners, pennons, surcoats or coats of arms, it was impossible for the heralds and other armorial experts to identify which individuals had been killed. Once they had also been robbed of their armour and garments, it was not even possible to tell a nobleman from a citizen militiaman.

Identifying the dead was made more difficult by the fact that so many of them had received head and facial wounds. One chronicle claimed that only eighteen out of some five or six hundred Breton dead could be identified "because all the others were so lacerated that no one could recognise them." This was in part because of the nature of the battle: the arrows had been aimed principally at the visors of the approaching enemy, and those men-at-arms who fell in the crush and the mud were dispatched by the archers, who raised their visors as they lay helpless and stabbed them with their daggers or struck them with their leaden mallets. Some of the dead must also have been the prisoners whose execution Henry had ordered when a French rally seemed likely. Again, head wounds are likely to have been a common cause of death, since the prisoners would all have been unhelmed. It may perhaps be significant in this context that when the body of Antoine, duke of Brabant, was discovered, two days after the battle, it was lying naked a little way from the field. He had a wound to his head but his throat had also been cut. One imagines that he was too important a prisoner to have been executed — but in the heat of battle his makeshift surcoat was evidently not enough to identify and protect him.[47]

The local Ruisseauville chronicler also claimed that "the king of England had 500 men well armed and sent them amongst the dead, to take off their coats of arms and a great quantity of armour. They had small axes in their hands and other weapons and they cut both the dead and the living in the face so that they might not be recognised, even the English who were dead as well as the others." Though he was not noted for his accuracy, his story may be substantially true. Le Févre de St Remy also records that Henry V ordered that all the armour, above and beyond that which his men could carry away, was to be gathered together in a single house or barn, which was then to be set on fire. While one can imagine that many of the corpses might have been disfigured in the process of removing their armour, especially as this must have been done in haste, this was not the object of the exercise, but incidental to it. The real purpose was to prevent such a vast cache of armour and weapons falling into the hands of the enemy, enabling them to mount an attack on the rear of the English army as it resumed its march to Calais.[48]

Before that march could begin, there were other tasks to perform. There were too many bodies lying on the battlefield for the English to contemplate giving them all a Christian burial; we do not even know whether they did this for their own compatriots. Certainly the corpses of some of the more eminent victims — in particular, Edward, duke of York, and Michael, earl of Suffolk — were recovered for removal to England. Given the length of time it would take to transport them, and the lack of facilities to embalm them or encase them in lead to prevent them putrefying, it was the medieval practice to quarter the bodies and boil them until the flesh came away from the bones. This pragmatic but unpleasant procedure meant that the bones could then easily be transported back to England in a simple chest or coffer, to be interred with all due ceremony in their final resting place. Who was responsible for carrying out this gruesome office we do not know, though we can guess that Thomas Morstede and his team of surgeons — if they were not too busy attending the living — were probably involved.[49]

It would be several days before the rest of the dead were buried. The families of the greater lords sent their servants and priests to search the battlefield for their loved ones. In this way, the bodies of the dukes of Alençon, Bar and Brabant were discovered, together with those of Constable d'Albret, Jacques de Châtillon, Galois de Fougières, the archbishop of Sens and the counts of Nevers and Roucy. Even at this late stage, some men were still found alive under the heaps of dead. Englebert van Edingen, sire de Kestergat, for instance, was discovered lying badly wounded three days after the battle, but even though he was carried to St Pol, he did not recover and died shortly afterwards. Every effort was made to take the dead back to their homes for burial beside their ancestors: the body of Philippe, count of Nevers, was embalmed and taken to the Cistercian abbey of Elan, near Mézières, in the Ardennes; the corpse of his brother the duke of Brabant was embalmed on the field and carried in a formal funeral procession through the grieving towns of his duchy to lie in state in Brussels, before being buried beside his first wife at Tervueren. The duke of Alençon was similarly embalmed so that his body could be taken for burial in the abbey church of St Martin at Sées, but his entrails were interred close to the great altar in the Franciscan church at Hesdin. Guillaume de Longueil, captain of Dieppe, was brought back to the town and buried with due honour in the church of St Jacques, together with one of the two sons who died at Agincourt with him; the body of his other son presumably could not be found.[50]

Many other members of the local nobility found a final resting place in the churches and abbeys of Artois, Picardy and Flanders, where they were joined by those for whom the journey home was just too far. It was said that so great a number of bodies were brought for burial to the churchyards of Azincourt and Ruisseauville that all further interments there had to be prohibited. The proximity of the two churches at Hesdin, some seven miles from the battlefield, meant that they also received so many corpses that they were obliged to resort to mass graves. Constable d'Albret, far from his native Gascony, was given the place of honour before the grand altar of the Franciscan church, but thirteen other noblemen were interred elsewhere in the building, including two "lords whose names we do not know," who were buried together by the holy water stoup in the nave. The great abbey church of Auchy-les-Moines at Hesdin provided a final resting place within its walls for fifteen noblemen, including Jacques de Châtillon, his brothers-in-law Gui and Philippe de la Roche-Guyon, who shared a single grave, Guichard Dauphin and eleven others. Despite the fact that four of these, including Galois de Fougières and "le petit Hollandes," the son of the *bailli* of Rouen, were interred together, space was at such a premium that twelve more corpses, among them that of Symmonet de Moranvilliers, the *bailli* of Chartres, had to be buried in a communal grave in the cemetery behind the choir. It can have been small compensation for such indignity that their names and places of burial were assiduously recorded by Montjoie king of arms, with the assistance of Ponthieu and Corbie kings of arms, numerous heralds and pursuivants and the servants of those who had died.[51]

In the end, it fell to the local clergy to make the necessary arrangements for the interment of the unidentified dead. Louis de Luxembourg, bishop of Thérouanne, in whose diocese Azincourt lay, authorised the consecration of a section of the battlefield. Under the direction of the abbots of Ruisseauville and Blangy, a series of long trenches were dug and somewhere in the region of six thousand corpses received a crude but Christian burial in these anonymous grave pits. A great wooden cross was raised over each mass grave, but no permanent memorial was erected until the nineteenth century and their location is still a matter of dispute today.[52] The dead of Agincourt were not the first, nor yet the last, to find an anonymous corner in the graveyard of Europe which is the Somme.

❖ CHAPTER SEVENTEEN ❖

THE RETURN OF THE KING

Walking back across the battlefield, through "the masses, the mounds, and the heaps of the slain," the English chaplain was not alone in weeping at the scale of the slaughter. Like his king, he was utterly convinced of the justice of the English cause and his fanaticism on this point made him blind to alternative or, indeed, opposing views. He was therefore unable to see the French dead simply as those who had given their lives in defence of their country against a foreign invader. He was also unaware of how many of them had put aside bitter party differences to do so, an altruism that made their deaths all the more poignant. Though his sympathy is expressed in terms that make uncomfortable reading for those who do not share his conviction, it was nevertheless totally genuine. He could not help but be touched by the thought that

> so great a number of warriors, famous and most valiant had only God been with them, should have sought their own deaths in such a manner at our hands, quite contrary to any wish of ours, and should thus have effaced and destroyed, all to no avail, the glory and honour of their own country. And if that sight gave rise to compunction and pity in us, strangers passing by, how much more was it a cause of grief and mourning to their own

people, awaiting expectantly the warriors of their country and then seeing them so crushed and made defenceless. And, as I truly believe, there is not a man with heart of flesh or even of stone who, had he seen and pondered on the horrible deaths and bitter wounds of so many Christian men, would not have dissolved into tears, time and again, for grief.[1]

Even the most impious soldier in the English army must have been given pause for thought by a victory that surely justified the term miraculous. Indeed, it was not long before rumours began to circulate that a miracle really had taken place. There were those who were prepared to testify that they had seen St George, the warrior patron saint of England, fighting on behalf of the English, just as he had aided the Normans against the Saracens in the battle of Cerami in 1063.[2] If St George did appear, neither the chaplain nor our other eyewitnesses noticed him. All were united, however, in attributing the victory to God. "Our England . . . has reason to rejoice and reason to grieve," the chaplain wrote in words that again echoed his king's sentiments. "Reason to rejoice at the victory gained and the deliverance of her men, and reason to grieve for the suffering and destruction wrought in the deaths of Christians. But far be it from our people to ascribe the triumph to their own glory or strength; rather let it be ascribed to God alone, from Whom is every victory, lest the Lord be wrathful at our ingratitude and at another time turn from us, which Heaven forbid, His victorious hand."[3]

This was, in essence, the view of almost all contemporaries, including the French themselves. Some Burgundians were quick to blame the Armagnacs, circulating rumours among the international representatives of the Church meeting at the council of Constance that Charles d'Albret and Charles d'Orléans had betrayed their own side by defecting during the course of the battle to throw in their lot with the English — a particularly distasteful attempt to ward off criticism of their duke's own absence from the battle. It was even said that the Agincourt news was received with joy in Paris because it was a defeat for the Armagnacs.[4]

Other chroniclers, regardless of party, pointed the finger of blame squarely at the leaders of the French forces. They were accused of being too hasty in not waiting for the arrival of their own archers and crossbowmen, which was patently untrue; of being too arrogant to accept the military assistance of these men because they were their social inferiors, which has some justice; and of failing to impose discipline, which was true of the small cavalry unit, but not of the huge numbers of infantry, who had patiently maintained their position for hours on end the evening before and the morning of the battle. Whatever practical explanations for the disaster could be found, French commentators regarded these as merely incidental. They had no doubt that the real reason for the defeat was divine punishment for their own sins. By this they meant both the personal moral failings, such as the sin of pride that they attributed to the nobility in taking their places in the vanguard, or the cowardice that had caused so many to flee the field, and the political ambitions and quarrels that had set Armagnac against Burgundian, plunged the country into civil war and enabled the English to invade in the first place.[5]

It is said that Henry seized an early opportunity to lecture his French prisoners on this subject, informing them that "he had done nothing, nor had the English; it was all the work of God and of our Lady and St George and due to your sins, for they say that you went to battle in pride and bombastic fashion, violating maidens, married women and others, and also robbing the countryside and all the churches; acting like that God will never aid you." Another version of the same anecdote has Henry tell Charles d'Orléans that God himself had opposed the French: "and, if what I have heard is true, it is not surprising; for it is said that there was never seen more discord or disorder caused by sensuality, mortal sins and evil vices than reigns in France today."[6]

Just how many prisoners were now in English hands is a matter as hotly disputed and as irresolvable as the number of combatants in the French army. The lowest contemporary estimate comes from an English source, Thomas Walsingham, who suggested that 700 men were captured at the battle; le Févre puts the figure at 1600 and says that they were "all knights or esquires," a statement that is likely to be true, given that anyone of lower rank would not be worth ransoming. Both the monk of St Denis, with 1400, and the chronicler of the nearby abbey of Ruisseauville, with 2200, are in the same sort of region, as is the report that went to the council of Constance suggesting 1500.[7]

Whatever their actual numbers, it is indisputable that they included some of the greatest men in the kingdom: Charles, duke of Orléans; Jean, duke of Bourbon; Charles, count of Eu; Louis, count of Vendôme; and Arthur, count of Richemont; together with the paragon of French chivalry Marshal Boucicaut. It was a disaster for the Armagnac cause on an epic scale. With the exception of the dauphin, who would die, unlamented, only a couple of months later in December 1415, the seventy-five-year-old duke of Berry, who would die the following year, and Louis, duke of Anjou (whose force of 600 men failed to arrive in time for the battle, turning tail and returning to Rouen without striking a blow when they encountered some of the French fleeing from the field), every Armagnac leader of any consequence had been killed or taken captive.

As evening approached and even the skies wept over the blood-soaked field of Agincourt, Henry decided that it was too late to resume his journey to Calais. However objectionable it might be to have to spend the night in such close proximity to the piles of unburied dead, his men were desperately short of rest and sleep. They needed to gather their strength, and the French baggage wagons, abandoned on the field, offered them a welcome and ready supply of provisions after the tight rationing of the previous weeks. The king himself retired to his former lodgings at Maisoncelle, where, as they were bound to do by the terms of their indentures, his captains surrendered to him all the princes of the blood royal and French commanders who had been captured. According to one source, written almost a quarter of a century later by an Italian under the auspices of Humphrey, duke of Gloucester, Henry required the most noble of his French prisoners to serve him at his feast that night. Though the story obtained popular currency because it was repeated by Tudor historians, it does not occur in any eyewitness or contemporary account, and seems to have been an embellishment. After all, as le Févre de St Remy pointed out, most of the prisoners had been wounded and therefore would not have been in a fit state to wait upon their conqueror. In any case, this was not a moment for the sort of ruthless humiliation of his prisoners which Henry had displayed at the public surrender of Harfleur. Instead, he treated them with grace and punctilious politeness, speaking courteously and comfortingly to them, ensuring that the wounded were treated and offering food and wine to them all.[8]

Very early the next morning, on Saturday 26 October, the king left his lodgings and escorted his prisoners in a final penitential act of walking over the battlefield. "It was a pitiful thing to see the great numbers of the nobility who had been killed there for their sovereign lord, the king of France," le Févre remarked: "they were already stripped naked as the day they were born." Even at this late stage the living could still be found under the piles of the dead. Those who were capable of identifying themselves as being of noble birth were taken prisoner; the rest, including those too severely wounded to travel, were put to death.[9]

The king now gave the command for his army to resume its journey towards Calais. The remarkable reversal in fortune that had befallen them the previous day was acknowledged by the decision that although they would still march in their customary battle formation, the order to wear coats of arms was rescinded; the English were no longer expecting or looking for a fight. Monstrelet tells us that three-quarters of them now had to travel on foot. Many horses on both sides were undoubtedly killed in the battle, despite the fact that all the English and most of the French had not used them for fighting. It is a matter of record in the royal accounts for the period that the king alone lost twenty-five, in addition to a further twenty that died on the march. Despite these heavy losses, the number of horses shipped back to England at the end of the campaign still outnumbered the men. Even the duke of York's retinue, which had suffered especially high casualties in the battle, returned with 329 horses as opposed to only 283 men. If three-quarters of the English army really did have to resume their march on foot, it can only have been because their horses were required for carrying the wounded, the prisoners and possibly booty, but it seems more likely that Monstrelet's claim was simply an exaggeration.[10]

Nevertheless, the English progress towards Calais was unusually slow. They had some forty-five miles to cover and it took them a full three days. After the high drama and tension of the journey to Agincourt, the remainder of the march was such an anticlimax that even the chaplain passed over it without any comment. This cannot have entirely reflected the actual mood of those in command, for Henry at least was aware that, despite his victory, his men were not yet out of danger. Jean, duke of Brittany, with his Breton forces, was not so far away at Amiens. Louis d'Anjou's six hundred men, under the command of the sire de Longny, were even closer, having come within three miles of the conflict before turning to flee. And no one knew for sure where John the Fearless was, or whether he would put in a belated appearance with the Burgundian forces he had claimed to be raising for so long. There could be no certainty that the alliances with the dukes of Brittany and Burgundy would hold in the light of the capture of the former's brother, Arthur, count of Richemont, and the deaths of both the latter's brothers, Antoine, duke of Brabant, and Philippe de Nevers, at Agincourt. The English could not afford to relax their guard against the possibility of an ambush until they finally reached the safety of the Pas-de-Calais.

In the event, the march passed off without any serious incident, though the accounts of the town of Boulogne record that some stragglers in the English army were captured by the men of the garrison and imprisoned in the belfry.[11] By the evening of Monday 28 October the army had reached the fortified town of Guînes, which lay within the Pas-de-Calais, and was second only to Calais in its importance. They were welcomed with all due solemnity by the captain of the garrison and Henry, together with his most notable prisoners, spent the night there. The rest of the army pressed on to Calais, which lay only a few miles further north. If they had expected a hero's welcome, they were mistaken. The citizens of Calais were understandably nervous about admitting almost six thousand half-starved and battle-hardened armed men through their gates. Provision had been made for the army's arrival: food, beer and medicines had already been sent over from London in abundant quantities, but a shortage of bread was almost inevitable. Anxious to avoid a clash between the soldiers and the citizenry, or the even worse prospect of gangs of armed men rampaging through the streets taking by force what they could not acquire by purchase, the town authorities gave orders that only the leaders of the English army were to be admitted within its walls. The rest, including the less important French prisoners, were to remain encamped outside.[12]

The wisdom of this move was readily apparent. There was much hard bargaining between the Agincourt veterans, who were desperate for food and drink, and the hard-nosed traders of Calais, who had an eye on the spoils of battle. The former naturally resented the latter, accusing them of exploiting their situation and forcing them to sell their booty and their prisoners at a mere fraction of their true value, simply in order to obtain the necessaries of life. In fact, a trade in prisoners, especially, was inevitable. Not everyone who had captured a Frenchman could afford to keep him indefinitely: in addition to paying for his living expenses, there was also the cost of his shipment back to England to consider. Many of the prisoners were also wounded and in need of medical care and treatment, which was an expensive luxury at the best of times, but an essential investment if the prisoner was to be kept alive for ransom. And the hope of obtaining large sums of money at some future date was not necessarily as attractive a prospect as that of realising cash in hand.

Unfortunately, we do not know the exact process by which the figure for the ransom was calculated, other than that it had to be agreed between the captor and his prisoner. A ransom of less than 10 marks (the equivalent of almost $4,444 today) was entirely at the disposal of the captor, whatever his rank, so there must have been a strong temptation to set this as the ceiling value. On the other hand, captors were under pressure from superior officers to obtain the best possible price. According to the terms of their indentures, anyone in the English army who captured a prisoner worth more than 10 marks was obliged to pay a third of the ransom to his own captain, whether that captain was head of a tiny retinue or the king himself. Where the captain had been personally retained by the crown, his indenture obligated him to pay a third of that third directly to the king.[13] With the eye of the king fixed firmly upon them, and a comprehensive list of all prisoners being drawn up by his clerks at Calais, underselling of ransoms was not likely to be a common practice.

Henry himself remained only a single night at Guînes, making a triumphant entry into Calais on Tuesday 29 October over the Nieulay bridge, which had been hastily repaired "against the arrival of the king after his victory at Agincourt," and along the causeway that led to the town gates. There he was welcomed by its captain, his old friend Richard Beauchamp, earl of Warwick, and a vast crowd of excited citizens. Escorted through the streets by the priests and clergymen of the town, clad in their ecclesiastical robes, bearing the crosses and banners from their respective churches and singing the *Te Deum*, he was hailed on every side by men, women and children crying, "Welcome to the king, our sovereign lord!" Making his way to the castle, where he was to lodge until his passage home could be organised, he paused only to give thanks at the church of St Nicholas for his victory. Ironically, eleven years earlier, the same church had witnessed the marriage of Richard II to the infant Isabelle of France, a union that had been intended to end the decades of warfare which Henry had now rekindled.[14]

Henry was committed to remaining in Calais until 11 November 1415. On that day, all those who had previously surrendered to him, both at the fall of Harfleur and at various stages on the march to Agincourt, were under oath to give themselves up to him again as his prisoners. To a man they did so. Unbelievable as it may seem to a more cynical modern world, they came voluntarily and without any compulsion, other than the power of chivalric ideology. They could have chosen to ignore their obligation: they were at liberty in their own country and the English were not in a position to round them up and throw them into jail. They could have claimed that their oaths were invalid because they were obtained under duress. They could have excused themselves on the grounds of sickness or the needs of their families. Instead, they chose honour before dishonour and keeping faith to perjury. They did so in the knowledge that they faced financial ruin, years in foreign captivity and possibly even execution.

Raoul de Gaucourt, the former captain of Harfleur, rose from his sickbed at Hargicourt, near Amiens, and, despite being wasted by the dysentery that had had him in its grip since the final days of the siege, made his way to Calais to surrender to Henry V. With him went at least twenty-five of his former companions, including Jean, sire d'Estouteville, Georges de Clère and Colard Blosset. As de Gaucourt later recounted, when he and d'Estouteville appeared before Henry, they demanded that, as they had fulfilled their part of the agreements concluded at the surrender of Harfleur, he should now keep those undertakings that had been given on his part. We do not know what those undertakings were, though de Gaucourt seems to have believed that, having come to Calais as required by his oath, he would now be released again on parole to raise his ransom. But whatever promises had been made by the king's negotiators, Sir Thomas Erpingham, Henry, Lord Fitzhugh, and the earl of Dorset, Henry himself refused to be bound by them: "he replied, that whatever these parties might have said to us, we should all remain prisoners."[15] As de Gaucourt and his companions were to learn to their cost, their defiance of the king in holding Harfleur for so long against him would be neither forgiven nor forgotten. Their captivity would endure long after most of the prisoners taken at Agincourt had been released.

The logistical problem of transporting such vast numbers of prisoners ensured that only the most important would be taken back to England. Those who were of lesser value, or who could provide security for their ransoms, were released on oath to raise the money within a specified term. Others, including those who were too sick or badly wounded to travel, remained in custody but were dispersed to various strongholds throughout the Pas-de-Calais. Not all of them survived: Robin de Hellande, *bailli* of Rouen, for instance, was still in captivity when he died on 15 December 1415, and two of the eleven prisoners in the custody of Ralph Rocheford, captain of Hammes, died during the course of 1416.[16] A contributory factor in the deaths of Rocheford's prisoners may have been that he was allowed only 3s 4d a week (the medieval equivalent of $111 today) for each man's living expenses: though this was about the same as a skilled workman could expect to earn at the time, it was considered to be the minimum amount necessary for a prisoner of knightly lineage, and contrasts sharply with the 10s 9d allowed to each of the Harfleur defendants during their imprisonment in the Tower of London. Medical expenses were an additional burden: the cure of Jean, sire d'Estouteville's long illness in 1418 cost the king 40s ($1,317 at modern values) "for divers medicines" purchased from the royal physician, Master Peter Altobasse.[17]

All those who had prisoners were obliged to enter into bonds with the king to pay him his portion of their ransoms. This could be costly. One of his retainers, Sir Henry Huse, for example, had to account for nine prisoners from Beauce, Eu, Vimeu, Beaugency and Abbeville in his possession: on 16 January 1416 he agreed to pay 200 marks to the king's treasurer at Calais by midsummer, giving him five months to collect the sum from his prisoners' families or raise it by other means. Another of the king's retainers, William Trussell, esquire, had captured nine prisoners at Agincourt, whose ransoms ranged in value from £6 13s 4d to £17 6s 8d: his bond obliged him to pay the king £40.[18]

Although both Huse and Trussell could expect to receive twice as much as the king for their personal cut of the ransoms, these were still relatively small amounts compared to the sums that others received for their prisoners. A bundle of forty-nine bonds preserved among the exchequer records lists individual ransoms worth £48 6s 8d, £55 11s 4d and even £163 6s 8d (the last almost $108,868 today). Yet these figures, too, pale by comparison to the phenomenal sums commanded for the great princes who had been captured at Agincourt. Such men belonged to the king as of right, and he was under no legal obligation to compensate their captors. Nevertheless, he clearly did so, for Sir John Grey of Ruthin, who had indented to serve with the relatively modest retinue of fifteen men-at-arms and forty-five foot archers, found himself 1000 marks ($444,360) richer after capturing Charles, count of Eu, and selling him to the king.[19] This was not merely a financial speculation on the king's part, for he had no intention of ransoming the count: like the dukes of Bourbon and Orléans, Marshal Boucicaut, Arthur, count of Richemont, and Raoul de Gaucourt, he was more valuable as a prisoner.

On 16 November, five days after de Gaucourt and his fellow-defenders of Harfleur had surrendered themselves at Calais, the king and his prisoners, including the princes captured at Agincourt, boarded ship and set sail for England.[20] The homecoming was an altogether quieter and humbler affair than the original invasion. The great fleet that had brought the English to France had disbanded many weeks earlier and, though the king had undertaken to pay for the return crossing, he no longer had the means to take his army back with him *en masse*. Instead, the veterans of the campaign had to find their own passage across the Channel. Each man was allowed two shillings for his own fare, together with a further two shillings for each horse, and it was left to the captains of the retinues to make the necessary arrangements privately with ship-owners and masters visiting the port.

The greatest part of the victorious army thus made its way back to England from Calais without flourish or fanfare. The men slipped quietly into the Cinque Ports in dribs and drabs, before dispersing to their homes in towns, villages and farmsteads the length and breadth of the country. The hero's welcome was reserved for their monarch. His passage home was marred by violent late fall storms, in which, it was said, two ships carrying Sir John Cornewaille's men were lost with all hands, and others, carrying prisoners, were driven ashore on the Zeeland coast. Whether or not it was true that the king's iron constitution and cheerful demeanour were the envy and admiration of the French prisoners on board his ship, the latter, particularly those still suffering from dysentery, must have suffered horribly during the many hours it took to effect the crossing. They landed at Dover, in a great snowstorm, just before nightfall.[21]

News of Henry's return spread swiftly, and when he set out for London the following morning, he found his road already lined with cheering crowds. His route naturally took him through Canterbury, but it was inconceivable that so pious a king could simply pass through the town without pausing to give thanks for the success of his campaign at England's premier cathedral. His arrival was obviously expected, for he was met by Henry Chichele, archbishop of Canterbury, at the head of a long procession of clergymen, who welcomed him and escorted him to the cathedral.

There was a double significance to this visit. Henry's official purpose was to pay his devotions and make offerings at the great shrine of St Thomas Becket in the Trinity Chapel behind the high altar of the cathedral. Flanking that shrine, however, were the tombs of two of Henry's own forebears. On one side was that of the great warrior Edward, the Black Prince, with its magnificent gilded and armour-clad effigy, his surcoat emblazoned with the quartered arms of England and France, and his feet bearing the spurs he won at the battle of Crécy: over this tomb, as yet another reminder of his victories at Crécy and Poitiers, hung his funeral achievements, the helm with its lion crest, shield, gauntlets and coat armour he had worn to battle.[22]

On the other side of the shrine was the tomb of Henry's father, Henry IV, who had been interred there just over two and a half years earlier. Though equally imposing in its own way, this tomb was very different from that of the warrior prince: the effigy, carved from marble, portrayed the king in civilian clothing and with a remarkably realistic and care-worn face, which must have been drawn from life. The only intimation of his royal stature was his gilded crown, the "crown Henry" or "Lancaster crown," the original of which his son had just pawned to his brother, the duke of Clarence, as security for his wages for the Agincourt campaign.[23]

The presence of the tombs of the Black Prince and Henry IV on either side of St Thomas Becket's shrine turned what might otherwise have been just an act of simple piety and thanksgiving into an altogether more momentous affair. As the victor of Agincourt, Henry V had won the right to take his place alongside the victor of Crécy and Poitiers. Perhaps more importantly, he had proved that he had been chosen by God to be the instrument of His will. The crime of his father's usurpation and the long shadow it had cast over the legitimacy of the Lancastrian kingship had been wiped out. Irrespective of the justice of his claims to the throne of France, no one could doubt any longer that Henry V was indeed, by the grace of God, king of England.

After visiting the cathedral, Henry made a second pilgrimage to the nearby church of St Augustine's Abbey, to give thanks at the tomb of the cathedral's founder and first archbishop. Having spent one, or possibly two nights as the guest of the abbot and his monks, he then set out once more for London. His progress was slow and it was not until six days after landing at Dover that the royal party finally arrived at the king's manor of Eltham on the outskirts of the city. The leisurely pace was deliberate, for it allowed the citizens time to complete their arrangements for the great pageant that was to mark his triumphal return. Londoners, who had contributed so much to the king's campaign in terms of finance, shipping and men, had followed his campaign with understandable nervousness. The absence of news during his march from Harfleur had been a cause of particular tension, especially since, on the very day of the battle of Agincourt, "a lamentable report, replete with sadness, and cause for endless sorrow, had alarmed the community throughout all the City, in the boundless grief that it caused." It took four days for news of the English victory to filter through, reaching London only on the day that the king himself entered Calais.[24] That same day, 29 October, was the customary occasion for the newly elected mayor to ride to Westminster Palace to be admitted formally to his office and sworn in before the barons of the exchequer. On learning the joyful news, Nicholas Wottone, the new mayor, decided to break with precedent. With his aldermen and "an immense number of the Commonalty of the citizens of the city," he went "like pilgrims on foot" to Westminster Abbey. There, in the presence of Henry's stepmother, Joan of Navarre, a host of lords spiritual and temporal, and some of the more substantial citizens, he made "devout thanksgiving, with due solemnity." Only after having given their due to God, his saints and especially "Edward, the glorious Confessor, whose body lies interred at Westminster," did he proceed to Westminster Palace to complete his inauguration. Always swift to guard their civic privileges, the mayor and aldermen went to great lengths to ensure that the reasons for this break with tradition were recorded for posterity, so that no future mayor should feel it incumbent upon himself to walk humbly, rather than ride in pomp, to Westminster.[25]

The spontaneous celebrations that greeted the news of Agincourt were as nothing compared to those which hailed the return of the victorious king. London was accustomed to festivities on a grand scale: royal progresses, coronations, jousts and tournaments, ceremonies to welcome or honour visiting dignitaries, had all been marked by processions through the streets, the ringing of church bells, allegorical and heraldic displays. On such occasions, too, it was customary for the public water pipes and fountains to run with wine, which no doubt encouraged a convivial atmosphere. The citizens had had almost a month to prepare for this event and the result was as elaborate and visually stunning a pageant as medieval ingenuity could devise. At first light on Saturday 23 November, the mayor and twenty-four aldermen rode four miles out of the city, as far as the heights of Blackheath, to meet the king. They were clad in their finest scarlet and accompanied by huge numbers of citizens, all dressed in red robes with parti-coloured hoods of red and white, or black and white. Each one proudly wore the distinctive and "richly fashioned badge" that marked his status as a member of one of the great London guilds and distinguished him from his fellows in other crafts or trades. At about ten in the morning, the king arrived, bringing with him only a modest personal retinue, but one that pointedly included his French prisoners. After formally congratulating him and thanking him "for the victory he had gained and for his efforts on behalf of the common weal," the citizens formed themselves up into a procession and, to the sound of trumpets, rode off to escort him in triumph to the capital.[26]

About a mile from the city, at St Thomas Waterings, just outside Southwark, the abbot of Bermondsey and a procession of London clergymen were waiting to receive the king. Bearing the holy relics, crosses and banners of their churches, they sang the *Te Deum* and acclaimed him (in Latin) with cries of "Hail, flower of the English and of the world, knight of Christ!"[27] Accompanied by an ever-growing train, Henry now approached the tower at the entrance to London Bridge, which marked the city boundary. Here two gigantic allegorical figures bearing the royal arms had been erected side by side, "like guards outside the gate." The male was armed with an axe in one hand and a lance, from which dangled the keys of the city, in the other; the female wore a scarlet mantle and "adornments appropriate to her sex." To the chaplain, viewing this display with barely concealed wonder, "they were like a man and his wife who, in their richest attire, were bent upon seeing the eagerly awaited face of their lord and welcoming him with abundant praise." (The more martial Adam of Usk was merely struck by their size, admiring the breadth of the enormous axe, "by which . . . an entire army might be slaughtered," and the physical bulk of the woman, which "was in truth fit not only to spawn gigantic demons, but also to bring forth the towers of hell.") From every rampart of the gatehouse tower hung the royal coat of arms and blazoned across its front wall was the legend "City of the King of Justice"; trumpeters and horn-players stationed within and on the tower made the place ring with their fanfares to welcome the king.[28]

As the royal party approached the drawbridge at the centre of the bridge, they saw that two large wooden pillars or turrets had been erected and hung with linen cloth, skilfully painted to give the appearance of marble. On one stood the figure of an antelope (the king's personal badge) with a shield of the royal arms round its neck and a royal sceptre cradled in its forefoot. On the other stood the lion of England holding the royal standard in its paw. At the far end of the drawbridge, and straddling the route, was another tower of similar construction whose centrepiece was a statue of St George, fully armed except for his triumphal helm and his shield, which were displayed on either side of him. His right hand rested on the hilt of his sword, in his left he bore a scroll with the legend "Honor and glory be to

God alone!" and on his head he wore the ancient symbol of victory, the laurel crown. A multitude of angel choirs — little boys dressed up in white robes and wings, with gold-painted faces, and laurel leaves wound through their hair — sang the anthem "Blessed is he that cometh in the name of the Lord" as the king approached.[29]

Another choir, this time of Old Testament prophets, "with venerable white hair, in tunicles and golden copes, their heads wrapped and turbaned with gold and crimson," was waiting for the king at Cornhill, where the water storage tower had been draped in crimson cloth and cunningly disguised as a great pavilion. Here again, the arms of St George, St Edward and St Edmund, the saints under whose patronage the campaign had been fought, were prominently displayed, together with those of England and of the king himself. As Henry rode past, the "prophets" chanted Psalm 98, "O sing unto the Lord a new song: for he hath done marvellous things," and released a huge flock of little birds, "of which some descended on to the king's breast, some settled upon his shoulders, and some circled around in twisting flight."[30]

The water storage tower at the entrance to Cheapside, which had been filled with wine, had been similarly draped with cloth and adorned with shields bearing the arms of the city. Beneath its awnings stood the twelve apostles and, rather less obviously identifiable, the twelve martyrs and confessors of the English royal line, "girt about the loins with golden belts, with sceptres in their hands, crowns upon their heads, and their emblems of sanctity plain to see." These, too, greeted the king by sweetly singing the appropriate verse from Psalm 44, "But it is thou that savest us from our enemies: and puttest them to confusion that hate us." Then, in a deft biblical allusion that would not have been lost upon Henry V, they offered him wafers of bread, mixed with wafers of silver, and wine drawn from the spouts of the water tower, just as Melchizedek, king of Salem, had done for Abraham, when he returned from his victory over the kings of Sodom and Gomorrah.[31] (Though they had already been lectured on the subject of their national vices and moral failings by Henry, one wonders how his French prisoners must have reacted to being equated so publicly with the most notorious of all biblical sinners.)

Queen Eleanor's stone cross in Cheapside, which had been erected as one of a series across the country to mark the places where her coffin had rested on its final journey to Westminster Abbey in 1290, was masked entirely by an elaborate wooden castle, three storeys high, complete with towers and a bridge leading to a gatehouse. A vast archway had been built on either side to link the castle with the buildings on each side of the street, and over both arches were inscribed the words "Glorious things of thee are spoken, city of God." As the king approached, a choir of singing maidens, clad in white and dancing to the sound of drums and stringed instruments, emerged from the castle, just like the ones who had greeted David on his return from slaying Goliath. The chaplain approved mightily of this display, noting with satisfaction that Goliath was a highly appropriate representation of the arrogant French. The virgins hailed Henry with a specially written song of congratulation, beginning, "Welcome Henry ye fifte, Kynge of Englond' and of Fraunce." This was particularly significant for two reasons: it was the only piece in the entire pageant to be performed in English and it was also the only one to address the king himself as the conquering hero. Every other tableau had relied on quotations in Latin from the Bible, especially the Psalms, and had ascribed the victory to God. Lest even this moderate bit of praise for the king's role be considered blasphemous, it was tempered by the singing of the *Te Deum* by a second host of little boys, dressed as angels and archangels, who showered the king with gold coins and laurel leaves.[32]

The "castle" contained one more surprise for the king. "Six citizens, magnificently dressed, came out of its iron gates carrying two basins made of gold and filled with gold, which were offered to the king." The basins themselves were said to have been worth five hundred pounds, and between them they held a thousand pounds, a most acceptable gift from the Londoners to a king whose campaign had left his cup of glory overflowing, but his coffers decidedly empty.[33]

More virgins were waiting at the other end of Cheapside, standing in a series of niches contrived out of the tower encircling the other water cistern. Crowned with laurels and wearing girdles of gold, these maidens held golden chalices from which they gently blew roundels of gold leaf upon the king's head. At the very top of the tower stood the figure of a golden archangel, surmounting a canopy painted to resemble a cloud-bedecked sky, beneath which sat a sun, enthroned in splendour, and emitting dazzling rays.[34]

> And . . . so great was the throng of people in Cheapside, from one end to the other, that the horsemen were only just able, although not without difficulty, to ride through. And the upper rooms and windows on both sides were packed with some of the noblest ladies and womenfolk of the kingdom and men of honour and renown, who had assembled for this pleasing spectacle, and who were so very becomingly and elegantly decked out in cloth of gold, fine linen, and scarlet, and other rich apparel of various kinds, that no one could recall there ever having previously been in London a greater assemblage or a more noble array.

At the epicentre of this maelstrom of extravagant pageantry and noisy demonstrations of popular joy rode the quiet, almost incongruous figure of the king. He had deliberately dispensed with all the usual trappings of triumph and royalty, just as he had done when making his formal entry into Harfleur. He wore no crown and bore no sceptre; his only concession to his regal status was his gown of purple, a colour associated only with emperors, kings and prelates. He was accompanied by just a small personal retinue and followed by a group of his most important prisoners, including Charles d'Orléans, whose twenty-first birthday would fall the following day, the duke of Bourbon and Marshal Boucicaut. Not one of them could, or would, have adopted a similarly humble attitude if their situations had been reversed.

A lesser man might easily have been seduced into joining the celebrations, if only by acknowledging the excitement and gratitude of the crowds, but Henry remained impassive throughout. "Indeed, from his quiet demeanour, gentle pace, and sober progress, it might have been gathered that the king, silently pondering the matter in his heart, was rendering thanks and glory to God alone, not to man."[35]

The celebrations drew to an appropriate end with services at both St Paul's and Westminster Abbey, where the king made offerings at the shrines of St Earconwald and Edward the Confessor, respectively, before retiring to his palace at Westminster. The following day, Sunday 24 November, in accordance with the king's command, a solemn requiem mass was held at St Paul's for all those, on both sides, who had been killed in the battle of Agincourt.[36] The remains of the duke of York were then carried to Northamptonshire and interred, as he had requested, in the choir of his new foundation, the collegiate church of St Mary and All Saints at Fotheringhay; building work had only just begun, under the supervision of Stephen Lote, the king's chief master mason, so the duke's premature end meant that his church would be built around the simple marble slab, with his figure engraved in brass upon it, which marked his final resting place. It would be left to his heir, several decades later, to complete the rebuilding of the church he had begun.[37]

Similar obsequies were taking place in towns and villages, churches and abbeys all over France. Despite the scale of the disaster, news of the defeat had been relatively slow to filter out to the regions. Disbelief must have played a part. The people of Abbeville, for instance, were so sure of a French victory that they prematurely held a celebratory civic feast as soon as the expected news reached them: a sad little marginal note was later added in the town accounts against the sum expended that the rumour "was not true." At Boulogne, where the whole town had been in a state of high tension for weeks and had deployed messengers throughout the vicinity to pick up any news they could find, they knew on 25 October that battle had been joined but had to wait till the following day to learn its outcome. Their first response was to protect themselves, for Boulogne lay on the English route to Calais and the garrison had been severely depleted when, on the orders of Constable d'Albret, the sire de Laurois had led a large force to join the French army. Letters were immediately dispatched to neighbouring Montreuil begging for crossbowmen to reinforce the town, to the king, the dauphin and the duke of Berry at Rouen, asking for provision to be made to secure the frontier, and to Philippe, count of Charolais, at Ghent, seeking "comfort and aid." Perhaps surprisingly, reinforcements did pour into Boulogne not only from Montreuil but also from as far afield as Amiens, Hesdin, St Riquier and St Laleu, continuing to arrive for several days after Henry had sailed for England.[38]

Other reactions to the French defeat were less altruistic. At Mantes, for instance, which lay between Rouen and Paris, guards were posted at the town gates so that "the men fleeing and returning from the host of the king should not pass through the town save in groups of 20 to 30 at a time." The town of Amiens was equally pragmatic in looking after its own. Messengers were sent to the battlefield to recover as much as possible of the town's property, which had been requisitioned for the army's use by their *bailli*. Among the items they managed to retrieve were three large cannon, two smaller ones, some battered shields belonging to their crossbowmen and scraps of tents. The town elections, which were traditionally held on 28 October, had to be abandoned in the general chaos caused by the influx of wounded and dying.[39]

All the towns of the region now looked to the king and the dauphin to provide them with some sort of leadership in the aftermath of the disaster. They were still at Rouen, together with the dukes of Berry and Anjou, and the large force that had been held in reserve to protect them. Now, more than at any other time, the dauphin should have provided a rallying point for those who had survived the battle, but when the shocking news was brought to him, he proved incapable of taking any decisive action. His paralysis was unhelpful but understandable. Until he knew for certain that Henry V had left France, there was every possibility that further military action might take place; his councillors were urging him to retake Harfleur, not merely to restore French pride, but to pre-empt its governor, the earl of Dorset, carrying out a strike against Rouen.[40] On the other hand, no one knew how John the Fearless would react in this crisis.

In the end, the dauphin's fear of the duke of Burgundy proved greater than his fear of the English. Ten days after the battle, the duke had at last set out from Dijon at the head of the Burgundian army that he had promised to send against the English. He had no intention of avenging the deaths of his two brothers at Agincourt, or even of belatedly going to the aid of his country. He was heading for Paris. The English had wiped out the Armagnac leadership for him and there was now no one standing between him and the control of the government of France. It was a chance not to be missed. In a further act of defiance, he took with him the Parisian leaders of the bloody pro-Burgundian coup in 1413, including Simon Caboche himself, all of whom were still under royal interdict. The dauphin responded by ordering that no prince of the blood should be allowed to enter Paris with an army and that all the bridges and ferries into the city should be removed.[41]

By 21 November the duke was at Troyes, some eighty miles south-east of Paris, with an army whose ranks were daily swelling as they were joined by the Burgundian veterans of Agincourt. The dauphin could no longer ignore the threat. Abandoning Rouen and the northern regions to their fate, he fled back to Paris, taking his father and the duke of Berry with him. Even now this hapless young man managed to offend his natural supporters by passing through St Denis without paying his respects at the abbey, as custom demanded. Bereft of his Armagnac councillors and protectors, most of whom had died or been captured on the field of Agincourt, he sent an urgent summons to Charles d'Orléans' father-in-law, Bernard, count of Armagnac, inviting him to come to Paris and take up the late Charles d'Albret's role as constable of France. Confident that his champion would soon arrive from Aquitaine with a host of seasoned Gascon men-at-arms in his train, the dauphin defied John the Fearless's demands for a personal audience and declared his intention of taking up the reins of government himself.

It was not to be. Although Bernard d'Armagnac set off promptly, by the time he arrived in Paris on 27 December, the eighteen-year-old dauphin had been dead and buried for more than a week. Although he had been persuaded to effect a perfunctory deathbed reconciliation with the wife he had abandoned, she left Paris almost immediately to return to her family. Her father, the duke of Burgundy, learnt of his son-in-law's death only when he heard the Parisian bells tolling for his passing.[42]

The shock of the disaster at Agincourt had failed to unite France, so it is perhaps not surprising that the death of Louis de Guienne also had no impact on the internal quarrels that were tearing the kingdom apart. His successor as dauphin was his seventeen-year-old younger brother Jean de Touraine, who had been brought up in the court of the duke of Burgundy's sister Margaret, countess of Hainault, and had recently married her fourteen-year-old daughter. The duke was determined that this dauphin would not reject his authority. Ignoring demands from Paris that the new heir to the throne should be returned to the capital, John the Fearless temporarily disbanded his army and withdrew to Brabant and Flanders, where he could keep a watchful eye on the dauphin and issue orders in his name.[43] He was, however, merely biding his time before launching another and more deadly assault on Paris. And in Bernard d'Armagnac, to whom the standard of Armagnac leadership had passed from the captive Charles d'Orléans, he had found an opponent as implacable, ruthless and opportunistic as himself. The civil war between Burgundian and Armagnac was by no means over. It was as if the battle of Agincourt had never taken place.

CHAPTER EIGHTEEN

THE REWARDS OF VICTORY

For Henry V, Agincourt was just the beginning. The euphoria that had greeted his victory did not start or end with the London pageant. Even before the king returned to England, his brother John, duke of Bedford, acting as his lieutenant, had summoned a meeting of Parliament at Westminster. Since many of those who would normally have taken their places in either the House of Lords or the House of Commons were still with the English army in France, it was a severely depleted gathering that met in the Painted Chamber of the Palace of Westminster on Monday, 4 November 1415. The king's half-uncle Henry Beaufort, bishop of Winchester, gave a rousing opening address on the theme "as he has done to us, so let us do to him," reminding those present that Henry had laboured continually to preserve peace, law and justice, but that he had been unable to regain his rights in France except by going to war. God had given him victory to the exaltation of his crown, the comfort of his lieges, the fear of his enemies and the perpetual profit of his realm. Now it was the duty of his subjects to enable him to complete what he had begun by granting him aid for a second expedition.[1]

Parliament responded with a generosity that was unparalleled in its history. The collection of the second of the two-tenths and -fifteenths that had been granted in 1414 was brought forward from February 1416 to December 1415, so that the king could pay his returning troops and redeem the jewels he had pawned as security for their wages. Yet another new tax of a tenth and fifteenth was approved for collection in November 1416. And, most extraordinary of all, the House of Commons granted Henry customs duty on all imports and exports, including wool and wine, for the rest of his life. This was a remarkable public demonstration of trust in, and approval of, Henry's kingship, for the right to grant taxes was a privilege that the Commons guarded closely as its main bargaining counter for receiving concessions from the king. There was only one precedent for a life grant of the wool levy and that had been extracted under duress by the autocratic Richard II. Though there may have been some arm-twisting by Henry's ministers in the background, and it was arguable that this depleted Parliament lacked proper authority since large swaths of England were unrepresented, there was no denying the fact that the Commons had made the life grant voluntarily, confident in the knowledge that Henry V would spend the money wisely and in the furtherance of their own best interests. It was, in effect, a vote for the continuation of the war in France.[2]

Henry's clerical subjects were just as eager to acclaim his achievement and prove their loyalty. The northern convocation voted him a tax of one-tenth on the value of all benefices in that province and the wealthier southern convocation voted him two. Important steps were also taken to ensure that Henry's victory could not be forgotten or passed over. At the king's personal request, Henry Chichele, the archbishop of Canterbury, decreed that henceforth 23 April, the feast of St George, "the special patron and protector of the [English] nation . . . by whose intervention, we unhesitatingly believe, the army of the English nation is directed against enemy attacks in time of wars," was to become a double festival in the Church calendar. This meant that, like other saints' days, it would remain a public holiday but additionally it would now become a day when people ought to go to church, as they did at Christmas. Less well known than this enhancement of the status of England's patron saint was a similar order enforcing the holding of public holidays on the festivals of three Welsh saints, Winifred, David and Chad. This was a gracious and politically astute acknowledgement of the role played by the Welsh archers and their patron saints in achieving the victory of Agincourt.[3]

Henry and his archbishop also ensured that the anniversary of the battle would be publicly celebrated with special masses and Church services. Since the cobbler saints of Soissons, Crispin and Crispinian had failed to exert themselves on behalf of the French at Agincourt and therefore might be considered to have given their blessing to their opponents, their feast day was shamelessly appropriated by the English. The king himself had immediately incorporated a mass in their honour into his daily religious observance, but as the preparations for a second campaign began the archbishop now ordained that their feast should be celebrated with increased reverence throughout the realm. Three masses were to be dedicated to each of the two saints on every anniversary of the battle, together with a further three in honour of the very English St John of Beverley.[4] The shrine of St John at Beverley Minster in Yorkshire had been a centre of pilgrimage since Anglo-Saxon times and his banner, like the French oriflamme, had been carried into battle by Yorkshire recruits to the royal army since 1138. (It is not known whether it accompanied Henry V to France in 1415.) In more recent years (perhaps to counterbalance a growing cult at York surrounding Archbishop Scrope, who had been executed by Henry IV in 1405 for his part in the Percy rebellion and was therefore revered by those hostile to the new king), St John, himself a former bishop of York, had been promoted as a Lancastrian patron. His shrine was said to have exuded holy oil when Henry IV landed in England to usurp Richard's throne, a miracle which, Archbishop Chichele informed convocation, had been repeated even more spectacularly on 25 October during the very hours that the battle of Agincourt was raging. As that day also just happened to be the Feast of St John's Translation, it was self-evident that the saint had striven on behalf of the English and should be venerated accordingly.[5] Agincourt had become part of the English Church calendar and no one in En-

gland or Wales would be allowed to forget either the anniversary of the battle or the part that God and his saints had played
in securing their victory.

Significantly, these innovations were not introduced in the
immediate heady aftermath of victory but months later, in the
midst of preparations for a second campaign whose objective
was no less than the reconquest of Normandy. Instead of being
purely pious acts of gratitude and thanksgiving for past support, they therefore became important tools in the propaganda
war preceding a far more ambitious and long-term campaign.
The king's subjects were not merely being reminded that God
and his saints favoured their cause, but also being taught that it
was their religious duty, as it was the king's, to carry out the
divine plan to recover England's lost rights and inheritances.

The English chaplain's eyewitness account of the Agincourt
campaign was also part of this propaganda offensive. Written in
the winter months preceding the launch of the second expedition in July 1417, it portrayed Henry as the humble instrument
of God's will and his victory as the culmination of God's plan. It
ended with a prayer for the success of the new campaign that
was nothing short of a rallying cry to the king's own subjects
and his allies in Europe.

> And may God of His most merciful goodness grant that, just as
> our king, under His protection and by His judgement in respect
> of the enemies of his crown, has already triumphed twice, so
> may he triumph yet a third time, to the end that the two Swords,
> the sword of the French and the sword of England, may return to
> the rightful government of a single ruler, cease from their own
> destruction, and turn as soon as possible against the unsubdued
> and bloody faces of the heathen.[6]

The chaplain's *Gesta Henrici Quinti* has been aptly described by
its editors as both "an illustration and a justification" of Henry's
aims as king. It follows the party line to such an extent that it
frequently echoes the arguments and phraseology of the official
documents by which Henry sought to woo other rulers into supporting his war in France. The idea that a united England and
France could lead the way for a new crusade, for instance, was

one that appealed to Henry personally, but also had extra reso-
nance at this particular time because the council of Constance
was still in session. The principal objectives of this gathering of
clerical and lay representatives from all over Europe were to
remove the rival claimants to the papacy from office and end
the thirty-year schism that had caused so much damage to the
Church.[7] Christian unity was the theme of the moment. The
council also provided Henry with a ready-made forum in which
to make his case. Before embarking on the Agincourt campaign,
and again when preparing for his conquest of Normandy, he circulated copies of the treaties of Brétigny and Bourges, together
with transcripts of the diplomatic negotiations that had taken
place in his own reign, "that all Christendom might know what
great acts of injustice the French in their duplicity had inflicted
on him." In February 1416 letters written under the privy seal
on "affairs intimately concerning the king" were also dispatched to the Emperor Sigismund and various German dukes,
earls and lords. Henry knew the value of choosing an appropriate messenger and it was no coincidence that the person appointed to carry those letters through Europe was the man who
held the newly created post of Agincourt herald.[8]

Although Henry's intention to invade France for a second
time had been announced even before his return from his first
campaign, it would take him eighteen months to complete his
preparations. In this respect, the organisation for the Agincourt
campaign provided a blueprint for the much larger operation
that would culminate in the invasion of Normandy in 1417. It
was particularly important to the king that he had the continuing support of those who had rallied to his banner two years
earlier: in the build-up to renewed war, he could not afford to
have the veterans of Agincourt feel disappointed or aggrieved.
Henry was never lavish in the granting of titles, but two loyal
servants received promotions for their good service. Sir John
Holland, who had served with a courage and distinction beyond
his years, was rewarded by having the final vestiges of his
father's attainder for treason swept away.[9] Within a year of
Agincourt, he had been restored by the king's grace to the title
of earl of Huntingdon, been made a Knight of the Garter and

been appointed lieutenant of the fleet. Henry's confidence in him would be amply repaid by decades of loyal and successful military service as one of the chief defenders of English interests in France. The king's half-uncle Sir Thomas Beaufort, earl of Dorset, who had commanded the fleet during the invasion and held Harfleur, despite French attempts to retake it in 1416, was elevated to the rank of duke of Exeter.[10]

There was bureaucracy to conquer, too. The payment of wages was a potential bone of contention between the king and his soldiers because the accounting process was unavoidably complex. According to the terms of the indentures of service, all wages were supposed to have been paid quarterly in advance, but the situation was complicated by the fact that the first half of the first payment was made before the expedition set sail and its objective had been secret. The king had therefore paid his retinue leaders at the Gascon rates, which were half as much again as those for France. Their payments for the second half of the first quarter therefore had to be adjusted accordingly. To add to the confusion, jewels and plate, rather than cash, had been pledged for the payment of the second quarter's wages, and most of the army had returned to England before the end of that quarter and at different times. The retinue leaders had not only paid their men for the first quarter, but had also, in most cases, advanced the wages due for the second quarter in cash from their own funds. To recoup this money, the leaders had to present their paperwork at the exchequer. By this means, the king's clerks could compare the numbers they had promised in the original indentures against the actual numbers they had produced, as revealed by the muster lists drawn up at various points in the campaign and by the official lists of the sick who had received permission to return home from Harfleur. Together with the certified lists drawn up by each captain, noting who had been killed, captured, fallen sick or left behind in the garrison of Harfleur, this evidence theoretically made it possible to work out the wage bill proportionately to the length of service performed.[11]

In order to settle the thorny question of how this could all be arranged fairly and amicably, the king held a meeting in his secret chamber at the Tower of London with his treasurer, the keeper of the privy seal, the archbishop of Canterbury and Sir Walter Hungerford. In answer to a series of questions put to him on behalf of the exchequer, the king decided to ignore the different dates at which the retinues had mustered and disbanded and fix the dates for the start and end of the campaign at 6 July and 24 November 1415. This created an accounting period of 140 days, which conveniently meant that each man-at-arms would receive a round £7 and each archer £3 10s for his services on the campaign. All those who had been killed, died or fell sick and returned home (but only so long as they did so with the royal licence) during the first quarter were to receive their wages for the whole of that quarter. Similarly, all those who had been killed at the battle of Agincourt were to be paid in full as if they had taken part in the entire campaign. The only ones not to receive wages were those who had mustered in England but had been left behind for lack of shipping.[12] Though it is tempting to see these rulings as an attempt to impose a relatively simple accounting solution to a complex financial problem, there is no doubt that the king's decisions were also dictated by a wish to be generous to those who had served him well and, in some cases, had paid for it with their lives.

Still, those who had indented to serve directly with the king soon discovered that they could not always expect full and prompt repayment of the money they had expended in his service. Eight years after the battle and a year after Henry V himself had died, Sir John Holland, despite being high in the king's favour, was still owed £8158 (the equivalent of $5,437,633 today) for wages for the Agincourt campaign. And he was by no means alone. In 1427, for example, the duke of Gloucester and the earl of Salisbury petitioned Parliament, claiming that they had suffered "very great personal loss and damage" because they had paid their men in full for the whole of the second quarter, whereas the Exchequer had knocked forty-eight days' pay off their own payments in line with the king's decision that the campaign had ended early.[13] In other words, they were having to stand the loss themselves.

Although it was expected that the higher nobility would, to a certain extent, bankroll the king's military campaigns, those lower down the social scale also sometimes found themselves with unpaid wage bills. Sir Thomas Strickland, who carried the banner of St George at Agincourt and served continuously in France from 1417 to 1419, claimed to have received no wages at all, except for the first half-year, and had therefore sold off the silverware that the king had given him in pledge to help fund his continuing military service. In 1424 he petitioned, "for the sake of God, and as an act of charity," that he should be allowed the £14 4s 10¼d value of the silver against the arrears he was owed, a plea that was granted. Ten years later, the widow of John Clyff similarly claimed for £33 6s in outstanding wages due to him and his company of seventeen minstrels for the Agincourt campaign. Unlike Strickland, she had returned the king's jewels, which were valued at more than £53, to the crown; nevertheless, she received only £10 towards her claim.[14] The problem extended further down the chain of command, especially when it was unclear who was ultimately responsible for paying wages. The leader of each retinue was legally bound by the terms of the indentures he had signed with his men to pay them their due, but what of those companies who, through no fault of their own, had lost their leaders before the campaign began? The men who had indented to serve with Richard, earl of Cambridge, and Henry, Lord Scrope, for instance, had no redress against the estates of their executed leaders because these had been forfeited to the crown. The difficulty of establishing responsibility for payment was illustrated by the case of Henry Inglose, a man-at-arms who had indented to serve with Sir John Tiptoft. In March 1417 Inglose was driven to sue Tiptoft in the Court of Chivalry, accusing him of having refused to pay him the wages due to himself and his men for the Agincourt campaign "against his own express promise and against the whole noble custom of arms." On the face of it, relying on the indentures, Tiptoft's obligation was clear. The difficulty arose because, having recruited his thirty men-at-arms and ninety archers, Tiptoft was then appointed seneschal of Aquitaine and departed for Bordeaux before the campaign began. Henry Inglose, Sir John Fastolf and others of his retinue did not go with him but were ordered by the king to join his invasion of France. Who, then, was responsible for paying their wages? Inglose could have pursued his case through the ordinary courts but chose instead to go before the Court of Chivalry, which was presided over by the constable and marshal of England and had jurisdiction over all disputes concerning arms. Although this choice was probably determined by the technical nature of the case, Inglose was taking a substantial personal risk: if he was unable to prove his case by means of witnesses and evidence, the constable could compel him to do so in person by fighting a judicial duel to the death.[15]

If it was sometimes difficult to obtain payment for wages, there were other compensations available. Humphrey, duke of Gloucester, was granted the castle and lordship of Lanstephan, which had been forfeited by the Welsh rebel Henry Gwyn, "who was killed at Agencourt in the company of the king's adversaries of France." As the king could not afford to redeem the jewels he had given as security to his friend Henry Lord Fitzhugh, he gave him possession of all the lands held in chief by the son and heir of John, Lord Lovell, during his minority, so that he could offset the income against the wages owed to him and his company. Another royal knight Sir Gilbert Umfraville was similarly granted a valuable wardship in lieu of his wages for the campaign, and Sir Roland Lenthale was rewarded with the wardship and marriage rights of the son and heir of Sir John Mortymer "in consideration of his great expense on the king's last voyage." (Conversely Sir Walter Beauchamp and John Blaket, who presumably had received the money due to them, were both pursued in the courts for non-return of the king's jewels: when Beauchamp failed to respond to several court orders, the local sheriff was ordered to seize lands to their value from him.)[16]

A rather less expensive way of rewarding loyal service, but nevertheless one that was much sought after and highly prized, was admission to the Order of the Garter. This prestigious chivalric order could never exceed twenty-six members, yet in the five years after Agincourt, thirteen of the new appointees were veterans of the battle. Five of them — Sir John Holland, Thomas, Lord Camoys, who had commanded the left wing, the

earls of Oxford and Salisbury and Sir William Harington —
were admitted in 1416 alone.[17]

Most knights and esquires could not aspire to such heights of
chivalry, but there was another, equally effective way of rewarding their prowess. This was to turn a blind eye to the unauthorised assumption of coats of arms by Agincourt veterans. On
2 June 1417 Henry ordered his sheriffs to proclaim that no one,
"of what estate, degree or condition soever he be," was to
appear at a muster for the new campaign wearing a coat of arms
to which he was not entitled either by ancestral right or official
grant, on pain of being stripped of his assumed coat of arms and
barred from taking part in the expedition. The sole exemption
to this was for "those who bore arms with us at the Battle of
Agincourt." The interpretation of this clause has been much
debated and for many years it was assumed that anyone who
had fought in the battle was automatically raised to the nobility.
This gave rise to Shakespeare's famous lines in which Henry V
promised his men before the battle

For he, today that sheds his blood with me,
Shall be my brother; be he ne'er so vile
This day shall gentle his condition.

Though a number of esquires were knighted during the Agincourt campaign, there was no explosion in the assumption of
coats of arms and the ranks of the nobility were not immediately swelled by hordes of ambitious archers, so we can safely
dismiss this interpretation. The most likely explanation of the
exemption is that it allowed those who had unofficially changed
their coat of arms in consequence of taking part in the battle to
bear these arms as of right in perpetuity. John de Wodehouse,
for example, changed the ermine chevron on his coat of arms to
one of gold (*or*, in heraldic terminology) scattered with drops of
blood, and later adopted the motto "Agincourt." Sir Roland de
Lenthale similarly added the motto "Agincourt" to his coat.
Rather more imaginatively, Richard Waller commemorated his
capture of Charles d'Orléans by adding the duke's shield to the
walnut tree that was his family crest.[18]

As for Charles d'Orléans himself, he and the other important French prisoners had endured the humiliation of defeat, capture and being paraded through the streets of London for the delectation of an English audience, followed by incarceration in the Tower of London to await the king's decision on their fate. This brought about a particularly poignant reunion for Arthur, count of Richemont, with his mother, the dowager Queen Joan, whom he had not seen since she left Brittany to marry Henry IV when he was a child of ten. Richemont was now twenty-two and, to his mother's annoyance and grief, he failed to recognise her among her ladies when he was brought into her presence. She too must have experienced some difficulty in recognising her son, for his face had been badly disfigured by wounds received at Agincourt. The meeting was not a happy one, and though Joan covered up her disappointment by giving him clothing and a large sum of money to distribute among his fellow-prisoners and guards, he never saw her again throughout the seven long years of his captivity.[19]

The terms of his imprisonment were not harsh, even by modern standards. As befitted their aristocratic status, the French prisoners were permitted to live as honoured guests in the households of their captors and were free to ride, hunt and go hawking as they pleased. The more senior ones were allowed to stay in the king's own palaces at Eltham, Windsor and Westminster, and were provided with state beds purchased for their own use. They were not separated or isolated, but generally kept in groups or at least allowed contact with each other. They were even allowed to make their captivity more comfortable by bringing over their favourite servants, horses and possessions — Marshal Boucicaut shared his captivity with his personal confessor, Frère Honorat Durand, and his barber, Jean Moreau, while one of the duke of Bourbon's first demands was that four of his falconers should be sent over to him. Generous sums were also allocated for their living expenses, though this was not entirely altruistic: these expenses were then added to the ransoms they were required to pay to obtain their freedom.[20]

It was only in times of particular danger that their liberties were curtailed. In June 1417, when Henry was about to invade

France for a second time, all his French prisoners were temporarily sent out to more secure custody in the provinces: Charles d'Orléans was sent to Pontefract Castle in Yorkshire (a particularly insensitive choice, since his first wife's first husband, Richard II, had been murdered within its walls), Marshal Boucicaut and the counts of Eu and Richemont were transferred to Fotheringhay Castle in Northamptonshire and Georges de Clère, the sire de Torcy, and a number of other prisoners were taken to Conwy and Caernarvon castles in north Wales. Even in these more remote places, the prisoners were generally allowed to take exercise outside the castle walls. When Charles d'Orléans and Marshal Boucicaut were held at Pontefract Castle, their jailer, Robert Waterton, regularly allowed them to visit his manor of Methley, six miles away, where the hunting was particularly good. In 1419, however, during the crisis following the murder of John the Fearless, there were rumours that Charles d'Orléans had been in contact with the Scottish duke of Albany, and Henry moved swiftly to clamp down on his privileges. He was not to be allowed to leave the castle under any circumstances, not even to go to "Robertes place or to any disport, for it is better he lack his disport than we were deceived."[21]

For all the comforts of their captivity,[22] it was still captivity. Less important prisoners, who had not crossed over to England, were being ransomed and set free in a steady stream throughout the weeks and months following the battle. At Boulogne, the city authorities dispensed wine to celebrate the return of those released from English prisons; from the beginning of November this was happening on almost a weekly basis, and the returnees included the mayor of Le Crotoy and Jehan Vinct, son of a former mayor of Boulogne. By the following June, some prisoners from England were also beginning to make their way home. On 3 June 1416 a safe-conduct was issued on behalf of Jean, sire de Ligne, a Hainaulter who had been captured at the battle by the earl of Oxford, together with his eldest son, Jennet de Poix, and David de Poix. This allowed the sire de Ligne to be released on licence so that he could raise the money for his ransom; his arrival at Boulogne was celebrated on 14 June, but this was premature, for he was under oath to return to England by

29 September. If he had raised the requisite sums, he could then expect to be set free; if not, then he would have to return to captivity.[23]

While it was customary for those released on licence to provide hostages as pledges for their return, the temptation not to go back must have been strong. This did happen on occasion. As we have already seen, the earl of Douglas and Jacques de Créquy, sire de Heilly, both broke their oaths so that they could remain at liberty.[24] Henry V's prisoners from Harfleur and Agincourt were more honourable. When Arthur, count of Richemont, was allowed to go to Normandy in the company of the earl of Suffolk in 1420, he refused to be complicit in a plot to rescue him: "he replied that he would rather die than break the faith and the oath that he had given the king of England."[25] Raoul de Gaucourt was also released on licence in 1416 and again in 1417, yet, despite feeling that Henry V had not honoured his promises to him, he returned to captivity each time. Uniquely, because the whole matter later became the subject of a court case before the Paris Parlement between himself and the heir of Jean d'Estouteville, we have de Gaucourt's first-hand account of his attempts to secure his freedom. His negotiations began with the king, who, instead of simply demanding a sum of money as the joint ransom for de Gaucourt and d'Estouteville, asserted that seven or eight score of his servants and subjects "were being very harshly treated as prisoners in France, and that if we desired our liberation, we should exert ourselves to obtain theirs." As these Englishmen were not as valuable as the two defenders of Harfleur, Henry suggested that he would take the opinions of two English and two French knights as to how much more they should pay to make up the difference. He also mentioned that he had lost some of his jewels in the attack on the baggage train at Agincourt, "which it would be a great thing for us if we could recover," and demanded two hundred casks of Beaune wine, which would also be taken into the final account.

Troubled by this unusual arrangement, de Gaucourt and d'Estouteville consulted Charles d'Orléans, the duke of Bourbon, the counts of Richemont, Eu and Vendôme, and Marshal Boucicaut, who gave it as their unanimous opinion that they should agree to the king's conditions if only to avoid the prospect of a long detention in England. Even though de Gaucourt "was by no means cured of my severe complaint," he received his safe-conduct from the king on 3 April 1416 and set off for France, where he managed to secure the liberation of all except twenty of the English "gentlemen, merchants and soldiers" who were being held prisoner. The jewels "were already dispersed, and in different hands," but de Gaucourt succeeded in finding the king's crown, coronation orb and golden cross containing the fragment of the True Cross, "as well as several other things which he was anxious to recover; in particular, the seals of the said King's chancery." He purchased the wine and, taking the seals with him, returned to England believing that he had done everything demanded of him.[26]

Henry, however, proved implacable. He declared that he was perfectly satisfied with the diligence that de Gaucourt had displayed, but that everything should be conveyed to London before he would authorise his release. The Frenchman therefore hired a ship, paid off the outstanding ransoms of the English prisoners, provided them all with new clothes and liveries and delivered them and the king's jewels to the Tower of London. A week later, a second ship carrying the casks of wine arrived. Once again, de Gaucourt and d'Estouteville thought they had fulfilled all the king's conditions and sought their release, but Henry left London without giving them an answer. Four and a half months later, without consulting them, without their knowledge or consent, and without compensating them, he ordered that the English who had been living at de Gaucourt's expense in the Tower should all be set free.[27]

On 25 January 1417, the same day that de Gaucourt had received his safe-conduct for his ship "with twelve or fourteen mariners" bringing back the prisoners and wine, he was also given licence to return to France. This was to allow him to complete his arrangements, but also because he had been entrusted with a special mission to the French court. In a secret meeting between the duke of Bourbon and Henry V, the king had said that he might be prepared to give up his own claim to the throne of France if Charles VI agreed to accept the terms of the Treaty of Brétigny and renounce all his rights to Harfleur. Bourbon had suggested that this offer was so reasonable that he would even do homage to Henry himself, as king of France, if Charles VI rejected it. Raoul de Gaucourt was chosen to convey Henry's terms and to urge Charles VI and his advisors to accept them. But it was another futile task. The offer was bogus. A second invasion of France was imminent and as Henry informed Sir John Tiptoft on the very day de Gaucourt's licence was granted, "I will not abandon my expedition for any agreement they make."[28]

All de Gaucourt's efforts had come to nothing. Although he had saved the dukes of Bourbon and Orléans the 40,000 crowns (around $4,443,600 today) which Henry had demanded from them as security for his return by 31 March, peace between England and France was no nearer. He was personally 13,000 crowns out of pocket in his attempts to secure his and d'Estouteville's release, yet they were still the king's prisoners. What is more, when Henry gave orders on his deathbed that certain of his French prisoners should not be released until his infant son came of age, de Gaucourt's name was one of them. It would be ten years after the battle of Agincourt before he finally achieved his freedom and only then because his ransom was needed to offset that demanded by the French for the release of John Holland, earl of Huntingdon.[29] His later career proved Henry's wisdom in keeping him captive. On his final return to France, de Gaucourt devoted himself to the service of the dauphin and fought in every military campaign against the English. Appointed captain of Orléans and governor of the Dauphiné, he distinguished himself both on and off the field, was an early champion of Joan of Arc and, with her, raised the English siege of Orléans and attended the dauphin's triumphant coronation at Reims. He lived long enough to see the reconquest of both Normandy and Aquitaine, and, by the time he died, in his eighties or early nineties, he had the satisfaction of knowing that he had been one of the chief architects of the final expulsion of the English from France.[30]

Another of Henry's prisoners who later played a leading role in the restoration of the French monarchy was Arthur, count of

Richemont. Prior to his capture at Agincourt, and despite his brother the duke of Brittany's alliances with England, he had been an active supporter of the Armagnac cause. While in captivity, he was persuaded by Henry V to change his allegiance so that he then became an active supporter of the Anglo-Burgundian alliance. He agreed to become an ally and vassal of the English king and, as we have seen, was therefore permitted to return to France on parole, so long as he remained in the company of the earl of Suffolk. Absconding after Henry's death, he married Margaret of Burgundy, John the Fearless's daughter and widow of the dauphin Louis de Guienne, a year later. In 1425 the dauphin Charles, as yet uncrowned and unanointed, offered him the post of constable of France, and in a second spectacular political volte-face the count of Richemont returned to his Armagnac roots. His reforms of the French army and his victories over the English at the battles of Patay (1429) and Formigny (1450) paved the way for the reconquest of Normandy.[31]

The brother and stepson of the duke of Bourbon — Louis de Bourbon, count of Vendôme, and Charles d'Artois, count of Eu — similarly took up arms against the English after their respective releases in 1423 and 1438. After twenty-three years in captivity, and now aged forty-five, Charles d'Artois had his revenge for his lost youth by becoming the French king's lieutenant in both Normandy and Guienne.[32] The duke of Bourbon himself never had that opportunity. In July 1420 he was offered terms that might have obtained his release, though Raoul de Gaucourt's experience did not augur well. He was allowed to return to France on licence to find a hundred thousand gold crowns for his ransom, on condition that he also persuaded his son, the count of Clermont, to join the Anglo-Burgundian alliance, and provided important hostages, including his second son. All his efforts to meet these terms proved unavailing and although Henry V died while he was still at liberty, unlike the count of Richemont he did not consider his obligations at an end. He returned to England, where his captivity did not prevent him fathering an illegitimate daughter, and died at Bolingbroke in 1434. Even in death he did not return home, for he was buried in the Franciscan church of London.[33]

Marshal Boucicaut, too, would never see France again. At forty-eight years of age when he was captured at Agincourt, he was already one of the oldest prisoners and, having spent all his life from the age of twelve in arms, he was now forced to end his days in involuntary retirement. This most pious of men, who reserved hours each day for his devotions, and every Friday wore black and fasted in memory of Christ's passion, had commissioned a Book of Hours in 1405–8. Twenty-seven miniatures of saints with special relevance to his life adorn the book. Ironically, the first and most important was dedicated to St Leonard, the patron saint of prisoners. Though it had been included in memory of the marshal's brief captivity after Nicopolis, it proved to be a prescient choice. All Boucicaut's efforts to obtain his release were in vain. He offered Henry V sixty thousand crowns as a ransom, but this was rejected out of hand. The pope tried to intervene on his behalf, sending ambassadors to England to offer forty thousand crowns and promising that Boucicaut would give his oath never to fight against the English again. Henry remained obdurate. Despairing of ever obtaining his freedom, Boucicaut added a codicil to his will a few weeks before he died, leaving a few tokens to his fellow-prisoners and the rest of his small estate to his brother Geffroi. On 25 June 1421, this internationally famous paragon of chivalry died in the obscurity of Robert Waterton's manor house at Methley in Yorkshire. It was the passing of an age and of the great Boucicaut name. The marshal's wife had died while he was in prison, he had no children and both his nephews, who inherited the estate from their father, died childless, too. His body, however, was taken back to France and buried, with honour, close to his father, the first marshal Boucicaut, in the chapel of the Virgin behind the choir of the Church of St Martin at Tours.[34]

The fate of Henry V's most important prisoner was equally pathetic. Charles d'Orléans was still legally a minor when he was captured at Agincourt. He celebrated his twenty-first birthday within days of landing in England and would spend the next twenty-five years of his life in captivity. His younger brother Philippe died in 1420, his only child Jeanne in 1432 and his wife Bonne of Armagnac at about the same time. Helpless to aid either his own cause or that of France, he could only watch from the sidelines as Henry V invaded France and conquered Normandy. The assassination of his father's murderer, John the Fearless, by the dauphin in 1419 might have been a cause for rejoicing, but it was short-lived. As a sixteenth-century prior remarked, when showing John the Fearless's skull to François I, "It was through this hole that the English entered into France."[35] The murder drove Philippe, the duke of Burgundy's son and heir, into open alliance with the English and led directly to the Treaty of Troyes, by which the dauphin was disinherited for his crime and Henry V, having achieved his long-held ambition of marrying Catherine of France, was legally recognised by Charles VI as the rightful heir to his crown.

Ironically, Henry V never became king of France, for Charles VI outlived his son-in-law by almost two months. Henry V's son was only nine months old when he inherited the crowns of England and France, and it was in neither the English nor the Burgundian interest to procure Charles d'Orléans' release. Until 1435, when Philippe, duke of Burgundy, abandoned his English alliance and made his peace with the dauphin, whom he now recognised as Charles VII, the only people who actively championed Charles d'Orléans' cause were his bastard brother Jean, count of Dunois, and Joan of Arc. It would take another five years before all sides came to the conclusion that Charles was more valuable as a potential peacemaker between England and France than as an impotent prisoner. He was formally set free in a ceremony at Westminster Abbey on 28 October 1440.

A month later, aged forty-six, he married for the third and last time. His fourteen-year-old bride would give birth to three children, one of whom would eventually succeed to the throne of France as Louis XII, but Charles himself had lost his appetite for politics. He retired to live quietly at his chateau at Blois, where he spent his time much as he had done in captivity in England: reading his impressively large library of books on philosophy, theology and science, pursuing his interest in clocks and other mechanical devices and writing the urbane and witty love poetry of which he had become a master craftsman during his years of enforced leisure.[36]

Though most of Charles d'Orléans' poetry belonged firmly in the courtly love tradition and should not be read as autobiographical, his personal plight surfaced occasionally. Seeing the coastline of France while on a visit to Dover, for instance, inspired a plea for the peace that would allow him to return home:

> *Peace is a treasure which one cannot praise too highly.*
> *I hate war, it should never be prized;*
> *For a long time it has prevented me, rightly or wrongly,*
> *From seeing France which my heart must love.*[37]

In another of his poems, "Complainte," he looked back to the causes of the French defeat at Agincourt and regretted that France, which had once been a pattern to all other nations for honour, loyalty, courtesy and prowess, had sunk into pride, lethargy, lechery and injustice. He urged his countrymen to return to the virtues that had once inspired its great Christian heroes, Charlemagne, Roland, Oliver and St Louis, so that the saints would forgive them and once more rally to their cause.[38]

Charles d'Orléans' poetry was part of an enormous literary response generated by the battle. The defeat was such a cataclysmic event that contemporaries often could not bear to refer to it by name. In fifteenth-century France "la malheureuse journée" (the unhappy or unfortunate day) was understood to mean Agincourt and needed no further explanation.

Alain Chartier's long poem, *Le Livre des Quatre Dames*, for instance, was written within two years of the battle and in direct response to it, but never mentions it by name. Disguised as a courtly love lyric, the poem is in fact a thinly veiled attack upon those whom Chartier considered responsible for the defeat. In it he describes meeting four ladies, all weeping copiously, who ask him to judge which of them is the most unhappy. All of them have lost their lovers at Agincourt. The first lady's was killed "on that accursed day," the second's was captured and now languishes in an English prison. The third lady claims that her fate is worse still: she waits in suspense, like a tower which has been mined but must fall in due course, for she does not know what has happened to her lover or whether he is dead or alive. Each one blames those who fled the field for the defeat and their personal loss. It is obvious that the fourth lady, whose lover survived, is the most unhappy. She bewails having given her heart to "a disgraced and cowardly fugitive, who stands condemned for dishonourable conduct": in his selfish anxiety to preserve himself, he had abandoned his comrades to death and imprisonment. "He polished up his bascinet and put on his armour, only to run away," she complains. "Alas! What a day!"[39]

Chartier was a Norman cleric and lifelong Armagnac who became secretary to the new dauphin, Charles, in 1417. Like Charles d'Orléans, he also wrote a number of works denouncing French knights for their moral failings and urging them to practise the ancient chivalric virtues so that victory against the English would one day be theirs:

One ought to consider more worthy of honour and praise the military commander who has the wisdom to know when, if necessary, to withdraw his army and keep it intact rather than risking its destruction through excessively rash contempt for danger, neglecting moderation and caution in the vain hope of acquiring a reputation for chivalric valour. I do not need to look for ancient examples from times past to prove what I am saying; something we have seen recently and in our own day serves as a better lesson. Let us remember in our hearts the case of the unhappy battle of Azincourt, for which we have paid dearly, and grieve still for our woeful misfortune. All the weight of that great disaster presses upon us and we cannot free ourselves from it, except by acting promptly, showing a wise perseverance and reining in our rash impatience with the safety of caution.[40]

In her *Letter Concerning the Prison of Human Life*, which she finished on 20 January 1417, Christine de Pizan also advised patience and fortitude, doling out measured words of comfort to Marie, duchess of Bourbon, whose son-in-law and cousins were killed at Agincourt, and whose husband, son and brother-in-law were all English prisoners. The French dead, she declared, were all God's martyrs, "obedient unto death in order to sustain justice, along with the rights of the French crown and their sovereign lord." After Henry launched his second campaign and the English advance through France appeared unstoppable, Christine's resignation gave way to indignation and a nationalism that was all the more ardent for being the adopted identity of this Italian-born writer. Her growing hatred of the English culminated in her premature celebration of Joan of Arc's successes. "And so, you English . . . You have been check-mated," she crowed. "You thought you had already conquered France and that she must remain yours. Things have turned out otherwise, you treacherous lot!"[41]

In England, the delight that greeted the victory at Agincourt found expression in a host of political songs and popular ballads. Adam of Usk, for instance, introduced an eight-line Latin epigram into his chronicle with the words, "This is what one poet wrote in praise of the king." Though obviously a scholarly production, the tone was unashamedly populist.

> *People of England, cease your work and pray,*
> *For the glorious victory of Crispin's day;*
> *Despite their scorn for Englishmen's renown,*
> *The odious might of France came crashing down.*[42]

This Latin epigram was one of many produced after the battle and comes from a long tradition of such work in chronicles. There is, however, a piece that stands out from the rest not only because it survives in an independent manuscript, complete with musical notation, but also because the verses were composed in English. The Agincourt carol was written in Henry V's lifetime for three voices: the six verses were to be sung in unison by two voices, but the Latin chorus, "To God give thanks, O England, for the victory," opened with a single voice, progressed to two-part harmony for the second phrase and was then repeated with variations by all three voices. Like the English verses sung at the London pageant, it managed to lavish praise on the king while attributing his success to God.

> Deo gracias, anglia, redde pro victoria
> *Our king went forth to Normandy, with grace and might*
> *of chivalry;*

There God for him wrought marv'lously,
Wherefore Englond may call and cry:
Deo gracias, Anglia, redde pro victoria.
Deo gracias, Anglia, redde pro victoria.
He set a siege, forsooth to say,
To Harflu town with royal array;
That town he won and made affray,
That France shall rue till Domesday:
Deo gracias.

Then went him forth our King comely;
In Agincourt field he fought manly;
Through grace of God most marvellously
He hath both field and victory:
Deo gracias.

There lordës, earlës and baron
Were slain and taken and that full soon,
And some were brought into London
With joy and bliss and great renown:
Deo gracias.

Almighty God he keep our king,
His people and all his well-willing,
And give them grace withouten ending;
Then may we call and safely sing:
Deo gracias anglia.[43]

The Agincourt carol was probably a production of either Henry's own royal chapel or a religious house and has been preserved in ecclesiastical archives. Undoubtedly many popular ballads in English and French must also have been composed for the gratification of the Agincourt veterans of all ranks. The minstrels in the retinues of the great lords, many of whom had accompanied the English army to France, were expected to celebrate the deeds of their patrons and Agincourt was the ideal topic for courtly and chivalric gatherings. It was also a gift for the wandering minstrels who earned their living by going from one knightly household to another to perform. By their very nature such compositions were ephemeral: they were part of the oral tradition of ballad-making and were never written down. Though no examples have survived, their impact on the popular imagination cannot be ignored. They ensured that news of the king's victory reached the more remote rural communities, encouraged a feeling of national pride and unity and were a powerful recruiting agent for Henry's new campaign. Indeed, it might be argued that they preserved the place of Agincourt in the national consciousness for centuries to come.

As the last vestiges of English power in France were slowly but inexorably eradicated, people looked back to the glory days of Agincourt with nostalgia. Ballads, chronicles and plays in English written for an increasingly literate bourgeoisie preserved the memory of the victory and served as a rallying cry for future wars in France. Just as the English chaplain wrote his *Gesta Henrici Quinti* in the build-up to Henry V's second invasion of Normandy, so *The First English Life of King Henry the Fifth* was written in anticipation of the launch of Henry VIII's war against France. As late as the 1940s, Winston Churchill, who was then prime minister, asked Laurence Olivier to make a film of Shakespeare's *Henry V* (omitting the Cambridge plot, since it suggested there had been dissent) to prepare the nation psychologically for the D-Day landings in Normandy, which were to liberate Europe from Nazi occupation.[44]

It has often been claimed that Agincourt had little or no impact on the course of history: it did not result in lands changing hands or in dramatic political changes, and, longer term, the English obsession with their rights in France proved to be a costly and ultimately futile distraction from more important issues. By reigniting the war with France, Henry V committed his country to decades of warfare and heavy taxation to pay for it; he has even been blamed for sowing the seeds that would lead to England itself being torn apart by civil strife in the Wars of the Roses. While there is a kernel of truth in all these hoary chestnuts, they are by no means the whole story.

It is useful to speculate, for instance, on what might have happened had Henry lost the battle of Agincourt, as everyone but the king himself expected him to do. If the French cavalry had succeeded in riding down and destroying his archers, then his tiny force of men-at-arms would not have been able to withstand the weight and numbers of the French advance on foot. The English army would have been swiftly overwhelmed and annihilated. Henry and his brother Humphrey, together with the cream of the English aristocracy and gentry, would have been killed or captured. In either case, the consequences for his own country would have been catastrophic. Henry had only been king for two years, and the remarkable changes he had wrought in that time could not have been sustained without him. Clarence would have become king and he had neither the tact nor the ability to unite and lead a country in the way his brother had done. He also lacked a legitimate son and heir, which would have again exposed the Lancastrian dynasty to other and better claims to the throne. The machinery of government at national and local levels would have descended into chaos without the great office holders of state and the members of Parliament, sheriffs and justices of the peace, whose sons would have been too young to take their place. The security of the realm would have been greatly endangered since the military resources of the kingdom had already been stretched to their furthest limits to provide the army for the Agincourt campaign. Backed by the victorious French, the Scots and Welsh rebels would undoubtedly have taken advantage of the situation to invade, plunder and even take control of the border regions.

Many estates, both great and small, would have been thrown into administration because their heirs were underage, with all the opportunities that provided for the unscrupulous and ambitious to line their own pockets at the expense of the future stability and economic success of the property and those dependent on it. The necessity of finding ransoms for those captured would also have been a heavy financial burden on the entire country, since a lord's ransom would ultimately have had to be paid by taxes on his tenants. Had Henry himself been taken prisoner, the ransom demanded would have been as ruinous as that demanded by Edward III for Jean II of France after his capture at the battle of Poitiers in 1356. And would Clarence, seeing an opportunity to seize power, have dragged his feet in collecting the money, just as Prince John had done when his brother, Richard the Lionheart, was captured on his return from crusade? Defeat at Agincourt would certainly have caused political, economic and social disaster in England — it might even have precipitated the country into civil war.

Henry's victory laid the foundations for the resurrection of an English empire in France. The conquest of Normandy in 1417–19 could not have been achieved so rapidly had not so many French officers of the crown, including local *baillis* and castellans, as well as a whole swath of the military profession, from princes to militiamen, been killed at Agincourt. Henry's successes in the field were arguably less important than the dauphin's assassination of John the Fearless in 1419 in bringing about the Anglo-Burgundian alliance that eventually forced Charles VI to disinherit his own son, marry his daughter to the English king and accept his new son-in-law as his heir. Nevertheless, Agincourt played a vital role in establishing that Henry had a moral right to the throne of France. God had approved his demand for the restoration of his just rights and inheritances in spectacular fashion. He had won the trial by battle.

Perhaps more importantly, Henry had proved beyond all doubt that he was also the true king of England. God had chosen to bless him with victory at Agincourt despite the fact that he was the son of a usurper. There could have been no more effective demonstration to the world that the sins of the father would not be held against this son. Henry V clearly enjoyed divine approval. And with God on his side, who could stand against him?

ACKNOWLEDGEMENTS

In writing this book I have incurred many debts. First and foremost, I am grateful to Alan Samson, who suggested the subject and commissioned this book on behalf of Little, Brown. I am equally indebted to Andrew Lownie, my agent, who reminded Alan that despite being better known as a nineteenth-century literary biographer, I am also a historian of medieval chivalry. It has been a joy to have a legitimate excuse to re-immerse myself in the world of Henry V.

It would be impossible to acknowledge each and every one of the hundreds of scholars whose detailed studies of different aspects of the period under-pinned the writing of this book: the extent of my debt will be obvious from my notes. On the other hand, it would also be impossible to write about Agincourt without acknowledging the work of two scholars whose names have become synonymous with the subject. James Hamilton Wylie (1844–1914) was the epitome of a Victorian antiquarian: an indefatigable (and sometimes undiscriminating) collector of historical minutiae, he had an unrivalled knowledge of the unpublished manuscripts of the Public Record Office. His great work, *The Reign of Henry the Fifth* (Cambridge University Press, 1914–29), the third volume of which was compiled from his notes after his death by William Templeton Waugh, is an indispensable source for the historian of Agincourt, though it is for his footnotes, rather than his chaotic text, that the book is valuable.

In more recent times, Dr Anne Curry has been equally industrious. She has pioneered a renaissance in Agincourt studies and made the subject more accessible, especially for those unable to read medieval Latin, French or manuscript hand. *The Battle of Agincourt: Sources and Interpretations* (Boydell Press, Woodbridge, 2000) is a sine qua non for anyone interested in Agincourt and it was the starting point for my own research. Her latest work, *Agincourt: A New History* (Tempus, Stroud, 2005), was published as this book was going to press and therefore too late for me to utilise its wealth of detail in my own account. Although, for the most part, our conclusions are broadly similar, I remain unconvinced by her argument that the French did not greatly outnumber the English at the battle. Surviving administrative records on both sides, but especially the French, are simply too incomplete to support her assertion that nine thousand English were pitted against an army only twelve thousand strong. And if the differential really was as low as three to four then this makes a nonsense of the course of the battle as described by eyewitnesses and contemporaries.

I could not have undertaken the task of writing this book without having had access to the Brotherton Library at the University of Leeds, which has one of the finest collections of historical texts in the country, and I am grateful to the authorities of the university for granting me permission to read there. Dr Marcus Ackroyd has, once again, incurred my gratitude for his cheerful, prompt and efficient assistance in locating more obscure texts and, on occasion, translating some of the French quotations that defeated me. Regrettably, I cannot blame him for any errors that remain. Manuscript material has played a smaller part than I would wish in a book of this kind, but it is nevertheless an important one, and I would like to thank the staff and governing bodies of The National Archives, the British Library, the Bodleian Library, the Gloucester Record Office and Norfolk Record Office for access to their archives and for permission to quote from them.

I am also indebted to many individuals who patiently and courteously shared their specialist knowledge with me, answering questions and making observations that have all had a formative influence on this book: chief among them are my son, Edward Barker, an undergraduate studying history at the University of St Andrews; Ian Chance of Wingfield College; Mr Mick Crumplin, MB, FRCS (Eng), FRCS (Ed), FINS, FHS; Professor Shaun Gregory of the University of Bradford; Dr Maurice Keen of Balliol College, Oxford; David McNeill, Assistant Map Curator of the Royal Geographical Society; Jonathan Riley and his family; Dr Ingrid Roscoe; and, finally, those officers, acting and retired, of the Duke of Wellington's Regiment, the Prince of Wales's Own Regiment of Yorkshire, the King's Own Yorkshire Light Infantry and others, with whom I have conversed informally on the subject while writing this book. His Honour Judge Shaun Spencer kindly lent me his personal copy of *The Master of Game, by Edward, Second Duke of York*; Richard Dobson drew my attention to Henry V's injury at the battle of Shrewsbury; Michael Gandy obtained copies of manuscript material on my behalf from The National Archives. Tim Whiting and Geoff Shandler of Little, Brown have been attentive and helpful editors.

My husband, son and daughter have, as usual, suffered most from my obsession with my subject. I would like to thank them (again) for their forbearance and encouragement, and apologise to them unreservedly (again) for making them spend their summer "holiday" of 2004 following in Henry V's footsteps through France on the Agincourt campaign. Although I perhaps ought to dedicate this book to them (again), there is another person to whom I owe a hitherto unacknowledged debt of gratitude. As an undergraduate at Oxford, I was fortunate enough to be taught by Maurice Keen, of Balliol College, whose quite exceptional abilities as a historian are matched only by his talents as a teacher. He not only inspired my own abiding love of the medieval period, and chivalry in particular, but also guided me through my doctorate on English tournaments and set me on the path to becoming a published author. For all these reasons, I can think of no one more appropriate to whom I should dedicate this book.

NOTES

PREFACE

1 *GHQ*, p. 93.
2 *St Albans*, p. 96.

CHAPTER ONE: JUST RIGHTS AND INHERITANCES

1 Monstrelet, iii, pp. 78–80; *St-Denys*, v, pp. 526–8.
2 Anna Comnena, *The Alexiad*, ed. and trans. by E. R. A. Sewter (Penguin, Harmondsworth, 1979), p. 416.
3 For map of Aquitaine (English Gascony), see above p. 3.
4 M. G. A. Vale, *English Gascony 1399–1453* (Oxford University Press, Oxford, 1970), pp. 2–3.
5 John Palmer, "The War Aims of the Protagonists and the Negotiations for Peace," in Fowler, p. 51.
6 Maurice Keen, *The Pelican History of Medieval Europe* (Pelican Books, Harmondsworth, 1969 repr. 1976), pp. 202, 122, 217; Barbara W. Tuchman, *A Distant Mirror* (Ballantine Books, New York, 1979), pp. 42–4. The persecution was unique to France, though the Templar order was suppressed throughout Europe and its assets transferred to the Knights Hospitallers.
7 Peter S. Lewis, *Later Medieval France: The Polity* (Macmillan, London and St Martin's Press, New York, 1968), pp. 39–41; Kenneth Fowler, "War and Change in Late Medieval France and England," in Fowler, p. 1. As late as 1522 Charles, duke of Bourbon, could declare himself to be seriously considering the English title to the French throne; the English did not finally renounce the title until the Treaty of Amiens in 1802.
8 Anne Curry, *The Hundred Years War* (Palgrave, London and New York, 1993), pp. 66–7; Maurice Keen, "Diplomacy," *HVPK*, pp. 182–4.
9 Since he was a minor at the time, the act could be repudiated as invalid.
10 Palmer, "The War Aims of the Protagonists and the Negotiations for Peace," pp. 54–5.

11 Vale, *English Gascony*, pp. 5, 27–8; *ELMA*, p. 289; Curry, *The Hundred Years War*, pp. 83–8.
12 G. L. Harriss, *Cardinal Beaufort: A Study of Lancastrian Ascendancy and Decline* (Clarendon Press, Oxford, 1988), pp. 23–5; Curry, *The Hundred Years War*, pp. 90–1.
13 McLeod, pp. 30–1, 56.
14 Vale, *English Gascony*, pp. 48–9, 53; *ELMA*, p. 320.
15 For a discussion of Charles VI's madness, which began in 1392, see Bernard Guenée, *La Folie de Charles VI Roi Bien-Amé* (Perrin, Paris, 2004).
16 Lewis, *Later Medieval France*, p. 114.
17 Vaughan, pp. 44–7, 67–81; McLeod, pp. 33, 38–40.
18 Vaughan, pp. 81–2; McLeod, pp. 58–66.
19 K. B. McFarlane, *Lancastrian Kings and Lollard Knights* (Oxford University Press, Oxford, 1972), pp. 103–4.
20 *ELMA*, p. 321; Vaughan, pp. 92–4.
21 Ibid., pp. 94–5; Vale, *English Gascony*, pp. 58–62.
22 Capgrave, p. 124 n. 2.
23 Monstrelet, i, pp. 451–2.
24 *St Albans*, pp. 65–7.
25 *ELMA*, pp. 322–3; Christopher Allmand, *Henry V* (Yale University Press, New Haven and London, new edn, 1997), pp. 56–8; Vale, *English Gascony*, p. 67. An audit of the Calais accounts cleared Henry of any misdoing.
26 Cornewaille's name is usually transcribed as "Cornewall" in modern texts (including *ODNB*) but I prefer the archaic spelling which is consistently used in medieval sources.
27 Vale, *English Gascony*, pp. 62–8; *ELMA*, pp. 321–2; McLeod, pp. 82–6, 275.

CHAPTER TWO: A KING'S APPRENTICESHIP

1 *ELMA*, pp. 322–3; W&W, iii, p. 427; Vale, *English Gascony*, p. 67.
2 Thomas Hoccleve, *The Regiment of Princes*, ed. by Charles R. Blythe (Western Michigan University, Kalamazoo, Michigan, 1999), pp. 97ff.
3 Christine de Pizan, *Le Livre du Corps de Policie*, summarised in Edith P. Yenal, *Christine de Pizan: A Bibliography* (Scarecrow Press, Metuchen, N.J. and London, 1989), pp. 65–6.
4 Kate Langdon Forhan, *The Political Theory of Christine de Pizan* (Ashgate, Aldershot, 2002), pp. 13, 30, 74. Christine had placed her son in the household of John Montagu, earl of Salisbury, a Francophile poet, patron of poets and favourite of Richard II; Salisbury was killed in revolt against Henry IV in January 1400 and Henry then took the boy into his own household.
5 Hilary M. Carey, *Courting Disaster: Astrology at the English Court and University in the Late Middle Ages* (Macmillan, London, 1992), p. 129.
6 McFarlane, *Lancastrian Kings and Lollard Knights*, pp. 233–8, 117.
7 *First English Life*, p. 17; Nicholas Orme, *Medieval Children* (Yale University Press, New Haven and London, 2001), p. 190; Nicolas, p. 389; John Southworth, *The English Medieval Minstrel* (Boydell Press, Wood-

bridge, 1989), pp. 113–14; Richard Marks and Paul Williamson (eds), *Gothic Art for England 1400–1547* (V&A Publications, London, 2003), pp. 121 (illus.), 157.

8 Orme, *Medieval Children*, p. 182.

9 John Cummins, *The Hound and the Hawk: The Art of Medieval Hunting* (Weidenfeld and Nicolson, London, 1988), p. 4.

10 Ibid., p. 53.

11 Juliet Barker, *The Tournament in England 1100–1400* (Boydell Press, Woodbridge, repr. 2003), pp. 33–40, 132–3; *St-Denys*, i, pp. 672–82.

12 Barker, *The Tournament in England*, ch. 7 *passim*; Philippe de Commynes, *Memoirs: The Reign of Louis XI 1461–83*, ed. and trans. by Michael Jones (Penguin, Harmondsworth, 1972), p. 71.

13 Geoffroi de Charny, *The* Book of Chivalry *of Geoffroi de Charny: Text, Context, and Translation*, ed. by Richard W. Kaeuper and Elspeth Kennedy (University of Pennsylvania Press, Philadelphia, 1996), p. 89.

14 James Hamilton Wylie, *History of England under Henry IV* (London, 1884–98), i, pp. 42–3; Maurice Keen, *Chivalry* (Yale University Press, New Haven and London, 1984), pp. 7, 65, 78; Charny, *The* Book of Chivalry *of Geoffroi de Charny*, pp. 167–71. By the fifteenth century, knights created at this type of ceremony were known as Knights of the Bath. According to one contemporary French source, Richard II had already knighted Henry on campaign in Ireland earlier in the year (see Desmond Seward, *Henry V as Warlord* [Sidgwick and Jackson, London, 1987], pp. 9, 11) but knighthood could not be conferred twice.

15 Allmand, *Henry V*, pp. 16–17.

16 Ibid., p. 27; *ELMA*, pp. 306, 313; for Orléans' campaign, see above pp. 17, 18–9.

17 Nigel Saul, *The Batsford Companion to Medieval England* (Barnes and Noble Books, Totowa, NJ, 1982), pp. 264–7; R. A. Griffiths, "Patronage, Politics, and the Principality of Wales, 1413–1461," in *British Government and Administration: Studies Presented to S. B. Chrimes*, ed. by H. Hearder and H. R. Loyn (University of Wales Press, Cardiff, 1974), pp. 74–5.

18 *ELMA*, p. 309; Allmand, *Henry V*, p. 21.

19 John de Trokelowe, "Annales Ricardi Secundi et Henrici Quarti," *Johannis de Trokelowe & Henrici de Blaneford . . . Chronica et Annales*, ed. by Henry Thomas Riley (Rolls Series, London, 1866), pp. 367–71; Ken and Denise Guest, *British Battles: The Front Lines of History in Colour Photographs* (HarperCollins, London, 1997), pp. 47–9.

20 C. H. Talbot and E. A. Hammond, *The Medical Practitioners in Medieval England: A Biographical Register* (Wellcome Historical Medical Library, London, 1965), pp. 123–4; Strickland and Hardy, pp. 284–5. Thomas Morstede, the royal servant at Agincourt (see below, pp. 138–40), must have witnessed the operation or read Bradmore's account of it. For his version of it see R. Theodore Beck, *The Cutting Edge: Early History of the Surgeons of London* (Lund Humphries, London and Bradford, 1974), pp. 75–6, 117, 13.

21 See plate 1. I owe this observation to Dr Ingrid Roscoe.

22 *Original Letters Illustrative of English History*, 2nd series, ed. with notes and illustrations by Henry Ellis (Harding and Lepard, London, 1827), i, pp. 11–13, 39–40.

23 *ODNB*; McFarlane, *Lancastrian Kings and Lollard Knights*, pp. 68, 108, 125; *The Beauchamp Pageant*, ed. and introduced by Alexandra Sinclair (Richard III and Yorkist History Trust in association with Paul Watkins, Donington, 2003), pp. 25–30.

24 Griffiths, "Patronage, Politics, and the Principality of Wales 1413–1461," pp. 76–8; Ralph Griffiths, "'Ffor the Myght off the Lande . . .': the English Crown, Provinces and Dominions in the Fifteenth Century," in Anne Curry and Elizabeth Matthew (eds), *Concepts and Patterns of Service in the Later Middle Ages* (Boydell Press, Woodbridge, 2000), p. 93 and n. 48.

25 *ELMA*, pp. 308, 315–16; Margaret Wade Labarge, *Henry V: The Cautious Conqueror* (Secker and Warburg, London, 1975), pp. 19, 23, 25.

26 G. L. Harriss, "Financial Policy," *HVPK*, pp. 168–9, 169 n. 10.

27 *ELMA*, pp. 316–18, 338–40; G. L. Harriss, "The Management of Parliament," *HVPK*, p. 139.

28 *ELMA*, pp. 124, 130.

29 Harriss, "The Management of Parliament," pp. 140–1.

30 *ODNB*. Chaucer was the son of Catherine Swynford's sister, Philippa Roet.

31 Harriss, *Cardinal Beaufort*, pp. 1–2, 4, 7–8, 16, 18, 24–5, 29–31, 33, 45, 47–8, 58, 68–9. A cardinal a latere was appointed temporarily and with a specific brief, at the end of which his title and powers lapsed.

32 Harriss, "The Management of Parliament," p. 143.

CHAPTER THREE: A MOST CHRISTIAN KING

1 Usk, p. 243. For differing interpretations of the omen, see Capgrave, p. 125; *St Albans*, p. 69.

2 Trokelowe, "Annales Ricardi Secundi et Henrici Quarti," pp. 297–300. The myth of Becket's holy oil was created in imitation of the Valois dynasty's claim that French kings were anointed with the heaven-sent oil of Clovis at their coronations: John W. McKenna, "How God Became an Englishman," *Tudor Rule and Revolution: Essays for G. R. Elton from his American Friends*, ed. by Delloyd J. Guth and John W. McKenna (Cambridge University Press, Cambridge, 1982), p. 28.

3 Powell, pp. 129–30; Harriss, "The Management of Parliament," pp. 139–40.

4 Powell, p. 57; Monstrelet, iii, p. 94; *GHQ*, pp. 52–3; le Févre, i, pp. 228–9. See also below, pp. 195–7.

5 *St-Denys*, vi, p. 380.

6 See, for example, A. J. P. Taylor, *A Personal History* (Hamish Hamilton, London, 1983), p. 180; Vaughan, p. 205 and Seward, *Henry V, passim*.

7 W&W, i, p. 200 and n. 8.

8 Powell, p. 130.

9 W&W, i, p. 3; *ODNB*. The four other sons of rebels knighted at the coro-

nation were the earl of March's brother, Roger Mortimer; Richard, lord le Despenser; John Holland, the future earl of Huntingdon; and his brother.

10 W&W, ii, p. 21; *ODNB*; *ELMA*, p. 353.

11 W&W, i, pp. 1, 13–14; *The Beauchamp Pageant*, pp. 30–1.

12 *Register of Henry Chichele, Archbishop of Canterbury, 1414–1443*, ed. by E. F. Jacob (Clarendon Press, Oxford, 1943) i, pp. xvi–clxx; Peter Heath, *Church and Realm 1272–1461* (Fontana, London, 1988), pp. 291–2, 294–5.

13 W&W, i, pp. 119–20.

14 Ibid., i, pp. 119–20, 324–5.

15 D'A. J. D. Boulton, *The Knights of the Crown: The Monarchical Orders of Knighthood in Later Medieval Europe 1325–1520* (Boydell Press, Woodbridge, 1987), p. 15. For brotherhood-in-arms, see below, pp. 153–4, 177.

16 W&W, i, pp. 507–8. The manner of Clarence's death in 1421 mournfully demonstrated that he could not be trusted to act in the best interests of either the king or the kingdom. In his anxiety to outdo his brother's success at Agincourt, he over-ruled wiser and more experienced soldiers to attack a much larger French army without waiting for his archers to arrive. The resulting battle of Baugé was the greatest military disaster of Henry's reign: Clarence himself, Lord Roos, Lord Grey of Heton and Gilbert Umfraville were killed and the earls of Huntingdon and Somerset, the latter's brother, Edmund Beaufort, and Lord Fitzwalter were all captured: ibid., iii, pp. 301–6.

17 Ibid., pp. 134–5 and n. 88; *CPR*, p. 331.

18 Powell, pp. 197–9.

19 Ibid., pp. 199–200; W&W, i, pp. 109–10.

20 It should be noted that legal actions were often concocted as a means of pressurising an opponent, for instance in a land dispute, to settle quickly. For the following discussion on law and order I have relied entirely on the magisterial study by Edward Powell, *Kingship, Law, and Society: Criminal Justice in the Reign of Henry V* (Clarendon Press, Oxford, 1989) and his article which preceded it, "The Restoration of Law and Order," in *HVPK*, pp. 53–74.

21 The figures also include Staffordshire, where there were similar problems and the same solution: Powell, "The Restoration of Law and Order," p. 65.

22 The six who served on the Agincourt campaign were John Burley, Richard Lacon, John Winsbury, Ralph Brereton, Robert and Roger Corbet. John Wele, constable of Oswestry, stayed behind to defend the Shropshire march: ibid., p. 72.

23 *Brut*, ii, pp. 595–6. On one occasion he summoned two brothers, William and John Mynors of Staffordshire, to appear before him to account for their crimes, then personally ordered his justices to pardon them: William later served on the Agincourt campaign and in the conquest of Normandy: Powell, p. 66.

24 Quoted in Powell, p. 275.

25 *ODNB*.

26 *Heresy Trials in the Diocese of Norwich, 1428–31,* ed. by Norman P. Tanner (Camden Fourth Series, vol. 20, London, 1977), pp. 10–22, 142.

27 Anne Hudson, *The Premature Reformation: Wycliffite Texts and Lollard History* (Clarendon Press, Oxford, 1988), pp. 110–11, 115.

28 *St Albans,* p. 71; Saul, *Batsford Companion to Medieval England,* pp. 273–5; Heath, *Church and Realm 1272–1461,* pp. 258–9; Hudson, *The Premature Reformation,* pp. 114–15, 339–40. Oldcastle may have hoped to initiate a similar scheme in England, introducing a bill in 1410 to confiscate the lands of the richest bishops and abbots in order to provide the king with an extra twenty thousand pounds of annual income for the defence of the realm. It failed because Henry V, who, as prince of Wales, was then head of the royal council, leapt to the Church's defence and strongly condemned the whole idea.

29 Ibid., pp. 116–17; Powell, pp. 146–8; *GHQ,* pp. 4–5.

30 For what follows on Oldcastle's revolt, see W&W, i, pp. 258–80; *ELMA,* pp. 244–6; Heath, *Church and Realm 1272–1461,* pp. 274–9; Powell, pp. 149–66.

31 Ibid., p. 150; W&W, i, p. 264 nn. 10, 11. John de Burgh, a carpenter, and Thomas Kentford were granted annuities of 10 marks each for detecting and revealing certain Lollards and their treasonable plots; Thomas Burton, "a royal spy," was rewarded for similar information at about the same time.

32 Oldcastle's pardon was revoked in March 1415 in the build-up to the Agincourt campaign. He was eventually caught near Welshpool, condemned by his peers in Parliament and suffered the dual penalty of hanging as a traitor and burning as a heretic on 14 December 1417: Powell, p. 164.

33 *ELMA,* pp. 245–6; Powell, pp. 161–2, 165–6.

34 Ibid., p. 166.

35 The Valois kings of France were traditionally styled "très-Chrétien," most Christian, to distinguish them from other kings, including those of England, whom they deemed less favoured by God: McKenna, "How God Became an Englishman," p. 26.

CHAPTER FOUR: THE DIPLOMATIC EFFORT

1 *Bourgeois,* pp. 29–31; W&W, i, pp. 170–1.

2 *Bourgeois,* pp. 32–3.

3 Vaughan, p. 100.

4 *Bourgeois,* p. 44; Vaughan, p. 101.

5 McLeod, p. 94; *Bourgeois,* p. 46.

6 Ibid., pp. 47–50.

7 According to French legend, the oriflamme had miraculously appeared to the emperor of Constantinople in a dream as a flaming lance in the hand of Charlemagne, hence its sacred quality. Having been lost several times on the field of battle, it appears that it also had a miraculous habit of reincarnating itself.

8 Vaughan, pp. 194–6, 197, 247–8; *Bourgeois,* p. 48; W&W, i, pp. 412–13 and n. 3.

9 Oliver van Dixmude, quoted in Vaughan, pp. 146–7.

10 *Bourgeois*, p. 53. See below, p. 269.

11 W&W, i, p. 397.

12 Vaughan, pp. 198–204.

13 Catherine's mother was Constanza of Castile, John of Gaunt's second wife.

14 W&W, i, pp. 84–5, 90–7, 93 n. 3; Christopher Allmand (ed.), *Society at War* (Boydell Press, Woodbridge, new edn, 1998), pp. 129–30; Anthony Goodman, "England and Iberia in the Middle Ages," in *England and her Neighbours 1066–1453: Essays in Honour of Pierre Chaplais*, ed. by M. Jones and M. G. A. Vale (Hambledon Press, London, 1989), pp. 86–8.

15 Michael Jones, "The Material Rewards of Service in Late Medieval Brittany: Ducal Servants and Their Residences," in Curry and Matthew (eds), *Concepts and Patterns of Service in the Later Middle Ages*, pp. 120–3; A. R. Bridbury, *England and the Salt Trade in the Later Middle Ages* (Clarendon Press, Oxford, 1955), p. 80.

16 *Foedera*, ix, pp. 80–7; W&W, i, pp. 102–4, 103 n. 6, 104 n. 4.

17 Powell, pp. 203–6; Charles Lethbridge Kingsford, *Prejudice and Promise in XVth Century England* (Clarendon Press, Oxford, 1925), pp. 83–4, 85–7; Felipe Fernández-Armesto, "Naval Warfare After the Viking Age, *c.*1100–1500," in Keen, *MW*, p. 235.

18 In the Leicester Parliament of 1414, Henry introduced another exceptional measure, extending the definition of high treason to include breaking a truce or a safe-conduct, or aiding someone else who did so; the punishment, as for all treasons, was drawing, hanging and quartering. The justification for including this new category of offence was that truces and safe-conducts were granted and guaranteed by the king's word or promise; breaches of them therefore impugned the king's honour and injured his majesty in the same way that other treasonable offences did. The Statute of Truces was deeply unpopular and had to be amended in 1416 to make allowances for letters of marque, but it was highly effective in curtailing acts of piracy by English subjects: *Rotuli Parliamentorum*, iv, pp. 22–3; John G. Bellamy, *The Law of Treason in England in the Later Middle Ages* (Cambridge University Press, Cambridge, 1970), pp. 128–9.

19 *Foedera*, ix, p. 84. See also below pp. 258–9.

20 *Foedera*, ix, pp. 35, 56–9; W&W, i, p. 152 and n. 2; Jean Juvénal des Ursins, *Histoire de Charles VI*, ed. by J. A. C. Buchon (Choix de Chroniques et Mémoires sur l'Histoire de France, iv, Paris, 1836), p. 478; *St-Denys*, v, p. 353.

21 W&W, i, pp. 153–5; *Foedera*, ix, pp. 58–9.

22 *Foedera*, ix, pp. 91–101.

23 Ibid., ix, pp. 102–4.

24 *St-Denys*, v, pp. 158, 228; Juvénal des Ursins, *Histoire de Charles VI*, pp. 487, 493. Juvénal des Ursins, an eyewitness of events in Paris, commented that "even the English princes were divided by the quarrel between Burgundy and Orléans, for the dukes of Clarence and of Gloucester, the king's brothers, and with them the duke of York, favoured

the Orléanists; while the king and the duke of Bedford, likewise his brother, were inclined to the Burgundians": ibid., p. 497.

25 Vaughan, p. 206.

26 *Foedera*, ix, pp. 136–8. Opening *negotiations* for other marriages did not breach Henry's undertaking to the French, which only gave his promise not to *contract* a marriage. A nice distinction but a legal one.

27 Ibid.; Hovyngham had negotiated the truces with Castile and Brittany.

28 Vaughan, p. 207; *Foedera*, ix, p. 138. The power to receive the duke's homage was given on 4 June 1414, the same day as the other instructions.

29 *POPC*, ii, p. 141.

30 *Foedera*, ix, pp. 131–2, 208–11.

31 Shakespeare, *Henry V*, Act I, Scene 2, ll. 261–3.

32 *St Albans*, p. 83; Usk, p. 253. For the tennis balls story, see, for example, *Brut*, ii, pp. 374–5; Capgrave, pp. 129–30; Thomas Elmham, "Liber Metricus de Henrico Quinto," *Memorials of Henry the Fifth, King of England*, ed. by Charles Augustus Cole (Longman and Co., London, 1858), p. 101.

33 Monstrelet, iii, pp. 59–62; *Bourgeois*, pp. 58–61.

34 *Foedera*, ix, pp. 212–14.

35 *Letter-Books*, p. 135; *Memorials of London and London Life in the XIIIth, XIVth, and XVth Centuries*, ed. by Henry Thomas Riley (Longmans, Green and Co., London, 1868), pp. 603–5.

36 W&W, i, p. 94–9.

37 See above, pp. 66, 68.

CHAPTER FIVE: SCOTS AND PLOTS

1 *ELMA*, pp. 305–6; E. W. M. Balfour-Melville, *James I, King of Scots, 1406–37* (Methuen, London, 1936), p. 22.

2 Ibid., pp. 25–6.

3 Ibid., pp. 26, 31–3.

4 Ibid., pp. 34–5; Patricia J. Bradley, "Henry V's Scottish Policy — a Study in Realpolitik," in *Documenting the Past: Essays in Medieval History Presented to George Peddy Cuttino*, ed. by J. S. Hamilton and Patricia J. Bradley (Boydell Press, Woodbridge, 1989), pp. 179–80.

5 W&W, i, pp. 34–6; Powell, pp. 136–7.

6 This had not prevented it being breached, spectacularly, on two recent occasions. In 1378 two men, who had refused to hand over to John of Gaunt a prisoner captured eleven years earlier at the battle of Najera, escaped from the Tower and fled to sanctuary at Westminster; they were pursued by the constable of the Tower and fifty armed men, who forced their way in, slew one of the men and the sacristan and abducted the other. Nine years later, in 1387, Sir Robert Tresilian, the chief justice, was accused of treason by the Appellants (of whom the future Henry IV was one) and claimed sanctuary at Westminster; he too was abducted by force, tried and executed: Heath, *Church and Realm 1272–1461*, pp. 209–11.

7 Ibid., p. 211.

8 W&W, i, p. 36; Powell, p. 138. Although this phrase is now commonly

rendered "hanged, drawn and quartered," this is not the order in which the process took place. The convicted person was drawn on hurdles to the place of execution, hanged and then quartered; sometimes the traitor was cut down from the gallows while still alive, disembowelled (his entrails being burnt before him), beheaded and then quartered. In either case, the body parts were displayed in prominent public places to deter other traitors.

9 Devon, pp. 325, 326–8, 332; *St Albans*, p. 77; *Brut*, ii, p. 373. It was said that Richard had been kind to Henry, when, as a child, he had been a hostage at the royal court (not that this had prevented the future Henry IV from returning at the head of an army to usurp the throne). Lancastrian propagandists even said that Richard had predicted that the young Henry would fulfill Merlin's prophecy that a prince should be born in Wales, whose praise would one day ring round the world. *St Albans*, p. 77, suggests that Henry venerated Richard as if he were his own father, but as this is said in the context of the reburial, it may be applicable only to that act. It does not seem to me to warrant the claims of later chroniclers and historians that the two had been like father and son.

10 Balfour-Melville, *James I, King of Scots, 1406–37*, p. 55; Bradley, "Henry V's Scottish Policy — a Study in Realpolitik," pp. 180–1.

11 Ibid., pp. 178, 181.

12 G. L. Harriss, "The King and his Magnates," in *HVPK*, pp. 31–51. Percy was to be partially reimbursed by Murdoch himself: Balfour-Melville, *James I, King of Scots, 1406–37*, p. 65.

13 *St Albans*, p. 86; W&W, i, pp. 517, 520 (where Talbot is wrongly called Henry); Balfour-Melville, *James I, King of Scots, 1406–37*, pp. 62–3; Bradley, "Henry V's Scottish Policy — a Study in Realpolitik," pp. 182–3; T. B. Pugh, "The Southampton Plot of 1415," in *Kings and Nobles in the Later Middle Ages: a Tribute to Charles Ross*, ed. by Ralph A. Griffiths and James Sherbourne (Alan Sutton, Gloucester and St Martin's Press, New York, 1986), p. 66; *CPR*, p. 339.

14 Balfour-Melville, *James I, King of Scots, 1406–37*, p. 63; *CCR*, p. 278; Bradley, "Henry V's Scottish Policy — a Study in Realpolitik," pp. 183–4.

15 *Original Letters Illustrative of English History*, pp. 45–6; Pugh, "The Southampton Plot of 1415," p. 65; "The Conspiracy of the Earl of Cambridge against Henry V," 43rd Report of the Deputy Keeper of Public Records (HMSO, London, 1882), App I, §5.

16 Pugh, "The Southampton Plot of 1415," pp. 83, 64.

17 The Scottish link, for instance, was established beyond doubt, which was not surprising, given the northern English origins of most of the conspirators, Cambridge included (Cambridge lived on his brother's charity at Conisburgh Castle, near Doncaster, in Yorkshire). Murdoch's abduction in Yorkshire makes sense if its purpose was to enable the plotters to use him as a bargaining counter with the Scots — and Cambridge was able to tell Grey that Murdoch was safe in their hands a week later. He was also able to produce a letter that he said was from the duke of Albany, offering to send him Percy and the "Mommet" in return for his son. A Welsh supporter of Oldcastle was captured near Windsor Castle, where King James

had been held; he was carrying large sums of money and a list of places between Windsor and Edinburgh (the medieval equivalent of a modern map), and confessed that he had been trying to assist the Scottish king's escape. As we have seen, there was indeed a Scottish invasion only nine days before March revealed the plot to Henry V, even though Umfraville routed it, rather than joined it. The "crown of Spain on a pallet," which Cambridge had promised to display in Wales, together with a banner of the arms of England, when March was proclaimed king, was actually in his possession: Henry V had given it to him as security for the wages of the men whom he had contracted to take with him on the Agincourt campaign.

It should not be forgotten, either, that the muster at Southampton provided the perfect cover for the plotters to raise an army. The leading conspirators were all committed to providing some of the biggest contingents of the forthcoming campaign. Cambridge and March had each undertaken to bring sixty men-at-arms and one hundred and sixty mounted archers, Scrope to bring thirty men-at-arms and ninety mounted archers. All in all, including the forty knights or esquires whom the Lollards had promised would desert from the muster to support an uprising, the conspirators could count on raising a force of almost eight hundred armed and fully equipped men from within their own ranks before they had even left Southampton: "The Conspiracy of the Earl of Cambridge against Henry V," p. 582; W&W, i, pp. 518–9; Bradley, "Henry V's Scottish Policy — a Study in Realpolitik," p. 183; Nicolas, pp. 373–4, 385; James Hamilton Wylie, "Notes on the Agincourt Roll," *Transactions of the Royal Historical Society*, 3rd series, vol. v (1911), pp. 136–7.

18 *ELMA*, p. 324.
19 *Brut*, ii, pp. 375–6; *St Albans*, pp. 87–8; W&W, i, pp. 507–8. Cambridge, who was probably illegitimate, had inherited nothing from his nominal father and was financially entirely dependent on the goodwill of his brother, Edward, duke of York. Grey, who had already been outlawed twice for failure to pay debts, received a payment in May 1415 of £120 from the exchequer in compensation for giving up his post as constable of Bamburgh Castle, a sale that may have been forced on him by his need to fulfil his contract with the king to raise twenty-four men-at-arms and forty-eight archers for the Agincourt expedition: *ODNB*; Pugh, "The Southampton Plot of 1415," pp. 71–3, 79; W&W, i, p. 517 n. 3.
20 Pugh, "The Southampton Plot of 1415," pp. 62–4, 67–9, 83–4; W&W, i, pp. 523–33; *CPR*, p. 409; Powell, p. 131.
21 *Original Letters Illustrative of English History*, p. 48; *CPR*, p. 349.
22 Bellamy, *The Law of Treason in England in the Later Middle Ages*, p. 222.
23 There was an ironic postscript to the story. Less than three months after Cambridge's execution, Edward, duke of York, was one of the two English magnates who fell at the battle of Agincourt. Had the earl of Cambridge remained loyal to Henry V, he would have inherited his brother's title, lands and wealth, and achieved the position of power and influence he craved, without resorting to the treason that cost him his life.

CHAPTER SIX: "HE WHO DESIRES PEACE,
LET HIM PREPARE FOR WAR"

1 Vegetius, *De Re Militari*, quoted by Pizan, *BDAC*, p. 27 n. 23.
2 W&W, i, pp. 38, 39 n. 9.
3 Ibid., pp. 45–6, 39 and nn. 1, 3–7.
4 Ibid., i, p. 41 and nn. 4–6. "Scuratores" was a Calais-specific term for scouts, and not "scourers" as W&W translate the word: see R. E. Latham, *Revised Medieval Latin Word-List* (published for the British Academy, Oxford University Press, London, repr. 1980), p. 170.
5 John Kenyon, "Coastal Artillery Fortification in England in the Late Fourteenth and Early Fifteenth Centuries," in Curry and Hughes, pp. 146–7; Michael Hughes, "The Fourteenth-Century French Raids on Hampshire and the Isle of Wight," ibid., pp. 133–7.
6 *Rotuli Parliamentorum*, iv, p. 53; Kenyon, "Coastal Artillery Fortification in England in the Late Fourteenth and Early Fifteenth Centuries," p. 146.
7 W&W, i, pp. 161, 160 n. 1.
8 During a lull in the fighting at Poitiers (1356), English archers ran forward to pull arrows from the ground, and from dead or wounded men and horses; they were then able to use these against the next French attack: Strickland and Hardy, p. 301.
9 Paul Hitchin, "The Bowman and the Bow," in Curry, *Agincourt 1415*, pp. 44, 46–7. The English were defeated at Ardres (1351) when the archers ran out of arrows too early: Strickland and Hardy, p. 231.
10 Hitchin, "The Bowman and the Bow," pp. 45–6 and illustration, though the "type 16" arrowhead is actually on the third row, not the second, as it is captioned.
11 Strickland and Hardy, p. 313; Robert Hardy, "The Longbow," in Curry and Hughes, p. 168.
12 Andrew Ayton, "Arms, Armour, and Horses," in Keen, *MW*, p. 205 and illus., p. 72; Jim Bradbury, *The Medieval Archer* (Boydell Press, Woodbridge, 1985, repr. 2002), pp. 146–50. Strickland and Hardy, pp. 34–48, effectively demolish the myth of the shortbow, a third category of weapon which was an invention of nineteenth-century military historians.
13 W&W, i, p. 159 n. 7; Ayton, "Arms, Armour, and Horses," p. 204; *Foedera*, ix, p. 224.
14 Hitchin, "The Bowman and the Bow," pp. 42–4; Ayton, "Arms, Armour, and Horses," p. 204; Bradbury, *The Medieval Archer*, p. 107. But see Strickland and Hardy, p. 227.
15 Ibid., pp. 17–18, 199, 30; Hardy, "The Longbow," p. 179.
16 Maurice Keen, "The Changing Scene: Guns, Gunpowder, and Permanent Armies," in Keen, *MW*, pp. 274–5 and illus. p. 156; Clifford J. Rogers, "The Age of the Hundred Years War," ibid., pp. 156–8; Richard L. C. Jones, "Fortifications and Sieges in Western Europe, *c*.800–1450," in ibid., pp. 180–2; Pizan, *BDAC*, pp. 122–3; Robert D. Smith, "Artillery and the Hundred Years War: Myth and Interpretation," in Curry and Hughes, pp. 156–7; Richard L. C. Jones, "Fortifications and Sieges in Western Europe, *c*.800–1450," in Keen, *MW*, p. 182.

17 Nigel Ramsey, "Introduction," in John Blair and Nigel Ramsay (eds), *English Medieval Industries: Craftsmen, Techniques, Products* (Hambledon Press, London and Rio Grande, 1991), p. xxxii; Pizan, *BDAC*, pp. 117–19; Jones, "Fortifications and Sieges in Western Europe, *c.*800–1450," p. 181.

18 *Foedera*, ix, pp. 159, 160; *CPR*, p. 292.

19 W&W, i, pp. 161 n. 2, 265 n. 2; Henrietta Leyser, *Medieval Women: A Social History of Women in England 450–1500* (Weidenfeld and Nicolson, London, 1995), p. 162; Jane Geddes, "Iron," in Blair and Ramsay (eds), *English Medieval Industries: Craftsmen, Techniques, Products*, p. 187.

20 Ibid., pp. 168, 170–2, 174–5.

21 Ibid., pp. 186 and 187 (fig. 86). See plate 5.

22 C. F. Richmond, "The War at Sea," in Fowler, pp. 111–12, 108.

23 This meant that although he was a clergyman, he had not progressed to the rank of priest nor taken his final vows as a monk. Most clerks in the royal services were of this rank and never became fully ordained.

24 Richmond, "The War at Sea," pp. 112–13; W. J. Carpenter-Turner, "The Building of the *Holy Ghost of the Tower*, 1414–1416, and her Subsequent History," *The Mariner's Mirror*, 40 (1954), p. 270; W. J. Carpenter-Turner, "The Building of the *Gracedieu*, *Valentine* and *Falconer* at Southampton, 1416–1420," ibid., p. 56.

25 Ibid., pp. 65–6; Richmond, "The War at Sea," pp. 112–13, 104–7.

26 Carpenter-Turner, "The Building of the *Gracedieu*, *Valentine* and *Falconer* at Southampton, 1416–1420," pp. 62–3; Carpenter-Turner, "The Building of the *Holy Ghost of the Tower*, 1414–1416, and her Subsequent History," pp. 271, 273. The sums involved equate to almost $1,352,400 and $2,999,430 in modern currency, but there was almost certainly further expenditure.

27 Richmond, "The War at Sea," pp. 121 n. 55, 113–14.

28 *CPR*, pp. 294–5; W&W, i, p. 448 and n. 2.

29 Fernández-Armesto, "Naval Warfare after the Viking Age, *c.*1100–1500," pp. 238–9; Ian Friel, "Winds of Change? Ships and the Hundred Years War," in Curry and Hughes, pp. 183–5.

30 *Foedera*, ix, pp. 215, 216; W&W, i, pp. 45, 104.

31 Vaughan, pp. 241–4. See above, pp. 62–3, 65–6 for the Anglo-Burgundian negotiations.

32 *Registres de la Jurade: Délibérations de 1414 à 1416 et de 1420 à 1422: Archives Municipales de Bordeaux* (G. Gounouilhou, Bordeaux, 1883), iv, p. 193.

33 *Foedera*, ix, p. 218; Antonio Morosini, *Chronique d'Antonio Morosini 1414–1428*, ed. by Germain Lefèvre-Pontalis and Léon Dorez (Librairie Renouard, Paris, 1899), ii, pp. 20–5, 34–5, 44–5.

34 *Foedera*, ix, pp. 224, 238–9, 248–9; *CPR*, pp. 325, 329, 343; *CCR*, p. 232.

35 *Foedera*, ix, pp. 250–1, 261; *CPR*, pp. 327, 346.

36 *Foedera*, ix, pp. 251–2, 253; *CCR*, pp. 214, 217, 218.

37 Ibid., p. 278; *Foedera*, ix, pp. 288–9; H. J. Hewitt, "The Organisation of War," in Fowler, pp. 81–2.

38 See, for example, Henry's writ of 26 May 1415 to the sheriff of Kent: *Foedera*, ix, p. 251.

CHAPTER SEVEN: OF MONEY AND MEN

1 Pizan, *BDAC*, p. 19.
2 Harriss, "Financial Policy," in *HVPK*, pp. 163–74. See also Edmund Wright, "Henry IV, the Commons and the Recovery of Royal Finance in 1407," in R. E. Archer and S. Walker (eds), *Rulers and Ruled in Late Medieval England: Essays Presented to Gerald Harriss* (Hambledon Press, London and Rio Grande, 1995), pp. 65–81.
3 Harriss, "Financial Policy," p. 163.
4 Ibid., p. 177.
5 Harriss, "The Management of Parliament," pp. 137–8, 156; Saul, *The Batsford Companion to Medieval England*, pp. 200–2.
6 See, for example, *Rotuli Parliamentorum*, iv, pp. 3, 15, 34; Harriss, "The Management of Parliament," pp. 143, 145.
7 Ibid., pp. 145–6, 158.
8 *Rotuli Parliamentorum*, iv, p. 34.
9 Ibid., iv, p. 35; W&W, i, p. 434.
10 *Memorials of London and London Life*, pp. 603–5; *Letter-Books*, pp. 135, 143; Nicolas, p. 14; Marks and Williamson (eds), *Gothic Art for England 1400–1547*, p. 206 and fig. 71a.
11 *Foedera*, ix, p. 241. The signet was a relatively new seal, introduced by Richard II as a means of bypassing the more ponderous administrations of the great seal (that is, the chancery) and privy seal offices: Saul, *Batsford Companion to Medieval England*, pp. 112–13.
12 *CPR*, p. 329; Nicolas, pp. 13, 14; *Foedera*, ix, pp. 285–6.
13 W&W, i, pp. 472–4; *Foedera*, ix, pp. 268–9; Allmand (ed), *Society at War*, pp. 136–40.
14 W&W, i, pp. 477–9; *Letter-Books*, p. 144.
15 *Webster's Biographical Dictionary*, p. 1570; *Foedera*, ix, p. 310; Sylvia L. Thrupp, *The Merchant Class of Medieval London (1300–1500)* (University of Chicago Press, Chicago, 1948), pp. 55, 374; W&W, i, pp. 147 and n. 5, 360–1, 365. For Hende, see Thrupp, op. cit., p. 127.
16 Morosini, *Chronique*, pp. 20–3; Jeremy Catto, "The King's Servants," in *HVPK*, p. 82; W&W, i, p. 474.
17 Ibid., i, p. 474 n. 4; *Foedera*, ix, pp. 271, 284, 312.
18 W&W, i, pp. 472 nn. 1–6, 473 n. 6.
19 Monstrelet, iii, p. 71.
20 *CPR*, p. 344.
21 Maurice Keen, *Origins of the English Gentleman* (Tempus, Stroud and Charleston, SC, 2002), p. 95; *Foedera*, ix, p. 216; *CCR*, pp. 270, 271–2. For examples of indentures for life service, including some issued by Henry as prince of Wales, see Michael Jones and Simon Walker, "Private Indentures for Life Service in Peace and War 1278–1476," *Camden Miscellany xxxii* (Royal Historical Society, London, 1994), pp. 1–190, esp. pp. 139–43.

22 *POPC*, ii, pp. 150–1; Curry, p. 414.
23 MS E101/69/5, TNA; MS E101/47/29, TNA. For published examples of indentures signed on 29 April 1415, see *Foedera*, ix, pp. 227–38; Nicolas, Appx ii, pp. 8–10. MS E101/45/5, TNA, summarises the terms of 210 indentures for the Agincourt campaign.
24 At the battle of Agincourt the ratio rose to five to one because so many men-at-arms were invalided home from Harfleur. See below, pp. 208, 219, 260–1, 283.
25 MS E101/69/5, TNA; *Foedera*, ix, pp. 223, 230. Welsh foot archers received only 3d a day in 1355 (Strickland and Hardy, p. 204). For the regard, see Ayton, "English Armies in the Fourteenth Century," in Curry and Hughes, pp. 24–5.
26 Ayton, "Arms, Armour, and Horses," in Keen, *MW*, p. 188; Thrupp, *The Merchant Class of Medieval London*, pp. 276–7, 224; Christopher Dyer, *Everyday Life in Medieval England* (Hambledon Press, London and Rio Grande, 1994), pp. 148, 167, 188; D. Knoop and G. P. Jones, *The Medieval Mason* (3rd edn, Manchester University Press, Manchester, 1967), pp. 72, 86–7.
27 Strickland and Hardy, pp. 204–5. The social status of archers had risen steadily throughout the fourteenth century as the demands of war (in particular, the *chevauchée*) required them to be mounted. Richard II's ordinances of war (1385) placed them on a par with men-at-arms, and distinguished them from foot archers, when setting out punishment. Ibid., p. 204.
28 MS E101/47/29, TNA. The payment for the first quarter was higher than for the second quarter because it was calculated at Gascon rates.
29 Nicolas, pp. 373–4.
30 MS E101/47/29, TNA; Nicolas, p. 15.
31 Ibid., pp. 16–18.
32 MS E101/69/5, TNA; *Foedera*, ix, pp. 227–8. For similar indentures, see ibid., pp. 228–30, 233–5, 244, 250.
33 Ayton, "Arms, Armour, and Horses," in Keen, *MW*, p. 191.
34 Ibid., pp. 191–2, 188, 195.
35 Ibid., p. 197. For a reference in the king's ordinances at Rouen in 1419 to "all maner of men, Ryding or taryeng wyth us in oure hoste or vnder our baner, thoughe they Receue no wages of vs or our Realme," see Allmand (ed), *Society at War*, p. 82.
36 MS E101/69/5, TNA. In January 1416, Sir John Grey received a thousand marks (£666 13s 4d) from the king in part payment for the Count of Eu, whom he had captured at Agincourt: Devon, pp. 344–5. See below, pp. 133, 327–8, for examples of ransoms of French prisoners after Agincourt.
37 Anne Curry, "Sir Thomas Erpingham: A Life in Arms," in Curry, *Agincourt 1415*, pp. 74–5 and pls. 23 and 24. For Chaucer's accounts see MS E101/47/29, TNA.
38 Ibid., p. 66; MS E101/45/5, TNA. See also Wylie, "Notes on the Agincourt Roll," pp. 107–8, 140, 111; Nicolas, p. 383.
39 *Foedera*, ix, p. 258; Nicolas, pp. 10–11; Maurice Keen, "Richard II's

Ordinances of War of 1385," in Archer and Walker (eds), *Rulers and Ruled in Late Medieval England*, pp. 35–6.

CHAPTER EIGHT: THE ARMY GATHERS

1 W&W, i, pp. 484–6; *Letter-Books*, p. 138.
2 *St-Denys*, v, pp. 512–27; Monstrelet, iii, pp. 73–4.
3 W&W, i, pp. 505–8; Morosini, *Chronique*, ii, pp. 34–7.
4 W&W, i, pp. 500–1.
5 Carey, *Courting Disaster*, pp. 93–6, 106–9; Christine de Pizan, *The Writings of Christine de Pizan*, selected and edited by Charity Cannon Willard (Persea Books, New York, 1994), pp. 17–21; Lewis, *Later Medieval France: The Polity*, pp. 24–5.
6 W&W, i, pp. 500, 502, 503–5.
7 Ibid., i, pp. 506–7, 505 n. 6.
8 *Foedera*, ix, pp. 223, 239–40, 243, 262; CPR, p. 353; POPC, ii, pp. 157, 168; *Public Record Office, London: Lists and Indexes Supplementary Series*, no. ix, vol. ii (Klaus Reprint Corporation, New York, 1964), Appx, p. 382.
9 *Foedera*, ix, p. 223; CCR, pp. 268, 280; Nicolas, p. 385; POPC, ii, pp. 145–7, 165.
10 *Foedera*, ix, pp. 255–6; Hitchin, "The Bowman and the Bow," p. 40.
11 Pizan, BDAC, p. 214; *Foedera*, ix, pp. 253–4; CCR, pp. 213–14, 218.
12 Ibid.; Heath, *Church and Realm 1272–1461*, p. 284. Arrays of clergy were more frequent in the see of York: they were also called out twice in 1417, again (with the see of Canterbury) in 1418, and several times in 1419. The only bishopric omitted from Henry's writ was that of Sodor and Man, which until *c*.1387 had been a Scottish see. Local clergymen who had mustered at Beverley fought against the Scots at the battle of Neville's Cross (1346), "taking off their shoes and their hoods, [they] showed themselves with swords and arrows at their waists and bows under their arms" (Strickland and Hardy, p. 190). See also ibid., p. 259.
13 Mowbray MS; ODNB; Harris, "The King and his Magnates," in HVPK, p. 41.
14 Mowbray MS, fo. 21. The earl had contracted to serve in person with four knights, forty-five esquires and 150 archers. Like many of those raising retinues, the number of men he actually engaged to fight in his service differed from the figure for which he had contracted, hence the importance of the muster. The earl had received his first payment at the higher Gascon rate; the second payment was made at the French rate. The fact that the earl paid his men at the French rate may indicate that a decision had been taken by 1 July to go to France, rather than Aquitaine. On the other hand, it may simply reflect his shortage of cash: an adjustment could have been made later.
15 Mowbray MS, fo. 21. A further fourteen men, whose status is unclear, were given payments ranging from 21s to 38s under a heading that appears to mean "Regard for Welshmen for the expedition": at least two of the names are obviously Welsh.

16 Mowbray MS fo. 21; *Forty-Fourth Annual Report*, pp. 561–3, 565–70; *CPR*, p. 370.

17 *Forty-Fourth Annual Report*, pp. 566, 561. The archer was John Riggele alias Power, in the retinue of Sir John Fastolf.

18 Mowbray MS, fo. 13.

19 Le Févre, i, p. 253. The French similarly cut down their lances to fight on foot at Poitiers (1356): Strickland and Hardy, pp. 234, 249.

20 Barker, *The Tournament in England*, pp. 23, 157–8. For a sixteenth-century example, see Marks and Williamson (eds), *Gothic Art for England 1400–1547*, p. 198.

21 Mowbray MS, fos 13, 15, 14.

22 Mowbray MS, fos 12, 11. The shields could have been for Mowbray's archers, though forty-eight would not have provided enough for even a third of his contingent.

23 *ELMA*, p. 181; Strickland and Hardy, p. 201; Mowbray MS, fo. 9. The earl bought thirty-eight "crosses" from Nicholas Armourer: ibid., fo. 13. For the wearing of St George's cross, see below, p. 162.

24 Mowbray MS, fos 14–16.

25 Harriss, "The King and his Magnates," in *HVPK*, p. 41; Nicolas, Appx. xvii.

26 Wylie, "Notes on the Agincourt Roll," p. 135; Powell, p. 235: MS E404/31/315, TNA. Only a handful of the Welsh archers were mounted.

27 MS E404/31/386, TNA; MS E101/45/5, TNA. Curry, p. 414, describes them as being from the Forest of Dean, but Greyndor was an Anglo/Welsh knight from south Wales.

28 MS E101/45/5, TNA; Nicolas, p. 386; *Public Record Office: Lists and Indexes*, no. ix, vol. ii, pp. 390–1. Examples are Gerard Van Willighen, Hans Joye, Frederick Van Heritt, Claus Van Roosty and Martin van Osket.

29 Benedeyt Spina, the envoy who was ordered to bring the brides, was in London on 8 June 1415, but apparently without his charges: as late as 30 October they were still in Aquitaine and the authorities in Bordeaux decided that it was too late in the season to send them: *Calendar of Signet Letters of Henry IV and Henry V (1399–1422)*, ed. by J. L. Kirby (HMSO, London, 1978), p. 197 no. 962; *Registres de la Jurade*, pp. 194, 232, 254, 279.

30 Nicolas, pp. 386, 388–9; Jim Bradbury, *The Medieval Siege* (Boydell Press, Woodbridge, 1992), pp. 197, 241–2, 270; MS E404/31/409, TNA lists only twenty-five cordwainers, led by George Benet, master cord-wainer, not twenty-six as in Nicolas, p. 388.

31 MS E101/45/5, MS E404/31/437 and MS E404/31/416, TNA; Nicolas, pp. 387–9; W&W, ii, p. 186 n. 2.

32 Nicolas, pp. 387–9; Wylie, "Notes on the Agincourt Roll," p. 139. For Bordiu, see *Henrici Quinti, Angliae Regis, Gesta*, ed. by Bernard Williams (English Historical Society, London, 1850), p. vii. The various identities suggested for the chaplain are discussed, but in the absence of positive evidence, no conclusion is reached in *GHQ*, pp. xviii–xxiii.

33 See, for example, the dancing nakerer in the fourteenth-century Luttrell Psalter: BL MS Add 42130 fo. 176.

34 *Foedera*, ix, pp. 255, 260; Southworth, *The English Medieval Minstrel*, pp. 113–14, 115, 174 n. 47.

35 Ibid., pp. 47 and n. 21, 117, 15.

36 *Foedera*, ix, pp. 255, 260; Southworth, *The English Medieval Minstrel*, pp. 113–14, 119, 143–6, 174 n. 47, 187. In 1433 Clyff's widow was still claiming £33 6s for his retinue's unpaid wages for the Agincourt campaign: see below p. 347.

37 Maurice Keen, *Chivalry* (Yale University Press, New Haven and London, 1984), pp. 126–7, 134–7, 138.

38 Ibid., p. 134.

39 Garter king of arms was nevertheless "taken prisoner . . . and his goods taken from him [by] the King's enemies" when travelling through France on a royal errand to the earl of Warwick in 1438: Devon, p. 436.

40 Nicolas, p. 387.

41 Nicolas, p. 387; *Foedera*, ix, pp. 235–6, 237–8, 252–3; Barbara Harvey, *Living and Dying in England 1100–1540: The Monastic Experience* (Oxford University Press, Oxford, 1993), pp. 83, 85–6, 232–4; Talbot and Hammond, *The Medical Practitioners in Medieval England: A Biographical Register*, p. 100.

42 Ibid., pp. 220–2; MS E404/31/359, TNA; *Foedera*, ix, pp. 235–6.

43 Beck, *The Cutting Edge*, pp. 85, 92, 79; *Foedera*, ix, pp. 237–8, 252–3.

44 Beck, *The Cutting Edge*, pp. 76–8; Talbot and Hammond, *The Medical Practitioners in Medieval England: A Biographical Register*, pp. 387–8.

45 Beck, *The Cutting Edge*, pp. 63, 67–8.

46 Thrupp, *The Merchant Class of Medieval London (1300–1500)*, pp. 260, 267 n. 75; Beck, *The Cutting Edge*, pp. 81–2.

47 Marie-Christine Pouchelle, *The Body and Surgery in the Middle Ages* (Rutgers University Press, New Brunswick, NJ, 1990), pp. 68–9.

48 Transcribed from the extracts of Thomas Morstede's *Fair Book of Surgery*, given in Beck, *The Cutting Edge*, pp. 105ff, esp. p. 108.

49 Ibid.; Pouchelle, *The Body and Surgery in the Middle Ages*, pp. 165–6.

50 Will of Hamon le Straunge: MS LEST AE 1, Norfolk Record Office; *Foedera*, ix, pp. 289–92.

51 Ibid.; Morgan, "The Household Retinue of Henry V and the Ethos of English Public Life," p. 65. The famous Gascon knight Jean de Grailly, Captal de Buch (d.1369), directed in his will that fifty thousand masses were to be sung for him in the year after his death: Keen, *Chivalry*, p. 155.

52 *St-Denys*, v, pp. 526–8.

53 Seward, *Henry V as Warlord*, p. 63.

54 *St-Denys*, v, pp. 526–8. See also Monstrelet, iii, pp. 78–81; le Févre, i, pp. 219–21; and Waurin, i, pp. 174–6.

55 *GHQ*, pp. 17–19.

56 Deuteronomy, ch. xx, v. 10. See also below, p. 174.

57 *Foedera*, ix, p. 298; CCR, p. 278; W&W, ii, p. 1; *GHQ*, pp. 20–1.

CHAPTER NINE: "FAIR STOOD THE WIND FOR FRANCE"

1 The opening line of Michael Drayton's seventeenth-century "Ballad of Agincourt."

2 *GHQ*, p. 21; *St Albans*, p. 89; Robert F. Marx, *The Battle of the Spanish Armada 1588* (Weidenfeld and Nicolson, London, 1965), p. 53.

3 Vale, *English Gascony 1399–1453*, pp. 13–14; Blair and Ramsay (eds), *English Medieval Industries: Craftsmen, Techniques, Products*, p. 341; Bridbury, *England and the Salt Trade in the Later Middle Ages*, pp. 80, 110–11, 114; Knoop and Jones, *The Medieval Mason*, pp. 46, 48. The river Don in Yorkshire supplied a boat for Henry V's second invasion of France in 1417, so it is reasonable to suppose that similar vessels were also used in 1415: Friel, "Winds of Change? Ships and the Hundred Years War," p. 189.

4 Ibid., pp. 183–5; Ayton, "Arms, Armour, and Horses," p. 198. Sir Robert Knollys's expeditionary force of 1370, which had a contracted strength of two thousand men-at-arms and two thousand mounted archers, took 8464 horses to France, according to exchequer records.

5 *Calendar of Signet Letters of Henry IV and Henry V (1399–1422)*, p. 161; Richmond, "The War at Sea," p. 114; *GHQ*, pp. 20–1; le Févre, i, p. 224; W&W, i, p. 525. The king later decided that those who mustered, but had to be left behind, were not to receive their wages: *Foedera*, ix, p. 52.

6 Carpenter-Turner, "The Building of the *Holy Ghost of the Tower*, 1414–1416, and her Subsequent History," p. 271.

7 W&W, ii, p. 2; Armstrong, "The Heraldry of Agincourt," p. 130.

8 Elizabeth Danbury, "English and French Artistic Propaganda during the Period of the Hundred Years War," in Christopher Allmand (ed), *Power, Culture and Religion in France c.1350–c.1550* (Boydell Press, Wood-bridge, 1989), p. 82. When Charles V of France reduced the number of lilies on the French royal coat of arms to three, Edward III followed suit: ibid., p. 87.

9 Richard Barber, *The Knight and Chivalry* (Sphere Books, London, 1974), p. 40.

10 Ibid., pp. 304–6; Keen, *Chivalry*, pp. 191, 184. For Werchin's challenge to the Garter knights and, separately, to Sir John Cornewaille, see MS Additional 21370 fos 1–14, esp. fo. 7v, British Library; Barker, *The Tournament in England*, pp. 41–2, 157.

11 W&W, ii, pp. 3–4; Armstrong, "The Heraldry of Agincourt," p. 130; *GHQ*, pp. 120–1.

12 Bacquet, p. 109, quoting the accounts of the city of Boulogne which had sent a messenger to Honfleur, "where monseigneur the constable is now."

13 Ibid., pp. 22–3.

14 Trokelowe, "Annales Ricardi Secundi et Henrici Quarti," p. 333; A. C. Reeves, *Lancastrian Englishmen* (University Press of America, Washington, DC, 1981), pp. 143–4; MS Additional 21370 fos 4v–14, esp. fo. 10, British Library. Cornewaille's side of the correspondence relating to the seneschal's challenge was carried by William Bruges, who was then Chester herald of the prince of Wales.

15 Catto, "The King's Servants," pp. 89–90; Reeves, *Lancastrian English-men*, p. 168; W&W, ii, p. 17 n. 2; Wylie, "Notes on the Agincourt Roll," pp. 136, 128–9.

16 *GHQ*, p. 23 n. 3; W&W, i, pp. 98, 344 and nn. 8 and 9, 345 and n. 2, 435, 536; W&W, ii, pp. 16–17; *CPR*, p. 359; Nicolas, p. 340.

17 Geoffrey Chaucer, *Canterbury Tales*, ed. by A. Kent Hieatt and Constance Hieatt (Bantam Books, New York, 1971), p. 54, l. 276; Barber, *The Knight and Chivalry*, pp. 208–9. A transcript of the agreement is given in Allmand (ed), *Society at War*, pp. 32–4.

18 Reeves, *Lancastrian Englishmen*, pp. 153, 151, 148; McLeod, pp. 85, 177, 186. Though Cornewaille evaded capture personally, he had to raise enormous sums for the ransom of his stepson, Sir John Holland (who had then become earl of Huntingdon), when he was captured at Baugé in 1421. He was only able to do it by means of assistance from the king, by exchanging one of his own most valuable prisoners and by remitting some of the ransom due to him. And at his death in December 1443, it was discovered that he held £2666 13s 4d in uncashed exchequer tallies, money that was therefore owed to him by the crown, together with debts of more than £723 owed to him for loans by others. As many of the other Agincourt veterans were to discover, receiving payment for their services was neither straightforward nor easy: Reeves, *Lancastrian Englishmen*, pp. 147, 169–70, 182; McLeod, pp. 252, 275; Michael Stansfield, "John Holland, Duke of Exeter and Earl of Huntingdon (d.1447) and the Costs of the Hundred Years War," in *Profit, Piety and the Professions in Later Medieval England*, ed. by Michael Hicks (Alan Sutton, Gloucester and Wolfeboro Falls, 1990), pp. 108–9.

19 Morgan, "The Household Retinue of Henry V and the Ethos of English Public Life," p. 74; W&W, ii, pp. 17 n. 2, 88, 119; Wylie, "Notes on the Agincourt Roll," p. 109 n. 1.

20 Rudolf Simek, *Heaven and Earth in the Middle Ages: the Physical World Before Columbus*, trans. by Angela Hill (Boydell Press, Woodbridge, 1996), pp. 41–4, 51–5, 20–1, 29–31, 37–8. See plate 15.

21 Ibid., pp. 42–3. For facsimile examples of medieval navigational maps, see Gabriel Marcel, *Choix de Cartes et de Mappemondes des XIV et XV Siècles* (Ernest Leroux, Paris, 1896), esp. the Cartes de Dulcert (1330), de Mecia de Viladestes (1413) and de Saleri (1385).

22 *St-Denys*, v, pp. 532–3; *GHQ*, pp. 24–5.

23 Ibid., p. 25.

24 http://membres.lycos.fr/valsoleil/hellandes/histoire_du_fief_de_hellande.htm; Monstrelet, iii, pp. 70–1, 117; W&W, i, p. 447 n. 1.

25 Bacquet, pp. 109, 110; Bouvier, p. 64.

26 Bacquet, p. 109.

27 W&W, i, p. 447 n. 1; *St-Denys*, v, pp. 532–4.

28 W&W, ii, pp. 17, 19 and n. 9; Monstrelet, iii, pp. 82–3; *GHQ*, pp. 22–5, 22 n. 1.

29 Ibid., p. 27.

30 Keen, "Richard II's Ordinances of War of 1385," pp. 33–43; Shakespeare, *Julius Caesar*, III.i.273. For Henry V's Mantes ordinances, see

F. Grose, *Military Antiquities Respecting the History of the English Army* (London, 1801), ii, pp. 65–79.

31 Keen, "Richard II's Ordinances of War of 1385," pp. 44–5. See below, p. 291.

32 *GHQ*, pp. 68–9; *St-Denys*, v, pp. 556–7; Pizan, *BDAC*, p. 41. The story of the soldier stealing the pyx (see below, p. 239) was used by Shakespeare, who, applying poetic licence, made the thief Bardolph, one of the king's former associates: Shakespeare, *Henry V*, III.vi.

33 W&W, ii, pp. 25–9 and n. 28; i, pp. 508–10.

34 *GHQ*, pp. 26–7.

CHAPTER TEN: HARFLEUR

1 Despite several visits in the summer of 2004, I was unable to gain access to the interior of the church: the best efforts of the very helpful ladies at the tourist information office and the *mairie* were unable to locate a keyholder or key.

2 *St-Denys*, v, p. 532; Monstrelet, iii, p. 225.

3 Allmand (ed), *Society at War*, p. 130; W&W, ii, p. 10; Allmand, *Henry V*, pp. xii, 67.

4 Most of my ensuing description of medieval Harfleur, including the *clos-aux-galées*, is drawn from the very useful information boards supplied by Parcours du Patrimonie on site, and an article by Bernard Perrot in *Le Havre Livre*, Sunday, 4 January 2004, p. 6.

5 *GHQ*, pp. 32–4. The paving stones lifted from the Montivilliers road were taken to Harfleur to be used as ammunition in the event of attack: Monstrelet, iii, p. 83; Waurin, i, pp. 181–2.

6 *GHQ*, pp. 26–31; W&W, ii, pp. 13–16; Jones, "Fortifications and Sieges in Western Europe *c*.800–1450," p. 175.

7 Bouvier, pp. 64, 35 and n. 3, 38–9, 46, 52; Denis Lalande, *Jean II le Meingre, dit Boucicaut (1366–1421): Étude d'une Biographie Héroïque* (Librairie Droz, Geneva, 1988), p. 94; McLeod, pp. 84–5, 121. See also Aubert de la Chenaye-Desbois et Badier, *Dictionnaire de la Noblesse* (Paris, 1866, repr. Kraus-Thomson Organisation, Liechtenstein, 1969), ix, pp. 33–5 and *Dictionnaire de Biographie Française*, ed. by M. Prevost, Roman d'Arnot and H. Tribout de Morembert (Librairie Letouzey et Ané, Paris, 1982), xv, p. 689. Both *Dictionnaires* contain glaringly obvious errors of fact and it is difficult to disentangle references to Raoul VI de Gaucourt and his father, Raoul V, in the chronicles. Some of the earlier references may relate to Raoul V, who also led an active military career until he was assassinated by Burgundian sympathisers at Rouen in 1417.

8 Allmand (ed), *Society at War*, pp. 25–7.

9 Bouvier, p. 64; *GHQ*, pp. 32–3. Monstrelet, iii, p. 83 and le Févre, i, p. 225 both place de Gaucourt in the garrison, which they number at four hundred men-at-arms (that is, including his contingent), though they do not mention how he, and they, got there.

10 *GHQ*, pp. 32–5.

11 Jean de Bordiu, writing on 3 September 1415, notes that the king's great army "increases every day": Curry, p. 445; *Registres de la Jurade*, p. 257.

12 Forhan, *The Political Theory of Christine de Pizan*, p. 136; *GHQ*, p. 35. For Henry's letter to Charles VI, quoting Deuteronomy, see above, p. 143.

13 Deuteronomy, ch. 20, vv. 13–14; *GHQ*, pp. 34–7.

14 *St-Denys*, v, pp. 536–7; *GHQ*, pp. 36–7; Curry, p. 445; *Registres de la Jurade*, p. 257.

15 *GHQ*, pp. 38–9; *St-Denys*, v, p. 536.

16 *Original Letters Illustrative of English History*, i, p. 95. Hostell is usually described as an archer, but Curry, p. 435, identifies him as a man-at-arms in the company of Sir John Lumley; he went on to fight at the battle of Agincourt.

17 *GHQ*, p. 39.

18 Ibid.

19 Pizan, *BDAC*, pp. 116, 136.

20 *First English Life*, p. 38; Barber, *The Knight and Chivalry*, p. 209; Seward, *Henry V as Warlord*, pp. 149–51.

21 *GHQ*, pp. 40–1. When Henry V invaded Normandy a second time, he hired miners from Liège, suggesting that lack of military experience had been a problem for the Welsh.

22 Ibid., pp. 42–3.

23 Curry, p. 445; *Registres de la Jurade*, p. 257.

24 *First English Life*, p. 38; Waurin, i, p. 182.

25 Curry, p. 445; *Registres de la Jurade*, p. 257.

26 Curry, p. 444; *Registres de la Jurade*, p. 256.

27 All the clinical information on dysentery which follows has been extracted from Healthlink Worldwide's online newsletter on the control of diarrhoeal diseases, *Dialogue on Diarrhoea*, which can be found at www.rehydrate.org/dd/su55.htm. Handwashing with soap is the only proven method of preventing transmission, but dysentery can be cured with anti-microbial drugs.

28 Henry lost thirty-three of his own horses to murrain during the campaign: W&W, ii, p. 186 n. 2.

29 Talbot and Hammond (eds), *The Medical Practitioners in Medieval England: A Biographical Register*, p. 222; *First English Life*, p. 36.

30 Monstrelet, iii, pp. 84–5; le Févre, i, p. 226; Waurin, i, p. 183.

31 *Foedera*, ix, pp. 288, 310, 312, 314; MS Mowbray, fos 22–4; William Beamont, *Annals of the Lords of Warrington* (Chetham Society, 1872), i, p. 239. Harington's account was debited for this amount, plus two extra pitchers of wine.

32 *Calendar of Signet Letters of Henry IV and Henry V (1399–1422)*, p. 196 no. 964; Curry, pp. 444–5; *Registres de la Jurade*, pp. 256–7; *Foedera*, ix, pp. 310–11.

33 *ODNB*; *Calendar of Inquisitions Post Mortem, xx, 1–5 Henry V (1413–1418)*, ed. by J. L. Kirby (HMSO, London, 1995), nos 460–1; *GHQ*, p. 45.

34 *ODNB*; *Calendar of Inquisitions Post Mortem*, nos 441–51, 452–9; Wylie, "Notes on the Agincourt Roll," p. 130. The earl himself had

brought a retinue of 40 men-at-arms and 120 archers: MS E101/45/5, TNA. For further victims of dysentery, see below, pp. 204–7.

35 *GHQ*, pp. 44–5, 47 n. 1.

36 Ibid., pp. 48–9.

37 *St-Denys*, v, p. 538; *GHQ*, pp. 48–9.

38 W&W, ii, pp. 52, 49 n. 1; Perceval de Cagny, *Chroniques*, ed. by H. Moranvillé (Société de l'Histoire de France, Paris, 1902), p. 95 n. 4. Jehan La Guette, otherwise known as Lescot (was he also a Scot?), was given the boat, which is described as a "galiotte" (a term usually used for a pirate vessel), and paid a salary, but ran the enterprise "at his own peril and fortune."

39 Monstrelet, iii, p. 84; le Févre, i, pp. 230–1. Both de Lille Adam and Brimeu would become founder members of the Burgundian order of the Toison d'Or in 1430; le Févre, who is the only chronicler to report this story, was the order's herald, so he must have heard this story from them. They evidently took some small comfort from the fact that their captor, Sir Lewis Robsart, a long-standing member of Henry V's household, was from Hainault.

40 W&W, ii, p. 53 n. 1; Monstrelet, iii, p. 93.

41 W&W, ii, pp. 52–3; *St-Denys*, v, pp. 538–41; *Bourgeois*, p. 77.

42 *St-Denys*, v, p. 540. There are some extant musters of the troops gathering at Rouen in September and October 1415; most are for very small companies of fewer than fifteen and do not give any indication of the size of the whole army. A number are summarised in René de Belleval, *Azincourt* (Paris, 1865), pp. 300–36.

CHAPTER ELEVEN: "OUR TOWN OF HARFLEUR"

1 *GHQ*, p. 49.

2 *Brut*, ii, p. 376; *St Albans*, pp. 90–1; W&W, ii, p. 49.

3 *GHQ*, pp. 48–51; *St Albans*, p. 90; *St-Denys*, v, p. 540.

4 Bacquet, p. 91. The rumours also reached Venice: see Morosini, *Chronique*, p. 62 and n. 6.

5 *St-Denys*, v, pp. 540–3. The monk places this three-hour assault on the morning of the actual handover of the town, 22 September, which is clearly impossible, as Henry would have executed the hostages if Harfleur had offered any resistance once the agreed time had elapsed.

6 *Memorials of London and London Life*, p. 619. The abbreviated version of this letter in *Letter-Books*, i, p. 131 and *Calendar of Signet Letters of Henry IV and Henry V (1399–1422)*, p. 197 no. 965 is misleading; the latter also wrongly dates the surrender to 15 September.

7 *GHQ*, pp. 54–5; Nicolas, Appx vi, p. 24.

8 See above, pp. 59–60.

9 *St Albans*, pp. 90–1; W&W, ii, p. 50; *GHQ*, pp. 50–1; *St-Denys*, v, pp. 540–3. The names of the hostages are given in *Chronicles of London*, ed. by Charles Lethbridge Kingsford (Alan Sutton, Gloucester, 1977), pp. 116–17.

10 Monstrelet, iii, p. 85; *First English Life*, p. 39.

11 *St-Denys*, v, p. 538.

12 *GHQ*, pp. 52–3; Usk, p. 255.

13 *First English Life*, p. 40; *GHQ*, pp. 52–3; Elmham, "Liber Metricus," p. 112. The *First English Life* attributes the words of surrender to Sir Lionell Braquemont, "the governor of the town," but the chaplain, who was an eyewitness, says that de Gaucourt handed over the keys.

14 Curry, p. 445; *Registres de la Jurade*, p. 257; *GHQ*, pp. 54–5; Monstrelet, iii, p. 94; *First English Life*, p. 40.

15 *GHQ*, p. 55; *Brut*, ii, pp. 377, 554; *St-Denys*, v, p. 544; le Févre, i, p. 229; W&W, ii, pp. 58–60. The unreliable *Chronique de Ruisseauville* claims that many of the refugees were robbed and raped by their fellow countrymen once their English escort had left them: Bacquet, p. 91.

16 Nicolas, Appx vi, p. 24; *GHQ*, pp. 54–7.

17 Ibid., pp. 56–9; Elmham, "Liber Metricus," p. 113; *Foedera*, ix, p. 313. *Foedera* wrongly dates the letter to 16 September (it was actually written on 26 September, the day before de Gaucourt's release) and mistranscribes "Guienne" as "Vienne."

18 Barker, *The Tournament in England 1100–1400*, pp. 158–61; Francis Henry Cripps-Day, *The History of the Tournament in England and in France* (Bernard Quaritch, London, 1918), p. 67 n. 4.

19 The chaplain, writing the "official" version of the campaign, had clearly been provided with a copy of the challenge, which he closely paraphrases in his text: *GHQ*, pp. 56–9.

20 The chaplain says that Henry released the French men-at-arms "with the intention and in the hope that by their instigation and good offices the peace which he so much desired might be the sooner restored": ibid., pp. 54–5. For de Gaucourt's later mission, see below, pp. 353–4.

21 *GHQ*, pp. 58–9.

22 Ibid.; Capgrave, p. 131; Elmham, "Liber Metricus," p. 113.

23 *Memorials of London and London Life*, p. 619; *Letter-Books*, i, p. 159; *Forty-Fourth Annual Report*, p. 576.

24 Devon, pp. 341–2; *Foedera*, ix, p. 314; CPR, p. 364; CCR, p. 236.

25 W&W, ii, pp. 64, 65 n. 3. For Curteys, see above, p. 97. For wages paid to masters of ships from Hull, King's Lynn, Winchelsea and London, for service from 1 August see *Foedera*, ix, pp. 315–17.

26 GHQ, pp. 58–9. Curry, *Agincourt: A New History*, p. 131, rightly observes that one cannot simply count names to ascertain the reduction in fighting strength of the army as some of those sent home were noncombatants, but the incomplete nature of the records of the sick and the identifiable losses to some companies do not support her conclusion that Henry V still had "at least" 8680 soldiers ("a minimum" 8732, p. 187) with him on his march to Calais.

27 W&W, ii, p. 66 n. 5, 67–8; ODNB; *Calendar of Inquisitions Post Mortem*, nos 654–71; MS Mowbray fo. 23. The medicines were all supplied in October 1415. For Arundel, see above, pp. 20, 33–4, 45.

28 W&W, ii, pp. 45–6; *Calendar of Inquisitions Post Mortem*, nos 302–5, 359–69, 441–51, 452–9, 460–1, 654–71. William Botiller, lord of Warrington, died on 26 September; Sir John Southworth on 5 October:

Abstracts of Inquisitions Post Mortem, made by Christopher Towneley and Roger Dodsworth, ed. by William Langton (Chetham Society, Manchester, 1875), pp. 112–14, 117.

29 Wylie, "Notes on the Agincourt Roll," p. 136; W&W, i, p. 3 n. 10; ii, p. 46 n. 6; *Calendar of Inquisitions Post Mortem*, nos 359–69. Ken Mourin, "Norwich, Norfolk and Sir Thomas Erpingham," in Curry, *Agincourt 1415*, pp. 80–1.

30 Monstrelet, iii, p. 85.

31 W&W, ii, p. 67 and n. 7; Wylie, "Notes on the Agincourt Roll," pp. 131–2, 139; MS E101/47/29, TNA.

32 *Calendar of Inquisitions Post Mortem: 1413–1418*, no. 343; GHQ, pp. 58–9.

33 Wylie, "Notes on the Agincourt Roll," pp. 128, 130; Allmand, *Henry V*, p. 212.

34 Wylie, "Notes on the Agincourt Roll," p. 112 n. 1; *Forty-Fourth Annual Report*, p. 577; Anthony Smith, " 'The Greatest Man of That Age': The Acquisition of Sir John Fastolf's East Anglian Estates," in Archer and Walker (eds), *Rulers and Ruled*, pp. 137–8.

35 GHQ, pp. 58–9; W&W, ii, p. 62 n. 8; Devon, pp. 345, 349.

36 Curry, p. 445; *Registres de la Jurade*, p. 257.

37 GHQ, pp. 58–9. Some of the ships had been released after six weeks' service: that is, on 12 September, ten days before the capitulation of Harfleur. See, for example, *Foedera*, ix, p. 315.

CHAPTER TWELVE: THE MARCH TO CALAIS

1 GHQ, p. 60.

2 GHQ, p. 58 n. 5; le Févre, i, p. 229; *First English Life*, pp. 42–3; Curry, pp. 429–30; Bacquet, p. 110.

3 GHQ, p. 61. For Fusoris, see above, pp. 122–3, 164–5.

4 See above, p. 33.

5 Pizan, *BDAC*, pp. 37–8.

6 Ibid., p. 38 n. 50.

7 Norbert Ohler, *The Medieval Traveller*, trans. by Caroline Hillier (Boydell Press, Woodbridge, 1989), p. 98; Pizan, *BDAC*, p. 50 n. 72. The English chaplain (GHQ, pp. 60–1) believed that Calais was only 100 miles away (it was actually 150 miles away), but his mistake was not shared by the king.

8 GHQ, p. 61.

9 W&W, ii, p. 88 n. 3; *St Albans*, p. 93; Elmham, "Liber Metricus," p. 114; GHQ, pp. 60–1. Those French chroniclers who attempted to give a date generally referred to "the first week in October": see, for example, Cagny, *Chroniques*, p. 97.

10 C. R. Cheney (ed), *Handbook of Dates for Students of English History* (Royal Historical Society, London, 1978), pp. 1–2. The Julian calendar was replaced by the Gregorian calendar throughout Christendom in 1582.

11 Ibid., pp. 3–6.

12 Ibid., pp. 12–13, 65–9. An added complication of using regnal years was that sometimes a moveable feast, such as Easter, either dropped out of a regnal year altogether, or occurred twice.

13 Monstrelet, iii, p. 103.

14 Cheney (ed), *Handbook of Dates for Students of English History*, p. 9; Harvey, *Living and Dying in England 1100–1540: the Medieval Experience*, pp. 154–5.

15 Ibid., pp. 155–6; Cheney (ed), *Handbook of Dates for Students of English History*, p. 9; Geddes, "Iron," in Blair and Ramsay (eds), *English Medieval Industries: Craftsmen, Techniques, Products*, pp. 178–9.

16 *GHQ*, p. 61; Cheney (ed), *Handbook of Dates for Students of English History*, p. 80.

17 W&W, ii, pp. 88ff. prefer the alternative dating, starting on 6 October, but for confirmation of 8 October, see below, n. 26.

18 W&W, ii, pp. 88–9. The fact that the English army was able to take the Montivilliers road indicates that the floods in the Lézarde valley had now disappeared completely: Henry must have breached his own dam and opened the sluices in Harfleur because he needed to re-establish the water supply on taking the town.

19 Beamont, *Annals of the Lords of Warrington*, p. 245. Curry, pp. 430–1, argues convincingly that reassignment to new retinues explains the difference in personnel that sometimes occurs between muster rolls and retinue lists. This is a more credible explanation than that the retinues were brought up to full strength by the recruitment of new men, as she suggests in Curry, *Agincourt: A New History*, pp. 130–1.

20 Curry, pp. 433–4. If the retinues of the dukes of Clarence and York had taken their allotted quota of horses in full, according to the terms of their indentures, Clarence would have set out with 1798, York with 646; they returned home with only 1225 and 282, respectively. York's losses, at almost exactly half, were proportionately higher than Clarence's, at just under a third. The earl of Oxford would bring home only half the horses reserved for his personal use, together with six horses to pull his carts; his thirty-nine men-at-arms still had sixty-nine horses between them but his eighty-four archers had only thirty-seven. The earl marshal, on the other hand, shipped home his full personal complement of twenty-four horses, all of which had survived siege, march and battle.

21 *Foedera*, ix, pp. 314–15. Bardolf, perhaps mistakenly, believed that the "notable knight" (that is, the sire de Laurois) was acting under the authority of the sire de Laviéville.

22 Bacquet, pp. 109–10; Monstrelet, iii, p. 78.

23 *St-Denys*, v, p. 550; Bacquet, p. 101.

24 Ibid., pp. 110–11; W&W, ii, pp. 110–11.

25 Nicholas Wright, *Knights and Peasants: The Hundred Years War in the French Countryside* (Boydell Press, Woodbridge, 1998), pp. 57, 97. The underground city of Naours is now open to guided tourist visits: my description which follows is based on such a visit and the information provided on site.

26 *GHQ*, pp. 60–1; Nicolas, p. 361; W&W, ii, p. 90 nn. 9–10. One of the archers was called Robert Roger; the other, together with the esquire, was from the retinue of the earl of Suffolk who had died at the siege of Harfleur: according to the exchequer accounts, this ambush took place on 8 October, confirming that this was the actual date that the march began.

27 *First English Life*, p. 42.

28 *Chronicles of London*, pp. 117, 304; Nicolas, p. 361; W&W, ii, pp. 91–2, 91 nn. 4–7, 92 n. 3. According to a plaque in the abbey church, Estold d'Estouteville was abbot of Fécamp 1390–1423 and was buried in the nave.

29 *Registres de la Jurade*, p. 257. See above, pp. 213–4 and, for Bordiu, p. 180.

30 *GHQ*, pp. 60–3.

31 Le Févre, i, pp. 231–2; Monstrelet, iii, pp. 95–6; *First English Life*, pp. 43–4; *GHQ*, pp. 62–3.

32 Ibid.

33 See, for example, le Févre, i, p. 231; Thomas Basin, *Histoire de Charles VII*, ed. and trans. by Charles Samaran (Société d'Édition "les Belles Lettres," Paris, 1933), i, p. 38.

34 *GHQ*, p. 65.

35 Vaughan, pp. 203–4. For the Cabochien revolt of 1413, see above, p. 56.

36 Vaughan, p. 204.

37 Ibid.

38 See above, pp. 96–7. For the proposed Anglo-Burgundian alliance of 1414, see above, pp. 66–7.

39 Vaughan, pp. 147, 199; W&W, ii, p. 394 and n. 4. The Armagnac duke of Bar, who was killed at Agincourt, also employed English mercenaries, and a hundred archers were still nominally in his pay more than three weeks after the battle: ibid., ii, p. 180 n. 1.

40 W&W, i, p. 416; le Févre, i, p. 251; Waurin, i, p. 205; *Foedera*, ix, p. 304; W&W, ii, p. 106 n. 1.

41 W&W, ii, p. 101; *Bourgeois*, pp. 62–4; Morosini, *Chronique*, i, p. 64.

42 W&W, ii, p. 103; *St-Denys*, v, p. 546. Even if the duke had sent the aid he promised, it was already too late for Harfleur, which had surrendered two days before he replied to the dauphin.

43 Monstrelet, iii, p. 90.

44 W&W, ii, pp. 52–3, 52 n. 11, 53 n. 1; Monstrelet, iii, p. 90.

45 Ibid., iii, pp. 90–3. This letter, which is given as an example, was addressed to Philippe d'Auxy, *bailli* of Amiens, who, together with his son and his two brothers, was killed at Agincourt: ibid., iii, p. 113.

CHAPTER THIRTEEN: CROSSING THE SOMME

1 Bacquet, p. 110.

2 Le Févre, i, pp. 232–3; *GHQ*, p. 64–5; Waurin, i, p. 189, says that the

story of the Gascon prisoner which follows was told him by le Févre, "who had been present throughout this campaign."

3 Ibid.; le Févre, i, p. 232. The coast as far as Cap Gris-Nez is clearly visible from the road between St Valery-en-Caux and Veules-les-Roses and from the long stretch between Eu and Ault.

4 Ibid.; *GHQ*, pp. 64–7; W&W, ii, p. 112; Cagny, *Chroniques*, pp. 97–8.

5 *GHQ*, p. 67; Monstrelet, iii, p. 96.

6 *GHQ*, p. 67. Despite having put patriotism before party, Vaudémont was killed at Agincourt.

7 Ibid., pp. 68–9; Bouvier, pp. 69–70, 69 n. 5.

8 *GHQ*, pp. 68–9; le Févre, i, p. 234.

9 Ibid.

10 W&W, ii, pp. 115–16; Nicolas, pp. 351, 374; *GHQ*, pp. 68–9; Monstrelet, iii, pp. 96–7. It is unlikely that Bourchier was involved in this skirmish as he had been assigned to the garrison of Harfleur: see above, pp. 236–7.

11 *GHQ*, pp. 68–71. The chaplain attributes the idea to the king, which seems most probable, but later English sources attribute it to the duke of York: see *First English Life*, p. 55; *Brut*, ii, pp. 378, 554–5.

12 Rogers, "The Age of the Hundred Years War," in Keen, *MW*, pp. 137–42; Matthew Bennett, "The Development of Battle Tactics in the Hundred Years War," in Curry and Hughes, pp. 15–16; Lalande, *Jean II le Meingre, dit Boucicaut (1366–1421)*, pp. 58–72.

13 W&W, ii, p. 116. Henry's decision to cut across to Nesle must have been taken after his arrival at Corbie, as it would have been quicker and easier to have gone there straight from Boves.

14 *GHQ*, p. 69.

15 *St Albans*, p. 93; *GHQ*, pp. 70–1; le Févre, i, p. 234.

16 Henry did not burn the villages but this does not prove that the location of the fords was betrayed to him by a local inhabitant; once he had found the crossings, his priority was to secure them and get his men across safely. He would have had neither the time nor the manpower to carry out his threat.

17 *GHQ*, pp. 71–3.

18 Ibid.; le Févre, i, p. 235; Waurin, i, pp. 193–4; Vegetius warned that armies were often caught in a trap at river crossings as a result of delays caused by the baggage-train: Pizan, *BDAC*, p. 38 n. 49. At Voyennes, the land rises steeply up the northern bank to a small plateau which would have been the obvious place for the vanguard to set up their bridgehead overlooking the crossing: at Béthencourt, the land on either side does not rise above the level of the river, suggesting that this would have been an easier route for the baggage carts. The Canal de la Somme, running alongside the river, has drained the marshes and reduced the flow in the river itself. Even so, the river is still wide, deep and fast-flowing, particularly at Béthencourt, with pools and submerged trees on either bank indicating the extent of the original marshes and giving an idea of how difficult it must have been to effect the crossings.

19 *GHQ*, pp. 72–3; le Févre, i, p. 235.

20 *GHQ*, p. 73.

21 Ibid., p. 75.

22 Le Févre, i, p. 236.

23 See above, p. 179.

24 Lalande, *Jean II le Meingre, dit Boucicaut (1366–1421)*, p. 94.

25 Le Févre, i, pp. 236–7. *GHQ*, p. 74 n. 4, following W&W, ii, p. 125, identifies two of the heralds as Jacques, sire de Heilly and Jean, sire de Graville, but this is a confusion with their different embassy to Henry V on the morning of 25 October (see below, pp. 272–4ff). Le Févre and *GHQ* identify the three messengers of 20 October as "officiers d'armes" and "haraldos" respectively; de Heilly and de Graville were both laymen. Curry, *Agincourt: A New History*, pp. 158–9, 161, 170–1, 248–9, argues that Henry V agreed to do battle at Aubigny on 24 October 1415 then reneged on his promise, but this story appears only in Bouvier, pp. 66–7, a devoted servant of Charles VII, who was writing forty years after the event. It is improbable that Henry V, who was punctilious in his observance of the law of arms, would have commited such a flagrant breach of protocol, or that such a breach would have passed unnoticed by his contemporaries.

26 *GHQ*, pp. 74–5; le Févre, i, p. 237.

27 *GHQ*, pp. 74–7, esp. p. 77; W&W, ii, p. 127 n. 2.

28 There is an unbearable poignancy in following this route today: the front line in 1916 lay between Péronne, Albert and Miraumont, and there are cemeteries and memorials to the British, Australian, Canadian and New Zealand dead seemingly by every ridge, village and roadside.

29 Le Févre, i, pp. 240–1. The reason for Henry's refusal to retrace his steps is completely misunderstood in W&W, ii, p. 128 (which wrongly places Henry at Blangy for the night of 23 October) and also in Curry, *Agincourt: A New History*, p. 166.

30 Le Févre, i, p. 242; *GHQ*, p. 77.

31 Vaughan, pp. 207–8, who nevertheless believes that the duke did intend to join the campaign against the English. For the duke's itinerary between 1 September and 24 October (when he was at Fleury-sur-Ouche), see W&W, ii, p. 106 n. 2.

32 For the justification for this claim, see above, pp. 188, 229–30.

33 Gilles de Roye, "Chronique, avec les Additions d'Adrien de But," *Chroniques Relatives à l'Histoire de la Belgique sous la Domination des Ducs de Bourgogne*, ed. by Kervyn de Lettenhove (Académie Royale des Sciences, des Lettres et de Beaux-Arts de Belgique, Brussels, 1870), i, p. 168; le Févre, i, pp. 238–40; Waurin, i, pp. 197–8.

34 *Foedera*, ix, pp. 297, 309; W&W, ii, p. 122 n. 9.

35 Cagny, *Chroniques*, pp. 101–2.

36 Waurin, i, p. 197; Bouvier, p. 67.

37 Nicolas de Baye, *Journal de Nicolas de Baye*, ed. by Alexandre Tuetey (Société de l'Histoire de France, Paris, 1888), ii, pp. 231–2; *St-Denys*, v, pp. 586–8.

38 Pizan, *BDAC*, pp. 21–2.

CHAPTER FOURTEEN: THE EVE OF BATTLE

1 *GHQ*, p. 79; Curry, p. 69; le Févre, i, p. 242; MS C1/68/213, TNA.

2 *GHQ*, p. 79.

3 Even the venerable W&W, ii, pp. 131–2, 207–10, while drawing attention to the more fanciful descriptions of previous historians, believed that the site was unchanged. Modern military historians and television documentaries frequently make the same mistake, as does the entertaining but far too Shakespeare-reliant Centre Historique Médiévale at Azincourt.

4 *GHQ*, pp. 74, 79. The "very little valley," which is no more than a long depression in the ground, can still be seen running parallel to the D104; the "certain wood" to the left of the English line is the woodland round Tramecourt. At this point the two armies were at right angles to their final positions.

5 Waurin, i, p. 211, claims that the space between the woods was so narrow that only the French men-at-arms could be deployed; there was not room for the bowmen.

6 Le Févre, i, p. 242, says that d'Albret did not arrive until later that evening, suggesting that Boucicaut alone was in charge at this stage. Waurin, who was in the French army, does not mention d'Albret's arrival, late or otherwise.

7 Bacquet, p. 102; Pizan, *BDAC*, p. 22.

8 Ibid., pp. 55, 53–4.

9 Monstrelet, iii, p. 102; W&W, ii, p. 130 n. 3.

10 *GHQ*, p. 81; le Févre, i, p. 243; *Brut*, ii, pp. 377–8; Elmham, "Liber Metricus," p. 121.

11 Le Févre, i, p. 243. W&W, ii, p. 141 and n. 1 wrongly translate this to mean that the prisoners should return to the king "with their masters" rather than "and to their masters," that is, to those who had captured them.

12 Bacquet, p. 93; Waurin, i, p. 244.

13 See, for example, Wolfram von Eschenbach, *Parzival*, trans. with an introduction by Helen M. Mustard and Charles E. Passage (Vintage Books, New York, 1961), pp. 94, 125, 139, 166 and 127.

14 Curry, p. 69.

15 *GHQ*, pp. 83, 87. For the long-running dispute about where the archers were placed, see W&W, ii, pp. 148–50; Bradbury, *The Medieval Archer*, pp. 129–30; Matthew Bennett, "The Battle," in Curry, *Agincourt 1415*, pp. 24–32; Strickland and Hardy, pp. 306–10.

16 Le Févre, i, pp. 244–5; Waurin, i, p. 203.

17 See below, pp. 261–2, 266–7.

18 *Brut*, ii, p. 378; *GHQ*, pp. 82–3 and 82 nn. 3 and 4. Waurin, ii, p. 199, following Monstrelet, iii, p. 100, puts the duke in charge of the vanguard as early as 22 October, but le Févre, i, p. 241, who relates the same incident and was in the English army, does not make that mistake. The choice of Camoys is puzzling as he was not yet a Garter knight and his military career had been undistinguished: see *ODNB*.

19 Bacquet, p. 104.

20 C. Philpotts, "The French Plan of Battle During the Agincourt Campaign," *English Historical Review*, xcix (1984), pp. 59–66; Allmand (ed), *Society at War*, pp. 194–5. This document detailing in writing not only the deployment of the French army but also the tactics to be adopted is one of only two medieval battle plans to have survived. The other extant plan was drawn up by John the Fearless on 17 September 1417 as he was approaching Armagnac-held Paris; it is given in full in Vaughan, pp. 148–50.

21 Despite being master of the crossbowmen of France, de Rambures did not personally lead them into battle. In 1411 his predecessor in the post had been forced to concede to Marshal Boucicaut the right to muster and review archers and cannoneers, and to have jurisdiction over them (Strickland and Hardy, p. 330). At Agincourt de Rambures fought in the vanguard with the other royal officers (see above, p. 265).

22 Louis de Bourdon's name is variously given as Bourbon, Boisredon and Bosredon in the different sources. He is not to be confused with Louis de Bourbon, count of Vendôme.

23 Bradbury, *The Medieval Archer*, p. 124.

24 Despite this absence of evidence, Curry asserts that the French army was only *c.*12,000 strong (as against *c.*9000 English), a figure she is unable to substantiate. While contemporaries vary wildly in their estimates of numbers, all agree that the French greatly outnumbered the English and that this was a contributory factor in their defeat. Although they also agree that French casualties were very high, not one of them goes so far as to suggest that half of all the French forces at the battle were killed, which follows inevitably from Curry's figures since she accepts that the dead numbered *c.*6000. Such a proportion of fatalities is unrealistic in a medieval battle. See Curry, *Agincourt: A New History*, pp. 187, 192, 233, 248.

25 Bacquet, pp. 101, 104. Juvénal des Ursins, a dedicated Armagnac, even went so far as to suggest that there were 8000 Frenchmen in the vanguard and main battle, but claimed that they were defeated by an English army 20,000–22,000 strong! There is a useful table giving the various chroniclers' estimates of numbers in both armies and of the dead on each side in Curry, p. 12, but it should be used with caution, as some of the figures (for example, those given for Morosini) are not accurate and others do not distinguish between the numbers of English who invaded and those present at the battle.

26 *GHQ*, p. 94; le Févre, i, p. 247; Waurin, i, pp. 206–7. Waurin's actual numbers add up to 28,400 but a rearguard of 7600 seems appropriate, given the size of the other battles.

27 Bradbury, *The Medieval Archer*, pp. 127–8; le Févre, i, pp. 247–8; Monstrelet, iii, pp. 103–4.

28 *St-Denys*, v, p. 558; Monstrelet, iii, pp. 103–4; Bouvier, p. 69; Bacquet, pp. 103–4. Fenin, *Mémoires*, p. 64.

29 Waurin, i, p. 206; le Févre, i, p. 248; *St-Denys*, v, p. 562; Bouvier, pp. 68–9. Monstrelet, iii, pp. 103–4, is alone in attributing the leadership of this wing to Guichard Dauphin but his text is obviously corrupt and unreliable at this point: Waurin and le Févre both correct this to Vendôme.

30 Bouvier, pp. 68–9; *St-Denys*, v, p. 560.

31 *St-Denys*, v, p. 560; Monstrelet, iii, p. 104; le Févre, i, pp. 85, 102, 105, 248, 288; Waurin, i, pp. 206, 213.

32 Bacquet, pp. 112–13. This account of Agincourt, in a court case of 1460, makes it clear that Bouvier, p. 69, is right in saying that the count of Marle and his company were in the main battle, not in the rearguard as in Monstrelet, iii, p. 104, Waurin, i, p. 206 and le Févre, i, p. 248.

33 *GHQ*, p. 81; Fenin, *Mémoires*, p. 64; Allmand (ed), *Society at War*, p. 195.

34 Le Févre, i, p. 248, using the phrase "tout le surplus des gens de guerre." *Gens de guerre* is a general term, meaning all soldiers; it is different from *gens d'armes* or *hommes d'armes*, which specifically refers to men-at-arms.

35 *St-Denys*, v, p. 548.

36 Ibid., v, pp. 558–60; Waurin, i, p. 206; W&W, ii, p. 53. The decision was not without precedent. Jean II had similarly dismissed most of the "poorly equipped and ill-disciplined foot-soldiers raised by the *arrière ban*" before the battle of Poitiers (1356) on the grounds that their presence at Crécy (1346) had hampered the more professional troops and contributed to the defeat. See Strickland and Hardy, p. 234.

37 See above, pp. 59–60.

38 *GHQ*, pp. 81–3.

39 Ibid., pp. 82–3; le Févre, i, p. 244.

40 It was customary practice to draw the wagons into a circle behind the lines, forming an enclosure with a single entrance that could be more easily protected from enemy attack. The horses of all of the dismounted men and the non-combatants sheltered within this laager. See Strickland and Hardy, p. 225.

41 Le Févre, i, p. 245 and n. 1. Certain manuscripts of this chronicle also add the banner of the Virgin Mary; this is also implied in *GHQ*, pp. 66–7, which refers to the army being under the protection of "the Glorious Virgin and the Blessed George." See also above, pp. 235, 240.

42 Le Févre, i, p. 253. Sir John Holland was allowed to use his standard as earl of Huntingdon, even though he was not yet fully restored to the earldom. See below, p. 344.

43 Pizan, *BDAC*, pp. 152–3.

44 Le Févre, i, pp. 245–6, 251. Curry, p. 158, wrongly translates this as "victory over *your* enemies" instead of "*our* enemies," a subtle but important difference of emphasis. Medieval archers, unlike modern ones, used only two fingers to draw their bows. Sir James Douglas (d. 1330), Robert the Bruce's lieutenant, was reputed to cut off the right hand or put out the right eye of any captured enemy archer, but it had been standard practice for centuries simply to execute them. See Strickland and Hardy, pp. 181, 79. After the English victory at Agincourt, the archers are said to have taunted the defeated French by sticking their two bowstring fingers up at them, a gesture which is still used vulgarly in England today to express contempt.

45 Bouvier, pp. 67–8; Elmham, "Liber Metricus," p. 118; Capgrave, p. 132;

Baye, *Journal*, pp. 224–5; W&W, i, pp. 135–6, 136 n. 1; ii, p. 125 n. 6. An investigation into the escape was ordered on 26 October 1415: *CPR*, p. 410. De Heilly had previously been captured fighting for the Scots at Homildon Hill (1402) but had been ransomed and released: Wylie, *History of England under Henry IV*, i, p. 293; ii, p. 61.

46 *First English Life*, pp. 57–8.

47 Le Févre, i, p. 251; *St-Denys*, v, p. 554; Basin, *Histoire de Charles VII*, i, p. 41. W&W, ii, pp. 132–3 place this parley the night before the battle and take the French accounts at face value.

48 Le Févre, i, p. 251.

CHAPTER FIFTEEN: "FELAS, LETS GO!"

1 Bennett, "The Development of Battle Tactics in the Hundred Years War," p. 11. See also Jean de Bueil, *Le Jouvencel*, ed. by Léon Lecestre (Société de l'Histoire de France, Paris, 1889), ii, p. 63, where de Bueil applies this dictum to Agincourt.

2 Le Févre, i, pp. 252–3; Bacquet, p. 93.

3 *GHQ*, p. 82; *St-Denys*, v, p. 558.

4 *GHQ*, pp. 85–7.

5 Curry, p. 72; *Brut*, ii, p. 555.

6 For Erpingham's career, see Curry, "Sir Thomas Erpingham: A Life in Arms," in Curry, *Agincourt 1415*, pp. 53–77.

7 *Brut*, ii, pp. 378, 555, 596; le Févre, i, p. 253; *An English Chronicle of the Reigns of Richard II, Henry IV, Henry V, and Henry VI. Written Before the Year 1471*, ed. by Rev. John Silvester Davies, Camden Society, 64 (1856), p. 41; Allmand, *Henry V*, p. 91 n. 17.

8 Guillaume Gruel, *Chronique d'Arthur de Richemont, Connétable de France, Duc de Bretagne (1393–1458)*, ed. by Achille le Vavasseur (Société de l'Histoire de France, Paris, 1890), p. 17; *St-Denys*, v, p. 560; Bouvier, pp. 70–1.

9 Waurin, i, p. 213; *GHQ*, pp. 86–7.

10 Waurin, i, pp. 206, 213; Monstrelet, iii, p. 255.

11 The word is variously given as "nesciecque," "nestrotque" and "nestroque" in French sources; it has been translated as "I do not know what" (that is, that Monstrelet, the reporter, did not know what Erpingham said), "Knee! Stretch!," the option favoured by W&W, ii, p. 156, and taken to be a command to the archers to shoot because they bent their knees when they did so, or, my own preferred option, "Now strike!," which seems the most logical command. Erpingham's Norfolk accent clearly confounded his auditors. See Monstrelet, iii, p. 106 and n. 1; Waurin, i, p. 212; le Févre, i, p. 253; W&W, ii, p. 156 n. 6. All three chroniclers have Erpingham give his signal before the English moved to their new position, so it may have been a general order to advance rather than a command to fire.

12 *St-Denys*, v, p. 560; *GHQ*, pp. 86–7; Gruel, *Chronique d'Arthur de Richemont*, p. 17; Alain Bouchart, *Grandes Croniques de Bretaigne*, ed. by Marie-Louise Auger and Gustave Jeanneau (Éditions du Centre

National de la Recherche Scientifique, Paris, 1986), ii, p. 253; "Chronique de Normandie de l'an 1414 à 1422," in *Henrici Quinti, Angliae Regis, Gesta*, p. 219.

13 Bouvier, p. 70 and n. 3; Monstrelet, iii, pp. 116, 118 n. 5.

14 Le Févre, i, pp. 198–9, 248, 309, 323, 330; Monstrelet, iii, p. 128. It is possible that Guillaume was the father, rather than the brother, of Hector and Philippe de Saveuses. Neither Hector nor Philippe took any further part in the battle after the death of their brother and, immediately afterwards, they were among those personally summoned to join the army that the duke of Burgundy was preparing for his march on Paris. Both men took a leading role in John the Fearless's attempts to seize the city and in its eventual capture in 1418.

15 Le Févre, i, pp. 205–6, 42. At Montendre in Aquitaine in 1402, de Brabant had also taken part in a combat of seven Frenchmen against seven English, celebrated in three ballads by Christine de Pizan: Bouvier, pp. 9–10 and 9 nn. 1 and 2.

16 Ibid., p. 21 and n. 3.

17 Ibid., p. 124 and n. 3. Katherine, Pierre de Giac's widow, was the daughter and heiress of Jean, sire de l'Île Bouchard, who was killed at Agincourt; her second husband, Hugues de Chalon, count of Tonnerre (Pierre de Giac was her third), was killed fighting against the English at the battle of Verneuil in 1424.

18 Ferry de Mailly was a Burgundian and close associate of the de Saveuses brothers: le Févre, i, pp. 248, 271, 275–6, 297, 327; Monstrelet, iii, p. 128.

19 But see below, p. 293.

20 Bouvier, p. 70. The fact that so many of them did escape capture or death appears to contradict the monk's claim that it was their men who turned tail and fled, abandoning their leaders to their fate: St-Denys, v, p. 560.

21 Monstrelet, iii, p. 105; le Févre, i, pp. 250–1.

22 *GHQ*, pp. 86–7; W&W, ii, p. 159 n. 4. In Beamont, *Annals of the Lords of Warrington*, i, p. 244, he is called Roger Hart.

23 Le Févre, i, p. 154.

24 David Nicolle, *French Armies of the Hundred Years War* (Osprey, Oxford, 2000, repr. 2002), pp. 18, 21; *The Beauchamp Pageant*, p. 65.

25 *GHQ*, p. 89. The "iron furnace" is a biblical reference (Deuteronomy 4.20) to Egypt and the slavery of the Israelites there.

26 Ibid., pp. 88–9; le Févre, i, p. 256.

27 *GHQ*, pp. 89, 91.

28 Ibid., pp. 90–1. Suffocation in similar circumstances was the main cause of death among the Scots at the battle of Dupplin Moor (1332) against the English. As at Agincourt, the losses were almost entirely on one side and the dead "fell in a remarkable way in a great heap." See Strickland and Hardy, pp. 184–5, 266.

29 Le Févre, i, pp. 249–50. Jehan de Croy, a leading Burgundian and grand butler of France, and his sons, Jehan and Archembaut, were all killed at Agincourt: Bacquet, pp. 77–8.

30 *GHQ*, p. 98; Curry, p. 62; St-Denys, v, pp. 570, 572; Monstrelet, iii,

pp. 119–20. Both the acts of striking off part of Henry's crown and wounding the duke of Gloucester, as well as killing the duke of York, were later falsely attributed to Jean, duke of Alençon. One of Charles d'Orléans' closest friends, the thirty-year-old Alençon had been created a duke on 1 January 1415, in recognition of his services against the duke of Burgundy. Like Orléans, he had been one of the most eager to fight the English, throwing caution to the winds and himself into the combat with such ardour that his men were not able to keep up with him and he was struck down. According to later legend, he was killed by Henry's body-guard as he was in the very act of surrendering himself to the king. By one of those terrible ironies so often created by the complexities of medieval intermarriage, he was distantly related to the king, his mother-in-law, Joan of Navarre, being Henry V's stepmother. As W&W, ii, pp. 165–6, point out, Alençon's own family chroniclers did not attribute such feats of valour to him, but French pride demanded the creation of a suitable hero.

31 Beamont, *Annals of the Lords of Warrington*, p. 246; Gruel, *Chronique d'Arthur de Richemont*, p. 18; Waurin, i, pp. 217–18; le Févre, i, p. 260. A French knight, Jean Valentin, was wounded trying to come to the aid of Charles d'Orléans: Belleval, *Azincourt*, p. 335.

32 *GHQ*, pp. 90–3.

33 Pizan, *BDAC*, pp. 169–70.

34 *GHQ*, pp. 91–3.

35 Le Févre, i, p. 258.

36 Seward, *Henry V as Warlord*, p. 80, suggests that there were perhaps as many as three thousand.

37 Ghillebert de Lannoy, *Oeuvres de Ghillebert de Lannoy: Voyageur, Diplomate et Moraliste*, ed. by Ch. Potvin and J.-C. Houzeau (P. and J. Lefever, Louvain, 1878), pp. xii–xiv.

38 Ibid., pp. 49–50.

39 See, for example, W&W, ii, p. 172 and n. 11; Curry, p. 472.

40 The Portuguese similarly executed their prisoners at the battle of Aljubarotta (1385) when threatened by a Castilian rally. See Strickland and Hardy, p. 254.

41 *St-Denys*, v, p. 564; Lannoy, *Oeuvres*, p. 50. Ghillebert de Lannoy's claim that it was the duke of Brabant's arrival which prompted the killing of the prisoners is supported by at least two other chroniclers from opposite sides of the French political divide, but others are equally adamant that there was a genuine rally behind the lines. The fact that this was attrib-uted in some sources to the leadership of Clignet de Brabant suggests that this might be where the confusion arose, as it was cries of "Brabant! Bra-bant!" which first alerted the English to the new danger and this war-cry was equally applicable to the duke and Clignet. The chaplain (*GHQ*, p. 91) is in no doubt about what he saw and heard: "a shout went up that the enemy's mounted rearguard (in incomparable number and still fresh) were re-establishing their position and line of battle in order to launch an attack on us, few and weary as we were." See also Basin, *Histoire de Charles VII*, p. 45; "Le Livre des Trahisons de France envers la Maison de Bourgogne," in *Chroniques Relatives à l'Histoire de la Belgique sous la*

Domination des Ducs de Bourgogne, ed. by M. le baron Kervyn de Lettenhove (Académie Royale des Sciences, des Lettres et des Beaux-Arts de Belgique, Bruxelles, 1870), ii, p. 129.

42 Serge Boffa, "Antoine de Bourgogne et le Contingent Brabançon à la Bataille d'Azincourt (1415)," *Revue Belge de Philologie et d'Histoire*, 72 (1994), pp. 259–62; Curry, pp. 172–3; Bacquet, pp. 93, 103.

43 See, for example, *St-Denys*, v, p. 564; Pierre de Fenin, *Mémoires de Pierre Fenin*, ed. by Mlle Dupont (Société de l'Histoire de France, Paris, 1837), p. 64.

44 Le Févre, i, p. 258. How the English archers obtained a new supply of arrows to carry out this bombardment is not explained, but it was standard practice to collect spent arrows from the battlefield during lulls in the fighting: see above, p. 379 n. 8.

45 Monstrelet, iii, p. 109; Waurin, i, pp. 215–16; le Févre, i, p. 257; Fenin, *Mémoires*, pp. 64–5; Bacquet, pp. 93–4.

46 See above, p. 262.

47 *GHQ*, p. 85; *Foedera*, ix, pp. 356–7.

48 Ibid.; Bacquet, p. 94; Fenin, *Mémoires*, pp. 64–5; Monstrelet, iii, pp. 109–10.

49 Curry, p. 72; le Févre, i, pp. 267–8.

50 Monstrelet, iii, p. 111. W&W, ii, p. 178, misunderstand the reason for Montjoie's presence, believing him to be an English prisoner.

CHAPTER SIXTEEN: THE ROLL OF THE DEAD

1 *St Albans*, p. 96; *GHQ*, pp. 95–7; Morosini, *Chronique*, ii, p. 85. Morosini actually lists twenty-seven dead barons, but his names are garbled and, in some cases, demonstrably wrong. The table in Curry, p. 12, should be treated with caution, as it does not distinguish between numbers of armigerous dead and overall figures that include commoners.

2 Le Févre, i, p. 258. The same number is given by Waurin, i, p. 217, but the two chronicles are interdependent and heavily reliant on Monstrelet, iii, p. 110, who gives six hundred dead, which is still probably too high a total, but which suggests that their sixteen hundred is a manuscript misreading for his lower figure.

3 McFarlane, *Lancastrian Kings and Lollard Knights*, p. 67.

4 *ODNB*; *Foedera*, ix, p. 309.

5 Ibid., ix, pp. 307–9; Marks and Williamson (eds), *Gothic Art for England 1400–1547*, p. 439 no. 327.

6 Edward, duke of York, *The Master of Game by Edward, Second Duke of York*, ed. by W. A. and F. Baillie-Grohman (Chatto and Windus, London, 1909), p. 1. See ibid., pp. 2–3, for his quotation from Chaucer's *The Twenty-Five Good Women*.

7 Cummins, *The Hound and the Hawk*, Appx. iii, p. 266.

8 Edward, duke of York, *The Master of Game*, pp. 8–9, 11–12.

9 See, for instance, Seward, *Henry V as Warlord*, p. 79. W&W, ii, p. 187 n. 5, point out that the description of the duke as "a fatte man" originates with John Leland's *Itinerary*, compiled in the 1530s and 1540s.

10 Harriss, "The King and his Magnates," in *HVPK*, p. 41.

11 W&W, ii, p. 186 n. 5. He lost almost exactly half his horses too: see above, p. 410, n. 18.

12 See below, p. 307.

13 Wylie, "Notes on the Agincourt Roll," p. 128. Thomas, Lord Camoys, for example, who led the English left wing, lost none of the twenty-six men-at-arms and fifty-five archers who accompanied him into battle. John Holland, the future earl of Huntingdon, lost only four archers (plus one who died afterwards at Calais) and one man-at-arms out of a combined company of eighty: ibid., pp. 128–9, 134.

14 W&W, ii, p. 185 n. 3, 188 n. 4; Beamont, *Annals of the Lords of Warrington*, i, pp. 244–5; *Abstracts of Inquisitions Post Mortem*, p. 116; Wylie, "Notes on the Agincourt Roll," p. 134 n. 1. Harington additionally lost from his personal retinue the archer Roger Hunt, who was killed by a gun in the battle: see above, p. 284. Another leader of a contingent of fifty Lancashire archers, Sir William Botiller, also died at Harfleur, leaving his men leaderless, but their fate is not recorded: see above, p. 204.

15 The only other named man-at-arms killed at Agincourt, apart from those mentioned in the text, is Sir John Skidmore, who had indented to serve himself, with three men-at-arms and twelve archers: Usk, p. 126, is the only source to mention that he was killed in the battle. For his retinue, see MS E101/45/5, TNA; Nicolas, p. 384.

16 *ODNB*; *St Albans*, pp. 61, 67.

17 W&W, ii, pp. 188–9, 188 n. 7, 189 n. 4, 218; Wylie, "Notes on the Agincourt Roll," p. 135. Vaughan's funeral effigy, wearing his Lancastrian SS collar, is in the chancel of Bredwardine church, near Hereford. Watkin Lloyd took only one mounted archer with him, which I take to be the meaning of Jeuan Ferour "cum equo cum Watkin Lloyd," not that Lloyd was Ferour's groom, one of the alternatives suggested by Hardy, "The Longbow," p. 163.

18 Bouchart, *Grandes Croniques de Bretaigne*, ii, p. 254.

19 Ibid., iii, pp. 112–13, 113 n. 1, 119–20; le Févre, i, p. 265. W&W, ii, p. 182, add the count of Dammartin, but see below, p. 311.

20 Monstrelet, iii, p. 118. The corruption of Monstrelet's text makes it impossible to give a definitive figure, as family names are sometimes given with titles and sometimes without, making it difficult to identify them as one or two people.

21 W&W, ii, p. 222, suggest this was a Burgundian institution, but see Barber, *The Knight and Chivalry*, pp. 137–8.

22 W&W, ii, p. 222; *St-Denys*, v, p. 572; Bacquet, p. 105. His nephew, Charles de Montaigu, sire de Marcoussis, was also killed in the battle: *St Denys*, v, p. 572.

23 See, for example, Monstrelet, iii, pp. 114–18, 117 nn. 3 and 7, 118 n. 5; le Févre, i, p. 267.

24 Nicolas, p. 375.

25 Monstrelet, iii, pp. 113–15, 117; Bacquet, pp. 76–81.

26 Monstrelet, iii, pp. 113, 116, 114; *Bourgeois*, p. 79; http://gilles.mailet.free.fr/histoire/recit/recit_duche_et_comte_de bourgogn.htm; http://membres.

lycos.fr/valsoleil/hellandes/histoire_du_fief_de_hellande.htm. For the *bailli* of Evreux, Pierre de Hellenvillier, see below, p. 312. Robin de Hellande, the *bailli* of Rouen, was captured but died of his wounds on 15 December 1415: see below, p. 343.

27 Bacquet, pp. 76–8, 80; www.defense.gouv.fr/gendarmerie/lexique/ aafcbcbefbf.htm; www.ville-auchydeshesdin.fr/default_zone/fr/html/ page-77. html.

28 See below, p. 356.

29 Monstrelet, iii, p. 112; Bouvier, p. 20 n. 3; *St-Denys*, v, p. 572.

30 Bouvier, pp. 68–9 and 68 nn. 4 and 5; Baye, *Journal*, ii, p. 224 and n. 1.

31 *St-Denys*, v, p. 570; le Févre, i, p. 242.

32 Monstrelet, iii, p. 118 n. 5; www2.ac-lille.fr/fjoliot-calonne/calonnort/ historiqueCalonne.htm; le Févre, i, 266; http://perso.wanadoo.fr/ jean-claude.colrat/enigmes.htm; *Liste*.

33 Monstrelet, iii, pp. 118 n. 5, 120 and n. 2; *Liste*; http://jarnou.free.fr/ degribauval.htm.

34 *Liste*; http://jarnou.free.fr/site078.htm; http://pascale.olivaux.free.fr/ Histoire/Pages/Picardie.htm; Monstrelet, iii, p. 113.

35 http://jeulin.chez.tiscali.fr/Normandie/Mesnieres/histoire/MesnBois.htm; Baye, *Journal*, i, pp. 95 n. 1, 98.

36 On 6 December 1415, "Theobaldus Chauntemarle," a prisoner, and two servants, were among a group of Frenchmen given safe-conducts to return to France to negotiate their ransoms. Perhaps he was unsuccessful and had to return to England, or died before he set off: *Foedera*, ix, p. 323.

37 http://jeulin.chez.tiscali.fr/Normandie/Mesnieres/histoire/MesnBois.htm.

38 Siméon Luce, *La France Pendant la Guerre du Cent Ans: Épisodes Historiques et Vie Privée aux XIVe et XVe Siècles* (Libraire Hachette et Cie., Paris, 1904), pp. 150, 166–70, 174–5.

39 Le Févre, i, pp. 266, 265, 248; Bouvier, pp. 68–9, 69 n. 1; Monstrelet, iii, p. 113; Allmand (ed), *Society at War*, p. 25.

40 Monstrelet, iii, pp. 104, 124; Luce, *La France Pendant la Guerre du Cent Ans*, pp. 176–7.

41 Ibid., pp. 183–8, 190–3; *St-Denys*, v, pp. 310–12.

42 www.ville-auchyleshesdin.fr/default_zone/fr/html/page-77.html. Their burial site was lost when the abbey was destroyed.

43 Curry, pp. 459–60.

44 Curry, p. 467. The petition was inspected under a *vidimus* of July 1416, by which date presumably nothing had changed.

45 Le Févre, i, p. 260; *GHQ*, p. 92.

46 Ibid., p. 93; le Févre, i, p. 260.

47 W&W, ii, pp. 176 n. 4, 220.

48 Bacquet, p. 95; le Févre, i, p. 260.

49 Ibid.; W&W, ii, p. 217 n. 6, quote other examples of this practice.

50 http://home.tiscali.be/lathuyfdlc/gen/pafg131.htm#2705; Bacquet, pp. 83, 84, 87.

51 Ibid., pp. 95–6, 83–4. The heralds' list, which was preserved in the duke of Brabant's library in Brussels, is reproduced in ibid., pp. 85–6.

52 Monstrelet, iii, p. 122; W&W, ii, p. 225. Monstrelet, and other Burgundian apologists, attribute the initiative to the charitable piety of Philippe,
count of Charolais, son of John the Fearless, who was absent from the
battle.

CHAPTER SEVENTEEN: THE RETURN OF THE KING

1 *GHQ*, p. 93.
2 Capgrave, p. 134; *Brut*, ii, p. 557; Elmham, "Liber Metricus," p. 123;
Keen, *Chivalry*, p. 47.
3 *GHQ*, p. 99.
4 W&W, ii, p. 190 n. 7; Bacquet, p. 103.
5 "Le Livre des Trahisons de France envers la Maison de Bourgogne,"
p. 129; Basin, *Histoire de Charles VII*, i, p. 44; W&W, ii, p. 202 n. 4;
St-Denys, v, pp. 558–60.
6 Le Févre, i, p. 261; Bacquet, pp. 94–5, 105.
7 *St Albans*, p. 97; le Févre, i, pp. 268–9; *St-Denys*, v, p. 574; Bacquet,
p. 95; W&W, ii, p. 243 n. 8.
8 Curry, p. 63; le Févre, i, p. 263.
9 *GHQ*, pp. 98–100; le Févre, i, p. 260; Monstrelet, iii, pp. 111–12.
10 Le Févre, i, p. 261; Monstrelet, iii, p. 112; W&W, ii, p. 186 and nn. 2, 5.
11 Bacquet, p. 112.
12 Le Févre, i, pp. 261–2; W&W, ii, p. 248 and nn. 3, 4; Devon, p. 342. On
2 November 1415, the men of Falkenham in Suffolk were ordered to send
ale and other victuals with all possible speed to Calais, "as it is well
known that [the king] is now at Calais in person with his army": *CCR*,
p. 237.
13 See above, p. 117.
14 Le Févre, i, p. 263; W&W, ii, p. 248 and nn. 7, 8, 10.
15 Nicolas, Appx vi, p. 24. The names of twenty-four are given in W&W, ii,
p. 252 n. 5. Jean, sire d'Estouteville, is not mentioned there, but it is clear
from de Gaucourt's account that the two men presented themselves to
Henry V together.
16 http://membres.lycos.fr/valsoleil/hellandes/histoire_du_fief_de_hellande.htm;
W&W, ii, p. 251 n. 9. The surviving nine prisoners were shipped to
England in February 1417 and sent to the Fleet prison in London.
17 W&W, ii, pp. 251 n. 9, 252 n. 5; Devon, pp. 355–6. Peter Altobasse
(d.1427), a Portuguese who was naturalised as an English citizen in 1420,
was physician and clerk to the first three Lancastrian kings: Talbot and
Hammond, *The Medical Practitioners in Medieval England: A Biographical Register*, pp. 246–7.
18 W&W, ii, p. 244 n. 3, p. 249 n. 6.
19 Ibid., ii, p. 249 n. 6; Devon, pp. 344–5.
20 *GHQ*, p. 100. De Gaucourt and the Harfleur prisoners clearly accompanied the king, since £40 11s 11d was paid by the treasurer of the king's
household for their expenses at Calais for five days only (that is, 11–16
November): they did not remain in Calais until 10 December, as sug-

gested by *GHQ*, p. 100 n. 1, based on conflicting statements in W&W, ii, p. 252 nn. 4, 6.

21 Le Févre, i, p. 264; Monstrelet, iii, p. 125; *St Albans*, p. 97. Later chroniclers, such as the *First English Life*, p. 64, built upon these reports to glorify Henry's insouciance in the face of danger and to denigrate the cowardice of the French, who were said to have been as afraid as they had been at Agincourt.

22 *GHQ*, p. 100; Elmham, "Liber Metricus," p. 124; Jonathan Alexander and Paul Binski (eds), *Age of Chivalry: Art in Plantagenet England 1200–1400* (Royal Academy of Arts, London, 1987), pp. 479–81.

23 See above, p. 114.

24 *GHQ*, p. 100; Elmham, "Liber Metricus," p. 124; *Memorials of London and London Life*, p. 621.

25 Ibid., pp. 621–2; *Letter-Books*, p. 144.

26 *GHQ*, p. 103; Usk, pp. 258–61.

27 Ibid.; *Brut*, ii, p. 558; le Févre, i, p. 264.

28 *GHQ*, p. 103; Usk, p. 261. The differing characters of the two men are also evident in the fact that Adam sees a lance, the chaplain only a baton, in the giant's hand.

29 Ibid.; Elmham, "Liber Metricus," pp. 125–6; *GHQ*, pp. 104–5.

30 *GHQ*, p. 107; Elmham, "Liber Metricus," p. 126.

31 *GHQ*, pp. 107–9; Elmham, "Liber Metricus," pp. 126–7.

32 *GHQ*, pp. 108–11; Elmham, "Liber Metricus," p. 127; Usk, p. 261. "Glorious things of thee are spoken" is from Psalms 44.8.

33 Ibid., p. 261; W&W, ii, pp. 268–9, where, following later sources, the presentation is placed on the day after the king's formal entry into London.

34 *GHQ*, pp. 110–13; Elmham, "Liber Metricus," pp. 127–8.

35 *GHQ*, p. 113; McLeod, p. 133. See also Elmham, "Liber Metricus," pp. 128–9.

36 *GHQ*, p. 113; Elmham, "Liber Metricus," p. 129; Usk, p. 263.

37 W&W, ii, p. 271 n. 5; Marks and Williamson (eds), *Gothic Art for England 1400–1547*, p. 439. The choir and the duke's tomb were destroyed during the Reformation; the nave, built by Richard, duke of York, survived as the parish church. The existing memorial to the duke in the church was erected later in the sixteenth century. The remains of Michael de la Pole, the young earl of Suffolk, were likewise removed from London for their interment, probably at Wingfield in Suffolk, though legend has it that he was buried in a silver casket at Butley Abbey in Suffolk. I am grateful to Ian Chance for this information. W&W, ii, p. 274, wrongly assert that he was buried at Ewelme, Oxfordshire: the family connection with this church did not begin until William de la Pole married Alice Chaucer over a decade later.

38 Jacques Godard, "Quelques Précisions sur la Campagne d'Azincourt Tirées des Archives Municipales d'Amiens," *Bulletin Trimestre de la Société des Antiquaires de Picardie* (1971), p. 134; Bacquet, p. 111.

39 Curry, p. 462; Godard, "Quelques Précisions sur la Campagne d'Azincourt Tirées des Archives Municipales d'Amiens," p. 135.

40 *St-Denys*, v, p. 582.

41 W&W, ii, pp. 282–3.

42 Ibid., ii, pp. 281, 286–7; *St-Denys*, v, pp. 586–8; Baye, *Journal*, ii, pp. 231–2.

43 Vaughan, pp. 208–10; W&W, ii, pp. 293–4.

CHAPTER EIGHTEEN: THE REWARDS OF VICTORY

1 *Rotuli Parliamentorum*, iv, p. 62.

2 Ibid., pp. 63–4; *GHQ*, pp. 122–5; Harriss, "The Management of Parliament," in *HVPK*, p. 147. The extraordinary and personal nature of the grant was reflected in the condition that it was not to establish a precedent for future kings.

3 Heath, *Church and Realm 1272–1461*, p. 281; *ODNB*; W&W, ii, pp. 238–9.

4 Allmand, *Henry V*, pp. 100–1.

5 Heath, *Church and Realm 1272–1461*, p. 281. St John's bones had been translated twice, so his other feast day, 7 May, was also upgraded in the church calendar.

6 McKenna, "How God Became an Englishman," pp. 35–6; *GHQ*, pp. xviii, xxiv, 181. The first of Henry's three victories referred to by the chaplain was over the Lollards.

7 Ibid., pp. xxviii–xxix; Keen, *The Pelican History of Medieval Europe*, pp. 288ff.

8 *GHQ*, p. 17; Keen, "Diplomacy," in *HVPK*, p. 195; Devon, p. 345.

9 *Rotuli Parliamentorum*, iv, pp. 100–1; *ODNB*; Harriss, "The King and his Magnates," pp. 36, 39.

10 *Rotuli Parliamentorum*, iv, p. 96; *ODNB*.

11 E358/6, TNA, is the final set of accounts for fifty-nine indentees, including the duke of York and Lord Camoys, to have survived. It records details of cash payments, jewels received in pledge, the value of war winnings and the numbers and status of men lost during the campaign and shipped home from Calais (with their horses) in each company.

12 *POPC*, ii, pp. 222–3, 225–7; Nicolas, Appx xi, pp. 50–2. The meeting was held on 6 March 1417.

13 Ibid., Appx xiii, pp. 55–8; Harriss, "The King and his Magnates," p. 41.

14 Nicolas, pp. 171–2; Devon, p. 423. Clyff's claim for wages alone would have amounted to £126, so he must have already received three-quarters of what the crown owed him.

15 Keen, *Origins of the English Gentleman*, p. 33. I am indebted to Maurice Keen for his personal comments on this case.

16 *CPR*, pp. 380, 385, 386, 395; Reeves, *Lancastrian Englishmen*, p. 94; Nicolas, Appx. xii, p. 54.

17 Nicolas, p. 174.

18 Ibid., pp. 170–1; Henry Paston-Bedingfield, "The Heralds at the Time of Agincourt," in Curry, *Agincourt 1415*, pp. 136–7; Elizabeth Armstrong, "The Heraldry of Agincourt: Heraldic Insights into the Battle of Agincourt," ibid., p. 132.

19 Gruel, *Chronique d'Arthur de Richemont*, pp. 19–20; M. G. A. Vale, *Charles VII* (Eyre Methuen, London, 1974), p. 35.

20 Devon, pp. 344, 345; *Foedera*, ix, pp. 324, 337; *Forty-Fourth Annual Report*, p. 578; McLeod, p. 134; Lalande, *Jean II le Meingre, dit Boucicaut (1366–1421)*, p. 171.

21 McLeod, pp. 145, 150; Lalande, *Jean II le Meingre, dit Boucicaut (1366–1421)*, p. 171; W&W, ii, p. 253 n.1. Waterton kept a lavish household, spending more than £340 (the equivalent of $226,624 today) in 1416–17: C. M. Woolgar (ed), *Household Accounts from Medieval England Part II*, Records of Social and Economic History, New Series xviii, pp. 503–22.

22 By comparison with other countries, the English had a reputation for treating their prisoners well. The Spanish "know not how to show courtesy to their prisoners" and, like the Germans, were notorious for holding even aristocratic captives in shackles and fetters in order to obtain greater ransoms. French merchants who were unfortunate enough to be apprehended in Normandy in 1417 by English, Burgundian and French forces in succession complained that the Burgundians treated them worse than the English, and the French were more cruel than Saracens. Barber, *The Knight and Chivalry*, p. 206; Lewis, *Later Medieval France: The Polity*, p. 50.

23 Monstrelet, iii, pp. 120–1; http://tyreldepoix.free.fr/Site/Histoire.htm; *Foedera*, ix, p. 360; Bacquet, p. 112.

24 See above, pp. 73, 272–3. For twenty-two prisoners in the Tower who were "plegges" for prisoners released on licence in 1423, see *POPC*, iii, 11.

25 The very personal nature of his view of this obligation — and the extreme narrowness of its definition — was demonstrated two years later when Henry V died. Having spent seven years as the king's prisoner, Richemont immediately returned to Brittany, considering himself to be released not only from his oath but also from his duty to pay a ransom. This was, by any standards, a highly debatable interpretation of the laws of war. Bouchart, *Grandes Croniques de Bretaigne*, pp. 271–2, 280.

26 Nicolas, Appx vi; *Forty-Fourth Annual Report*, p. 578.

27 Nicolas, Appx vi.

28 *Forty-Fourth Annual Report*, p. 586; *Calendar of Signet Letters of Henry IV and Henry V (1399–1422)*, p. 164 no. 800; *Foedera*, ix, p. 430; W&W, ii, pp. 39–41.

29 *Foedera*, ix, pp. 424–6; Nicolas, Appx vi; *Foedera*, ix, p. 337; Stansfield, "John Holland, Duke of Exeter and Earl of Huntingdon (d.1447) and the Costs of the Hundred Years War," pp. 108–9. De Gaucourt returned to France once more to arrange a joint ransom of twenty thousand crowns, with authority from d'Estouteville to sell one of the latter's estates to raise his share; instead, de Gaucourt raised all the money himself, relying on d'Estouteville to repay him. On his deathbed, d'Estouteville charged his son to repay de Gaucourt the seventeen thousand crowns he now owed him but the son repudiated the debt and de Gaucourt therefore sued him in the Paris Parlement.

30 Raoul de Gaucourt was "eighty-five years old, or thereabouts" when he gave evidence on 25 February 1455 to enable the pope to reverse the judgement against Joan of Arc. He is said have died on 21 June 1462. See *Procès en Nullité de la Condamnation de Jeanne d'Arc*, ed. by Pierre Duparc (Société de l'Histoire de France, Paris, 1977), i, p. 326; Chenaye-Desbois et Badier, *Dictionnaire de la Noblesse*, ix, pp. 33–5; Prevost, d'Arnot and de Morembert (eds), *Dictionnaire de Biographie Française*, xv, p. 689. After 1453 the only part of mainland France still in English hands was Calais.

31 Vale, *Charles VII*, pp. 35–7; http://xenophongroup.com/montjoie/richmond.htm.

32 Vendôme, who was a prisoner of Sir John Cornewaille, was effectively exchanged in 1423 for John Holland, earl of Huntingdon, who had been captured at Baugé: *Foedera*, ix, p. 319; Stansfield, "John Holland, Duke of Exeter and Earl of Huntingdon (d.1447) and the Costs of the Hundred Years War," pp. 108–9.

33 McLeod, pp. 153, 161, 190, 192; Bacquet, p. 88.

34 Lalande, *Jean II le Meingre, dit Boucicaut (1366–1421)*, pp. 171–4; John Harthan, *Books of Hours and Their Owners* (Thames & Hudson, London, 1977, repr. 1978), p. 73. See plate 33.

35 W&W, iii, p. 187.

36 *ELMA*, pp. 389–93, 396–8; www174.pair.com/mja/chuck.html. In 1414, Charles d'Orléans had paid £276 7s 6d for 960 pearls which were to be sewn onto his sleeve in the form of the words and music of his chanson, "Madame je suis plus joyeulx": ibid., p. 8 n. 36. See also plate 35.

37 www.unibuc.ro/eBooks/lls/MihaelaVoicu-LaLiterature/CHARLES%20DORLEANS.htm p. 2.

38 McLeod, pp. 171–2.

39 Alain Chartier, *The Poetical Works of Alain Chartier*, ed. by J. C. Laidlaw (Cambridge University Press, Cambridge, 1974), pp. 198–304, esp. pp. 262 (ll. 2138–45), 275–6 (ll. 2585–99).

40 Alain Chartier, *Le Quadrilogue Invectif*, ed. and trans. by Florence Bouchet (Honoré Champion, Paris, 2002), p. 89. It should be pointed out that Chartier himself does not necessarily agree with this view, which is enunciated by his fictional knight on behalf of his class.

41 Pizan, *The Writings of Christine de Pizan*, p. 339; Forhan, *The Political Theory of Christine de Pizan*, p. 72. Nevertheless, the importance of peace was the single most prominent recurring theme in Christine's work: ibid., p. 141.

42 Usk, p. 259. The last word of every line ends in "osa," a scholarly device typical of medieval Latinists: ibid., p. 258.

43 *Musica Britannica: A National Collection of Music, vol. iv, Medieval Carols*, ed. by John Stevens (Royal Musical Association, London, 1952), p. 6, no. 8. See plate 30.

44 Richard Olivier, *Inspirational Leadership: Henry V and the Muse of Fire* (Industrial Society, London, 2001), p. xxiii. In more recent times *Henry V* has been used to put across an anti-war message. Kenneth Branagh's film

version was made after the Falklands War; the National Theatre's stage version, with a black actor in the title role, came in the wake of the US-led invasion of Iraq. Curry, pp. 260–359, provides an excellent overview of the literary response to Agincourt throughout the centuries, and cites many valuable examples of the different genres.

BIBLIOGRAPHY

I: Abbreviations. Frequently cited sources have been abbreviated as follows:

Bacquet: Gérard Bacquet, *Azincourt* (Scop-Sadag Press, Bellegarde, 1977).

Bourgeois: *Journal d'un Bourgeois de Paris 1405–1449*, ed. by A. Tuetey (Paris, 1881).

Bouvier: Gilles le Bouvier, dit Le Héraut Berry, *Les Chroniques du Roi Charles VII*, ed. by Henri Courteault and Léonce Celier (Société de l'Histoire de France, Paris, 1979).

Brut: *The Brut or The Chronicles of England*, ed. by Friedrich W. D. Brie (Early English Text Society, London, 1908), vol. ii.

Capgrave: John Capgrave, *The Book of the Illustrious Henries*, ed. and trans. by Francis Charles Hingeston (Longman and Co., London, 1858).

CCR: *Calendar of the Close Rolls, Preserved in the Public Record Office: Henry V, vol. I, AD 1413–1419* (HMSO, London, 1939).

CPR: *Calendar of the Patent Rolls, Preserved in the Public Record Office: Henry V, vol. I, AD 1413–1416* (HMSO, London, 1910).

Curry: Anne Curry, *The Battle of Agincourt: Agincourt 1415: Sources and Interpretations* (Boydell Press, Woodbridge, 2000).

Curry, *Agincourt 1415*: *Agincourt 1415: Henry V, Sir Thomas Erpingham and the Triumph of the English Archers*, ed. by Anne Curry (Tempus, Stroud, 2000).

Curry and Hughes: *Arms, Armies and Fortifications in the Hundred Years War*, ed. by Anne Curry and Michael Hughes (Boydell Press, Woodbridge, 1994, repr. 1999).

Devon: *Issues of the Exchequer; Being a Collection of Payments Made out of His Majesty's Revenue, from King Henry III* to *King Henry VI Inclusive*, ed. and trans. by Frederick Devon (John Murray, London, 1837).

ELMA: Maurice Keen, *England in the Later Middle Ages* (Methuen and Co., London, 1973).

First English Life: *The First English Life of King Henry the Fifth written in 1513 by an anonymous Author known commonly as The Translator of Livius*, ed. by Charles Lethbridge Kingsford (Clarendon Press, Oxford, 1911).

Foedera: *Foedera, Conventiones, Literae et Cuiuscunque Generis Acta Publica inter Reges Angliae*, ed. by Thomas Rymer (2nd edn, J. Tonson, London, 1729), vol. ix.

Forty-Fourth Annual Report: *The Forty-Fourth Annual Report of the Deputy Keeper of the Public Records* (London, 1883).

Fowler: *The Hundred Years War*, ed. by Kenneth Fowler (Macmillan, London, 1971).

GHQ: *Gesta Henrici Quinti*, ed. and trans. by F. Taylor & J. S. Roskell (Clarendon Press, Oxford, 1975).

HVPK: *Henry V: The Practice of Kingship*, ed. by G. L. Harriss (Oxford University Press, Oxford, 1985).

Keen, MW: *Medieval Warfare: A History*, ed. by Maurice Keen (Oxford University Press, Oxford, 1999).

Le Févre: Jean le Févre, *Chronique de Jean le Févre, Seigneur de St Remy*, ed. by François Morand (Société de l'Histoire de France, Paris, 1876–81), 2 vols.

Letter-Books: *Calendar of Letter-Books Preserved Among the Archives of the Corporation of the City of London at the Guildhall, Letter-Book I, circa AD 1400–1422*, ed. by Reginald R. Sharpe (printed by Order of the Corporation, London, 1909).

Liste: *Liste des Morts Français à Azincourt le Vendredi 25 Octobre 1415: http://home.nordnet.fr/~amenec/page3Azincourt.html*.

McLeod: Enid McLeod, *Charles of Orléans: Prince and Poet* (Chatto and Windus, London, 1969).

Monstrelet: Enguerrand de Monstrelet, *La Chronique d'Enguerran de Monstrelet*, ed. by L. Douet d'Arcq (Société de l'Histoire de France, Paris, 1859), vol. iii.

Mowbray MS: Account roll of Robert Southwell, receiver general to John Mowbray, earl marshal, Michaelmas 1414–Michaelmas 1415: Microfiche MF1480, Gloucestershire Record Office. The original manuscript is at Berkeley Castle.

Nicolas: Nicholas Harris Nicolas, *The History of the Battle of Agincourt* (3rd edn repr., H. Pordes, London, 1971).

ODNB: *Oxford Dictionary of National Biography*, ed. by Colin Mathews and Brian Harrison (Oxford University Press, Oxford, 2004): online version: www.oxforddnb.com.

Pizan, BDAC: Christine de Pizan, *The Book of Deeds of Arms and of Chivalry*, ed. and trans. by Charity Cannon Willard and

Sumner Willard (Pennsylvania State University Press, Pennsylvania, 1999).

POPC: *Proceedings and Ordinances of the Privy Council of England*, ed. by Sir Harris Nicolas (Commissioner of Public Records, 1834), vol. 2.

Powell: Edward Powell, *Kingship, Law, and Society: Criminal Justice in the Reign of Henry V* (Clarendon Press, Oxford, 1989).

St Albans: *The St Albans Chronicle 1406–1420*, ed. by V. H. Galbraith (Clarendon Press, Oxford, 1937).

St-Denys: *Chronique du Religieux de Saint-Denys*, ed. by M.-L. Bellaguet (Crapelet, Paris, 1844), 6 vols.

Strickland and Hardy: Matthew Strickland and Robert Hardy, *From Hastings to the Mary Rose: The Great Warbow* (Sutton, Stroud, 2005).

TNA: The National Archives, formerly The Public Record Office, at Kew, London.

Usk: *The Chronicle of Adam Usk 1377–1421*, ed. and trans. by C. Given-Wilson (Clarendon Press, Oxford, 1997).

Vaughan: Richard Vaughan, *John the Fearless* (Longman, London and New York, 1966; repr. Boydell Press, Woodbridge, 2002).

W&W: James Hamilton Wylie and William Templeton Waugh, *The Reign of Henry the Fifth* (Cambridge University Press, Cambridge, 1914–29), 3 vols.

Waurin: Jehan de Waurin, *Recueil des Croniques et Anchiennes Istories de la Grant Bretaigne, A Present Nomme Engleterre*, ed. by William Hardy (Rolls Series no. 39, London, 1868).

II: Printed Primary Sources

Abstracts of Inquisitions Post Mortem made by Christopher Towneley and Roger Dodsworth, ed. by William Langton (Chetham Society, Manchester, 1875).

Basin, Thomas, *Histoire de Charles VII*, ed. and trans. by Charles Samaran (Société d'Édition "les Belles Lettres," Paris, 1933), vol. 1.

Baye, Nicolas de, *Journal de Nicolas de Baye*, ed. by Alexandre Tuetey (Société de l'Histoire de France, Paris, 1888), vol. 2.

The Beauchamp Pageant, ed. by Alexandra Sinclair (Richard III and Yorkist History Trust in association with Paul Watkins, Donington, 2003).

Bouchart, Alain, *Grandes Croniques de Bretaigne*, ed. by Marie-Louise Auger and Gustave Jeanneau (Éditions du Centre National de la Recherche Scientifique, Paris, 1986), vol. 2.

Bueil, Jean de, *Le Jouvencel*, ed. by Léon Lecestre (Société de l'Histoire de France, Paris, 1889), 2 vols.

Cagny, Perceval de, *Chroniques*, ed. by H. Moranvillé (Société de l'Histoire de France, Paris, 1902).

Calendar of Inquisitions Post Mortem, xx, 1–5 Henry V (1413–1418) ed. by J. L. Kirby (HMSO, London, 1995).

Calendar of Signet Letters of Henry IV and Henry V (1399–1422), ed. by J. L. Kirby (HMSO, London, 1978).

Charny, Geoffroi de, *The* Book of Chivalry *of Geoffroi de Charny: Text, Context, and Translation*, ed. by Richard W. Kaeuper and Elspeth Kennedy (University of Pennsylvania Press, Pennsylvania, 1996).

Chartier, Alain, *Le Quadrilogue Invectif*, ed. and trans. by Florence Bouchet (Honoré Champion, Paris, 2002).

Chartier, Alain, *The Poetical Works of Alain Chartier*, ed. by J. C. Laidlaw (Cambridge University Press, Cambridge, 1974).

Chaucer, Geoffrey, *Canterbury Tales*, ed. by A. Kent Hieatt and Constance Hieatt (Bantam Books Inc., New York, 1971).

Chronicles of London, ed. by Charles Lethbridge Kingsford (Alan Sutton, Gloucester, 1977).

"Chronique de Normandie de l'an 1414 à 1422," in *Henrici Quinti, Angliae Regis, Gesta*, ed. by Benjamin Williams (English Historical Society, London, 1850), pp. 165–262.

Commynes, Philippe de, *Memoirs: The Reign of Louis XI 1461–83*, ed. and trans. by Michael Jones (Penguin, Harmondsworth, 1972).

Comnena, Anna, *The Alexiad*, ed. and trans. by E. R. A. Sewter (Penguin, Harmondsworth, 1979).

Deputy Keeper of Public Records, "The Conspiracy of the Earl of Cambridge against Henry V," *43rd Report of the Deputy Keeper of Public Records* (1882), Appx 1.

Edward, duke of York, *The Master of Game by Edward, Second Duke of York*, ed. by W. A. and F. Baillie-Grohman (Chatto and Windus, London, 1909).

Elmham, Thomas, "Liber Metricus de Henrico Quinto," *Memorials of Henry the Fifth, King of England*, ed. by Charles Augustus Cole (Longman and Co., London, 1858).

An English Chronicle of the Reigns of Richard II, Henry IV, Henry V, and Henry VI. Written Before the Year 1471, ed. by Rev. John Silvester Davies, Camden Society, 64 (1856).

Eschenbach, Wolfram von, *Parzival*, trans. with an introduction by Helen M. Mustard and Charles E. Passage (Vintage Books, New York, 1961).

Fenin, Pierre de, *Mémoires de Pierre Fenin*, ed. by Mlle Dupont (Société de l'Histoire de France, Paris, 1837).

Gruel, Guillaume, *Chronique d'Arthur de Richemont, Connétable de France, Duc de Bretagne (1393–1458)*, ed. by Achille le Vavasseur (Société de l'Histoire de France, Paris, 1890).

Henrici Quinti, Angliae Regis, Gesta, ed. by Benjamin Williams (English Historical Society, London, 1850).

Heresy Trials in the Diocese of Norwich, 1428–31, ed. by Norman P. Tanner (Camden Fourth Series, vol. 20, London, 1977).

Hoccleve, Thomas, *The Regiment of Princes*, ed. by Charles R. Blyth (Western Michigan University, Kalamazoo, Michigan, 1999).

Kempe, Margery, *The Book of Margery Kempe*, trans. and ed. by Lynn Staley (W. W. Norton, New York and London, 2001).

Lannoy, Ghillebert de, *Oeuvres de Ghillebert de Lannoy: Voyageur, Diplomate et Moraliste*, ed. by Ch. Potvin and J.-C. Houzeau (P. and J. Lefever, Louvain, 1878).

"Le Livre des Trahisons de France envers la Maison de Bourgogne," in *Chroniques Relatives à l'Histoire de la Belgique sous la Domination des Ducs de Bourgogne*, ed. by M. le baron Kervyn de Lettenhove (Académie Royale des Sciences, des Lettres et des Beaux-Arts de Belgique, Bruxelles, 1870), ii, pp. 1–258.

Marcel, Gabriel, *Choix de Cartes et de Mappemondes des XIV et XV Siècles* (Ernest Leroux, Paris, 1896).

Memorials of London and London Life in the XIIIth, XIVth, and XVth Centuries, ed. by Henry Thomas Riley (Longmans, Green, and Co., London, 1868).

Morosini, Antonio, *Chronique d'Antonio Morosini, 1414–1428*, ed. by Germain Lefèvre-Pontalis and Léon Dorez (Librairie Renouard, Paris, 1899), vol. ii.

Musica Britannica: A National Collection of Music, vol. iv, Medieval Carols, ed. by John Stevens (Royal Musical Association, London, 1952).

Original Letters Illustrative of English History, 2nd series, ed. with notes and illustrations by Henry Ellis (Harding and Lepard, London, 1827), vol. i.

Pizan, Christine de, *The Writings of Christine de Pizan*, selected and ed. by Charity Cannon Willard (Persea Books, New York, 1994).

Procés en Nullité de la Condamnation de Jeanne d'Arc, ed. by Pierre Duparc (Société de l'Histoire de France, Paris, 1977), vol. i.

Register of Henry Chichele, Archbishop of Canterbury, 1414–1443, ed. by E. F. Jacob (Clarendon Press, Oxford, 1943–7), 4 vols.

Registres de la Jurade: Délibérations de 1414 à 1416 et de 1420 à 1422: Archives Municipales de Bordeaux (G. Gounouilhou, Bordeaux, 1883), vol. iv.

Rotuli Parliamentorum (London, 1767–1832), 7 vols.

Roye, Gilles de, "Chronique, avec les Additions d'Adrien de But," in *Chroniques Relatives à l'Histoire de la Belgique sous la Domination des Ducs de Bourgogne*, ed. by M. le baron Kervyn de Lettenhove (Académie Royale des Sciences, des Lettres et des Beaux-Arts de Belgique, Brussels, 1870), vol. 1.

Trokelowe, John de, "Annales Ricardi Secundi et Henrici Quarti," *Johannis de Trokelowe & Henrici de Blaneford . . . Chronica et Annales*, ed. by Henry Thomas Riley (Rolls Series, London, 1866), pp. 155–420.

Ursins, Jean Juvénal des, *Histoire de Charles VI*, ed. by J. A. C. Buchon (Choix de Chroniques et Mémoires sur l'Histoire de France, iv, Paris, 1836).

III. Secondary Sources

Alexander, Jonathan, and Binski, Paul (eds), *Age of Chivalry: Art in Plantagenet England 1200–1400* (Royal Academy of Arts, London, 1987).

Allmand, Christopher (ed), *Power, Culture and Religion in France c.1350–c.1550* (Boydell Press, Woodbridge, 1989).

Allmand, Christopher, *Henry V* (new edn, Yale University Press, New Haven and London, 1997).

Allmand, Christopher (ed.), *Society at War: The Experience of England and France during the Hundred Years War* (new edn, Boydell Press, Woodbridge, 1998).

Archer, R. E., and Walker, S. (eds), *Rulers and Ruled in Late Medieval England: Essays Presented to Gerald Harriss* (Hambledon Press, London and Rio Grande, 1995).

Armstrong, Elizabeth, "The Heraldry of Agincourt: Heraldic Insights into the Battle of Agincourt," in Curry, *Agincourt 1415*, pp. 123–38.

Ayton, Andrew, "English Armies in the Fourteenth Century," in Curry and Hughes, pp. 21–38.

Ayton, Andrew, "Arms, Armour, and Horses," in *Keen, MW*, pp. 186–208.

Balfour-Melville, E. W. M., *James I, King of Scots, 1406–37* (Methuen, London, 1936).

Barber, Richard, *The Knight and Chivalry* (Sphere, London, 1974).

Barber, Richard, and Barker, Juliet, *Tournaments: Jousts, Chivalry and Pageants in the Middle Ages* (Boydell Press, Woodbridge, 1989).

Barker, Juliet, *The Tournament in England 1100–1400* (Boydell Press, Woodbridge, 1985, repr. 2003).

Beamont, William, *Annals of the Lords of Warrington for the first Five Centuries after the Conquest* (Chetham Society, Manchester, 1872), vol. i.

Beck, R. Theodore, *The Cutting Edge: Early History of the Surgeons of London* (Lund Humphries, London and Bradford, 1974).

Bellamy, John G., *The Law of Treason in England in the Later Middle Ages* (Cambridge University Press, Cambridge, 1970).

Belleval, René de, *Azincourt* (Paris, 1865).

Bennett, Matthew, "The Development of Battle Tactics in the Hundred Years War," in Curry and Hughes, pp. 1–20.

Bennett, Matthew, "The Battle," in Curry, *Agincourt 1415*, pp. 21–36.

Blair, John, and Ramsay, Nigel (eds), *English Medieval Industries: Craftsmen, Techniques, Products* (Hambledon Press, London and Rio Grande, 1991).

Boffa, Serge, "Antoine de Bourgogne et le Contingent Brabançon à la Bataille d'Azincourt (1415)," *Revue Belge de Philologie et d'Histoire*, 72 (1994), pp. 255–84.

Boulton, D'A. J. D., *The Knights of the Crown: The Monarchical Orders of Knighthood in Later Medieval Europe 1325–1520* (Boydell Press, Woodbridge, 1987).

Bradbury, Jim, *The Medieval Archer* (Boydell Press, Woodbridge, 1985, repr. 2002).

Bradbury, Jim, *The Medieval Siege* (Boydell Press, Woodbridge, 1992).

Bradley, Patricia J., "Henry V's Scottish Policy — a Study in Realpolitik," in *Documenting the Past: Essays in Medieval History Presented to George Peddy Cuttino*, ed. by J. S. Hamilton and Patricia J. Bradley (Boydell Press, Woodbridge, 1989), pp. 177–95.

Bridbury, A. R., *England and the Salt Trade in the Later Middle Ages* (Clarendon Press, Oxford, 1955).

Carey, Hilary M., *Courting Disaster: Astrology at the English Court and University in the Later Middle Ages* (Macmillan, London, 1992).

Carpenter-Turner, W. J., "The Building of the *Gracedieu, Valentine* and *Falconer* at Southampton, 1416–1420," *The Mariner's Mirror*, 40 (1954), pp. 55–72.

Carpenter-Turner, W. J., "The Building of the *Holy Ghost of the Tower*, 1414–1416, and her Subsequent History," *The Mariner's Mirror*, 40 (1954), pp. 270–81.

Catto, Jeremy, "The King's Servants," in *HVPK*, pp. 75–95.

Chenaye-Desbois et Badier, Aubert de la, *Dictionnaire de la Noblesse* (Paris, 1866, repr. Kraus-Thomson, Liechtenstein, 1969).

Cheney, C. R. (ed), *Handbook of Dates for Students of English History* (Royal Historical Society, London, 1978).

Cripps-Day, Francis Henry, *The History of the Tournament in England and in France* (Bernard Quaritch, London, 1918).

Cummins, John, *The Hound and the Hawk: The Art of Medieval Hunting* (Weidenfeld and Nicolson, London, 1988).

Curry, Anne, *The Hundred Years War* (Palgrave, London and New York, 1993).

Curry, Anne, "Sir Thomas Erpingham: A Life in Arms," in Curry, *Agincourt 1415*, pp. 53–77.

Curry, Anne, and Matthew, Elizabeth (eds), *Concepts and Patterns of Service in the Later Middle Ages* (Boydell Press, Woodbridge, 2000).

Curry, Anne, *Agincourt: A New History* (Tempus, Stroud, 2005).

Danbury, Elizabeth, "English and French Artistic Propaganda during the Period of the Hundred Years War," in *Power, Culture and Religion in France c.1350–c.1550*, ed. by Christopher Allmand (Boydell Press, Woodbridge, 1989), pp. 75–97.

Dyer, Christopher, *Everyday Life in Medieval England* (Hambledon Press, London and Rio Grande, 1994).

Edbury, Peter, "Warfare in the Latin East," in Keen, *MW*, pp. 89–112.

Fernández-Armesto, Felipe, "Naval Warfare after the Viking Age, c.1100–1500," in Keen, *MW*, pp. 230–52.

Forhan, Kate Langdon, *The Political Theory of Christine de Pizan* (Ashgate, Aldershot, 2002).

Fowler, Kenneth, "War and Change in Late Medieval France and England," in Fowler, pp. 1–27.

Friel, Ian, "Winds of Change? Ships and the Hundred Years War," in Curry and Hughes, pp. 183–93.

Geddes, Jane, "Iron," in *English Medieval Industries: Craftsmen, Techniques, Products*, ed. by John Blair and Nigel Ramsay (Hambledon Press, London and Rio Grande, 1991), pp. 167–88.

Godard, Jacques, "Quelques Précisions sur la Campagne d'Azincourt Tirées des Archives Municipales d'Amiens," *Bulletin Trimestre de la Société des Antiquaires de Picardie* (1971), pp. 128–35.

Goodman, Anthony, "England and Iberia in the Middle Ages," in *England and her Neighbours 1066–1453: Essays in Honour of Pierre Chaplais*, ed. by M. Jones and M. G. A. Vale (Hambledon Press, London, 1989), pp. 73–96.

Gottfried, R. S., *Doctors and Medicine in Medieval England, 1340–1530* (Princeton University Press, New Jersey, 1986).

Griffiths, R. A., "Patronage, Politics, and the Principality of Wales, 1413–1461," in *British Government and Administration: Studies Presented to S. B. Chrimes*, ed. by H. Hearder and H. R. Loyn (University of Wales Press, Cardiff, 1974), pp. 69–86.

Griffiths, Ralph, "'Ffor the myght off the Lande . . .': the English Crown, Provinces and Dominions in the Fifteenth Century," in *Concepts and Patterns of Service in the Later Middle Ages*, ed. by Anne Curry and Elizabeth Matthew (Boydell Press, Woodbridge, 2000), pp. 80–98.

Grose, F., *Military Antiquities Respecting the History of the English Army* (London, 1801), 2 vols.

Guenée, Bernard, *La Folie de Charles VI Roi Bien-Amé* (Perrin, Paris, 2004).

Guest, Ken, and Guest, Denise, *British Battles: the Front Lines of History in Colour Photographs* (HarperCollins, London, 1997).

Hardy, Robert, "The Longbow," in Curry and Hughes, pp. 161–81.

Harriss, G. L., "Financial Policy," in *HVPK*, pp. 159–79.

Harriss, G. L., "The King and his Magnates," in *HVPK*, pp. 31–51.

Harriss, G. L., "The Management of Parliament," in *HVPK*, pp. 137–58.

Harriss, G. L., *Cardinal Beaufort: a Study of Lancastrian Ascendancy and Decline* (Clarendon Press, Oxford, 1988).

Harthan, John, *Books of Hours and Their Owners* (Thames & Hudson, London, 1977, repr. 1978).

Harvey, Barbara, *Living and Dying in England 1100–1540: The Monastic Experience* (Oxford University Press, Oxford, 1993).

Heath, Peter, *Church and Realm 1272–1461* (Fontana, London, 1988).

Hewitt, H. J., "The Organisation of War," in Fowler, pp. 75–95.

Hitchin, Paul, "The Bowman and the Bow," in Curry, *Agincourt 1415*, pp. 36–52.

Hudson, Anne, *The Premature Reformation: Wycliffite Texts and Lollard History* (Clarendon Press, Oxford, 1988).

Hughes, Michael, "The Fourteenth-Century French Raids on Hampshire and the Isle of Wight," in Curry and Hughes, pp. 121–43.

Jones, Michael, and Walker, Simon, "Private Indentures for Life Service in Peace and War 1278–1476," *Camden Miscellany xxxii* (Royal Historical Society, London, 1994), pp. 1–190.

Jones, Michael, "The Material Rewards of Service in Late Medieval Brittany: Ducal Servants and their Residences," in *Concepts and Patterns of Service in the Later Middle Ages*, ed. by Anne Curry and Elizabeth Matthew (Boydell Press, Woodbridge, 2000), pp. 119–44.

Jones, Richard L. C., "Fortifications and Sieges in Western Europe, c.800–1450," in Keen, *MW*, pp. 163–85.

Keen, Maurice, *The Pelican History of Medieval Europe* (Pelican, Harmondsworth, 1969, repr. 1976).

Keen, Maurice, *Chivalry* (Yale University Press, New Haven and London, 1984).

Keen, Maurice, "Diplomacy," in *HVPK*, pp. 181–99.

Keen, Maurice, "Richard II's Ordinances of War of 1385," in *Rulers and Ruled in Late Medieval England: Essays Presented to Gerald Harriss*, ed. by R. E. Archer and S. Walker (Hambledon Press, London and Rio Grande, 1995), pp. 33–48.

Keen, Maurice, "The Changing Scene: Guns, Gunpowder, and Permanent Armies," in Keen, *MW*, pp. 273–91.

Keen, Maurice, *Origins of the English Gentleman: Heraldry, Chivalry and Gentility in Medieval England, c.1300–c.1500* (Tempus, Stroud and Charleston, SC, 2002).

Kenyon, John, "Coastal Artillery Fortification in England in the Late Fourteenth and Early Fifteenth Centuries," in Curry and Hughes, pp. 145–9.

Kingsford, Charles Lethbridge, *Prejudice and Promise in XVth Century England: The Ford Lectures 1923–4* (Clarendon Press, Oxford, 1925).

Knoop, D., and Jones, G. P., *The Medieval Mason* (3rd edn, Manchester University Press, Manchester, 1967).

Labarge, Margaret Wade, *Henry V: The Cautious Conqueror* (Secker and Warburg, London, 1975).

Lalande, Denis, *Jean II le Meingre, dit Boucicaut (1366–1421): Étude d'une Biographie Héroïque* (Librairie Droz, Geneva, 1988).

Latham, R. E., *Revised Medieval Latin Word-List* (published for the British Academy, Oxford University Press, London, 1965, repr. 1980).

Lewis, Peter S., *Later Medieval France: The Polity* (Macmillan, London and St Martin's Press, New York, 1968).

Leyser, Henrietta, *Medieval Women: A Social History of Women in England 450–1500* (Weidenfeld and Nicolson, London, 1995).

Luce, Siméon, *La France Pendant la Guerre du Cent Ans: Épisodes Historiques et Vie Privée aux XIVe et XVe Siècles* (Libraire Hachette et Cie., Paris, 1904).

Marks, Richard, and Williamson, Paul (eds), *Gothic Art for England 1400–1547* (V&A Publications, London, 2003).

Marx, Robert F., *The Battle of the Spanish Armada 1588* (Weidenfeld and Nicolson, London, 1965), p. 53.

McFarlane, K. B., *Lancastrian Kings and Lollard Knights* (Oxford University Press, Oxford, 1972).

McKenna, John W., "How God Became an Englishman," in *Tudor Rule and Revolution: Essays for G. R. Elton from his American Friends*, ed. by Delloyd J. Guth and John W. McKenna (Cambridge University Press, Cambridge, 1982), pp. 25–43.

Morgan, David, "The Household Retinue of Henry V and the Ethos of English Public Life," in *Concepts and Patterns of Service in the Later Middle Ages*, ed. by Anne Curry and Elizabeth Matthew (Boydell Press, Woodbridge, 2000), pp. 64–79.

Mourin, Ken, "Norwich, Norfolk and Sir Thomas Erpingham," in Curry, *Agincourt 1415*, pp. 78–90.

Nicolle, David, *French Armies of the Hundred Years War* (Osprey, Oxford, 2000, repr. 2002).

Ohler, Norbert, *The Medieval Traveller*, trans. by Caroline Hillier (Boydell Press, Woodbridge, 1989).

Olivier, Richard, *Inspirational Leadership: Henry V and the Muse of Fire* (Industrial Society, London, 2001).

Orme, Nicholas, *Medieval Children* (Yale University Press, New Haven and London, 2001).

Palmer, John, "The War Aims of the Protagonists and the Negotiations for Peace," in Fowler, pp. 51–74.

Paston-Bedingfield, Henry, "The Heralds at the Time of Agincourt," in Curry, *Agincourt 1415*, pp. 133–8.

Philpotts, C., "The French Plan of Battle During the Agincourt Campaign," *English Historical Review*, xcix (1984), pp. 55–66.

Pouchelle, Marie-Christine, *The Body and Surgery in the Middle Ages* (Rutgers University Press, New Brunswick, NJ, 1990).

Powell, Edward, "The Restoration of Law and Order," in *HVPK*, pp. 53–74.

Prevost, M., d'Arnot, Roman, and de Morembert, H. Tribout (eds), *Dictionnaire de Biographie Française* (Librarie Letouzey et Ané, Paris, 1982).

Public Record Office, London: *Lists and Indexes Supplementary Series*, no. ix (Klaus Reprint Corporation, New York, 1964), vol. 2.

Pugh, T. B., "The Southampton Plot of 1415," in *Kings and Nobles in the Later Middle Ages: A Tribute to Charles Ross*, ed. by Ralph A. Griffiths and James Sherbourne (Alan Sutton, Gloucester and St Martin's Press, New York, 1986), pp. 62–89.

Reeves, A. C., *Lancastrian Englishmen* (University Press of America, Washington, DC, 1981).

Reid, E. J. B., "Lollards at Colchester in 1414," *English Historical Review*, 29 (1914), pp. 101–4.

Richmond, C. F., "The War at Sea," in Fowler, pp. 96–121.

Rogers, Clifford J., "The Age of the Hundred Years War," in Keen, *MW*, pp. 136–60.

Saul, Nigel, *The Batsford Companion to Medieval England* (Barnes and Noble Books, Totowa, NJ, 1982).

Seward, Desmond, *Henry V as Warlord* (Sidgwick and Jackson, London, 1987).

Simek, Rudolf, *Heaven and Earth in the Middle Ages: the Physical World Before Columbus*, trans. by Angela Hill (Boydell Press, Woodbridge, 1996).

Smith, Anthony, " 'The Greatest Man of That Age': The Acquisition of Sir John Fastolf's East Anglian Estates," in *Rulers and Ruled in Late Medieval England: Essays Presented to Gerald Harriss*, ed. by R. E. Archer and S. Walker (Hambledon Press, London and Rio Grande, 1995), pp. 137–53.

Smith, Robert D., "Artillery and the Hundred Years War: Myth and Interpretation," in Curry and Hughes, pp. 151–60.

Southworth, John, *The English Medieval Minstrel* (Boydell Press, Woodbridge, 1989).

Stansfield, Michael, "John Holland, Duke of Exeter and Earl of Huntingdon (d.1447) and the Costs of the Hundred Years War," in *Profit, Piety and the Professions in Later Medieval England*, ed. by Michael Hicks (Alan Sutton, Gloucester and Wolfeboro Falls, 1990), pp. 102–18.

Steel, A., "Receipt Roll Totals under Henry IV and Henry V," *English Historical Review*, 47 (1932), pp. 204–15.

Talbot, C. H., and Hammond, E. A., *The Medical Practitioners in Medieval England: A Biographical Register* (Wellcome Historical Medical Library, London, 1965).

Taylor, A. J. P., *A Personal History* (Hamish Hamilton, London, 1983).

Thrupp, Sylvia L., *The Merchant Class of Medieval London (1300–1500)* (University of Chicago Press, Chicago, 1948).

Tuchman, Barbara W., *A Distant Mirror* (Ballantine Books, New York, 1979).

Vale, M. G. A., *English Gascony 1399–1453* (Oxford University Press, Oxford, 1970).

Vale, M. G. A., *Charles VII* (Eyre Methuen, London, 1974).

Walker, Simon, "Richard II's Views on Kingship," in *Rulers and Ruled in Late Medieval England: Essays Presented to Gerald Harriss*, ed. by R. E. Archer and S. Walker (Hambledon Press, London and Rio Grande, 1995), pp. 49–64.

Webster's Biographical Dictionary (G. and C. Merriam Company, Springfield, MA, 1974).

White, John T., *A Complete Latin–English and English–Latin Dictionary* (Longmans, Green, and Co., London, New York and Bombay, 1896).

Woolgar, C. M. (ed), *Household Accounts from Medieval England Part II*, Records of Social and Economic History, New Series xviii, pp. 503–22.

Wright, Edmund, "Henry IV, the Commons and the Recovery of Royal Finance in 1407," in *Rulers and Ruled in Late Medieval England: Essays Presented to Gerald Harriss*, ed. by R. E. Archer and S. Walker (Hambledon Press, London and Rio Grande, 1995), pp. 65–81.

Wright, Nicholas, *Knights and Peasants: The Hundred Years War in the French Countryside* (Boydell Press, Woodbridge, 1998).

Wylie, James Hamilton, *History of England under Henry IV* (London, 1884–98), 4 vols.

Wylie, James Hamilton, "Notes on the Agincourt Roll," *Transactions of the Royal Historical Society*, 3rd series, vol. v (1911), pp. 104–40.

Yenal, Edith P., *Christine de Pizan: a Bibliography* (Scarecrow Press, Metuchen, NJ and London, 1989).

INDEX

Glen Ford
∘ Big Heat
∘¹ Gilda